Writing
Style and Grammar

Writing

Style and Grammar

James D. Lester, Sr.
James D. Lester, Jr.

GoodYearBooks

An Imprint of ScottForesman
A Division of HarperCollinsPublishers

GoodYearBooks

are available for most basic curriculum subjects plus many
enrichment areas. For more GoodYearBooks, contact your local
bookseller or educational dealer. For a complete catalog with
information about other GoodYearBooks, please write:

GoodYearBooks
ScottForesman
1900 East Lake Avenue
Glenview, IL 60025

Acknowledgments
p. 165: From *American Heritage Dictionary*. Boston: Houghton Mifflin, 1985.
Reprinted by permission.
p. 166: From *Roget's II: The New Thesaurus*. Boston: Houghton Mifflin, 1980.
Reprinted by permission.
p. 167: From *WordStar* word processing software package. WordStar International
Corporation, 1986, 1990. Reprinted by permission.

ISBN 0-673-36093-8

TABLE OF CONTENTS

THE WRITING PROCESS

1

CHAPTER

GETTING STARTED

Communication begins when we make an initial choice to speak or to record our ideas on paper. When we speak, our words disappear quickly, so we are often lax about our grammar since no record of what we say remains. When we write, however, we produce a public record of our knowledge, our opinions, and our skill with language, so we try to make our writing accurate, forceful, and honest.

Perhaps this difference between the spoken and the written word explains why normal, talkative people sometimes have writer's block. Writing—whether it be a history report, a poem, or a research paper—commits our personal concerns to public knowledge. Many people can examine our written document and then make judgments about our beliefs. That scrutiny may make us nervous.

For example, the authors of this text, J. D. Lester and his son Jim Lester, decided to write a composition book. Why, you ask, would anybody want to write a textbook? Commitment! We made the decision to share our ideas about the writing process. We identified an audience (high school students) and a thesis: **Writing is a complicated process that requires many choices.** Thus, we offer young writers a book that explains the choices: finding a well-focused topic, discovering a reason for writing about it, choosing a format, and then doing the writing with as much grace and style as the writer can muster.

If it were possible, we would give you a quick formula for writing, one similar to a mathematics equation or a cake recipe; unfortunately, writing cannot be reduced to a formula. Our writing is affected by the richness of our language, by our cultural backgrounds, by our targeted audience,

and finally by the form of expression we choose—
fiction, persuasion, or personal narration, to name
a few. Therefore, we want to explore the options
with you, explain the terminology, give examples,
and provide regular checklists that will help you
monitor your progress.

This book is not the usual text with assignments, exercises, and chapter exams. Instead, it
offers you a ready reference to the skills and
tasks required for good writing. It is a book that
will serve your needs for several years.

Our first bit of advice is this: keep a writing
journal. A journal is a notebook in which you
collect materials for developing your essays, fiction,
or poetry. You can jot down various ideas,
experiment with form and style, doodle, and
collect clippings from magazines and newspapers.
Talk to yourself in the journal, meditate, create,
and log your impressions about people and
events. A journal captures your ideas in words
until you need to retrieve those ideas for use in a
writing project. Unlike a diary, which is about
personal, daily activities, the journal can become
a warehouse of your thoughts and ideas on
specific issues. Kept diligently, a journal can
become a treasure trove of ideas. You will see
samples of journal notations here and there

throughout the first chapter. You should also understand that you belong to a community of writers, so you may find it helpful to discuss your ideas with family and friends, to let your teacher scan your first drafts, and to solicit feedback from your fellow students. On occasion, you might even write in collaboration with others as a member of a writing team.

Here's one final piece of advice before you start any writing task: complete each stage of the writing process conscientiously and without undo haste. The stages are:

1. generating ideas,
2. drafting,
3. revising, and
4. editing, polishing, and submitting the manuscript.

These four stages are discussed in detail in the sections that follow. Good luck. Perhaps when the school year is over you will be able to take pride in your writing portfolio, which will be a collection of your best works.

1a GENERATING IDEAS

Finding a topic for writing is no easy task. You must start with a general subject, generate ideas about it, and then narrow the focus of it to fit your point of view. Even if your teacher suggests a topic, for example "The Family" or "Drugs and Teenagers," you must generate ideas to find your own focus and format for that topic.

Writing in your journal, talking with others, and reading will help you generate ideas for an essay. You must also consider how a topic will affect you and how it will voice your feelings. Like a fingerprint, your essay will show what makes you a unique person. So let's watch as three writers generate ideas using five brainstorming techniques in their journals.

LISTING KEY WORDS: JOURNAL NOTATION 1

One good strategy for generating ideas is to develop a list of key words about a topic that interests you; then select one item from the list as the primary issue that will be your subject. Other items on the list might serve as subtopics. Let's look at Martin's journal and how he prepared to write an essay about first aid in relation to the assigned topic of "The Family." Martin began by developing a list based on a summer class in first aid.

Things a family needs to know how to do:

CPR	antidotes
Heimlich maneuver	tourniquets
ointments and medication	dressings

With this brief list, Martin could begin making choices. He could write on one first aid technique or use the list as a preliminary outline for writing about all of them.

In the next example, Kimberly began listing ideas for a paper her teacher assigned on "Teenagers and Drugs."

KIMBERLY'S JOURNAL NOTATION

alcohol

tobacco

marijuana

sniffing glue and solvents

Like Martin, Kimberly could choose one topic or develop all four.

In the next example, Ramon selected his own topic—his work at a grocery store.

RAMON'S JOURNAL NOTATION

my job at the grocery store

not enough time to study

my boss is hard to satisfy

customers are weird

hours are long

Ramon had several possible topics: lacking study time, satisfying the boss, and dealing with weird customers. He could choose one of these ideas as a narrow focus or decide to write about all three.

Clustering: Journal Notation 2

Another technique for finding and developing your topic is the cluster (or web), which is a chart of related topics and subtopics. First, write your topic in the center of a sheet of paper and draw a circle around it. Then jot down related ideas, circle them, and draw connecting lines to the main topic. Each major circle should have its own set of satellite subtopics, as shown in this example from Martin's journal.

1a

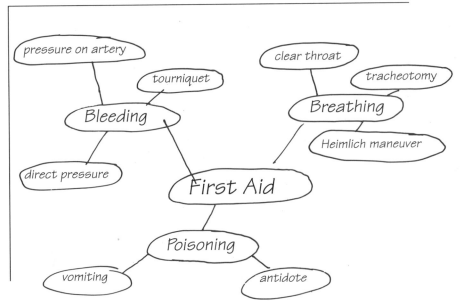

Clustering helped Martin connect his main topic to three subtopics (bleeding, breathing, and poisoning) and to the satellite subtopics.

On the next page, Ramon also clusters his major ideas.

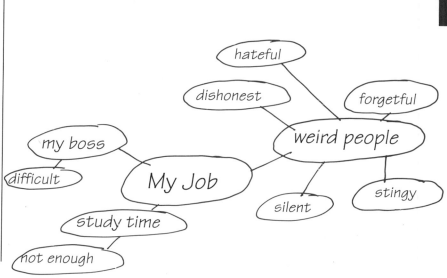

Ramon's choices in clustering began to show his primary interest—the customers. He might decide to explore in more detail his interest in his "weird" customers.

Asking Questions: Journal Notation 3

Yet another useful strategy is to ask yourself a set of questions about your topic. Even if you cannot answer all of them, the questions alone will help you generate ideas. To start, use the questions typically used by journalists: who? what? when? where? why? and how?

MARTIN'S JOURNAL NOTATION

Who can give first aid?

What training is necessary?

Where can a person get training in CPR?

Why do families need to know first aid?

Kimberly used a different set of questions to help her analyze the problems of drug use among teenagers. Note how she has begun to focus on household products.

KIMBERLY'S JOURNAL NOTATION

How do I define "huffing"?

What are the effects of inhaling solvents?

What is the process for getting high on paint thinner?

How does "huffing" compare with smoking marijuana?

Why do young people use these dangerous products?

Kimberly's answers will help her develop a significant part of her rough draft.

Freewriting: Journal Notation 4

This next activity, freewriting, is similar to writing a rough draft except for one thing: it is uncontrolled and spontaneous. Therefore, in your journal, begin a freewheeling, nonstop period of writing for five or ten minutes. Let ideas come tumbling out without concern for form, style, or correctness. Table 1.1 shows a few guidelines for freewriting. Here is one of Ramon's journal entries from a five-minute freewriting session.

RAMON'S JOURNAL NOTATION

One of my regular ladies, Miss Lucy, often shows up with a black eye. I feel sorry for her. She dates this local thug-- just a big ugly guy who always waits outside while she shops. Last week old man Grundy caught her shoplifting. The boss watched from the balcony office while she loaded her purse with all sorts of drugs--antihistamines, decongestants, sleeping pills, and so forth. Man, her purse was bulging. She comes to my counter with a carton of Winstons and a $20 bill. But 'bout that time, old man Grundy rushed up and grabbed her.

"Call the police, Ramon!" he ordered. The old grouch likes to give orders. Then he ripped open her purse and poured all the drugs onto the counter.

She began to cry. "Please, no police. Please? I have money. I'll pay for the drugs."

"No way," cried Grundy. "Ramon, dial 911 now!"

As I dialed 911, I could see Miss Lucy's boyfriend, the thug, leaning against the car, blowing smoke rings, unaware that we had caught his accomplice.

"Mr. Grundy," I said, "there's the one we need to arrest." I pointed to Miss Lucy's boyfriend.

"Oh God," cried Miss Lucy, "now he's really going to beat me."

And sure enough, he did. When I saw her the next morning in the courtroom, she had a cut lip, another black eye, and a bandage on her ear.

I kept my mouth shut, but I wanted to say, "Miss Lucy, you're weird."

Freewriting has helped Ramon draft one character sketch. If he finds it useful, Ramon can include the sketch in his first draft.

TABLE 1.1   Freewriting

---

1. Begin with a subject of interest to you and write whatever comes into your mind.
2. Write quickly for five or ten minutes without pausing to judge, edit, or reflect on your sentences.
3. Explore any aspect of the topic from any conceivable point of view.
4. Switch to different topics if you go blank so that you continue to write without stopping.

Clippings: Journal Notation 5

You may also find it useful to search newspapers and magazines for articles, columns, cartoons, and editorials on your subject. If the newspaper or magazine belongs to you, clip out the interesting material to paste in your journal; otherwise, make a photocopy of the material to paste in your journal. Always make a note of the name of the author, the title and page numbers of the article, the name and location of the publisher, and the year of publication. That way, if you decide to quote from these clippings, you will be able to cite the sources properly (we'll talk more about citing sources later on).

Martin found a helpful drawing of mouth-to-mouth resuscitation and pasted a photocopy of it in his journal.

MARTIN'S JOURNAL

I found this drawing in a book at home: <u>Health for Life</u>, Teacher's Resource Book. Glenview, IL: Scott, Foresman and Company. 127.

Some writers keep a separate clip file, a folder into which they place any article that interests them. It becomes a repository of ideas and topics.

Other Strategies for Generating Ideas

Finally, there are several methods for generating ideas outside the journal. **Reflect** during quiet moments about your subject, **recall** images and ideas, and **make associations** between your personal experiences and the subject at hand. By recalling images of the past and by reflecting on how things might be, you can sharpen your thinking on a topic. Another way to discover ideas is to **discuss** your topic with friends, teachers, family members, and others. Then listen to what they have to say. Make notes during the discussion or soon thereafter. Sometimes a teacher will encourage **brainstorming** sessions in which several students sit together and share ideas. You may also want to conduct an **interview** with a knowledgeable person. If time permits, **read** a story, newspaper report, or magazine article on your subject. For example, let's suppose your topic is "satellite dishes." You would want to find the latest information about the technology, so you would need to examine popular science magazines as well as specialty video magazines.

1b NARROWING THE TOPIC

To keep your topic manageable, you need to find a specific slant or angle for your essay, one that will reflect your interests and viewpoints. You can use your journal to explore whatever special interests you have in your subject.

Narrowing: Journal Notation 6

To narrow your topic to explore a particular angle, write a proposal in your journal that identifies these ingredients:

- your subject,
- your purpose or reason for writing, and
- your target audience.

In later proposals, you can also identify:

- a thesis sentence (explained later in this chapter) and
- a form, such as personal narration or how-to (see Chapter 2).

Here's how three students developed writing proposals to narrow their subjects.

MARTIN'S JOURNAL NOTATION

I want to focus on family first aid because our car almost burned up on the highway one day, and we had no fire extinguisher. Dad burned his hand and arm pretty bad. Thank goodness an old farmer in a battered pickup truck arrived in time. Since then, I have finished courses in home safety, CPR, and other first aid techniques. I think every family should have one member who knows basic first aid.

Martin's writing proposal establishes:

- his subject,
- his purpose or reason for writing,
- a target audience, and
- an explanatory format (see Chapter 2).

RAMON'S JOURNAL NOTATION

I work part-time as a checker at a neighborhood grocery. I deal with people every day. Most folks are nice, but some are weird. I think I'll focus on some of the people who drive me crazy almost every day. I think almost everybody will enjoy hearing about some of my experiences.

Ramon's writing proposal establishes:

- his subject,
- his purpose or reason for writing,
- a general audience, and
- a descriptive format that will feature character sketches.

Martin and Ramon both drew upon personal experience. However, in the next example, Kimberly focused on the subject, not on her personal experiences. She purposely withdraws into the background.

KIMBERLY'S JOURNAL NOTATION

A craze for some teens is "huffing," which involves inhaling various kinds of solvents, sprays, or petroleum products. I can't speak from experience, but I want to explain the highs and lows of "huffing," especially to warn students and parents about its dangers.

Kimberly's writing proposal establishes:

- her subject,
- her purpose or reason for writing,
- a clearly defined target audience,
- an explanatory format, and
- a preliminary thesis (the dangers of "huffing").

Like these three writers, you may find it helpful to develop a writing proposal that outlines your narrow focus and establishes your voice and your version of the experience at the heart of the essay.

1c DEVELOPING A PRELIMINARY THESIS SENTENCE

Almost all pieces of writing have an expressed or implied thesis, which is a theory or opinion about the narrowed topic. Your thesis is the special idea that you want to share with the reader or an issue that you want to explore in depth.

Developing a Thesis Sentence: Journal Notation 7

To develop a preliminary thesis sentence, use your journal to consider answers for three questions:
1. How do I feel about the topic?
2. What aspect will interest somebody else?
3. What is the issue?

Answering these three questions should help you develop a thesis. We have highlighted the thesis in the following notations.

Ramon's Journal Notation

I work part-time as a checker at a neighborhood grocery store. I worry about the hours and loss of study time. I get angry with my boss sometimes, but mostly I must deal with customers every day. Most folks are nice, but some are weird, others are constantly angry, and a few are downright crazy. I've decided that dealing with the public is a lesson in human behavior

Kimberly's Journal Notation

I'm going to focus on "huffing," which describes the way teenagers are inhaling glue, aerosol sprays, butane, paint thinners, and other solvents. I can warn about the dangers, but, mainly, parents need to wake up because the drugs their kids are abusing are right under the kitchen sink and in the workshop.

Martin's Journal Notation

It worries me that most families seem totally unprepared for emergencies. Don't people know that most accidents happen at home? I have studied home safety, CPR, and other first aid techniques, so I want to share that information. The key thing is this: At least one member of every family should learn first aid.

Here are a few specific methods for developing a thesis sentence:

1. State an argument for or against an issue.

Television talk shows capitalize on human emotions by exploring shocking topics.

Insurance rates are unfair to most teenagers.

2. Offer advice or give directives.

People need to become aware of the effect, causes, and cures of dyslexia.

Either we recycle our garbage and waste products or we will live in the middle of them.

3. Suggest consequences.

Children who grow up in a dysfunctional family may become addicted to disorder and carry it into their adult lives.

Christmas has become too commercial--a free-for-all money-grab for retailers, charity organizations, and the media, all of which are intent upon shoving Christmas down our throats until we see evergreens and reindeer everywhere we turn.

4. Give instructions.

Edging is an absolutely necessary part of skiing a slalom race.

Use natural lighting for your photography, not flash; three techniques make natural lighting effective.

5. Offer your personal judgment.

I have found that sensible weight loss and maintenance requires me and others to deal with the psychological and physical dependence on food.

Television is not an atrocious monster and does not turn our minds to mush.

6. Make an interpretation.

Although complicated, William Faulkner's story "The Bear" clearly stands as a symbol for humanity's destruction and demolition of nature and all things natural.

Walter Mitty, in James Thurber's "The Secret Life of Walter Mitty," tries to capture the essence of a child's freedom to make believe. Nowadays, we label this the "Peter Pan Syndrome" for men who refuse to grow up.

7. Suggest or imply a thesis (common in fiction and poetry).

Last line of a poem: Down narrow gravel roads we traveled that day / And passed a Century along the way.

First line of a short story: Stewart's journey into the deep pit of despair began on a foggy September morning with the doctor's casual remark, "We need to do some blood work."

A thesis sentence, as shown above, expresses your key point; it establishes an issue; it gives you a reason for writing; it offers readers an insight into your outlook on the topic. In addition, it will direct the form of the paper, as explained in Chapter 2.

These initial steps, seven journal notations in all, may seem like overkill to you, but methodical preparation will pay off when you begin drafting the actual paper. Your choices about subject, audience, and thesis will be recorded in your journal and will be readily available during your writing of the first draft.

2

CHAPTER

ORGANIZING AND WRITING A FIRST DRAFT

So far, your preliminary journal writing has been spontaneous. You have identified key words, discovered ideas and issues, and framed a working thesis. Now you must make additional choices so that your first draft will be complete. Preplanning requires two steps:

1. You need to choose an appropriate form.

2. You need to organize the material to fit the form.

2a

Form is the framework you choose for communicating your message, such as a personal letter, a poem, or a memo. The word "composition" is like an umbrella: it covers many possible forms. Therefore, we suggest that you make two decisions: which **type** of writing you will develop and which specific **form** best fits your purpose and your thesis sentence (see Table 2.1).

Within your essay, you may, and often should, use more than one type of writing. For example, a persuasive essay will often include an explanation and perhaps a personal experience to illustrate a point. You may also mix forms. For example, a character sketch might require history and reminiscence.

Expressive Writing

In **expressive writing**, the thesis sentence introduces your feelings about a key event or episode in your life, which you will further develop through reminiscence, meditation, or personal narration. You will want to share your private exploration of where, when, and what happened, who was involved, and why it was important. Because you are a central player in the experience you are describing, you should feel free to use "I."

You may choose to write an entire essay that explores one event in your life, or you may want to use a brief anecdote from your life to introduce or conclude an expressive essay. You can organize an expressive piece chronologically, by going from the beginning of the episode to the end, or you may decide to begin at a crucial moment in the episode and then use flashbacks to provide the necessary background.

It is often important in expressive writing to provide a description of the scene and to use dialogue to show the emotions and thoughts of the various people involved. You should use action and dialogue to advance the narration so that you are showing rather than just telling what happened. In concluding an expressive essay, you should imply or openly express why this episode or event made such a strong impression on you.

Explanatory Writing

Explanatory writing is informative writing, so the thesis sentence introduces the subject you are going to describe, interpret, or analyze. In writing an explanatory essay, you need to focus

TABLE 2.1 Types and Forms of Discourse

Type	Purpose	Tone	Form
Expressive writing	Discloses personal feelings	Exploratory, spontaneous, freewheeling, reflective	Journal Freewriting Personal narration Reminiscence Meditation Private letter Opinion paper
Explanatory writing	Communicates basic ideas, information, how-to, and process	Practical, direct, informative, functional	Report Research paper Biography How-to essay Process essay History Analysis
Persuasive writing	Influences others to change opinions and behaviors	Aggressive, forceful, articulate, intensive	Argumentative essay Letter to the editor Editorial Advertisement Political pamphlet Poster Speech Sermon
Creative writing	Explores interest in language, symbolism, and imaginative characters and plots	Inventive, imaginative, experimental	Story Poem Play Sketch Screenplay Television script

primarily on the subject, not your personal feelings or experiences, so you should avoid using "I."

In your opening, focus on defining and describing the subject. Then, provide practical and precise facts about your subject. You can use explanatory writing to describe, explain, and interpret your subject; provide historical background; describe memorable characters; classify parts of your subject and analyze each one; or give how-to instructions. You may also need to use definition, description, comparison and contrast, examples, and other methods to explain the complexity of your subject (these will be discussed in more detail in Chapter 5).

Persuasive Writing

In **persuasive writing**, the thesis sentence sets forth the primary argument with which you hope to encourage your readers to change their behavior or opinions. Your argument will focus your reader's attention on the evidence that supports your position.

In opening a persuasive essay, focus on your cause—defining it and establishing its importance. Then defend your position, suggest the consequences of ignoring your recommendation, and give readers enough details to reach their own decisions. You should also anticipate opposition to your position and offer reasons why your position is the most sensible one. In concluding, you should simply reaffirm your answer, solution, or recommendation.

Creative Writing

In **creative writing**, your spontaneity will prompt you to write a story, a poem, a play, or some other imaginative work that usually features an implied thesis. In writing creatively, you have the freedom to create interesting characters, imaginative scenes, and dramatic plots. However, creative writing isn't just about making up stories; you will best serve your reader if your creative writing addresses a central issue or theme about life.

Your most important role in creative writing is as the narrator. You may choose to use the third-person point-of-view and speak as an outside observer of the action, or you may want to use first-person and speak through one of your characters.

Creative writing generally requires specific forms. For example, short stories usually feature a chronological description of the action with appropriate flashbacks to set the scene. Poems and songs require special line breaks, figurative language, and sometimes special rhyme schemes. Plays and screenplays take careful plotting and precise use of dialogue.

By choosing one of these four types of writing and identifying a specific form, you can organize your first draft. For now, let's look at how Martin used different types of writing in his first draft.

Expressive Writing in Martin's Draft

Martin chose to write a brief anecdote from his life to introduce an explanatory essay on his narrowed topic. Drafting an expressive, personal narration required him to make journal notations about a key event in his life. The notes established where, when, and what happened, who was involved, and why it was important.

Martin organized his draft chronologically, describing the episode from the beginning to the end. He provides description to set the scene, and he uses dialogue to show the emotions and thoughts of various characters.

Martin's use of the first-person "I" is natural because he is a central player in the episode, and he openly expresses why this event made such an impression on him.

MARTIN'S DRAFT (EXPRESSIVE WRITING)

One hot August afternoon, our old Pontiac caught fire on Interstate 40, miles from nowhere. Dad stopped quickly and rushed us to a grass embankment. He raised the hood, and we could see flames flickering on the engine. Dad began to beat at the flames with one of the floor mats, but he jumped back when the flames seared his hand and arm.

Just then, a farmer in a battered green pickup truck rattled to a stop, jumped out with a fire extinguisher, and put out the fire.

"Got here just in time, huh?" he said. He took off his black baseball cap, wiped his brow, and smiled a toothy grin toward me and Mom.

"Yes, thank you very much," said Dad.

"Let's see your burns," the farmer said, examining Dad's lobster-colored hand.

He went back to his truck, returned with a first aid kit, and doctored Dad's hand. Then he carried us all to the next exit where we could get a wrecker and repair work.

We thanked the farmer for his kindness, and he drove off muttering, "Time to feed the stock." A few hours later, our car was repaired and we continued our journey.

> But that's not the end of the story. I kept
> thinking about the farmer and how well-prepared he
> was for an accident. I vowed that I, too, would do
> the same. It has influenced me to study first aid.

Explanatory Writing in Martin's Draft

In an explanatory portion of his draft, Martin focuses on his subject by providing detailed description. He withdraws into the background, avoiding any use of "I." Next, he gives the readers plenty of specifics. He classifies the various stages involved in performing the Heimlich maneuver and explains each one.

MARTIN'S DRAFT (EXPLANATORY WRITING)

> The Heimlich maneuver has saved lives at the
> kitchen table and in restaurants all over the
> world. What happens is that people choke on a piece
> of food, usually when they're trying to talk
> and eat at the same time. They begin to gasp for
> air and point to their throat, and a helpless
> feeling can strike the victim as well as the
> people at the table. The Heimlich maneuver, though,
> is pretty simple. Just stand behind the person,
> place your hands in a ball just below the sternum,

and quickly pull upward. The thrust of air upward
into the windpipe will usually dislodge the object.
Then, everyone can go quietly back to the meal.

Persuasive Writing in Martin's Draft

Martin also experimented with beginning his
draft persuasively; he wants to persuade his
readers of the importance of learning first aid.
After an opening sentence that states his argument, he provides examples to defend his position. Then he suggests the consequences and
gives readers enough details to help them reach
their own decision.

MARTIN'S DRAFT (PERSUASIVE WRITING)

A knowledge of first aid is a valuable
possession. Accidents occur every day, everywhere,
and without regard to age, race, sex, or class.
People just get hurt. The baby sprays carpet
cleaner in her eyes, Dad falls from the ladder
while cleaning the gutters, or Mom cuts her hand
while slicing a block of cheese. Calling the rescue
squad is important, but more vital is the immediate
action by other family members. Too many things can

go wrong while you wait for the ambulance and police: the baby screams in hysteria, Dad lies unconscious, Mom's hand spurts blood. Yet there is an answer. Every family needs a good first aid kit and at least one person who knows basic first aid techniques.

2b METHODS FOR DRAFTING THE COMPOSITION

The suggestions about form and content suggest a careful, planned approach to writing. This method has many benefits. For one, preplanning often results in a more complete draft with a recognizable introduction, body, and conclusion. However, you need to write with whatever method works best for you. Many writers find one of the following methods more to their liking.

Spontaneous writing of the draft is an impulsive explosion of ideas as you attempt to discover what you know or think about a subject. Spontaneous writing is generally not very well organized, however, and needs careful revision.

Step-by-step writing can be useful for writing a little passage here and a little passage there. Then you must pull all the pieces into a whole. Step-by-step writing requires you to know your subject well and to keep in mind the necessary ingredients of your form; otherwise, you may end up with a hodgepodge of only marginally related material.

For a change of pace, let's look at Kimberly's first draft.

KIMBERLY'S FIRST DRAFT

Huffing

A new craziness for teens is "huffing." Huffing can be defined as getting high by inhaling the organic solvents used to make aerosol sprays and petroleum products. The cost of drugs such as cocaine and pot continues to tower, so teens between the ages of 11 and 14 find it tough to purchase these drugs. Even cigarettes are out of reach in price. The teens have found a cheaper way to get high, but it can be more deadly than any other drug. The drugs kids have discovered now include products like fabric protector, butane, and paint thinner, to name just a few. So parents need to wake up, because the drugs the kids are abusing are right there under the kitchen sink and in the garage.

Why do it? One reason would be the low cost; for example, a can of butane can be purchased for under a dollar. Also, parents purchase most of the items: fabric protector, nail polish, nail polish remover, cooking sprays, glues, gasoline, hair spray, propane gas, and so on. The stuff is all over the house. Another reason for huffing is convenience. I know a student who puts paint thinner on the sleeve of his shirt and sniffs on it all day. Some kids spray an inhalant on a handkerchief or into a plastic ziplock bag and sniff away at school or at parties. Parents and teachers never know. Also, huffing is easy. There are no needles, pills, or smelly tobaccos.

When babies start crawling and walking, parents hide all harmful household products. When children get to be teens, parents stop hiding the products. So while the parents worry about getting to soccer practice on time, the children worry about which bottle or can to inhale next. If a mother notices her daughter using more hair spray than normal, does the thought ever cross her mind that her daughter may inhale it? No, she doesn't think twice about it--but she should.

The dangers are real. A kid in my class died last year in his garage. Nothing was said in public, but we knew he was sniffing. Yet I've got friends who dared me to try sniffing butane at a party last week. I took a little sniff, but I didn't inhale like they were doing. I hate to think about what it might be doing to their brains.

REVISING

To revise means *to reexamine* and *to alter.* To revise your first draft, you will want to rework it as a whole; merely reading it again will not suffice. You may think your essay says everything necessary, but you must keep in mind that your readers have three primary expectations:

1. They want an introduction that names the subject and establishes an issue.

2. They expect a well-developed body that examines several key issues with specific details.

3. They require a conclusion that offers an idea worth thinking about.

Therefore, you should revise your draft by using one or more of the checklists in this chapter. The checklists suggest specific methods for rebuilding the draft with additional sentences and paragraphs that expand on and support your main idea.

3a CHECKLIST 1: ANSWERING QUESTIONS ABOUT YOUR FIRST DRAFT

As you revise, you may find it helpful to respond to a series of tough questions about your draft. The following checklist offers some possible questions to consider; the responses are by Kimberly about her first draft, "Huffing."

REVISING CHECKLIST: GLOBAL CONCERNS

1. Is the main idea expressed clearly?
   Yes, I explain "huffing" and I warn about the dangers of "sniffing."

2. Is the main idea supported and illustrated with any of these details?

   Examples Yes, I have several examples.
   Definitions Yes, I define "huffing."
   Descriptions A few, but maybe I could describe a neighborhood scene of boys sniffing paint thinner in the garage while the parents watch television.
   Comparisons Huffing is compared to pot, cocaine, and cigarettes.
   Processes Several methods of huffing are mentioned.
   Classifications Four reasons for huffing are listed.
   Causes and effects The paper warns about the dangers.
   Personal narration Yes, I mention my experience with huffing.
   Expert testimony None, but I know that <u>Redbook</u> has an article about it.

3. Does the paper reach a conclusion?
   I mention the dangers, but maybe I can make a stronger argument against the practice.

Armed with her answers, Kimberly could begin revision. However, there are additional checklists that you might find useful.

3b CHECKLIST 2: OUTLINING THE ROUGH DRAFT

You should always examine your essay to be sure that you have three essential parts—an introduction, a body, and a conclusion. Even if you started with a rough outline, now is a good time to outline what you have actually written in the draft. You can use the questions in the following checklist to check your outline.

REVISING CHECKLIST: OUTLINING THE ROUGH DRAFT

1. Does the draft have an identifiable introduction that names the subject and provides a thesis sentence?
2. Does the draft have a body of paragraphs that expand on and support the main idea?
3. Does the flow of ideas seem logical? Is the material well organized?
4. Was anything left out or does anything need further discussion?
5. Does the conclusion give the readers something to think about? Does it summarize my position?

In outlining your draft, list your main ideas on the left side of a piece of paper and, on the right, make notes about ways you might improve the organization of the essay. Here is Kimberly's outline of her draft.

Introduction

Defines "huffing"   Add description of boys in
                          the garage

Has little or no cost
                          Add a quotation from an
                          expert
Gives examples

Gives a warning
(the thesis)

Body

Low cost   Make each of these a full,
                          separate paragraph

Convenient

Easy to do

Adults easily fooled   Comment more on parents,
                          especially if both work

Conclusion

The dangers   Add a quotation from a
                          user, a parent, an expert?

Examples   Make a serious, final
                          statement

You should be certain that early in your composition you have named your subject and provided a thesis sentence. There are many techniques you can use to invite the reader into your
essay, story, or poem. Consider the following
checklist of options.

REVISING CHECKLIST: THE INTRODUCTION

1. Do I need to provide background information or historical facts?
   What happened in the past that has affected our view
   of this topic? Why is it significant today?
2. Should I give biographical facts about key people?
   Who are the key people? What did they do? Why are
   they significant?
3. Would it help to describe a scene?
   Can the reader visualize this setting? Why is the place
   significant? How does it contribute to the issues that the
   essay will examine?
4. Should I provide an interesting narrative sketch?
   What significant event occurred? How does it relate to
   the subject matter of the essay? What issue might the
   narration raise in readers' minds?
5. Should I use a question to present the issue?
   What is the issue at hand? How does it affect me and
   others? How can it be defined?

6. Can I compare past events with present circumstances? What happened? Why was it significant? How does it affect us today? How does it differ today from yesterday?

7. Do I need to define complex terms?
   What does this term mean? Can I give examples? Can I compare it with other things with which my readers might be familiar?

8. Should I offer quotations from others?
   What do the experts say about this topic, as drawn from contemporary magazines? What do the great thinkers say about the subject, as drawn from a dictionary of quotations?

9. Do I provide a thesis sentence?
   Review pages 20–24 if necessary.

The example that follows shows Kimberly's revision notes for her introduction.

Huffing

A new craziness for teens is "huffing." Huffing can be defined as getting high by inhaling the organic solvents used to make aerosol sprays and petroleum products. The cost of drugs such as cocaine and pot continues to tower, so teens between the ages of 11 to 14 find it tough to purchase these

Describe a neighborhood scene: boys in garage huffing while their parents watch TV.

Add this quote from Redbook: Neil Rosenberg, a Denver neurologist, says, "The sobering truth is that inhalants are more poisonous to drugs. Even cigarettes are out of reach in price. The teens have found a cheaper way to get high, but it can be more deadly than any other drug. The drugs kids have discovered now include products like fabric protector, butane, and paint thinner, to name just a few. So parents need to wake up, because the drugs the kids are abusing are right there under the kitchen sink and in the garage.

the body than all other drugs combined" (qtd. in "Fatal Attraction" 78)

Kimberly plans to strengthen her opening by adding a description and a quotation. She will edit the wording later; right now she wants to build the substance of the essay.

3d CHECKLIST 4: REVISING THE BODY

The body of your paper should provide fundamental information that supports your thesis sentence. For example, Kimberly's thesis warns parents about the dangers of huffing. In the middle paragraphs of her essay, she, like you, must decide how to organize and discuss her material. Consider the questions in the following checklist as you revise the body of your essay. Please note that the explanations of these strategies will be found in Chapter 5.

✔ REVISING CHECKLIST: THE BODY

1. Should I classify the issues (see 3b above)?
2. Do I need to explain the problem?
3. Should I give reasons for present conditions?
4. Would it help to suggest consequences unless things change?
5. Should I compare and contrast two or more items?
6. Do I need to give a quotation from an outside source?
7. Should I trace a process or a sequence of events?
8. Should I show both negative and positive conditions?
9. Would it be useful to ask questions and give answers?
10. Should I give an illustration or example?
11. Should I tell a story?
12. Do I need to define technical and unusual terms?

Shown below are Kimberly's notations for revising the middle two paragraphs of her rough draft. You will see that she responded to the checklist in several ways.

Why do it? One reason would be the low cost; for example, a can of butane can be purchased for under a dollar. Also, parents purchase most of the items: fabric protector, nail polish, nail polish remover, cooking sprays, glues, gasoline, hair spray, propane gas, and so on. The stuff is all over the house. Another reason for huffing is convenience. I know a student who puts paint thinner on the sleeve of his shirt and sniffs on it all day. Some kids spray an inhalant on a handkerchief or into a plastic ziplock bag and sniff away at school or at parties. Parents and teachers never know. Also, huffing is easy. There are no needles, pills, or smelly tobaccos.

When babies start crawling and walking, parents hide all harmful household products. When children get to be teens, parents stop hiding the products. So while the parents worry about getting to soccer practice on

Make reason #1 a paragraph.

Make "convenience" a separate paragraph; add more examples.

Move down to be the fourth reason. Build into a full paragraph that shows how easy it is—sniffing a loaded cloth, inhaling from a sack or plastic bag, or sucking butane directly from the pressurized can.

time, the children worry about which
bottle or can to inhale next.
If a mother notices her
daughter using more hair spray
than normal, does the thought
ever cross her mind that her
daughter may inhale it? No, she
doesn't think twice about it--
but she should.

*Here's the
fourth
reason--adults are
easily fooled.*

3e CHECKLIST 5: REVISING THE CONCLUSION

In your conclusion, try to write more than a summary of your primary ideas. Instead, express your concern about the problem you have discussed and thereby leave your readers with something to remember. Consider the following checklist as you revise to frame an effective conclusion.

REVISING CHECKLIST: THE CONCLUSION

1. Should I offer a solution?
2. Should I interpret the facts?
3. Would it be helpful to ask a final question and answer it?

4. Do I need to elaborate upon my thesis sentence?
5. Should I quote an expert on the subject?
6. Should I give directions or a call to action?
7. Should I affirm the future?
8. Do I need to reach a judgment about personal experiences?

Again, let's look at Kimberly's revision notations for her conclusion.

The dangers are real. A kid in my class died last year in his garage. Nothing was said in public, but we knew he was sniffing. Yet I've got friends who dared me to try sniffing butane at a party last week. I took a little sniff, but I didn't inhale like they were doing. I hate to think about what it might be doing to their brains.

I really need to rework this part to focus on the dangers, maybe use another quote, and ask two key questions. Is a two-minute high worth the risk? Parents, do you know what your children are doing with your hair spray?

3f WRITING THE SECOND DRAFT

On rare occasions, you might move directly from the first draft to a polished manuscript; however, if you have revised conscientiously in the manner shown by Kimberly's notes, you will need a second draft so that you can concentrate wholly on editing, which will be explained in Chapter 4.

Shown below is Kimberly's second draft. In addition to some rewording, Kimberly added some new material, which is shown in boldface.

```
                    Huffing

    On a quiet suburban street, several sets of
parents relax in their family rooms, comfortable in
the knowledge that their sons are at Jason's home
making model airplanes in the garage.  Meanwhile,
the 13-year-old boys are sniffing glue and giggling
absurdly with the reaction to their central nervous
systems.  Unknown to their parents, the boys are
"huffing."
```

Huffing is the new craziness for teens, who get high by sniffing or inhaling the solvents used to make aerosol sprays and petroleum products. The cost of drugs such as cocaine and pot continues to tower, so teens between the ages of 11 and 14 find it tough to purchase these drugs. Even cigarettes are out of reach in price. The teens have found a cheaper way to get high, but it can be more deadly than any other drug. The drugs kids have discovered now include products like fabric protector, butane, and paint thinner, to name just a few. **Neil Rosenberg, a Denver neurologist, says, "The sobering truth is that inhalants are more poisonous to the body than all other drugs combined" (qtd. in "Fatal Attraction" 78).** So parents need to **check out the boys in the garage** because the drugs the kids are abusing are right there in the garage or under the kitchen sink.

Why do it? One reason would be the low cost; for example, a can of butane can be purchased for under a dollar. Also, parents purchase most of the items: fabric protector, nail polish, nail polish remover, cooking sprays, glues, gasoline, hair spray, propane gas, and so on. The stuff is all over the house.

Another reason for huffing is convenience. I know a student who puts paint thinner on the sleeve of his shirt and sniffs on it all day. Some kids spray an inhalant on a handkerchief or into a plastic ziplock bag and sniff away at school or at parties. **A can of butane is easily carried in a purse or pocket and shared with friends in the bathrooms. A can of hair spray can sit in a school locker without triggering questions.**

Also, huffing is easy. There are no needles, pills, or smelly tobaccos. **All one needs to do is douse a cloth with lighter fluid or paint thinner and take a deep breath through the cloth. It's also easy to stick a canister of butane in your mouth and shoot a blast down your throat. After all, the products are not illegal, like pot, and no age limit exists for purchasing the items, like alcohol.**

Parents and teachers never know. When babies start crawling and walking, parents hide all harmful household products. When children get to be teens, parents stop hiding the products. So while the parents worry about getting to soccer practice on time, the children worry about which bottle or can to inhale next. If a mother notices her daughter using more hair spray than normal, does the thought ever cross her mind that her daughter may inhale it? No, she doesn't think twice about it--but she should.

Two questions come to mind--one for the teens
and one for their parents. First is the two-minute
high worth the risk? The dangers are real. A kid
in my class died last year in his garage. Nothing
was said in public, but we knew he was sniffing.
Yet I've got friends who dared me to try sniffing
butane at a party last week. I took a little
sniff, but I didn't inhale like they were doing.
I hate to think about what it might be doing to
their brains. Dr. Rosenberg says huffing can
cause blindness, brain damage, lung failure, and
injury to the kidneys and liver (qtd. in "Fatal
Attraction" 78). Second, parents, do you know what
your children are doing with your hair spray or the
propane gas in your outdoor grill? Hundreds of
products can be sniffed, so you can't hide them
all. The best answer, perhaps the only answer, is
this one: communicate with your children daily.

4

CHAPTER

EDITING AND POLISHING THE COMPOSITION

To edit means *to correct* a composition in preparation for your readers. Therefore, after you have revised your composition, you should make several trips through the material to edit it for specific problems. The checklists in this chapter, with explanations, will show you how to edit your papers.

Please note that this chapter provides only the editing checklists.

To learn more, see the in-depth analysis provided in the following chapters:

Chapter 5 Writing Effective Paragraphs
Chapter 6 Writing Effective Sentences
Chapter 7 Using Language Effectively
Chapter 8 Bringing Your Writing to Life

4a EDITING CHECKLIST 1: EXAMINE EACH PARAGRAPH FOR UNITY

If your paper has *unity*, it sticks to the main point and does not drift beyond the essential issues. To edit your paper for unity, work through the following checklist.

EDITING CHECKLIST: UNITY

1. What is my thesis sentence? Does each paragraph include material that explains and defends my position? Each paragraph should give different information, yet each one should be centered on your narrowed topic. Kimberly, for example, has seven paragraphs to develop her thesis. Two paragraphs point forward to the issue, four paragraphs explain why youngsters huff, and the conclusion arrives at the warning to teens and parents.

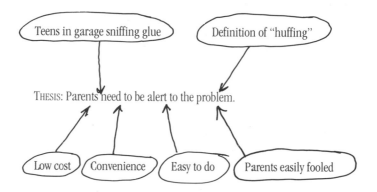

CONCLUSION: the dangers and the need for parent-child communication

Can you make a similar diagram of your paper?

2. What is the topic sentence for each of my paragraphs? Does each sentence explain and develop my position? The topic sentence of a paragraph, which is often the first sentence, serves as the subject of the individual paragraph and sets the direction for all sentences in that one paragraph. The topic sentence serves the reader, who will read it and then look for specific supporting information. Kimberly, for example, begins her final paragraph with this sentence:

Two questions come to mind--one for the teens and one for their parents.

This sentence acts as a contract with her reader; she must now provide two questions and, perhaps, give her answers. In another place, she opens a paragraph with this sentence:

Another reason for huffing is convenience.

For unity, the sentences that make up the rest of the paragraph must show how convenient "huffing" can be.

If any sentence in a paragraph does not support the topic sentence, delete it, move it, or alter it.

4b EDITING CHECKLIST 2: EXAMINE EACH PARAGRAPH FOR COHERENCE

Coherence means that each sentence flows smoothly into the next one. A coherent paragraph moves readers from one idea to the next through the use of transitions and the repetition of key words. Consider the following checklist as you edit your paper for coherence.

 EDITING CHECKLIST: COHERENCE

1. Does every sentence relate logically to its neighbors?
   Each sentence in a paragraph should build on the one that precedes it. Any paragraph that contains sentences that don't seem to relate to one another is not coherent. For example, Kimberly shouldn't use a sentence about the convenience of huffing in a paragraph on the dangers of huffing.
2. Do key words appear more than once?
   Using key words several times within a paragraph helps keep readers on track by keeping their minds on the

topic at hand. Be careful not to cross the line into repetitiveness, however. Using synonyms for key words is often just as helpful.

3. Have I used transitional words (such as *for example, the next day, in another part of the house,* and *shortly thereafter*) to help readers move from one idea to the next? Coherent paragraphs move from one idea to another. You can help readers see the movement by using a variety of transitional devices.

4. Have I used pronouns to rename key words? If you feel you are using key words too often and cannot find good synonyms, try to use pronouns in the place of key words.

Let's look at Kimberly's revision to check for coherence in one of her paragraphs. Revisions are shown in boldface.

Why do it? One reason would be the low cost **or no cost at all for inhalants. First,** a can of butane **or a tube of glue** can be purchased for under a dollar. **Second,** parents purchase most of the items: fabric protector, nail polish, nail polish remover, cooking sprays, glues, gasoline, hair spray, propane gas, and so on. **Inhalants are** all over the house.

By establishing two elements—low cost or no cost—Kimberly gains coherence by using "first" and "second" to open two of her sentences. Repetition of the word "inhalants" brings additional coherence and allows Kimberly to eliminate the slang word "stuff."

4c EDITING CHECKLIST 3: EDIT EVERY VERB

We suggest that you make one trip through your paper to look carefully at the verb of each sentence. Verbs report actions and, on occasion, show a state of being. With action verbs you can show change, activity, motion, sensations, moods, process, and conditions. Use the following checklist to be sure that your verbs are correct and useful.

EDITING CHECKLIST: VERBS

1. Do I express important actions as verbs, not as nouns?

DULL: The principal will use **suspension** to punish three students.

REVISED: The principal will **suspend** three students.

2. Do I use too many boring linking verbs (*am, is, are, was, were, being, been*)?

Using too many common linking verbs can deaden your writing. As you edit your essay, look for opportunities to drop common linking verbs in favor of linking verbs with more precision (such as *appear, become, feel, grow, look, remain, seem, smell, taste,* and *stand*). You can also change linking verbs to action verbs.

DULL: The teacher **was** wise to our practical jokes.

REVISED: The teacher **grew** wise to our practical jokes.

3. Do I use too many verbs in transitive passive voice that could be changed to active voice?

In active voice, the subject performs the action; in passive voice, the subject receives the action—it does not act. In passive voice, the actor appears in a prepositional phrase or sometimes does not appear at all. See **10b** for a detailed explanation of passive and active voice.

DULL: Fire safety is **encouraged** in all schools, so fire drills **are held** each month.

REVISED: Schools **practice** fire safety with drills each month.

4d EDITING CHECKLIST 4: REPLACE GENERAL WORDS WITH SPECIFIC NOUNS, ADJECTIVES, AND ADVERBS

Again, make a trip through your composition to judge your choice of words. Use the following checklist to look for ways to add specific nouns and precise modifiers.

EDITING CHECKLIST: USING PRECISE WORDS

1. Have I selected the best possible word from all the words I know, not just the first word that came to mind? You have an internal vocabulary list of words that you have stored away in a memory bank year after year, and you can remember useful synonyms if you will only pause and think for a moment. Given the word *car*, for example, you can quickly think of *auto*, *Thunderbird*, *convertible*, *wheels*, and so on. Therefore, edit your essay for the most precise words:

   sweltering afternoon   timeworn dairy barn

   /   /

   On a [~~very hot day~~] in July, the [~~old building~~] burned.

   In the example above, the writer has searched her mind for more specific words and made her selections:

HOT: scorching, sizzling, **sweltering**, torrid, blistering, fiery

DAY: midday, noon, morning, dawn, **afternoon**, evening

OLD: ancient, aged, **timeworn**, age-old, weather-battered

BUILDING: barn, **dairy barn**, milking shed

In like manner, you must scan your internal list of words and, at times, expand your choices by using a thesaurus or a computer's wordfinder.

2. Have I used concrete and specific modifiers so my readers can visualize a scene?

Try to show your readers rather than merely tell them. The following sentence needs specific language:

VAGUE: The teacher was hurt when she fell at school.

REVISED: Mrs. Roberts, the geometry teacher, tumbled headfirst down a flight of stairs, but luckily she only twisted an ankle.

3. Do my modifiers imply the right feeling or image?

Your choice of words can have a great impact on your readers. Be as precise as possible in choosing modifiers that will create the right image for your readers.

gruesome

/

The students viewed the [ugly] carcass of a dead cat.

repeatedly.

/

He took the SAT exam a [lot of times].

4. Have I used inappropriate slang words, stuffy words, and cliches?

delivered an excellent

/

The school players [~~are totally awesome in their thespian~~] interpretation of King Lear.

The writer above eliminated a slang word (*awesome*) and a stuffy word (*thespian*).

5. Have I used any biased or sexist language?
Edit any sexist or biased language that may appear in your prose ("the doctor . . . he" or "the nurse . . . she") by using more precise terminology instead. Use *he* and *him* if your principal is Robert G. Searcy; likewise, use *she* or *her* to replace Principal Gloria Stanton. Otherwise, change references to neutral alternatives (*personnel*, not *manpower*; *flight attendant*, not *stewardess*).

a

/

Every high school coach in the county must submit [~~his~~] final basketball schedule by October.

4e EDITING CHECKLIST 5: AVOID WORDINESS

Good writers often repeat key words; but wordiness is a different matter, and it comes in several forms. Work through the following checklist to avoid wordiness in your essay.

EDITING CHECKLIST: ELIMINATING WORDINESS

1. Do I use any words or phrases that merely repeat the same idea?

   WORDY: First of all, the initial down payment for fees will be $5.

   REVISED: The down payment for fees will be $5.

   WORDY: The play that the group chose to perform was a play by Shakespeare that he named <u>King Lear</u>.

   REVISED: The group chose to perform Shakespeare's <u>King Lear</u>.

2. Have I used a primer style?
   A primer style of writing uses many short sentences—the *see Dick run/see Jane run* style. Edit any string of simple sentences into more varied sentence forms.

   PRIMER STYLE: William Shakespeare wrote <u>Julius Caesar</u>. It is a play about dirty politics. The setting is the Roman Empire, and Julius Caesar seemed to be the invincible conqueror. His enemies quietly plot behind his back. Marcus Brutus was an idealist. Caius Cassius was a realist. Mark Antony was a scheming orator.

REVISED: William Shakespeare's <u>Julius Caesar</u> concentrates on the dirty politics of the Roman Empire. Julius Caesar seemed to be an invincible conqueror, but Marcus Brutus, an idealist, and Caius Cassius, a realist, plotted against him. Julius Caesar was followed in office by the scheming orator Mark Antony.

3. Do I have any sentences that begin with expletives? The expletives *there, what,* or *it* delay important ideas, so begin your sentences with good adjectives and nouns.

delete

/

[~~There is a chance that~~] Snow days may cause school sessions to continue into June.

delete   delete

/   /

[~~It was~~] The speech instructor [~~who~~] identified my French accent.

4f EDITING CHECKLIST 6: BE GRAMMATICALLY CORRECT

Errors in grammar and mechanics can be glaring, and they seriously undermine the reader's confidence in your ability as a writer. As you edit, use the questions in the following checklist to help you find and correct grammatical errors.

 EDITING CHECKLIST: CORRECT GRAMMAR

1. Have I misspelled any words?
   Check and double-check your spelling, watching especially for words that sound alike but are spelled differently and for words that you mispronounce.

   accept   a lot   athletes

   /   /   /

   If we [except] them into the club, we'll have [~~alot~~] of [~~atheletes~~] join.

   See **4g** for information on using your computer to check your spelling.
2. Have I written any fragments?
   A fragment appears when you allow a phrase or subordinate clause to pose as a sentence. See **7a** for additional details.

FRAGMENTS: The members of the pep band were ready. Starting at the top. Playing their very best. The district ribbon was on the line.

REVISION: Starting at the top, the members of the pep band were ready to play their very best. The district ribbon was on the line.

3. Do I have any dangling modifiers that need to be attached to the correct word?
   A modifier dangles if it does not logically and clearly refer to the noun, pronoun, or verb that you mean to describe. Be sure modifying phrases have a clear reference.

DANGLING MODIFIER: Stuttering at the beginning of every sentence, the speech teacher tried to help me.

The speech teacher did not stutter, so the writer must edit the sentence.

REVISED: Stuttering at the beginning of every sentence, I sought help from the speech teacher.

4. Have I made any errors in punctuation?
   Check the accuracy of your punctuation, especially the use of commas (see Chapter 11 for additional information).

The pep band played last week at the district festival [,] but it came home without any type of trophy.

5. Have I made any other grammatical mistakes?
   Watch for any other grammatical errors, such as the wrong form of the verb or incorrect subject-verb agreement.

WRONG FORM: Everyone on the team **getting their** new track shoes this week.

REVISED: Everyone on the team **will get** a pair of new track shoes this week.

REVISED: Team members **will get** their new track shoes this week.

4g EDITING CHECKLIST 7: USING A COMPUTER

A word processor can help you make both major and minor changes in the text and to print various drafts. Use the following checklist to be sure you are getting the most out of your computer.

EDITING CHECKLIST: USING THE COMPUTER

1. Have I checked my spelling with the computer?
   If you type your paper on some computers, the software will check your spelling and identify misspelled words. Be aware, however, that these programs will not alert you if you have used *their* instead of *there* or *to* instead of *too*.

2. Have I used the grammar software?
   Some computer programs examine your grammar, locating passive voice, wordiness, and punctuation errors. You should pay attention to these warnings, but remember that a computer can't read for individual style.

3. Have I used the FIND and FIND/REPLACE features to edit?

The FIND (or SEARCH) function of your computer will move the cursor quickly to a troublesome word or a common grammatical error.

a. Words commonly misused. Do you sometimes use *alot* rather than a *lot* and *to* rather than *too*? If so, order a SEARCH for *alot* and then for *to* and correct your errors accordingly. You know your weaknesses, so use the computer to search for problem words, such as these.

accept/except	farther/further
adapt/adopt	its/it's
advice/advise	lay/lie
all ready/already	on/onto
among/between	passed/past
cite/site	suppose to/supposed to
criteria/criterion	use to/used to

A spelling checker will accept these words as spelled correctly, so the FIND function is necessary.

b. Contractions. Avoid overusing contractions (*can't, won't, didn't*). You can easily correct them by searching for the apostrophe (').

c. Pronouns. *He, she, it, they,* and *their* can be troublesome because who or what these pronouns refer to can be unclear. For example, FIND *he* to be sure that it refers specifically to one man.

Stonewall Jackson served General Lee valiantly in the battles against Union forces. He was a man of raw courage.

The cursor blinking at *He* encourages a change to:

Stonewall Jackson served General Lee valiantly in the battles against Union forces. Jackson, like Lee, was a man of raw courage.

A search for the word *this* might uncover:

One teacher gave this advice: "Reading has more staying power than television." This is a good point, but it dismayed the couch potatoes in the audience.

The first highlighted *this* serves correctly as an adjective, but the second acts as a subject. Change it from a subject to an adjective:

This point dismayed the couch potatoes in the audience.

d. Punctuation. Use FIND to locate every comma (,) and every semicolon (;) to establish your accuracy (see Chapter 11). If you employ parentheses regularly, search for the opening parentheses and check visually for a closing one.

e. Abbreviations. Use the FIND and REPLACE function to put into final form any abbreviated words or phrases employed in the early draft(s). For example, you might have saved time in drafting your paper by typing SL for *The Scarlet Letter.* Now is the time to SEARCH for each instance of SL and to replace it automatically with the full title.

Designing the Manuscript with a Computer

You can use a computer to realign sentences, adjust paragraphs, and format entire pages. You can also add, delete, or rewrite material anywhere within the body.

Computers also allow you to create graphic designs and transfer them into your text. Some computers will allow you to create bar, line, or pie graphs as well as spreadsheets and other original designs. Such materials can enhance the quality of your presentation. Note how the following writer used graphics to embellish the text.

We need to accept the existence of global communication networks that have shrunk the globe. All nations have become neighbors by means of satellites in space and the receiving dishes on the ground. We can not only talk across the oceans, but we can also look down and see what is happening within any

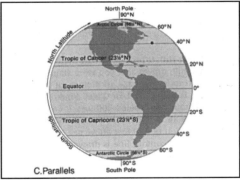

```
square mile around the globe. As a result, all
nations ought to be good neighbors with all others,
but it is just not so.
```

Use graphics only where appropriate. Do not substitute graphics for good solid prose or use them to dazzle the reader when your information is flimsy.

4h PROOFREADING

To proofread means *to read and correct.* Get into the habit of proofreading your final manuscript carefully. Marring a page with corrections is better than leaving an error in your paper. Learn to use these standard proofreading symbols.

error in spelling (m*i*stake)
close up (mis‿take)
delete and close up (mis⁄take)
insert (mi︠s︡take)
transpose elements (mi︡ts︠ake)
delete a letter (mistake͢e)
capital letter (m̲istake)
insert paragraph ¶

The following example shows how Kimberly edited two paragraphs of her second draft.

~~Another reason for~~ Huffing is convenience, **to** I

know a student who puts paint thinner on the sleeve

of his shirt and sniffs on it all day. Some ~~kids~~ **students**

spray ~~an~~ **a** inhalant**s** on ~~a~~ **a** handkerchief**s** or into ~~a~~ **a**

plastic ziplock bag**s** and sniff away at school or at

parties. **Students can easily carry a can of butane** ~~A can of butane is easily carried~~ in a

purse or pocket and shared **it** with friends in the

bathrooms. A **Student can set a** can of hair spray ~~can sit~~ in a school

locker without triggering questions.

Why do it? ~~Also~~ huffing is easy. **Sniffing requires** ~~There are~~ no needles,

no pills, or smelly tobaccos. **A teen can merely** ~~All one needs to do is~~

douse a cloth with lighter fluid or paint thinner

and take a deep breath through the cloth. **More daring, but** ~~It's also~~

also easy is ~~easy~~ to stick a canister of butane in your mouth

and shoot a blast down your throat. After all, the

products are not illegal, like pot, and no age

limit exists for purchasing the items, like

alcohol.

4i PREPARING THE MANUSCRIPT

Your teachers will provide specific information about the format required in their classes. In general, you should double-space throughout the paper, whether handwritten or typed. Provide your name and course information in the upper left corner of the first page. Place your last name and the page number at the top right margin of every page. Do not use a plastic cover. Do not write a separate title page. Do not write "The End" to close your paper. A sample final manuscript with the teacher's grade and comment follows.

                                          Spann 1

Kimberly Spann

English, Mrs. Roomer

April 6, 1993

                    Huffing

    On a quiet suburban street, several sets of

parents relax in their family rooms, comfortable in

the knowledge that their sons are at Jason's home

making model airplanes in the garage. Meanwhile,

the 13-year-old boys are sniffing glue and giggling

absurdly with the reaction to their central nervous

systems. Unknown to their parents, the boys are
"huffing."

Huffing is the new craziness for teens, who
get high by sniffing or inhaling the solvents used
to make aerosol sprays and petroleum products. The
cost of drugs such as cocaine and pot continues to
tower, so young teens of 11 to 14 find it difficult
to purchase these drugs. Even cigarettes have
become too expensive. The teens have found a
cheaper way to get high, but it can be more deadly
than any other drug. The drugs teens have
discovered include products like nail polish
remover, butane, and paint thinner, to name just a
few. Neil Rosenberg, a Denver neurologist, says,
"The sobering truth is that inhalants are more
poisonous to the body than all other drugs
combined" (qtd.in "Fatal Attraction" 78). So
parents need to check out the boys in the garage
because the teens now abuse drugs found in the
garage and under the kitchen sink.

Why do it? One reason would be the low cost or
no cost at all for inhalants. First, a teen can
purchase a can of butane or a tube of glue for
under a dollar. Second, parents purchase most of
the items: fabric protector, nail polish, nail
polish remover, cooking sprays, glues, gasoline,

hair spray, propane gas, and so on. Inhalants appear on shelves all over the house.

Why do it? Huffing is convenient. I know a student who puts paint thinner on the sleeve of his shirt and sniffs on it all day. Some students spray inhalants on handkerchiefs or into a plastic ziplock bag and sniff away at school or at parties. Students can easily carry a can of butane in a purse or pocket and share it with friends in the bathrooms. A student can set a can of hair spray in a school locker without triggering questions.

Why do it? Huffing is easy. Sniffing requires no needles, pills, or smelly tobaccos. A teen can merely douse a cloth with lighter fluid or paint thinner and take a deep breath through the cloth. More daring, but also easy, is to stick a canister of butane in your mouth and shoot a blast down your throat. After all, the products are not illegal, like pot, and no age limit exists for purchasing the items, like alcohol.

Why do it? Parents and teachers never know. When babies start crawling and walking, parents hide all harmful household products. When the children get to be teens, parents stop hiding the products. So while the parents worry about getting to soccer practice on time, the children worry about which substance to inhale next. If a mother notices her daughter using more hair spray than normal, does she suspect that her daughter may be inhaling it? No, she doesn't think twice about it and, in fact, buys even more hair spray.

Two questions come to mind--one for the teens and one for their parents. Is the two-minute high worth the risk? The dangers are real. A kid in my class died last year in his garage. Nobody said anything in public, but we knew he was sniffing. Yet I've got friends who dared me to try sniffing butane at a party last week. I squirted some into my mouth, but I didn't inhale deeply like they did. I hate to think about what it might be doing to their brains. Dr. Rosenberg says huffing can cause blindness, brain damage, lung failure, and injury to the kidneys and liver (qtd. in "Fatal Attraction" 78). Parents, do you know what your children are doing with your hair spray or the propane gas in your outdoor grill? Hundreds of products can be sniffed, so you can't hide the products. The best answer, perhaps the only answer, is this one: communicate with your children daily.

Works Cited

"Fatal Attraction: How 'Huffing' Kills." <u>Redbook</u>
March 1993:78+.

Kimberly,

You now have an A paper on an important topic. I like the way
you developed the four issues of low cost, convenience, ease,
parental control, and the consequences to the child who
"huffs." You have warned youngsters and their parents about
the dangers.

Part 2

PARAGRAPHS

5

CHAPTER

WRITING GOOD PARAGRAPHS

The term **paragraph** identifies a unit of related sentences, as shown in this example:

Downtown, brilliant lights flash green and red. Crowds gather at some store windows to watch animated Christmas pageants. Drivers honk their horns in bursts of impatience, and shoppers step around the blackened snow lying in heaps on the sidewalk edges. The hustle and tussle of Christmas downtown differs from the tranquility of my neighborhood. Here, the gently falling snow settles in white beauty on the streets and lawns, silencing the splashing and sloshing of auto tires but allowing the nostalgic music to echo among the houses. Several rooftops exhibit replicas of Santa Claus and his eight reindeer, and others display outlines of blue lights. Open drapes show a Christmas tree in every home.

This paragraph has several features that you might wish to imitate.

1. It forms a **visual unit** on the page, with the first line indented and the last line ending short of the right margin.

2. It has an expressed **topic sentence** that explains the theme of the paragraph. All sentences relate to and support the topic sentence. Note: some paragraphs have an implied topic sentence.

3. It has **unity** (every sentence focuses on the primary subject) and **coherence** (the sentences connect one with another in a logical manner).

4. It has an **effective style**. It **contrasts** the Christmas scene downtown with that in the suburbs. It features **repetition** of the subject-verb structure (*lights flash, crowds gather, horns honk*); it uses **alliteration** to repeat initial consonant sounds (silencing the *s*plashing and *s*loshing of auto tires); it uses **descriptive**

images to bring to life the two places—downtown and the suburban neighborhood. It has a **play on words** by changing the cliché "hustle and bustle" to "hustle and tussle" to better describe the struggles of the shoppers.

Some of these terms may be new to you, but they will be explained in more detail as you work your way through the book.

5a WRITING UNIFIED PARAGRAPHS

You will need a **cluster of paragraphs** in order to build a composition. We seldom write a single paragraph, except as a classroom exercise. Therefore, think of the paragraph as one part of a larger unit, just as the sentence is one part of the paragraph and a word is one part of the sentence.

Each paragraph in the composition should develop one aspect of the general subject to defend your central thesis. The paragraphs must flow into and expand out of each other. Therefore, you must write each paragraph to correspond with all other paragraphs in the composition, especially with the one that precedes it and the one that follows.

Let's look now at Martin's composition on first aid in order to examine the correspondence of his paragraphs to each other. The questions and answers in the margins explain various aspects of paragraph unity. Later in the chapter, we will discuss specific methods for shaping your paragraphs.

First Aid

Most families seem totally unprepared for emergencies. Don't people know that most accidents happen at home? I have studied home safety, CPR, and other first aid techniques, so I want to share that information. The key to survival may be this: At least one member of every family should learn first aid.

One hot August afternoon, our old Pontiac caught fire on Interstate 40, miles from nowhere. Dad stopped quickly and rushed us to a grass embankment. He raised the hood, and we could see flames flickering on the engine. Dad began to beat at the flames with one of the floor mats, but he jumped back when the flames seared his hand and arm.

WHAT TECHNIQUE DOES MARTIN USE IN HIS INTRODUCTION?
- **PERSONAL BACKGROUND**
- **A QUESTION**
- **A THESIS SENTENCE**

WOULD YOU DESCRIBE THE NEXT SET OF PARAGRAPHS (2-8) AS EXPRESSIVE, EXPLANATORY, OR CREATIVE? EXPRESSIVE

HOW DOES THE PERSONAL NARRATION CORRESPOND TO THE FIRST PARAGRAPH? BY REINFORCING THE THESIS WITH AN ANECDOTE FROM REAL LIFE.

Just then, a farmer in a battered green pickup truck rattled to a stop, jumped out with a fire extinguisher, and put out the fire.

"Got here just in time, huh?" he said. He took off his black baseball cap, wiped his brow, and smiled a toothy grin toward me and Mom.

"Yes, thank you very much," said Dad.

"Let's see your burns," the farmer said, examining Dad's lobster-colored hand.

He went back to his truck, returned with a first aid kit, and doctored my Dad's hand. Then he carried us all to the next exit where we could get a wrecker and repair work.

We thanked the farmer for his kindness, and he drove off muttering, "Time to feed the stock." A few hours later, our car was repaired and we continued our journey.

But that's not the end of the story. I kept thinking about the farmer and how well-prepared he was for an accident. I vowed that I, too, would do the same. It has influenced me to study first aid.

NARRATION/
DESCRIPTION
REQUIRES WHAT
SORT OF
DEVELOPMENT?
- A TIME
  SEQUENCE
- SPECIFIC
  IMAGERY
- DIALOGUE
- CHARACTERI-
  ZATION
- A CLIMACTIC
  EVENT OR
  PROBLEM
- A RESOLUTION

THE USE OF DIALOGUE
REQUIRES WHAT SPE-
CIAL PUNCTUATION?
- QUOTATION MARKS
- A NEW PARAGRAPH
  FOR EACH NEW
  SPEECH

PARAGRAPH 9 CON-
CLUDES MARTIN'S PER-
SONAL NARRATION AND
GIVES A REASON FOR
TELLING THE STORY.
WHAT IS THAT REASON?
THE PARAGRAPH
SHOWS HOW THE
FARMER INFLUENCED
MARTIN TO STUDY
FIRST AID.

5a

Let me describe one technique--the Heimlich maneuver--that you might use someday to save a choking person. The Heimlich maneuver has saved lives at the kitchen table and in restaurants all over the world. What happens is that people choke on a piece of food, usually when they're trying to talk and eat at the same time. They begin to gasp for air and point to their throat, and a helpless feeling can strike the victim as well as the people at the table. The Heimlich maneuver, though, is pretty simple. Just stand behind the person, place your hands in a ball just below the sternum, and quickly pull inward. The thrust of air upward into the windpipe will usually dislodge the object. Then, everyone can go quietly back to the meal.

In addition to the Heimlich maneuver, several other techniques have importance, but they require training. CPR, for example, can cause more harm than good if misapplied. The same is true with tourniquets to stop bleeding

HOW DOES MARTIN FORM A BRIDGE FROM PARAGRAPH 9 TO PARAGRAPH 10? HE HAS STUDIED FIRST AID AND NOW HE WILL DESCRIBE ONE TECHNIQUE.

IS THE PARAGRAPH ON THE HEIMLICH MANEUVER EXPRESSIVE, EXPLANATORY, OR PERSUASIVE? EXPLANATORY; IT EXPLAINS THE PROCESS.

WHAT IS THE PURPOSE OF PARAGRAPH 11? TO GIVE THREE EXAMPLES OF TECHNIQUES THAT AMATEURS SHOULD NOT ATTEMPT AND TO INTRODUCE THE MESSAGE THAT BEGINS THE LAST PARAGRAPH.

5a

or antidotes to counteract poisoning.
Without training, you better call 911
and hope the rescue squad makes good
time.

A knowledge of first aid is a
valuable possession. Accidents occur
every day, everywhere, and without
regard to age, race, sex, or class.
People just get hurt. The baby sprays
carpet cleaner in her eyes, Dad falls
from the ladder while cleaning the
gutters, or Mom cuts her hand while
slicing a block of cheese. Calling the
rescue squad is important, but more
vital is the immediate action by other
family members. Too many things can go
wrong while you wait for the ambulance
and police: the baby screams in
hysteria, Dad lies unconscious, Mom's
hand spurts blood. Yet there is an
answer. Every family needs a good first
aid kit and at least one person who
knows basic first aid techniques.

**HOW DO THE
FIRST AND LAST
SENTENCES OF
THE LAST
PARAGRAPH
BRING THIS
PAPER TO A
CONCLUSION?
BY REINFORC-
ING THE SAME
IDEA THAT
PEOPLE NEED
TO KNOW
FIRST AID AND
LIFE-SAVING
TECHNIQUES.**

**WHAT IS THE PURPOSE
OF THE MIDDLE
SENTENCES IN THE
CONCLUSION?
TO PROVIDE VIVID
EXAMPLES OF
THINGS THAT CAN
GO WRONG AT
HOME.**

5a

5b DEVELOPING PARAGRAPHS TO MEET THE DEMANDS OF FORM AND STRUCTURE

The purpose of a composition is to develop fully one subject. Every writer must discover the form that best fits his or her subject and thesis sentence. And each method of development—whether definition, description, or cause/effect—makes different demands on the writer. The essay might classify several issues, analyze each one, compare them, and give examples. The topic sentence of each paragraph will dictate in part the method of development, but you also need a checklist of the criteria for each form. Therefore, this section serves two purposes: (1) it discusses the role of the topic sentence, and (2) it provides the criteria for the basic modes of development.

First, let's look at a few topic sentences, some short and some long, to discover how they invite development.

> The shopping mall is the happening place on Friday night.

This topic sentence requires a list of reasons to explain why the mall entices activity and also description to bring the scenes to life. Perhaps the reasons people go to the mall are to see friends, to meet a date, to watch fights in the parking lot, to check out the latest fashions, and so forth. Each one deserves a full description. Let's look at another example:

In gentle ways, grandparents shape our lives.

This topic sentence requires classification that will list, in sequence, the wisdom gained from the grandparents, such as honesty, compassion, creativity, and even your family history. An essay with this topic sentence may also include a narrative sketch to show the grandparents in action.

The anxious Christmas shoppers swarmed like bees, buzzing from counter to counter and aisle to aisle in search of sweet gifts for loved ones.

This topic sentence makes a comparison that can be extended through the paragraph with a full description of the shoppers fluttering from place to place.

To write varied paragraphs, you need to know how to develop comparison, description, cause and effect, and analysis. Thus, your teacher may ask you to write a description of your most embarrassing moment or to write a comparison of anthropoids and crustaceans. In addition, the questions on standardized tests frequently make specific demands in these areas. For example, you need to know how to compare and contrast for questions such as the following:

> Explain the differences and similarities between a democratic and a socialist state.

Use the following guidelines to frame your compositions. Most of your writing will require a combination of methods. Martin, for example, used narration, description, process, example, and cause and effect.

Writing with Narration

Narration tells a story or traces a series of events. A narrative supports a topic sentence with a convincing incident from real life or with a short story. You need not always tell a complete story; narrate only those events that develop your point. Include these ingredients if possible:

- a time sequence that uses flashbacks to previous events as necessary;
- a narrator who may be a central player in the story or one who observes the activities of other characters;
- foreshortening that skips mundane matters so that your story remains focused on the primary events;

- characterization that focuses on a key, pivotal figure but that also distinguishes each person in the story;
- dialogue that brings characterization to life;
- a climactic event or a problem that drives the story forward;
- a resolution; and
- description (see below) that provides a picture of people and places.

For an example, see paragraphs 2–8 of Martin's essay.

Writing with Description

Description provides a picture of a person, scene, or activity. With the use of specific details, it builds one dominant impression. It adds a touch of reality by its appeal to the readers' senses—sight, hearing, taste, smell, and touch. The readers will imagine whatever you create. The more specific your prose, the more vivid will be the reader's interpretation. Description may be a personal, subjective view of the subject or a scientific study, in which case you must report objectively with scientific precision and terminology. Include these ingredients if possible:

- a point of reference (standing in the doorway, looking from the car window, walking along the canyon, viewed through a telescope);

- a clear focus on the subject;
- logical movement for the shift of focus from left to right, top to bottom, and so forth;
- concrete, specific words that show action and that appeal to the senses ("the eager blue jay snapped open the sunflower seed" rather than "the bird was feeding itself"); and
- figurative language if appropriate ("Her eyes seemed bright but somehow shallow, like cubic zirconium").

Here is an example in which Cathy describes an important person:

A preacher once asked who I wanted to be like when I grew up. My answer, "Grandma," embarrassed the white-haired woman at my side, but I felt her squeeze my hand as a gesture of thanks.

Grandmother was in so many ways like a valuable pearl, a priceless object hidden within a deceptively coarse outer shell. She had no need for fancy clothes or nail polish, for she had the plain look of a hardworking farmer's wife. I have many mental images of her, asleep in a chair with her Bible in her lap, working in the garden underneath an old straw hat, greeting guests at the back door wearing work clothes and standing with her feet bare.

However, the strongest image that comes to mind is the one of her cooking. Oh, the smells--ham, eggs, red-eye gravy, biscuits, pear preserves, strong black coffee--swirling about the silver-haired, bespectacled woman, buzzing from pot to oven, measuring her life and the next supper with pots and pans that she coordinated to finish at precisely the same moment.

Writing with Definition and Examples

Definition explains a word, phrase, image, or the characteristics of a subject. Formal definition does two things. First, it names the class to which the subject belongs and, second, it shows how the subject differs from various members of its class. For example, *applique* (subject) is a *piece of material* (class) that *is cut out and attached ornamentally to another piece of material* (differentiation). Informal definition also names a subject, but uses examples, description, comparison, and other techniques to clarify the meaning of the term or concept.

Examples serve as models and samples to demonstrate a point that you raise in the topic sentence. Good examples do more than list: they provide specific pictures of a general idea and thereby arouse interest. A paragraph, as well as an entire essay, can feature one extended example or many short ones, depending on the subject matter.

When using description and examples, use the following strategies if possible:

- give name, class, and differentiation;
- provide specific examples;
- offer comparison and contrast;
- describe the subject;
- provide categories that classify the subject;
- offer a personal definition to explain your point of view;
- tell what the subject is not;
- use expert testimony to add an authoritative voice; or
- explain a process.

For an example, see Martin's definition of the Heimlich maneuver, paragraph 10, page xx.

Writing to Classify, to Analyze, or to Explain a Process

When you **classify** the subject, you divide it into basic parts. When you **analyze**, you examine each element in depth. When you describe a

process, you show stages of progress or development. **Classification** begins with a plural subject (apples, types of gasoline, choice of motorcycles) to establish the basic categories for analysis. **Analysis** begins with a singular subject—one thing (red delicious apple), one issue (the state gasoline tax), or one activity (the backhand stroke). You must then study the subject's structure to discover its basic make-up. For example, coaches analyze their players' free throw technique, teachers analyze a student's method for solving a math problem, and you may analyze the pros and cons of the automobile you wish to buy.

5b

Process serves three purposes: (1) it explains how to do something ("How to swim the breaststroke"), (2) it tells about a system of nature ("From seed to food: vegetables"), or (3) it traces the history and development of something ("The growth of music videos").

Consider using the following strategies if they are appropriate for your composition:

- divide the subject into its basic parts;
- describe the steps in the process;
- establish the categories;
- give how-to directives;
- examine each category, part, issue, or period with in-depth analysis;

- use comparison and contrast to explain the differences and similarities between the items discussed; or
- use scientific terminology if it is appropriate to the analysis.

In the following example, Jennifer describes a process, analyzes specific stages, and compares and contrasts the positive and negative aspects:

5b

When skiing a slalom course, a skier wants to get as close to the poles as possible and turn as little as possible when between the two poles. Edging is an absolutely necessary part of skiing a slalom race. It is the sharp edge of the ski that enables one to actually make the turn around a pole. If a skier doesn't use the edges and turn on flat skis, the turn will be very round, thereby making the course longer and the skier's time longer. The skier must use his or her edges in order to navigate the course in the shortest amount of time.

But edging also presents disadvantages to a skier. One drawback in racing is that skis glide faster when they are flat on the snow as opposed to being angled to the ground. Therefore, it is imperative that a skier be on the ski's edges for the least amount of time in every turn, just enough to get around the pole. The skier can then benefit from a solid upward thrust when moving off the edge and onto a flat ski, gaining momentum. Even the best skiers can improve timing by shortening the length of time spent on the edge.

Another complication to edging is that the angled ski, when digging into the icy, crusty snow may "catch its edge." In this case, a skier may fall down or lose time as a result of the ski becoming caught in a rut or chattering around the turn rather than gliding smoothly. A skier can avoid both of these misfortunes by turning early or "high" in the turn.

Writing to Show Causes or to Discuss Effects

Cause and effect enables you to establish why something happens, to explore the results, and to forecast the consequences. You can explore scientific occurrences ("Why the earth spins"), historical events ("Why the Persian Gulf War was a battle for oil rights"), and social issues ("Why movies have a PG-13 rating"). Consider using the following strategies if they are appropriate to your composition:

- classify the various causes or reasons;
- list the known or foreseeable consequences;
- trace recent history to explain a current condition;
- compare your subject with one from the past to emphasize the possible outcome and to discuss positive or negative aspects;
- search out contributory causes as well as the main cause; or
- maintain a logical sequence so that one cause or one effect logically follows from the preceding cause or effect.

A set of paragraphs by Elysia demonstrates the use of cause and effect:

The system confines students to school. Students graduate from high school because they acquire a set number of credits, and they go to college for four more years--all the while isolated from society. If the high school curriculum required students to do community service work, perhaps 75 hours, the student would quickly learn about the "real" world faced by government employees and social workers.

First, service work benefits everyone. It helps the homeless, elderly, physically and mentally ill, and the different charities. It helps the young person doing the work because the person broadens his or her knowledge of the differences in social standards.

Second, the young person discovers people in all their various forms, faces, and fears. In some settings, the youngster will learn about poverty or about wealth, a lesson that might encourage them to work hard.

Third, it helps the community that will receive several thousand hours of free service. It will ease the tax burden. It will free city workers to pursue meaningful projects. It will make the community proud.

Fourth, the students gain self-esteem. Joanne S. Gillespie says that community service work helps to build "a feeling of self-worth" and that the students see "that their help is essential" (89).

Writing with Comparison and Contrast

Comparison enables you to examine one thing by showing its similarity to another ("The two-handed tennis stroke is similar to a baseball swing"). You can show the similarities of two or more items to explain them or sometimes to show the superiority of one over the others.

An **analogy** usually compares a complicated topic to something common and well-known ("the human heart is like a water pump," or "two tiny cells, the sperm and the ovum, contain a complete blueprint to guide development of the embryo").

Contrast shows the differences between topics that appear to be similar but are not ("all regional high schools are not alike," or "weight lifting and bodybuilding are two different exercises with unrelated results").

Consider using the following strategies if they are appropriate to your composition:

- compare your primary subject with another to show similarities that will clarify and define the subject;
- contrast your primary subject with another to show differences that will distinguish your subject from others;
- use analogy to explain something unfamiliar by comparing it with something well-known;
- compare your subject with numerous items, not just one;
- use a two-subject focus to examine first one and then the other item (television soaps and sitcoms);
- use a point-by-point focus to examine both subjects in relation to a series of issues (violence, love, and humor on television soaps and sitcoms);

- use a past-to-present pattern to compare the way things used to be with the present (the deterioration of the Parent-Teacher Associations); and
- express clearly your reason for making the comparison.

In the following paragraph, Luis uses comparison to develop one view of a short story by Edgar Allan Poe:

In "The Masque of the Red Death," Poe predicted that certain diseases, like the Red Death, would eventually destroy humanity. At the time, Poe was probably thinking about his wife's diagnosis of tuberculosis, the most deadly disease at that time. Today, readers make the connection of the Red Death with AIDS. Poe's wife died of tuberculosis, and anyone contracting the AIDS virus usually dies. Even though AIDS seems to spread quickly, let us hope that this next quotation never occurs: "And Darkness and Decay and the Red Death [AIDS] held illimitable dominion over all" (Poe 129).

You might also want to explore these other methods for developing your paragraphs:

- give a history of the subject;
- explore positive and negative issues related to the subject;
- furnish a set of questions and answers;
- provide a quotation;
- give a biographical sketch of a person;
- tell what something is *not*;
- use dialogue.

The following sample paragraphs demonstrate methods for building full paragraphs.

Communication with our parents plays a major role in our lives and theirs.	**TOPIC SENTENCE**
The problem of bickering within families can be resolved through the underlying strength of communication.	**CAUSE AND EFFECT**
Talking with one another around the kitchen table gives a family strength, just as the root system enables a tree to send out strong, independent branches that nevertheless remain firmly connected to the trunk.	**ANALOGY**
As the generation gap between teenager and parent grows, as it always does, effective communication is perhaps the only ingredient strong enough to bind the two sides.—Pamela Roddy	**CONSEQUENCE**

Life is precious, but some lumber companies seem determined to destroy it on several levels. First, they kill the trees and haul off the timber. At the same time, they kill many creatures. In time, other animals die because the environment is damaged. Finally, we all may die because of changes in the earth's ecological balance.—Scott Haskins

TOPIC
SENTENCE

CLASSIFICATION
OF
CONSEQUENCES

5b

The attic housed many precious relics of the past. The stairs leading to the most neglected part of the house showed a fine layer of dust, and the boards creaked with each step I took. When I opened the attic door, a stale, moist odor hit my senses. To the left of the square room were old forgotten toys, such as a fuzzy bear with buttons as eyes; an old aquarium filled with race cars, a race track, and a train set; and

TOPIC SENTENCE

DESCRIPTION

a faded red wagon with only three wheels. To the right of the entrance were large boxes filled with clothes that have gone out of style. The far corner to the left had Grandmother's old sewing machine and a black and white television. The low ceiling and sticky spider webs caused me to retreat back downstairs.—Sonja Griffin

5c EMPHASIZING KEY IDEAS WITHIN A PARAGRAPH

Several techniques will help you to build good paragraphs with emphasis on the correct words and sentences.

1. Use Transitional Words and Phrases to Keep the Reader Focused on Your Best Ideas

A transition connects (coheres) ideas. Transitional words or phrases show the shift from one idea to the next. A paragraph without transitional points may confuse the reader. Can you identify the words and phrases in the following passage that direct the reader from one idea to another?

A flower is a miniature version of the cycle of life. First, the seed, which is planted in the soil by hand or by the wind, carries the cell of existence. Then, the elements, especially the sun and moisture, help launch a life. Soon, the body springs upward and, as time passes, its branches wave gracefully in the breeze. In its prime, the flower blooms in glorious color, but time quickly cuts into this life. Nevertheless, there is no reason for sadness; autumn winds blow the flower's seeds near and far, and life continues its cycle.
—Bonnie Richman

Answers: cycle, first, then, soon, as time passes, in its prime, but, nevertheless, cycle. Note how the word *cycle*, coming early and also late, provides an echo effect to reinforce the implied thesis, "cycles of nature."

Use Table 5.1 to find appropriate transitional words and phrases.

TABLE 5.1   Transitional Words and Phrases

Purpose	Example
To introduce an example: for example to illustrate for instance specifically	Too many demands are made on members of the band. **For example**, we play at all pep rallies, games, concerts, and at least three parades every year.
To signal a time change: meanwhile soon after a short time after before the next day when immediately shortly thereafter finally at the end of the day one year later	A group of band members expressed their feelings to the director. **The next day**, he said pep rallies and two of the parades would be optional.
To move to a new place: above below nearby on the next counter in the hallway opposite to your right close just beyond the wall	The band formation required me to begin on the 30-yard line. **To my righ**t was a tuba and **to my left** was a trombone. I had to march five steps **forward**, **turn right**, and hope the tuba turned the same way.

5c

Purpose	Example
To add information: first second next in addition and also besides this one furthermore additionally	**In addition to left and right turns**, we also did several complete reversals. **First**, the tuba bumped me in the shoulder. **Next**, the trombone smacked me in the head.
To show contrast: however notwithstanding on the contrary nevertheless but yet although even though still on the other hand	**Nevertheless**, learning new formations and drills provides plenty of funny episodes, **although** I hate to be the one who makes a mistake.
To compare: in like manner in the same way also likewise similarly in comparison	Band practice is almost always dull, and it seems to last forever. **In the same way**, choir rehearsals seem tiresome. I guess I like performing, not practicing.

5c

Purpose	Example
To show cause or effect:	**Consequently,** I am subject to frowns and
for this reason	scowls from the directors.
consequently	
as a consequence	
as a result	
therefore	
so	
thus	
in effect	
To conclude:	**Therefore,** I usually get a B in music courses,
in conclusion	**even though** I play and sing extremely well.
in short	
therefore	
to sum up	
accordingly	
in closing	

2. Repeat Key Words and Phrases

It is helpful to repeat key words to keep them in the readers' minds. Most of the time, repeating your key word will be clearer than finding a synonym. Also, you might repeat the word in a different grammatical form (*fight, fought, fighting*). For example, a paper about aerobics has more coherence if you repeat the word "aerobics" several times rather than using "workout," "calisthenics," "bodybuilding," "jazzercise," and then "slimnastics":

> I have been feeling sluggish lately and
> downright lazy, so I joined an **aerobics** program to
> lose about five pounds. That may seem
> insignificant, but I'd rather use **aerobics** now
> rather than try a strict diet later on. I find
> **aerobic** workouts enjoyable, like a sport, so I
> participate four times a week. Who knows? I might
> lose 10 pounds!—Shamika Turner

3. Use Pronouns to Keep Readers Focused on the Subject

After you establish your primary subject by using a noun (the antecedent), you may want to refer to the noun with a pronoun (*he, she, it, they, them*). Consider how *it* or *its* is used to refer to *grass* in the following sentences:

> Everything has a reason for existence. Even
> grass has its role in the life cycle. It absorbs
> sunlight and produces energy to help us in two
> ways. Through photosynthesis it splits water into
> oxygen and hydrogen. The hydrogen helps produce
> glucose in the grass to nourish cattle and other

grass-eating animals. Additionally, the oxygen escapes from the grass into the air, enabling us to breathe.—Tammy Wafford

Pronouns must clearly refer to a noun; if in doubt, repeat the noun, as this writer did, on occasion, with the word *grass*.

4. Place Your Topic Sentence Conscientiously

As a general rule, you should position your best thoughts at the beginning or the end of a paragraph. Your opening sentence (probably your topic sentence) may announce an idea.

When I feel angry at the crazy way some people act, I recover my sanity by recalling the peaceful loneliness of life in the deep country. I lived in the country from the time I was five years old to age thirteen. We lived on a small farm down a long gravel road, many miles from town. We had no heavy traffic, no neighbors crowding us, and no mobs of people at the local general store. At the time, I felt isolated from the world. Now, I would enjoy just a week back on the farm.—Scott Haskins

The final sentence of a paragraph will often confirm a significant idea, as shown by the following example:

> Alexander Hamilton wanted people of wealth and prestige to govern the nation, but Thomas Jefferson felt that the common folk should participate in the government. Hamilton wanted an industrial nation, Jefferson a farming one. Hamilton wanted a strong federal government; Jefferson favored states' rights. **Yet despite their conflicts and public turmoil, both patriots meant well for the nation, just as Democrats and Republicans mean well today.**
> —Eric Smith

Putting an idea in the middle of a paragraph will usually bury that idea. However, you can point forward to a primary idea in the middle and then expand up to it:

> Most of the time, we conform to standards set by television advertising or the demands of the group we belong to. Look around in the halls at school for four or five guys clustered together and all wearing similar clothes, talking in the same slang, and thinking identical thoughts. Such conformity is not the same as having personality. **Personality is like a registered trademark.** If you

have to go in search of a personality, you don't
have it. If you copy anybody else, you don't have
it. If you even think about it, you don't have it.
—Sammy Valpone

5. Match Your Point of View to Your Purpose

Keep in mind three guidelines about voice
and point of view:

a. Consistently use the first person *I* when writing about yourself in a narrative paragraph. It is best to avoid pulling the reader into your story with the word *you*, as with, "You would not believe what happened to me last week." Instead, tell what happened to you with the first person *I*:

> When **I** saw the snow begin to fall, **I** immediately
> ran to **my** room to polish **my** boots and wax **my** skis.
> **I** couldn't wait to begin schussing down **my** favorite
> slopes.

b. When your paragraph explains or describes something or somebody, keep your focus on the subject by using a third person pronoun (*it, he, she, they*):

> The skiing term schussing means that a skier points
> straight down the slope; **it** generates speed. The term
> traversing means a skier works down the slope at an

5c

angle to the fall line; **it** decreases the speed and **it** requires many turns during the descent.

c. **When you write persuasively, invite the reader into the argument of the paragraph by using the pronoun *we*.** Rather than asserting "I believe," say instead, "we need to address the issues" or "together we can change this condition."

Reports indicate that two logging companies want to begin operations on nearby ski slopes. **We** will need a unified effort by all citizens in the county if **we** hope to stop the pilfering of timber and the devastation of the slopes.

6. Use Dialogue to Emphasize Key Issues

A **dialogue** (a form of direct quotation) features the conversation of two or more people. Distinctive personalities emerge as each person speaks. Using dialogue adds emphasis, a sense of reality, and immediacy to a paragraph. In using dialogue, you should follow two guidelines:

1. Start a new paragraph each time a different person begins to speak.
2. Enclose each speech within quotation marks.

For an example, see paragraphs 2–8 of Martin's paper.

CREATING FORCEFUL SENTENCES

CHAPTER

Forceful, effective sentences will:

- Express your opinions, not conventional thinking;
- Provide forceful phrasing to strengthen your key ideas;
- Show variety in form and style.

To achieve these goals, you will need to make wise choices from numerous sentence patterns that will come to mind.

INTRODUCTION 117

6a GIVING ORIGINALITY TO YOUR SENTENCES

6a

As you write, face the world on your terms. That is, examine your feelings, analyze the issues as they affect you, and be your own person, even to the point of taking risks in what you say. Make the difficult choices and be willing to disagree with others. For example, how did this next writer achieve his originality?

> Let's face facts here. Greed, not charity, drives the Christmas season. Even in giving, we take fiendish glee in doing the right thing. Servicing our ego is a type of greed.—Les Margowitz

These sentences might offend some readers, but the writer's decision to emphasize greed provides the originality. He has a reason for writing, a position to defend, and an argument to develop.

How has the next writer used language to give originality of style to her passage?

> I must confess the truth. I am a ham. I want to be the center of attention, like the actress who works her way upstage.

Backstage   Backstage
    ↘   ↙
      Stage right   Stage left
          ↘   ↙
              Center stage
                    ↓
                Upstage

> That's me, moving upstage at every chance.
> Something comes over me when an audience is
> present, whether it's a huddle of guys in the hall,
> relatives nesting in the living room, or my fellow
> students diddling, fiddling, and piddling in the
> auditorium.—Wendy Mason

This writer also made unconventional choices. She designed the page with a drawing of the stage and also used descriptive language—the guys "huddle," the relatives "nest," and the students "diddle, fiddle, and piddle."

What Can Go Wrong with Originality?

Readers want "news," which means they want new information. Unless you find a way to be original in content or style, your writing may suffer from the following problems:

1. Conventional thinking (you conform to general wisdom);
2. Triteness (you use commonplace wording);
3. Cliches (you employ worn-out figures of speech).

How does the following example show conventional thinking, trite wording, and a cliche?

> During the Christmas season, my mother gets busy as
> a bee trying to shop and decorate and do all the
> things that have to be done.

All mothers get busy. The phrase *do all the things that have to be done* is shallow and wordy. The simile *busy as a bee* is too familiar.

How does the writer make better choices in the revised sentence, below?

> Like a queen bee, my mother at Christmas attracts each little honey bee to her colony, where she nurtures them with special types of pollen that she calls candy cane, fudge, and divinity.—Amy Majors

The writer has extended the simile to include a "queen bee," "each little honey bee," "her colony," and "pollen." She also provides specific wording.

6b GIVING FORCEFUL PLACEMENT TO WORDS AND PHRASES

The subject and the predicate affect the reader far more than the other parts of speech. The subject usually comes first and the predicate energizes it. Which words carry the message in this next sentence?

> We fell asleep during the lecture on Darwin's theory.

The subject has one word; the predicate has eight. Obviously, the predicate activates the sentence.

If the subject has importance to you, then enrich it with concrete or proper nouns and with specific modifiers. Which of the next two sentences has the richer subject?

> Marci Broadman, who has perfect attendance and a 4.0 grade point average, will serve as valedictorian.

> The choice for salutatorian will be announced tomorrow.

The first sentence has a specific subject, which makes the sentence more interesting. The point should be clear: the predicate will activate most sentences, but you can also use the subject to activate sentences when appropriate.

To give them the most impact, place your key ideas at the beginning or the end of your sentences. Does this next sentence open and close with force?

> Deadly dangers lurk in school hallways, so our schools need some form of gun control.—Juanita Rodriguez

In this forceful sentence, readers encounter first the "deadly dangers" and learn the solution, "gun control," at the end.

What Can Go Wrong with Forceful Placement of Key Ideas?

If you do not pay attention to where you place your key ideas, you might bury an idea in mid-sentence. What is the main idea of this next sentence?

> When a student finds part-time work, grades may suffer unless the student can manage time well.

The fact that grades may suffer is the key idea, so put it up front or at the end:

> Grades may suffer when a student takes part-time work.

> or

> Part-time work may cause a student's grades to suffer.

What is wrong with placement of the key idea in this next sentence?

> When the debate team won the state championship, it was the last week of school.

The main idea, winning the debate championship, is buried in a subordinate adverb clause. The main idea should be part of the main clause.

> The debate team won the state championship during the last week of school.

Another common error is *anticlimax*, in which the main clause is followed by needless details that distract the reader. Which words could be deleted from the following sentence?

> The debate team won the state championship during the last week of school, which was the time when everybody was so terribly busy with graduation activities.

The last thirteen words provide needless details that can be cut without damaging the meaning of the sentence.

6c REPEATING KEY WORDS AND PHRASES

Repeating a key word or phrase can give force to your sentences. What word or phrase is repeated in the following sentence?

> Neither congressional hearings on voluntary gun control nor national conferences on mandatory gun control can help our cities, which face street warfare because the local neighborhoods have no control over guns.—Butch Ray

The words *gun control* dominate and give force to the sentence.

What Can Go Wrong with Repetition of Words?

You will be guilty of *needless repetition* (also known as *redundancy*) if your sentences use a word or phrase several times without a reason. What word or phrase is repeated needlessly in the following sentence?

> Like a leopard striking its prey, the coach was like
> an animal, like when he jumped on a player for
> something like a ball-handling mistake.

The word *like*, above, is redundant. However,
the next sentence employs *like* effectively:

> Like a leopard striking its prey, the coach jumped on
> the player for a ball-handling mistake; but, like a
> forgiving parent, he hugged the player after the
> game.

6d ADDING FORCE WITH PARALLELISM AND THE SERIES

Repeating a grammatical structure as well as
a key word adds force to your ideas. Can you
identify the sentence structure repeated by the
next writer?

> Sometimes my parents sound like owls, especially
> when I'm going out with friends—Who is your date?
> Who will be there? Who will bring you home? Who do
> we call if we need you?—Norma Ledbetter

The series of four questions, each beginning
with *who*, drives home the writer's point about
her parents.

To reinforce a sequence of related ideas with
parallelism, you must select a grammatical unit
and repeat it several times. For example, in the

following sentence, what grammatical unit does the writer use in a three-part series?

> The young diver accidentally fell off the platform, onto her back, and into deep trouble.

The three prepositional phrases (*off the platform, onto her back, into deep trouble*) in a series give force to the diver's fall. Parallel units may appear anywhere in the sentence. Can you identify the parallelism in the following sentence?

> The choir will sing a portion of Handel's Messiah, a medley of church hymns, and a collection of folk songs.

The direct object of will sing is actually a set of direct objects. Note that each item in the series above has the same identical structure: adjective, noun, preposition, adjective, noun. Can you identify the two parallel series in the following sentence?

> From the start the new student disliked the class, distrusted everybody in it, and displayed her antagonism, frustrations, and disdain.

This sentence uses a parallel series for the three verbs (*disliked, distrusted, displayed*) and another series for the objects of the verb *displayed*.

What Can Go Wrong with Parallelism and the Series?

Faulty parallelism disrupts the meaning of your sentences. For example, how does parallelism fail in the following sentence?

> Our history teacher criticized the students in the class for not reading the assignment and because too many students did not even bring their books to class.

The prepositional phrase *for not reading the assignment* is not parallel in structure with the adverb clause *because too many students did not even bring their books to class.* You can make the sentence parallel by changing the clause to a prepositional phrase:

> Our history teacher criticized the students in the class for <u>not reading the assignment</u> and <u>for not bringing their books to class</u>.

Note: Missing parts will cause parallelism to fail. To make sentence elements parallel, you must often repeat articles (*a, an, the*), prepositions (*by, for, in,* and so on), the infinitive *to,* and some auxiliary verbs (*has, will*). Without all the matching parts, your sentence will not be parallel.

> Some say that a proper diet can keep us slim and trim
>
> that
>
> /
>
> but exercise keeps us healthy.

The second *that*, added above, is necessary to introduce the second half of a compound noun clause. Some say what?

> that a proper diet can keep us slim and trim
>
> but
>
> that exercise keeps us healthy

6e GIVING FORCE TO YOUR KEY IDEAS WITH ACTIVE VERBS

To write forceful sentences, think about your verbs, not your nouns. Nouns may name things, but verbs put the nouns into action. For example, find the words that activate the following sentence:

> Our principal warned us about drug abuse, cautioned us about alcohol, and preached a message about abstinence.

The verbs—*warned, cautioned, preached*—give force to the sentence.

What Can Go Wrong with Verbs?

Do not choose the lifeless "to be" verbs when active verbs will serve your needs. Which sentence below is lifeless and which one is forceful?

Trial and error learning is to learn by practice.

Trial and error learning requires practice, practice, practice.

The second sentence has an active verb and effective repetition. Judge the next two sentences:

The morning fog was heavy in the valley, but several people were out walking and jogging on streets that were wet and icy.

The morning fog floated across the valley, but several people walked or jogged along the wet and icy streets.

The second sentence has the forceful verbs *floated, walked,* and *jogged,* while the first sentence relies too heavily on the "to be" verbs *was, were,* and *were.*

6f SHOWING, NOT TELLING

You can also add force to your sentences by allowing your readers to hear, see, and feel the activities in your essays and stories. Rather than just telling readers what happened, use the following strategies.

1. Show the action

TELLING: He was angry.

SHOWING: He threw his soda bottle at my head.

2. Use detailed description

TELLING: The weather was bad, reflecting his angry mood.

SHOWING: Matching his angry mood, the moon refused to shine that night, the storm clouds swirled in angry circles, and the wind blew icy gusts against his neck.

3. Use dialogue

TELLING: I made it plain that we needed to leave the party, but he said that he wanted to stay for one more dance. Reluctantly, I agreed.

SHOWING: "Let's go home now," I urged.
"Come on, the night's still young," he replied. "Let's stay for one more dance."
"Okay, but that's all—just one more dance," I insisted.

4. Give concrete details

TELLING: On the way home, he drove the car so recklessly that he frightened me.

SHOWING: On the way home, he raced his Cherokee through the narrow streets, slashed onto Morgan Boulevard, ran two red lights, and squealed to a stop in my driveway. I sat gasping in fear, unable to speak or to open my door.

6g ADDING FORCE TO SENTENCES WITH METAPHORS AND SIMILES

A new metaphor or simile can give force to your writing by making unusual comparisons. A metaphor is a comparison in which you *imply* the similarity of unlike things; a simile expresses the comparison with *like, as, looks like, became,* and similar expressions. What comparison does this sentence make?

The cat's eyes hypnotized me.

The writer's metaphor implies the similarities between a cat's eyes and a hypnotist. What comparison does this next writer express?

The cat's eyes glowed in the dark like cool jade.

The writer's simile compares the cat's eyes to jade. Again, how does the next sentence develop a simile?

The broken power lines twisted on the ground like a writhing snake.

The writer's simile expresses the comparison of the power lines to a snake. What simile does this next sentence develop?

Bouncing the ball at the free throw line, I looked nervously at the edge of rim, which was as small as a thimble.

The writer's simile reduces the rim to thimble size, so the basketball may never go in.

6h USING THE ACTIVE VOICE, NOT THE PASSIVE

When you write with the active voice, you show the subject performing the action of a sentence. Which of the following sentences shows the subject in action?

> The hallway was crowded, so announcements could not be heard.

> Students and teachers crowded the hall, so nobody could hear the announcements.

The second sentence activates the students and teachers. Which of the next two sentences uses active voice?

> The new homecoming queen was crowned by the football captain.

> Tim Johnson, the football captain, crowned Jessie Walters as the new homecoming queen for 1994.

The second sentence uses active voice.

What Can Go Wrong with Active Voice?

You may get so preoccupied with the object of your sentence that you forget the actor. Does this next sentence name an actor?

The exam was finally finished.

The writer uses passive voice, not active, and does not name the actor. Passive voice requires the writer to use the object as the subject and to use a "to be" verb (*was*) with a past participle (*finished*). Active voice, with the actor as subject, is forceful:

I finally finished the exam.

When you use the passive voice, you transfer the action of the verb back to the subject rather than allowing the subject to act. The passive verb often hides the actor. Note that the passive voice requires more words:

PASSIVE VOICE: Finally, after many years, the tyranny of England was brought to an end, and a new period for the American colonies was started in 1783 with the signing of the Treaty of Paris.

ACTIVE VOICE: Finally, after many years, the tyranny of England ended, and a new period for the American colonies began in 1783 with the signing of the Treaty of Paris.

The passive voice requires thirty-three words, while the active voice requires only twenty-eight. Which of the next two sentences uses active voice? How do you know?

> The Thanksgiving assembly has been presented every year by the school choir.

> The school choir has presented the Thanksgiving assembly every year.

6h

In the first sentence of twelve words, the subject (*The Thanksgiving assembly*) receives the action and the actor (*the choir*) serves only as the object of a preposition. In the second sentence of only ten words, the actor (*the choir*) serves as the subject.

Note: In some cases, you may wish to use the passive voice to focus attention on the object, not the actor, as in the next two examples:

> The new computers will be installed this week.

In this sentence, the writer wants to focus on the computers, not the installers.

> Sarah Lester was elected president on the third ballot.

In this sentence, Sarah Lester, the recipient of the action, is more important than the actors (the voters) themselves.

6i USING SENTENCE MODIFIERS TO ADD FORCE TO YOUR KEY IDEAS

A sentence modifier is a cluster of words that can give force to your main ideas. It can appear before, after, or between major words in the main clause.

An **anticipating modifier** appears before the main clause to signal that something important will follow. How does the opening modifier in the following sentence foreshadow the news of the main clause?

> One afternoon in early autumn when the warm afternoon temperatures cooled quickly at dusk and football practice lasted until dark, a mysterious illness infected several members of the team.

The opening modifier hints at a condition, warm days and cool nights, that anticipates and prepares the reader for the illness that afflicts team members.

A **trailing modifier** follows the main clause, adds specific detail, and shows what the main clause may only tell. Look first at a main clause:

> Blood is essential for human life.

This main clause makes a clear statement, but it does not provide specific details. The sentence becomes more forceful with a trailing modifier:

Blood is essential for human life, providing nutrients and oxygen to all the cells in the body and washing poisonous wastes from the system.

In short, this pattern enables you to say something general and to give it force with specific modifying elements. Here is another example:

The sky darkened.

The sky darkened, sending deep shadows across the valley and hiding the campground from the helicopter search parties.

A **sentence interrupter** provides you with another effective way to emphasize an idea. A common sentence pattern begins with a subject, then uses an interrupter to raise the tension and build momentum, and then follows with a verb. Let's look first at the main clause:

The members of the street gang watched us approach.

A sentence interrupter can make the sentence more forceful:

The members of the street gang, some snarling with curled lips and others smiling with fiendish anticipation, watched us approach.

6j WRITING WITH VARIOUS SENTENCE TYPES

The four sentence types—simple, compound, complex, and compound-complex—can be used to reinforce your ideas in different ways. Being able to use all four types of sentences reflects your maturity as a writer.

Simple Sentences

A **simple sentence** has one independent clause and focuses attention on one central idea:

SIMPLE SENTENCE: We skipped classes on Tuesday.

The simple sentence has force at the beginning of paragraphs, at the end of paragraphs, or as a transitional break between paragraphs.

What Can Go Wrong with Simple Sentences?

If you write with too many simple sentences, you will write in a primer style, which means you break your thoughts into separate short sentences. This slip-up is also known as period faults.

PRIMER STYLE: The little puppy darted through the hallways. It was racing to freedom. The puppy was being chased by the assistant principal. Luckily, it escaped capture.

You can edit this type of writing by joining your ideas with compound and complex sentences, as explained next.

Compound Sentences

A **compound sentence** has two independent clauses and balances the ideas in one clause against the other. You can use it to compare, to contrast, to give cause and effect, and to be positive or negative. The following compound sentence develops a cause-effect relationship:

COMPOUND SENTENCE: We will march in position 22 in the Thanksgiving parade, so you and Dad need to watch for us on television at about 11:00 a.m.

What Can Go Wrong with Compound Sentences?

You may fall into the habit of joining two clauses into a compound sentence for no justifiable reason. As explained above, the two clauses should work against each other for a purpose (to name and give an example, to show cause and effect, to name and define, to classify and analyze, to show progression). Which of the following two compound sentences has a justifiable reason for the coordination?

The men worked in the fields, the women labored over the wash tubs, but the children frolicked in the farm pond.

The men worked in the fields, and in the winter the family had something to eat.

The first sentence shows parallelism in the three clauses (*the men worked, the women labored,* but, in contrast, *the children frolicked*). The second sentence has a weak connection between working and eating.

Complex Sentences

A **complex sentence** contains one main clause and one or more dependent clauses. It emphasizes the main idea by putting minor ideas into phrases and dependent clauses. It thus allows you to show the reader which idea is important. The writer of the following sentence gives force to which idea—skipping class, feeling smug, or not getting a letter jacket?

COMPLEX SENTENCE: While we skipped classes on Tuesday, feeling smug and downright cocky, the coach awarded letter jackets to all players except us.

The subordinate clause is *While we skipped classes on Tuesday.* The phrase is *feeling smug and downright cocky.* The important information is in the independent clause and tells that the coach *awarded letter jackets.*

What Can Go Wrong with Complex Sentences?

Be careful that you do not put your main idea in the dependent clause, the one that starts with *after, because, before, if, when,* or *where.* The following sentence buries the key idea in the dependent clause that begins with which:

> Plasma is mostly water, which forms about 60 percent of a person's blood.

To correct this error, position the main idea effectively:

> Plasma, which is mostly water, forms about 60 percent of a person's blood.

Compound-Complex Sentences

A **compound-complex sentence** has two or more independent clauses and one or more dependent clauses. It elevates two important thoughts while subordinating one or more minor ideas:

> COMPOUND-COMPLEX: As red blood cells pass through blood vessels in your lungs, **a protein called hemoglobin picks up oxygen,** and then, as the red blood cells carry the

oxygen to all parts of your body, **the hemoglobin releases the oxygen for use by the cells**.

Boldface type highlights the main clauses above. They contain the primary information. The two dependent clauses that begin with *as* contain supporting information.

6j

7

WRITING CORRECT SENTENCES

For writing to be effective, each sentence must be grammatically correct. For questions about the grammar of your sentences, check Chapters 15 and 16, which provide a review of the grammar rules with examples.

As you write and review your compositions, examine each paragraph for the controlling sentence and the clarifying sentences. A sentence that controls, which is usually the topic sentence, will name the subject of the paragraph and suggest an idea that requires detailed development. A sentence that clarifies will contain specific information that develops and completes the topic sentence.

The following paragraph begins with a controlling sentence that is followed by several clarifying sentences:

> Blood makes a vital journey through your body. As it cruises through the network of arteries and veins, it distributes oxygen into the cells and collects carbon dioxide from the cells. The blood returns briefly to the heart, which sends it to the lungs, where the blood disposes of the carbon dioxide and gathers a new supply of oxygen. The lungs return the blood to the heart, which then sends it on another journey through your body.

These sentences have four features that are necessary for all correct sentences. The sentences are:

COMPLETE: The sentences combine ideas in a graceful, unified manner.

CLEAR: Every word appears in the best position to connect the various ideas.

PRECISE: The sentences avoid wordiness by focusing on key ideas.

ACCURATE: The sentences get the facts right.

Let's look at these four characteristics in more detail and study methods for editing sentences.

7a WRITING COMPLETE SENTENCES

To be complete, a sentence needs two vital ingredients—a subject and a predicate. Sentences may also contain various complements and modifiers. The following sentence is complete:

subject   verb   direct object

The dance instructor praised each performer.

A sentence is not complete until you connect all of its parts, especially in the case of compound sentences:

> The referee blew his whistle and pointed at me, so I had committed four fouls in the first period.

In this sentence, two independent clauses are joined correctly by the comma and the coordinate conjunction *so*.

Editing for Completeness

Be on guard for fragments when you edit. A **fragment** occurs when incomplete sentence parts pose as a sentence. That is, you might begin a phrase or a subordinate clause with a capital letter and end it with a period, even though the parts do not form a complete sentence. These are fragments:

Before the sun set.

Running the engine on full throttle.

On the first day of school when we lost our books.

In editing your compositions, look for these two types of fragments.

1. Fragments that have no subject and/or verb. Can you find the fragment in this example?

The shoplifter lingered at the jewelry counter without buying anything. And tried to disappear among other shoppers.

The second unit has a verb, *tried*, but no subject. It can be joined to the main clause to correct the fragment:

The shoplifter, lingering at the jewelry counter without buying anything, tried to disappear among other shoppers.

This correction uses a sentence interrupter between the subject *shoplifter* and the verb *tried*. The next correction uses a compound verb (*lingered and tried*):

The shoplifter lingered at the jewelry counter without buying anything and then tried to disappear among other shoppers.

2. Other fragments have a subject and verb but begin with a subordinating conjunction or a relative pronoun, such as *after, before, whoever, whenever,* and so forth. They function as subordinate clauses, and all subordinate clauses must be connected to a main clause. Can you identify the fragment in the next passage?

The clerk noticed the girl stealing a scarf. Which was now tied neatly around her neck.

The fragment, the second unit, can be corrected by attaching it to the main clause:

The clerk noticed the girl stealing a scarf, which she had tied neatly around her neck.

In addition to writing fragments, writers sometimes omit words that will make the meaning of a sentence complete. What word is missing from the following sentence?

The teacher saw Mary needed help with the math lesson.

The teacher did not "see Mary," the teacher saw "*that* Mary needed help." How is the next sentence incomplete?

In the student council race, Thomas Badge won more votes.

The reader needs more information: Thomas Badge won more votes than whom?

> In the student council race, Thomas Badge won more votes than Peggy Ward.

7b WRITING CLEAR SENTENCES

Clear thinking makes writing readable, but on occasion our brains betray us by switching too quickly from one idea to another. As a result, our writing can become vague, cloudy, and—without our intention—humorous. In brief, place the words in every sentence in the best position to connect ideas clearly.

Remember that most of your paragraphs will need plenty of clarifying sentences, as demonstrated by this next example:

> The human nervous system resembles a powerful computer. Both transmit information by using stimulating, electrical signals. Both receive, store, and process information. Both use a tiny but powerful unit to do their work: the human nervous system has a nerve cell, and a computer has a microchip.

This paragraph develops quite clearly the similarities suggested in the opening controlling sentence.

Editing for Clarity

Sentences become unclear when we connect the parts carelessly or don't connect them at all. For example, what is unclear about the next sentence?

> Worried that he might flunk the mathematics exam, the tutor gave Paul five special lessons.

Is the tutor worried? The next version makes it clear that it is Paul who is worried about flunking the examination:

> Worried about flunking the mathematics exam, Paul paid a tutor for five special lessons.

Three errors cause most of the problems with sentence clarity:

- Failure of agreement.
- Misplaced parts.
- Dangling modifiers.

Lets examine each error for ways to correct the problems.

1. Failure of Agreement

To be clear, a sentence's subject and verb must agree and all pronouns must make clear reference to their antecedents. Can you find the lack of agreement in this next passage?

> The teachers at our high school is planning a Thanksgiving program for Wednesday morning. Each performer must have their lines memorized for Monday's practice.

In the first sentence, the subject *teachers* requires a plural verb, *are planning*. In the second sentence, the subject *performer* requires a singular pronoun, *his and her*, or it needs to be plural, *all performers*, in order to agree with the plural pronoun *their*.

2. Misplaced Parts

A **misplaced part** is a word or phrase that is separated from the word it modifies. Here are a few guidelines for editing your adjectives and adverbs.

a. Keep adjectives (words, phrases, and clauses) next to the word they modify. What is wrong with the following sentence?

> After the tournament game, the coach awarded rings to the players with "Champions" engraved on each one.

The players do not have "Champions" engraved someplace on their bodies, but the rings do, as shown in the next sentence:

> After the tournament game, the coach awarded rings engraved with "Champions" to the players.

b. Adverbs, unlike adjectives, need not appear next to the word they modify; however, try to avoid three errors with your adverbs, as explained next.

First, place limiting words (*only, almost, just, even, scarcely, hardly, nearly, merely*) immediately before the words they modify. Can you identify the problem with this next sentence?

> We knew scarcely anyone at the party last night.

The writer probably means to say, "We scarcely knew . . . ."

Second, avoid *squinting modifiers*, which appear to modify the preceding words as well as the following words. What is confusing about the next sentence?

> The teachers said the next day they would go on a strike.

The sentence should make clear that the teachers will speak the next day or they will go on a strike the next day.

> The teachers said that they would go on a strike the next day.

Third, in most cases, do not separate the preposition *to* from the verb in an infinitive phrase.

SPLIT: The team wanted <u>to</u> only <u>wear</u> red jerseys at home games.

CORRECT: The team wanted <u>to wear</u> only red jerseys at home games.

3. Dangling Modifiers

Clarity will be lost if a modifier does not connect logically to its referent (such modifiers are said to be dangling). For example, what is unclear about the following sentence?

Quietly but viciously, we watched the snake make a strike at the baby chicken.

Who is vicious? Are *we* vicious or is the *snake* vicious? The adverb phrase *quietly but viciously* should be placed near *the snake make*, not next to *we*:

We watched the snake quietly but viciously make a strike at the baby chicken.

What is unclear about the next sentence?

By developing a study group, the exam should be easy to pass.

Logic tells us that an exam cannot develop a study group, so the writer needs to provide a subject that can perform the action:

> By developing a study group, we should pass the exam easily.

7c WRITING SENTENCES THAT ARE PRECISE

Precise wording in your sentences will help readers stay focused on key ideas. Be direct and clear by using natural, candid language:

> PRECISE: The metrical sounds of Edgar Allan Poe's "The Bells" move from light and merry to dark and somber.

Precision in your sentences requires specific wording, especially words that appeal to the senses—sight, sound, taste, touch, and smell. It is more precise to refer to *sliced ham and cheese with rye bread* than to the general word *sandwich*. Which of the following two sentences features precise wording?

> I began to feel sick during the game.

> In the third quarter, I suddenly felt dizzy and I could not focus my eyes.

The second sentence has precision; the first one does not.

Editing for Precise Wording

Try to avoid *wordiness*, also known as *redundancy*, which will clutter your sentences with unnecessary words. Can you identify phrases that seem redundant in this sentence?

> The sounds that a poem makes, like Edgar Allan Poe's "The Bells," can contribute to the meaning of a poem so that readers have another way of understanding the meaning.

Revised, the sentence might read like this:

> The sounds of Edgar Allan Poe's "The Bells" contribute to its meaning.

What could you strike from the next sentence?

> The team members trudged back again to the very same ten-yard line where they had started.

Strike *again, very same*, and *where they had started*.

The word *clutter* describes sentences loaded with unnecessary and distracting words:

> CLUTTERED: At this point in time, we are experiencing heavy precipitation, so the officials have met privately in a meeting and postponed the game for one hour.

7c

CLEAR: The current rainstorm has forced officials to postpone the game for one hour.

CLUTTERED: It is interesting to note that male students perform at an elevated level on the ACT and SAT exams but that female students achieve academic superiority on college grades.

CLEAR: Male students score higher on the ACT and SAT exams, but females make better grades in college.

Try to mix short words with long words to avoid a string of monotonous short words or a string of hard to pronounce long words. The following sentence uses too many small words:

WORDY: The coach was not happy with what the team did on the play, and so he signaled for the team to call a time-out.

PRECISE: Angry with his players, the coach signaled time-out.

Deadwood is another term that refers to unnecessary words. How would you edit deadwood from this next sentence?

WORDY: At this point in time, I know that the Academic Honors banquet has been penciled into the school schedule for May 14.

PRECISE: The Academic Honors banquet will be held May 14.

Flowery language ruins the precision of a sentence. It occurs when writers use too many adjectives and adverbs, too many elaborate words, or too many similes and metaphors.

FLOWERY: Like a dance with death, like a knock on the coffin, and like a suicidal ritual, bungee jumping has afflicted my noble boyfriend and captivated his heart like a crazed lover.

PRECISE: Although it is a dance with death, bungee jumping has captivated the attention of my boyfriend.

Trite words, cliches, and *euphemisms* also cause wordiness.

Overused phrases are trite:

in the due course of events
after a short period of time
what this school needs at the present time

Overused metaphors are cliches:

he passed by the skin of his teeth
happy as a clam
innocent as newborn babies

Inoffensive words are euphemisms:

preowned automobile (a used car)
misstatement (a lie)
a role player (a third-string quarterback)

WORDY: I bought a preowned car from a local automobile emporium that specializes in Ford and Mercury products.

PRECISE: I bought a used Mustang at Bell's Motor Company.

7d GETTING THE FACTS RIGHT

You have an obligation to your reader to supply accurate facts. You should research your topic as necessary by using textbooks, reference books, and magazines. Can you find an error in the next sentence?

Baton Rouge (the name means <u>red river</u>) has been ruled by three different governments—France, Spain, and the United States.

In truth, careful research would reveal that *Baton Rouge* means "red stick" and that seven governments have ruled Baton Rouge—France, Spain, Great Britain, Republic of West Florida, Republic of Louisiana, Confederate States of America, and the United States. The following passage is factually correct:

Baton Rouge, the capital of Louisiana, serves as a major port for the United States, despite the fact that it lies about 80 miles inland from the gulf.

Plagiarism

Plagiarism is a serious error. When you borrow specific ideas and words, rather than material that is common knowledge, you must cite the material accurately and identify the source by name and page number.

Let's look first at the information found by one student about the novel *A Separate Peace*.

> "I think it is the best-written, best-designed, and most moving novel I have read in many years. Beginning with a tiny incident among ordinary boys, it ends by being as deep and as big as evil itself."—Aubrey Menen

Can you identify plagiarism in the next sentence?

> The novel A Separate Peace begins with a tiny incident among ordinary boys, but it ends by being as deep and as big as evil itself.

This sentence misuses the source in four ways:

1. It uses the original wording of Aubrey Menen without giving proper credit.
2. It fails to use quotation marks.
3. It does not mention Menen.
4. It does not give a page number.

Look now at the correct way to cite the source:

> According to Aubrey Menen, the novel A Separate Peace begins with "a tiny incident among ordinary boys," but the conclusion is "as deep and as big as evil itself" (ii).

The correct version cites the author, places quotation marks around key passages, and provides a page number. At the end of the paper, the student would need to cite the book:

Menen, Aubrey. Prefatory Matter. <u>A Separate Peace</u>. By John Knowles. New York: Bantam, 1959. ii-iv.

7d

LANGUAGE

LANGUAGE

PART 3

8 FINDING THE APPROPRIATE WORD

CHAPTER

Since childhood, you have developed and expanded your storehouse of words. Nevertheless, to be an effective writer, you need to build your vocabulary even more by using a good dictionary and thesaurus and by developing vocabulary exercises. The right word expresses an idea exactly, so choosing just the right word will improve your messages, whether spoken or written.

Every composition you write tests your knowledge of words. Similarly, each community—be it home, the classroom, or the workplace—tests your ability to use appropriate words. The classroom, in particular, tests and enriches your vocabulary almost daily. Knowing the terminology of a subject gives you an edge for passing most examinations.

Being able to use the most appropriate word is vital to all writers. To find the most accurate word, writers scan their minds for **synonyms**, which are words that have the same general meaning but that differ in their specific application (*run, sprint, dash, race, jog*, and so forth). Unfortunately, we cannot always depend on our general vocabularies to provide the appropriate word. For example, does the following sentence contain any words that could be more specific?

> Principal Jones said, "Classes will be dismissed at noon because of the heavy snowfall."

Did you identify the word *said*? Although it is grammatically correct, the word *said* is general and overused. The writer needs to go in search of a more specific word. To find the best word, the writer will search his or her mind for synonyms or will consult a list of similar words, such as these:

announced	barked
declared	muttered
proclaimed	growled
disclosed	groaned
stated	grumbled

The choices are varied, but any one of these words is probably more effective than *said*. A strong verb can show the attitude of the speaker as well as the nature of the speech.

Let's look now at methods for finding the appropriate word.

8a USING A DICTIONARY TO FIND APPROPRIATE WORDS

Studying lists of synonyms may help you to clarify the meaning of closely related words and to choose the word that best expresses your intended meaning. Three common sources provide synonyms—a good dictionary, a thesaurus, and a computer word-finder.

Let's suppose that you write this sentence:

Saturday will be our last opportunity to take the SAT exam.

Is the word *last* appropriate? As shown below, a dictionary not only provides synonyms for the word *last*, but it also distinguishes each synonym from the others on the list.

Last

Synonyms: *last, final, terminal, eventual, ultimate.* These adjectives refer to that which marks an end or conclusion. *Last* applies to that which brings a series, sequence, or any collection of like things to an end: *the last day of the month; the last piece of candy. Final* refers to the end of a progression or process, and stresses the definiteness of the conclusion: *his final remark; our final offer. Terminal* is applied to that which marks a limit or boundary in space, time, development, or operativeness: *the terminal point of enemy penetration; the terminal state of tuberculosis. Eventual* refers to an outcome or issue: *eventual date of publication*; sometimes it implies a foreseeable or inevitable result: *the eventual downfall of a corrupt government. Ultimate* is applied to that which marks the termination of a lengthy progression and beyond which there exists no other: *our ultimate fate; an ultimate goal; the ultimate authority.* —*American Heritage Dictionary*, Boston: Houghton Mifflin, 1985.

Which word from the dictionary list seems appropriate to you?

Saturday will be our final opportunity to take the SAT exam.

Since it refers to the end of a process, *final* is probably the best choice.

8b USING A THESAURUS TO FIND THE APPROPRIATE WORD

A thesaurus, which is essentially just a collection of synonyms, also provides distinctions between various synonyms based on usage and meaning. As shown on the following page, a thesaurus shows four uses for *last* as an adjective, with synonyms for each use, and one use for *last* as a noun, with one synonym.

last *adjective*

1. Coming after all others: *the last act.*
   Synonyms: closing, concluding, final, terminal

2. Of or relating to a terminative condition, stage, or point: *the last days of Pompeii; a last farewell; last rites.*
   Synonyms: final, latter, terminal, ultimate

3. Bringing up the rear: *the last car in the gas line.*
   Synonyms: endmost, hindmost, lattermost, rearmost

4. Next before the present one: *last night.*
   Synonyms: foregoing, latter, preceding, previous

last *noun*

The last part.
   Synonym: end

—*Roget's II: The New Thesaurus.* Boston: Houghton Mifflin, 1980.

8c USING A COMPUTER'S WORD-FINDER

Many word processing programs also feature a thesaurus. As you type at the keyboard, you can use the computer to search for synonyms. The software WordStar 6.0, for example, gives this list for the verb *infer*:

infer: read, understand, study, comprehend, decipher, decode, interpret, peruse;

imply, insinuate, connote, hint, implant, lead, offer, put forth, seed;

deduce, derive, analyze, conclude, construe, draw, educe, gather, glean, guess, interpret, presume, surmise;

understand, think, assume, believe, comprehend, conceive, estimate, expect, fathom, gather, grasp, guess, imagine, presume, suppose, know, surmise, suspect, trust.

Each group of synonyms differs in meaning, and each synonym has a precise meaning with its own denotative and connotative values. Be sure you have found the exact word for your intended meaning before you use it.

WRITING CHECKLIST: FINDING THE APPROPRIATE WORD

A dictionary or thesaurus will help you in these ways:

1. To find the precise word. Consider how the words in the list below seem more specific than *questioned*.

The lawyer **questioned** the defendant.

cross-examined	Contested previous statements
interrogated	Questioned intensely and formally
grilled	Questioned severely and heatedly
quizzed	Tested with a series of questions
challenged	Raised a formal objection

2. To recall a familiar but forgotten word or to discover new words. Consider how the words in the list below seem more precise than *read*.

Mrs. Rodriguez **read** a passage from *A Day No Pigs Would Die.*

deciphered	Made clear the handwriting of the passage
decoded	Translated the secret meaning of the passage
interpreted	Explained the meaning of the passage for others
perused	Examined a passage carefully and thoroughly

3. To replace overworked or general words, such as *thing, do, make,* and *very*. Consider how the words in the list on the following page seem more precise than *make things*.

Simon likes to **make things** in the woodworking shop.

8c

invent toys	Design something that did not exist before and build a prototype
construct toys	Build and put together
create toys	Design but not necessarily build toys
produce toys	Finance and supervise the manufacture of toys

8d USING LANGUAGE DEVELOPMENT ACTIVITIES

In addition to a dictionary or a thesaurus, you need to practice other skills to improve your vocabulary. These are practical techniques that will serve you in different circumstances.

Learning the Vocabulary of a Subject

Try to memorize the important and unfamiliar words in every class you take. Knowledge of these academic words will serve you in two ways. First, knowing the words will help you pass examinations in each class. Second, the words will become part of your overall vocabulary. Therefore, keep a notebook of all unfamiliar words that you read or hear. Jot down new words so that you can study the spelling and the meaning.

3d

For example, one student, knowing that the teacher might test the class for reading and comprehension, examined D'Arcy Niland's short story, "The Parachutist." In the third paragraph alone, he noted seven words that were unfamiliar to him:

> The hawk, ruffled in misery, brooding in *ferocity*, came forth in hunger and hate. It struck off into the *abyss* of space, scouring the earth for some *booty* of the storm—the sheep lying like a heap of wet *kapok* in the sodden *paddocks*, the *bullock* like a dark bladder carried down on the swollen stream and washing against a tree on the river flats, the rabbit, driven from its flooded *warren* and squeezed dead against a log.

The student found the following definitions for the unfamiliar words:

ferocity	frenzy and brutality
abyss	canyon, gorge, gulch
booty	prize, bounty, plunder
kapok	fibers of a silk-cotton tree used for stuffing pillows

paddocks	barn, stable, stall
bullock	bull or steer
warren	a small space where rabbits live and breed

This student was prepared for the teacher's pop quiz as well as a vocabulary test.

This same process will serve you well in all classes. For science classes, you may need to memorize the spelling and meaning of such words as *glucose, mitosis, photosynthesis*, and *chlorophyll*. For such classes, you must learn the scientific terminology or risk failure.

Practicing Word Games in Your Writing Journal

Experiment with words and writing techniques in your journal. Try using new words and new phrasing. Play with sounds. Create a poem. Copy slogans and sayings that catch your fancy. Here is one student's journal entry:

I saw a billboard today for Wendy's. It said,

> LETTUCE

> fill you up

It's a pun, a word used two ways. Get it? Pretty cute. Maybe

I can do one with onion, chili, or ketchup. How about this—

Don't be chilly,

And don't be silly

Come to Wendy's

For some good hot chili.

As shown above, the writer is experimenting with language. Try to use your writing journal to practice word games, rather than merely to record daily activities.

Modeling Your Writing after Excellent Writers

Good readers make good writers. That is a known fact. What do readers learn from the best authors? Phrasing and word usage! Reading will make you conscious of the variations in tone, color, and meaning of a well-turned phrase.

Modeled writing requires you to find well-written passages during your reading. You should first copy a sentence or a paragraph onto a page of your journal, and then (1) try to use effectively a key word or two of the original in a sentence of your own, or (2) rewrite the passage in your own words but with the same tone and style as the original. Let's watch one student conduct this kind of exercise. First, Martina copied the original passage from the first page of John Knowles' novel, *A Separate Peace*:

"In the deep, tacit way in which feeling becomes stronger than thought, I had always felt that the Devon School came into existence the day I entered it, was vibrantly real while I was a student there, and then blinked out like a candle the day I left."

Then, Martina checked the meaning of *tacit* (unspoken or silent) and tried using it and a few other phrases in her own sentences:

I understood in a tacit way that my days as first-string catcher could end with one play.

Life is vibrantly real while I send signals to the pitcher, catch the pitch, and try to throw out the runner stealing second.

I was right, my days as catcher blinked out like a good dream when I failed to throw out four baserunners from Springfield High.

By studying how another writer used certain language, Martina was able to write three sentences that may be more lively and specific than she would have written otherwise.

8d

9

CHOOSING BETWEEN FORMAL AND INFORMAL LANGUAGE

Your language makes you a unique, interesting person, and it can make you an entertaining writer. Your choice of words affects both the message and the originality of your essay, thereby sending a specific impression to the reader. Nobody else could write your essay quite like you.

9a USING STANDARD ENGLISH FOR COMPOSITIONS

As a writer, you must make choices from a language that operates on several levels, from conversational to standard English and from informal to formal. A good rule to follow is this one: use words that fit the occasion. Talking "trash" may be appropriate in the hallways, but not in the classroom. Similarly, using a conversational style is acceptable in letters to friends, but not in academic essays.

Most of us have grown up learning and using **conversational English**, which is the language that displays our personal opinions, regional influences, cultural differences, and even vulgar expressions. When you speak, your dialect tells the listener something about your social, geographic, and ethnic background. In speech, you might say:

I'm gonna tell you guys about computer graphics.

The words affecting the listener will be the contraction *I'm*, the clipped word *gonna*, the regional expression *you guys*, as well as the pitch and accent of your voice.

When you write, however, you can communicate without revealing your regional or ethnic background:

This report explains computer graphics.

Note that this formal written version lacks the regional flavor of conversational English. That is an important distinction. Therefore, keep in mind three rules:

1. Cultivate your own rich dialect.
2. Use your dialect in appropriate contexts.
3. Avoid using your dialect in academic writing.

In writing an essay or a speech, use **standard, informal English**, which is the language that does not differ from one area of the country to another or from one ethnic group or social class to the next. Just as you would not wear blue jeans to a prom or a tuxedo to a picnic, so you should not use conversational language in an academic composition.

Yet you should not consider standard, informal English as "correct" and conversational English as "incorrect." Each has its place, so your task is to make suitable choices. Your "post-it" notes on the refrigerator door can be written in conversational English, but a book report must be written in standard, informal English.

9a

Some compositions will require **formal English**, as explained in the next section. Undoubtedly, you have the ability to handle conversational English and—in most cases—standard, informal English, but you may need to build your vocabulary for any type of scholarly composition.

TABLE 9.1   Three Levels of Language Usage

Conversational	Informal	Formal
Talking in the halls	English theme	Research paper
Personal letter	Speech	Scientific article
Journal note	Newspaper article	Technical report
Post-it notes	Classroom lecture	Legal brief

9b DISTINGUISHING BETWEEN FORMAL AND INFORMAL ENGLISH

A written composition can be casual and informal or serious and highly formal, so you face a choice every time you begin to write: Should you use formal or informal language?

Informal English is the language that the average person uses every day:

INFORMAL ENGLISH: The family feud between the Montagues and the Capulets is a big problem in <u>Romeo and Juliet</u>. One thing we know for sure, the families forced Romeo and Juliet into making some really bad decisions.

Informal English is appropriate for important letters, some school reports, some essay examinations, and personal essays. As shown above, informal English allows the reader to hear your voice and capture your personal style. It permits the use of the first-person *I*, some contractions, and the basic words of your vocabulary.

Formal English is the language that scholars use when writing about a serious subject for an educated audience:

FORMAL ENGLISH: The significant theme of <u>Romeo and Juliet</u> resides not in the story of the star-crossed lovers, but in the hostile relationship between the Montagues and the Capulets.

9b

Formal English is appropriate for academic papers. Use it to present the subject matter objectively. Try to keep yourself in the background and avoid any use of *I*. Let your readers focus entirely on the subject.

Let's look closely at the ingredients of the three levels of language use.

1. Conversational English (everyday speech that you can also use for dialogue in your compositions to capture the sound of voices on the street) typically has these ingredients:

contractions
many one-syllable words
slang
excessive use of *you*
vulgar words
sentence fragments
frequent use of *I*

> "You gonna have a garden this summer?" asked Connie.
>
> "No, I'm givin' up," said Jason. "Past three summers were too hot, you know? Plants just wilted on the vines."

2. Informal English (which you can use for themes and essay exams) typically has these ingredients:

a few contractions
a balance of one-, two-, and three-syllable words
a cautious use of slang words (usually enclosed within quotation marks)

use of *you* only in how-to essays

no vulgar words

no sentence fragments

use of *I* in personal narration but not in
explanatory essays and reports

> Plants in the garden will often wilt, especially in
> hot, dry weather. <u>Osmosis</u> is the word that describes
> the action involved. In simple terms, plant cells swell
> up and stand straight when they absorb enough water
> or they go limp when water leaks out.

3. Formal English (which you should use for
research papers and scientific reports) typically
has these ingredients:

no contractions

generous use of two-, three-, and four-syllable
words

no slang words

no use of *you*

no vulgar words

no sentence fragments

no use of *I*

a reasonable use of scholarly terminology

9b

<u>Osmosis</u> names a chemical action by which the diffusion of water occurs through a selectively permeable cell membrane. Osmosis causes plant cells to expand or contract.

9c WRITING WITH AND WITHOUT JARGON

Formal English often requires the use of the specialized language of a particular field of study (jargon), such as *rhythm, rhyme,* and *metaphor* for a paper about a poem or *membrane, chromosomes,* and *mitosis* for a science paper about cell division. You should use scientific jargon when writing about cell division or the process of fermentation. Similarly, you should use literary jargon in writing about a poem:

> The rhythm and the rhyme of this poem fit the general form of a Shakespearean sonnet.

This sentence effectively uses the words *rhythm, rhyme,* and *Shakespearean sonnet*; it has a language level appropriate to this field.

There may be occasions, however, when you will want purposely to misapply a word from another field to achieve a certain effect:

> The students **made a strategic withdrawal** into the classroom when the principal appeared in the hall.

The military phrase, *made a strategic with-drawal*, gives a humorous slant to this sentence.

What Can Go Wrong with Formal English?

Research papers written in formal English may require you to use unusual and difficult words, so be careful. Trying to use technical and scholarly words that you do not understand can obscure your meaning. The following sentence uses psychological jargon when a perfectly good word, *self-confidence*, is available:

> self-confidence
> /
> Children who have trouble reading may not have ~~psychic~~ ~~stamina~~.

This writer uses **pretentious language**, which is showy, fancy language, rather than precise wording. By using long words, the writer has attempted to sound formal but has failed to communicate the ideas clearly.

Euphemisms are bland, inoffensive words and phrases. How has this writer attempted to avoid the word *dismissal* or *suspension?*

> The principal's out-placement of three disorderly students was endorsed by the school board.

9c

The euphemism *out-placement* obscures meaning and requires more words than precise, clear language.

Why does the following sentence *not* qualify as formal English?

> The human spinal cord zips along from the bottom of the brain down toward the fanny.

This sentence contains slang (*zips along*) and conversational English (*down toward the fanny*). This version is more formal:

> The human spinal cord extends from the brain stem to the base of the spine.

Finally, can you identify the unnecessary jargon in the following sentence?

> A Shakespearean tragedy has a five-act flow chart in which the screen idol has success for three acts, but moral bankruptcy and villainous foreclosures ruin him in the fourth and fifth acts.

The business term, *flow chart*, and the legal words, *bankruptcy* and *foreclosures*, are inappropriate to the literary context. A better sentence might be:

> A Shakespearean tragedy has three acts in which the hero or heroine has success but two final acts in which human failures and villainous treacheries bring ruin.

9c

10

CHAPTER

WRITING WITH FORCEFUL WORDS

Dynamic writing will entertain as well as communicate with readers. For this reason, successful writers need to make choices about the right word in combination with the best phrasing. Good writing requires that each noun, verb, and modifier work in harmony with the individual sentence and with the composition as a whole.

10a USING FORCEFUL NOUNS

Nouns name the subject of a sentence—a person, place, object, condition, or idea. How you use nouns will affect your writing and give you style.

When you start a sentence or paragraph with a general noun, you will need to follow up with specific details:

The **person** next to me fainted.

The sentence above needs one of two things: a specific noun (*stranger, coworker, Ted Jones, bachelor, brother, soldier*) or trailing details:

> The person next to me in the cafeteria line fainted. I did not know him, but he was tall, blond, and a tumble of arms and elbows as he fell against me. As I struggled to keep my balance, I heard somebody call him Ted.

or

> My boyfriend Ted fainted in the cafeteria line, falling against me in a tumble of arms and elbows.

The choice is yours: be specific with your nouns at the very start or be general and follow with specifics. Both methods have merit. Which style do you prefer? The first passage below moves from general to specific nouns; the second begins with specific nouns:

> Many of the original rock stars are aging, and their lifestyles have mellowed. No longer do groupies crowd backstage, and drug dealers no longer hover in the hallways. Mick Jagger, Paul McCartney, Bob Dylan, and Neil Young all need Ben-Gay more than cocaine, and they hold their grandchildren instead of some young groupie on their knees.

> Mick Jagger is forty-nine, Paul McCartney is fifty-one, and Tina Turner is fifty-three, but their rock-and-roll fans continue to pack arenas that younger stars can't fill. Ben-Gay and grandchildren have replaced drugs and groupies for these old rockers, and the Grateful Dead have come back to life.

Nouns can be abstract or concrete, general or specific. **Abstract nouns** express ideas, attitudes, and qualities: *welfare, happiness, college education.* **Concrete nouns** refer to items that we can see, touch, hear, taste, or smell: *a government check, a kiss on the cheek, a diploma.* In addition, concrete nouns can be general or specific: *a government check* is general, *$467.92* is specific; a *Saturday night date* is general, *a goodnight kiss* is specific.

- General: flower
- Concrete: rose
- Specific: American Beauty Rose

By using concrete and specific nouns, you enable your readers to visualize more precisely what you are writing about. Note how the next passage moves from the general to the specific:

> Homecoming is the very best time! It provides a chance for the alumni to visit the school once again. Bonfires, floats for the parade, the crowning of a queen and her court, the football game--all these and more represent Homecoming.

In general, then, make it a practice to write with concrete nouns. Which nouns in the next sentence could be made more specific?

> The woman sat quietly, holding the cat in her lap.

Revised, the sentence features forceful nouns:

> Sarah Molroney sat quietly, holding her kitten Maypie in her lap.

Can the next sentence gain force with specific nouns?

> The workers finished in one room and began work in another.

Revised, the sentence might read:

> The painters finished the kitchen and began work in the dining room.

Note: You can also use adjectives to enhance nouns (see **10c**):

> The three, lazy painters, careless and unorganized, finally finished the kitchen.

Using a Series of Nouns

You put more force behind your nouns by listing them in a series:

Homecoming is the bonfire, the parade, the queen, the alumni, and the game itself.

The length of the series shows the reader your commitment to the subject. The longer you make the series, the more you show your exuberance and the more you face the dangers of clutter. Therefore, keep the nouns specific and properly punctuated. Which description below do you prefer? Why?

She heard the whistling wind and the sound of her heart.

She heard the shouts from friends below, the sound of her heart, the blast of gas rushing into the balloon, and then the eerie silence of life high above the trees.

The first sentence above uses a two-part series; the second uses a four-part series. The four-part series has strong, specific nouns—*shouts, sound, blast,* and *eerie silence.* Let's look at one more example, first at a short main clause and then at that main clause expanded with trailing noun phrases:

The horses stood.

The horses stood, **eyes darting** wildly toward the approaching stranger, **hooves thrashing** in the

10a

gray dust of the corral, **tails swishing** quietly but held high on alert.

Eyes darting, hooves thrashing, tails swishing— these noun phrases give force to a dull main clause.

Using Nouns That Have Sound Effects

Some nouns feature **onomatopoeia**, which means they form a sound that resembles the object they name (for example, the word *hiss* sounds like a hiss). This next writer uses a series of onomatopoeic words:

> The snake approached me in the dimly lit cave, for I heard **the scratching** against the crumbling rocks, **the r-r-r-rattling** of its warning system, and then **the hissing** through its now-glistening fangs. I **gasped** in fear, but then the snake slithered into a crevice, out of sight but not out of mind.

These nouns gain force by appealing to the reader's sense of sound, just as other nouns appeal to sight, taste, and so forth.

Using Nouns with Favorable or Unfavorable Connotations

Depending on your purpose for writing, you can use denotations for exact word meanings

10a

and connotations to add emotional colorings to your writing.

A word's **denotation** is the dictionary meaning of a word. According to the dictionary, a *watermelon* is a large oblong or roundish fruit with a hard green or white rind, often striped, containing a watery pink or red pulp with many seeds.

The **connotation** of a word is what the word suggests or implies, including the emotions or associations that surround it. *Watermelon*, for instance, may connote refreshment, juices dripping down the chin, picnics, or childhood memories.

To various readers, and in various contexts, each noun you use may have a unique connotative value. For instance, *motorcycle, motor scooter, hog, moped, chopper,* and *three-wheeler* all denote the same thing, a motorized form of transportation, but each has a specific connotation:

motorcycle	freedom and excitement out doors
motor scooter	childish excitement
hog	loud, gas-guzzling splendor
moped	sightseeing and riding for leisure

| *chopper* | customized, individual uniqueness |
| *three-wheele*r | outdoor, backwoods riding through mud and muck |

If the connotation of a word does not seem appropriate for your purpose, your audience, or your subject matter, you should use a different word. When a more appropriate word does not come quickly to mind, use a dictionary or thesaurus for a list of synonyms (see **8a** and **8b**).

10b USING FORCEFUL VERBS

In many ways, verbs resemble nouns: they are abstract and concrete, literal and figurative, and sometimes onomatopoeic. However, verbs present an additional feature—they can enliven a sentence by showing action or they can freeze the action to show a state of being. Both types have significant roles to play.

Using the "To Be" Verb Effectively

The *to be* verbs—*am, are, is, was, were, being, been*—show no action, but they do show certainty and thereby suggest a firm position on the subject. For that reason, they have value for:

DEFINITION A kiosk **is** a temporary public structure for selling refreshments, newspapers, jewelry, and similar items.

DENIAL A kiosk **is not** a permanent structure.

CERTITUDE This kiosk **will be** the first to sell this brand of t-shirt.

DESCRIPTION The kiosk **was** red with yellow trim and a light blue counter.

COMPARISON The kiosk **is** like any retail store except for its size, inventory, and the cost of the lease.

The *to be* verbs appear frequently in textbooks because they join the subject with a complement—one item equals and defines the other:

Viruses **are** noncellular units that **are** many times smaller than the cells they invade. Viruses **are** so small that scientists must use electron microscopes to study them.

However, the *to be* verbs might occur too frequently in your writing, as shown in this example:

I **was** ill during the holidays, but I **was** well enough to read two novels. I **was** in bed for five days, but it **was** five days well spent because I **am** finished with my reading assignments.

You can change *was* into other verbs that also show a state of being, such as:

10b

become	feel	remain	taste	seem
appear	grow	smell	sound	look

> I **became** ill during the holidays, but I **felt** well enough to read two novels. I **remained** in bed for five days and **finished** my reading assignments.

How would you change the verb *was* in the next sentence?

> Famished and growing weak, I found an apple. It **was** rotten, but I ate it anyway.

Did the apple *taste* rotten, *look* rotten, *smell* rotten? The writer could have a made a better choice.

Using Verbs That Show Action

Action verbs, unlike the *to be* verbs, activate the nouns and energize the sentence:

> The teacher **scampered** rapidly down the hall and **hopped** quickly into the principal's office.

The verbs *scampered* and *hopped* show the teacher in action, unlike the following wording:

> The teacher went down the hall to the principal's office.

Can you think of a verb that will activate the following sentence?

> The heavy surf was bad for the beach.

Revised, the sentence might read:

> The heavy surf pounded the beach, eroded the sand dunes, and ripped out the sea grass.

How would you activate the following sentence?

> The principal walked in the hall and appeared suspicious.

Revised, the sentence might read:

> The principal stalked the hallway and searched several lockers.

Using Transitive Active Verbs Rather than Passive Verbs

A transitive active verb activates a sentence by making the noun perform the action of the sentence:

> The vandals **smashed** several desks and **spray-painted** vulgar graffiti on the walls.

By contrast, a verb in transitive passive voice can deaden a sentence by making the focus of the action something other than the noun, which is acted upon rather than acting:

> Several desks **were smashed** and the walls **were spray-painted** by vandals.

In passive voice, the noun actor, *vandals*, gets lost in a prepositional phrase and has little force. The verbs *were smashed* and *were spray-painted* can only describe what was done to the nouns.

Transitive active voice is concise, vigorous, and forceful, so use it often. Use the passive voice only when you need to emphasize the receiver, not the actor.

How would you edit the following sentence?

When the building was struck by lightning last night, all computer files were erased.

Revised, the sentence might read:

When lightning struck the building last night, all computer files were erased.

The sentence above emphasizes the importance of the computer files.

Lightning struck the building last night and erased all computer files.

But this sentence emphasizes the action of the lightning.

You must make the choice, but generally the best verb will be active, not passive:

PASSIVE VOICE: The transformer in the parking lot **was destroyed** by a lightning bolt, and my car **was scorched** by sparks from a hot wire.

ACTIVE VOICE: A lightning bolt **destroyed** the transformer in the parking lot, and sparks from a hot wire **scorched** my car.

As you can see, active verbs energize your sentences:

PASSIVE VOICE: The ball **was caught** by the receiver who **was able** to run into the end zone for a touchdown.

ACTIVE VOICE: The receiver **seized** the ball with one hand and **dashed** into the end zone for a touchdown.

Changing Weak Nouns to Action Verbs

Try to avoid using weak nouns that are derived from verbs, such as:

intention	investigation	approach
ownership	discussion	resistance

Your sentences will have more force if you use the verbs themselves:

10b

WEAK NOUN: The teacher's **intention** is to give four examinations.

ACTION VERB: The teacher **intends** to give four examinations.

How might you activate the following sentence?

Our discussion centered on a pay raise.

Did you decide to change the noun *discussion* to a verb?

> We **discussed** a pay raise.

How might you activate the next sentence?

> We have the expectation that funding is available.

Did you decide to change *expectation* to the verb form, *expect*?

> We **expect** that funding is available.

Here are a few more examples; the forceful phrasing is on the right:

A review of the data	We will review the data.
A need for study time	The students need study time.
The ownership of the car	I own the car.
A discovery of gold	He discovered gold.

Using a Verb Series

Like a series of nouns, a cluster of verbs in a sentence enforces the action and duplicates or mimics the occurrences:

While the coach **paced** the sidelines, **shouted** at the referees, **threw** his headphones to the ground, and **encouraged** every player, the fullback **smashed** off tackle for six yards, the quarterback **squirted** up the middle for twelve yards, and the flanker **danced** into the end zone with a pass of eight yards.

Using Verbs That Have Sound Effects

Like nouns, verbs can feature onomatopoeia to duplicate the sound being named:

The teacher's chalk **rasped** and **screeched** against the board, and my teeth **clattered** in shock.

10c WRITING FORCEFULLY WITH ADJECTIVES AND ADVERBS

As you have seen, nouns and verbs serve as the heart and soul of every sentence you write; in addition, adjectives and adverbs supply picturesque details to support the ideas and the actions of your sentences. **Adjectives** give force to mild or bland nouns:

sensitive, sunburned skin that **throbbed**

Adverbs give force to mild or bland verbs:

the sunburned skin burned **intensely for two days**

Strive to use adjectives and adverbs that reinforce the action of your verbs:

Weak: The **strong** storm knocked down several old trees.

Forceful: The **violent** storm, **frightful in its fury**, knocked down several **ancient oak** trees.

Weak: The storm wrecked every house on the block.

Forceful: **Without warning** the storm wrecked every house on the block **with tornado-strength winds**.

Like nouns and verbs, adjectives and adverbs have degrees of specificity. Try to use specific adjectives and adverbs, such as those on the right below:

the smooth face	the unblemished face
the loud noise	the blaring, booming noise
the dirty shirt	the blood-stained shirt
the quiet street	the hushed street, muffled by snow
the sour taste	the bitter taste, like acid
spoke quietly	spoke in harsh whispers
approached quickly	approached rapidly with scampering steps

fell awkwardly	fell in somersaulting
	tumbles down the stairwell

If you use specific adjectives and adverbs in your sentences, you give your readers forceful words that add to the visual qualities of your writing.

Placing Adjectives and Adverbs

You should place adverbs strategically so they reinforce the verb. Adverbs can appear almost anywhere in a sentence:

> **With flashing speed**, the cooper hawk scooped up the field mouse and disappeared **quickly into the woods**.

> The cooper hawk, **with flashing speed**, scooped up the field mouse and **quickly** disappeared **into the woods**.

Adjectives, however, are limited to three positions:

1. Immediately before the noun:

> Hawthorne's **dark, somber** novels

2. Immediately after the noun:

> Hawthorne's novels, **dark and somber**

3. To complete a linking verb:

> Hawthorne's novels are **dark and somber**

Use a variety of these positions for your adjectives. In particular, avoid piling too many adjectives in front of the noun:

> My **soft, gentle, warm,** and **compassionate** grandmother was good to me.

These adjectives lack force because they fall together in a similar form. Variety of placement gives adjectives force:

> My **gentle** grandmother, so **soft** and **warm** to children, was a **compassionate** soul.

Using Adjectives and Adverbs Objectively and Subjectively

Like nouns, adjectives and adverbs have connotations; that is, they add emotional coloring to your writing. In expressive writing about yourself or in fiction and poetry, you may and should use subjective coloring to enrich your attitudes about the subject:

> His **sloppy and careless** ground strokes allowed his **incompetent but aggressive** opponent back into the match, so Garrison decided to destroy this **slimy** opponent by rushing the net after each of the guy's **squirrelly** serves.

In contrast, writing that must be factual and objective should depend almost entirely on denotative modifiers; that is, the words should be as specific as possible:

> Mass measures the size of an object. Weight measures the force of gravity on the object. The same golf ball will fly higher and farther in Denver than in Miami because of differences in gravity, not mass.

This type of objective writing has no room for subjective comments. Why is this next sentence emotional, subjective writing, not scholarly writing?

> It seems unfair that a high-jump record can be set at high altitudes, such as in Denver. NCAA rules are pretty stupid for not considering scientific evidence that affects sporting events.

A scholarly presentation would sound something like this:

> Athletes participating in events that defy gravity, such as the high jump, have an advantage in high-altitude cities such as Denver or Mexico City. However, governing bodies such as the NCAA do not factor environmental conditions into their records.

You should present factual material objectively in most academic assignments and reserve your subjective tone for personal and creative compositions:

> TOO SUBJECTIVE: Hawthorne's story is **stupid** to me.

BETTER: Hawthorne's story seems **terribly** out of date.

OBJECTIVE: Hawthorne's story, while out of date, explores a contemporary problem--the child born out of wedlock.

Removing subjective modifiers, as shown above, may be a necessary part of editing your academic papers.

Using a Series of Adjectives or Adverbs

As with nouns and verbs, adjectives and adverbs can be quite powerful when used in series. While you don't want to string too many together, a series of three adjectives or adverbs is reasonable:

Four pages long, difficult, and nerve-racking, the geometry test separated those who were **wise, persistent, and well-prepared** from the **desperate, hopeless, and failing** students.

The teacher explained the geometry problems **clearly, exactly, and patiently**.

If you list more than three adjectives or adverbs, you will show your emotional commitment to the topic or you will suggest the absurdity of the issue:

The judge said to the convicted banker, "Your behavior in this case has been **ugly, vicious, slovenly, disrespectful, and overwhelmingly criminal.**"

This accumulation of adjectives above shows the emotional involvement of the speaker. In the following sentence, a series of adverb phrases captures the absurd, rich nature of New Orleans's Bourbon Street:

Within the French Quarter the tourist will be overwhelmed **by smells of French pastries and shrimp gumbo, by the pounding throb of rock music in a battle with Bourbon Street jazz, by sights of panhandlers mixed with elegant Creole ladies, and by hawkers at open doors who make intimidating offers of wealth, fame, pleasure, gadgets, food, and--yes--even salvation.**

Again, you must make the choice: (1) to be reasonable by limiting the sentence to one, two, or three adjectives or adverbs, or (2) to release your subjective imagination with a series of five, six, or seven adjectives or adverbs.

Using Adjectives and Adverbs as Words, Phrases, or Clauses

Adjectives and adverbs have several forms,

and you need to choose the one appropriate to
your sentence:

SINGLE WORDS: The **outdated** laboratory serves
nobody.

She screamed **hysterically**.

PHRASES: **Out-of-date**, the laboratory serves nobody.

She screamed **with hysteria**.

CLAUSES: The chemistry laboratory, **which is woe-fully out-of-date**, needs new funding.

The girl **who screamed with hysteria**
has been taken to the infirmary.

10d USING METAPHORS AND SIMILES TO ENFORCE YOUR MEANING

Metaphors and similes compare one subject
or idea with a particular quality of another. They
help readers see the subject in a new and different light.

A **metaphor** is a figure of speech that makes
an implied comparison between two unlike
things:

LITERAL: The eye is an organ of sight.

COMPARATIVE: A camera, like an eye, has a lens.

METAPHOR: The cat's **eyes were jewels** glowing in
the night.

The metaphor implies the similarity of jewels
and eyes.

A **simile** is an expressed comparison using
the words *like* or *as*:

SIMILE: The action at the pep rally was **like a three-
ring circus**.

SIMILE: The broken power line twisted **like a snake**
on the wet grass.

As shown above, similes and metaphors bring
your writing to life in several ways:

- They enrich your language by showing the
  reader a new, fresh comparison.
- They reveal your special, perhaps unusual,
  view of the world.
- They may associate an abstract thought
  (*beauty*) with something visible and tangible
  (*a rose*) in order to dignify it (*my love is a
  rose*) or to degrade it (*my love is a thorn in
  my side*).
- They give clarity to a complex subject when
  the simile or metaphor is extended through a
  paragraph.

10d

Writing With Different Types of Metaphors and Similes

To create fresh and lively similes and metaphors, you can compare dissimilar things in a variety of ways:

1. Compare people and human features to non-human ones—vegetables, furniture, animals, automobiles, and so on:

   Rhonda bought her father a new cologne for Christmas, but her mother thought it made him smell **like a pickle factory**.

   Robbie was a slug in the one-mile race at Owens Track.

   Caleb chomped on the carrot sticks **like a happy bunny**.

10d

2. Use a comparison that gives human traits and qualities to animals and objects (**personification**):

   The house **sat** on the hill, **watching** for the family to return.

3. Use a gross exaggeration or overstatement (**hyperbole**) to say that the subject is far more or far less than in reality:

   The new cashier at the supermarket was slower than **a dead turtle**.

4. Use a part for a whole **(synecdoche)**:

> This **watercolor** is my favorite in the show.

5. Write an extended metaphor to explain a complex subject (allegory):

> Proteins in human cells are like an orchestra director who controls the various sections--strings, brass, percussion, and so forth. Each person's protein director waves the baton to determine bone size, eye and hair color, height, muscular frame, and so forth. All parts usually work in harmony like a good orchestra.

Creating Original Figures of Speech

Teachers will encourage you to write metaphors and similes in your essays, so try to conform to the following rules for using the figures of speech:

1. Metaphors and similes should be original and clear, not obvious. Trite metaphors (**clichés**) have appeared in print so often that they have become commonplace:

cool as a cucumber	beat around the bush
happy as a lark	seen but not heard
irony of fate	sharp as a razor
selling like hotcakes	light as a feather
easier said than done	green with envy

10d

playing with fire   blind as a bat

busy as a bee   beat around the bush

quick as a flash   dead as a doornail

The cure for these trite expressions is to avoid them or to give one a new twist or wrinkle (*quick as a flush, beat around the goal post,* or *easier said than groaned*).

2. Figures of speech should be in harmony with the seriousness or the playfulness of your tone. What do you think is wrong with the following sentence?

> Concerned about the treatment of students with AIDS, the principal chastised the students like Lucy scolding Charlie Brown.

Above, the reference to comic strip characters does not fit the seriousness of the message. The passage needs revision:

> Concerned about the treatment of students with AIDS, the principal chastised the students like a preacher on Sunday morning.

3. Figures of speech should be uniform with each other within a sentence. A **mixed metaphor** changes images midway through a comparison. What two images are mixed in the following sentence?

The swimmer kicked like a mule down the length of the pool and slithered to reach the touch pad.

A mule and snake do not mix, so the writer needs to eliminate one simile, as shown below:

The swimmer kicked like a mule and pulled with all his strength to reach the touch pad.

What is wrong with the following sentence?

Like a playful kitten, he poisoned the computer's software.

This comparison mixes the kitten with poison, an unlikely comparison. This revision cures the error:

Like a kitten in a sandpile, he soiled the computer software.

or

Like a sly apothecary of medieval days, he poisoned the computer software.

4. Figures of speech should be varied. The simile is popular, but give variety to your prose by using metaphors and other special forms— personification, synecdoche, hyperbole, and others.

The chalkboard preached the lesson of the day: "The wheels of learning turn slowly."

Above, *chalkboard* is synecdoche (a part that represents the learning environment), *preached* is personification (the chalkboard is like a preacher), and *wheels* is a metaphor (learning is like the slow turning of a wheel).

Nouns serve well as metaphors:

> Spaghetti is life in a meal--the dangling pasta, the slurping flavor, the spontaneous consumption.

In effect, the writer renames something: life is spaghetti. You might want to create metaphoric nouns such as these:

> Good times are chalkboards, too easily erased.

> A motorcycle is a purring leopard.

> The teacher thinks he is David Letterman.

Try your hand at creating a noun metaphor:

1. The flooding river is a brown, wrinkled blanket covering the wheat fields.

   The flooding river is a _____

2. Angela was three elements in one—the prayer, the deliverance, and the salvation.

   Angela was the _____

3. The soccer ball became a mud-encrusted gargoyle, so heavy and so lopsided it refused to roll.

   The soccer ball became a _____

10d

4. You are a boxer in the ring of life, punching fate in the midsection but receiving a crushing left hook to the jaw.

You are _____

Verbs also serve well as metaphors. A metaphoric verb is a condensed simile; for example, in the sentence below, the home is *like an old person who watches and withers with the years*:

The old family home **watched** the years go by and **withered** at the encroaching subdivisions.

What is the implied metaphor in the following sentence?

The mower engine **trembled** for a moment, **stumbled**, and then **ran** with excitement across the meadow.

The engine is like *a young, awkward animal that needs time to learn grace and efficiency*.

Try your hand at creating metaphoric verbs:

1. The swimmer **slithered** into his wet suit.

The swimmer _____

2. We watched the butterflies **rock and roll** among the zinnias.

We watched the butterflies _____

10e USING CURRENT WORDS WITHOUT USING SLANG

New words enter the language weekly, some valid and valuable and others short-term slang. Try to use words that a general audience would understand, but avoid words that only your special friends would recognize. Slang has a short life. The trendy words in the following sentence may be out of date by the time you read them:

neighborhood   realm
/   /

Gangs that roam the hood want to protect their turf.

Do not, under any circumstances, use vulgar words; they will mark you as insensitive and tactless.

Computer terminology is often trendy. As computer usage continues to grow, many words have become common—*modem, byte, database, floppy disk*. Other computer terms, however, may be too trendy for the average reader:

> If your **hard drive crashes**, be careful about asking a **chip head** for technical advice. Some of these **hackers** will tear into your **motherboard** and destroy your CPU.

Revised, the passage means:

If computer data disappears from your computer, be careful about asking amateurs for technical advice. Some hobbyists might alter internal circuits and destroy the central processing unit.

As you can see, time spent choosing just the right nouns, verbs, adjectives, and adverbs is time well-spent, for these are the elements that bring your writing to life.

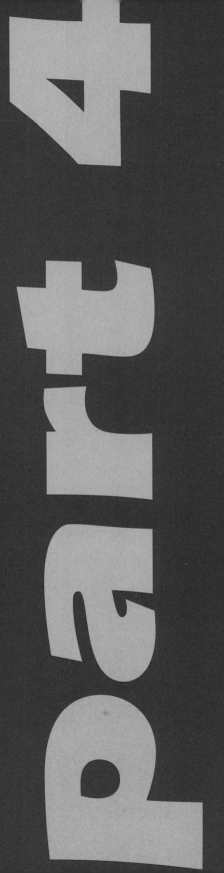

Part 4

PUNCTUATION AND MECHANICS

11

CHAPTER

USING PUNCTUATION EFFECTIVELY

Punctuation, like other writing decisions, involves choices. Your use of a comma, a semicolon, or another mark will affect the meaning of your sentences. This chapter examines the roles of various punctuation marks, especially for beginning, interrupting, or ending your sentences and for connecting the various parts. Exceptions exist, but three basic rules will serve you well.

1. Set off introductory phrases and clauses:

   Known nationwide for its CNN headquarters, one southern metropolis is Atlanta.

2. Set off phrases and clauses that interrupt the main clause:

   One southern metropolis, **known nationwide for its CNN headquarters**, is Atlanta.

3. Set off trailing adjectives but not trailing adverbs:

   One southern metropolis is Atlanta, **known nationwide for its CNN headquarters**.

   Atlanta is the southern metropolis **where Ted Turner headquarters his CNN television empire**.

Let's examine these options in more detail.

11a PUNCTUATING PHRASES AND CLAUSES AT THE BEGINNING OF SENTENCES

As a general rule, introductory phrases and clauses that precede the main clause should be set off by the comma. Consider this example:

While we hunted, Jennifer pitched the tent and started a fire.

The comma separates an introductory adverb clause, *While we hunted*; otherwise, the sentence reads, "While we hunted Jennifer. . . ."

In effect, the comma signals the end of the introductory matter and the beginning of the main clause. Many introductory phrases and clauses function as adverbs to establish *where, when, why,* or *how* with regard to the action in the main clause:

> **After his successful career as a player for several professional teams**, Frank Bernard turned to coaching.

Other introductory phrases are adjectives that modify the subject of the main clause:

> **Smiling with joy**, Jenny raced across the finish line.

The participial phrase, *smiling with joy*, serves as an adjective to describe Jenny. In the following sentence, a long introductory prepositional phrase requires a comma:

> **Like a yellow beast in the early morning fog**, the school bus growled and groaned in its climb up the hillside.

You should also set off single introductory words for emphasis, if that choice strengthens your meaning:

> **Exhausted**, the firefighter rested against the engine.

11a

You can also set off contrasting expressions:

Unlike many of his friends, Drew went to class on senior skip day.

When in doubt, insert a comma after introductory matter. You will never be incorrect by including it, but you can confuse the reader if you omit it. How does the addition of the comma improve the reading of these sentences?

At first, the computer seemed to be another typewriter. Later, I realized its tremendous advantages. Now, after just one week, I could never go back to using my old typewriter.

In this sentence, the commas set off transitions of time (*at first, later, now*) to show the writer's progress in learning to use a computer.

11b PUNCTUATING INTERRUPTIONS WITHIN SENTENCES

At times, you will need to interrupt the main clause by inserting extra information that is not essential to the meaning of the sentence. You should enclose such material within commas, dashes, or parentheses, as shown by these sentences:

Nancy Johnson, **who withdrew last week as**

> **a candidate for class president**, has now transferred to another school.

The main clause gives the essential information—Nancy Johnson has transferred. The commas set off the nonessential adjective clause (shown in boldface), which provides extra information about Nancy.

> Algebra, geometry, and trigonometry--**my next three mathematics courses**--will improve my knowledge but wreck my grade-point average.

The writer above, having named specific courses, uses dashes (which are typed as two hyphens) to distinguish the nonessential comment from the main clause.

> The epidermis (**the outer layer of the skin**) contains dead cells and emerging new cells. The dermis (**the inner layer of the skin**) contains living cells that form blood vessels, fat cells, nerves, and sweat glands.

Since the *epidermis* and the *dermis* are named, the definitions in the parentheses above contain nonessential information.

In deciding how to punctuate interrupting elements in the middle of sentences, follow these basic guidelines:

1. Use commas to set off nonessential elements but not essential ones. Can you discern

11b

the difference of meaning in the next two sentences to explain why one requires the commas and one does not?

My brother who attends Penn State will major in pre-med.

My brother, who attends Penn State, will major in pre-med.

In the first sentence, the writer probably has more than one brother, so the essential phrase explains which brother will major in pre-med. Because this information is essential, it is not set off with commas. In the second sentence, the writer clearly has only one brother, who happens to attend Penn State, which is nonessential information for this sentence. Word units that describe indefinite pronouns (*everyone* or *something*) are usually essential and do not require commas:

The teacher knew by first name everyone who entered the room.

Verbal phrases and prepositional phrases should be set off by commas when they are not essential to the sentence:

Situation comedies, **usually featuring satire**, are popular television entertainment.

The participial phrase *usually featuring satire* gives additional but nonessential information about all sitcoms. Compare that with an essential phrase:

Wrestling matches **featuring masked bullies** are standard fare.

Adjective clauses that follow the noun or pronoun they modify and begin with *who, whom, whose, which, where,* and *when* are generally nonessential:

The research paper, **which I wrote last semester**, only received a grade of B.

The highlighted clause, while it adds information about the modified noun, does not specify or limit. Compare that with an essential adjective clause:

The student director cut the scene **that seemed rather vulgar**.

As a general rule, use *that* to introduce essential clauses and use *which* with nonessential clauses:

The classic Thunderbird **that drove past us** turned into the parking lot of our apartment complex.

Old Thunderbirds, **which are true classics**, have always interested me.

Use commas with **nonessential appositives**, which merely rename a noun or pronoun without limiting it:

William Shakespeare's first comedy play, <u>A Comedy of Errors</u>, has two sets of twins who are constantly misidentified by other characters in the play.

The phrase *first comedy play* limits the meaning to one drama, so the appositive *A Comedy of Errors* is not essential and requires the commas.

2. **Use commas with transitions that interrupt the main clause.** Interrupting transitional words and phrases, such as *for example, in fact, in my opinion, in the first place, unfortunately*, and *certainly*, should be set off by commas:

I submitted three different fund-raising plans. My ideas, **unfortunately**, were overlooked.

High school football attracts many fans. Friday evenings, **consequently**, become a time for celebrations.

Note: Commas are unnecessary when the meaning is clear or when the adverb modifies a nearby verb:

His attitude **no doubt** influenced the teachers.

You should also set off other types of expressions that are clearly parenthetical and transitional in nature:

The trick basketball play, **as most of you know**, was illegal.

Similarly, you can use commas to create

11b

interruptions that duplicate the hesitant voice of a speaker:

> I yearn, well, I must admit, I lust, yes, that is the only word for it, I lust for chocolate fudge ice cream.

3. **Use dashes to indicate a sudden break in thought**. Use dashes on occasion, rather than commas, to set off a summary, restatement, amplification, explanation, or interruption:

> Collectible coins--**especially Franklin half dollars**--will increase in value.

> The team's goal--**to win the district tournament**--will only happen if they play as a unit.

4. **Use parentheses to enclose supplemental information.** Use parentheses to enclose some digressions, afterthoughts, nonessential remarks, in-text numbering, and page citations to source materials:

> Alaska (**the forty-ninth state**) and Hawaii (**the fiftieth state**) both joined the United States in 1959.

> The teacher stated that a topic sentence includes three ingredients: (**1**) a limited topic, (**2**) an attitude or opinion, and (**3**) a clear direction for development.

> Rowan explores the mythic elements in Faulkner (**81**).

11b

Do *not* use a comma before an opening parenthesis:

delete this comma

/

Mark Spitz's eight gold medals in swimming, (won in the 1972 Olympic Games) have not been equaled.

Do use a comma after a closing parenthesis if the material in parentheses comes at the end of an introductory remark or some other material that would normally be followed by a comma:

The residents prepared for the hurricane (the first of the season), but it came ashore 300 miles to the north.

5. Use brackets to insert your own comment into the quotation of another person:

One sports reporter cautioned, "In the heat of the season the coach **[Bob Knight of Indiana University]** has little patience with irrelevant questions."

The superintendent maintained that "allowing this **[an after-school program]** will bankrupt the school budget."

Convention allows you to replace an ambiguous word with a bracketed word or phrase to clarify the meaning:

The superintendent maintained that "allowing **[an after-school program]** will bankrupt the school budget."

The Latin word *sic* within brackets is used to indicate that an error occurred in the original quotation:

> The cowboy in the movie said, "They was hung [**sic**] from a huge oak tree."

Using *sic* shows that the writer knows that the correct phrasing should be *were hanged*, but the writer wants to reproduce the original exactly.

6. **Use ellipsis to interrupt and omit passages.** The ellipsis (three spaced periods) marks the omission of words and phrases from a direct quotation. The ellipsis enables you to interrupt a quotation and omit some words in order to concentrate on essential, relevant wording. Here is a passage that a writer might wish to quote, along with methods of elliptical omission:

> ORIGINAL: "There are many ways of enjoying ourselves, and one of the pleasantest is to meet interesting people."—Marchette Chute.

> Marchette Chute has insisted that "there are many ways . . . to meet interesting people."

You should add a fourth dot, denoting a period, if the ellipsis occurs at the end of a sentence:

> Marchette Chute has insisted that "there are many ways of enjoying ourselves. . . ."

11c PUNCTUATING TRAILING PHRASES AND CLAUSES

As a general rule, do not use a comma to set off adverb phrases and clauses that follow a main clause:

> no comma required
> /
> Jeremy collapsed when he raced across the finish line.

However, you should set off with commas any adjectives that appear after the main clause:

> The puppy wagged its tail, expectant, nervous, and lonesome.

You should also use a comma to separate an **absolute phrase** (see **15e**) that follows the main clause:

> The two boxers pounded each other relentlessly, **gloves soggy with sweat and faces battered.**

The trailing absolute phrase, *gloves soggy with sweat and faces battered*, modifies the entire main clause, not the subject or the verb of the main clause; therefore, it is set off by the comma.

11c

11d PUNCTUATING THE END OF THE SENTENCE

The period is usually the mark of choice to close various types of sentences:

DECLARATIVE SENTENCE: I enjoyed Raold Dahl's short story "Lamb to Slaughter."

REQUEST: Be sure to turn in your science project by Friday.

MILD EXCLAMATION: I can't believe I made a B on my report.

INDIRECT QUESTION: She asked if our game was at home or away.

Exclamation marks and question marks should be used only if the sentence is a genuine exclamation or a direct question. Use a **question mark** for all direct questions:

Is our Saturday game at home or away?

Your use of a period or a question mark will clarify whether you are asking a question or making a statement:

He really said that? (You are asking a question.)

He really said that. (You are making a statement.)

Question marks may also be used for an informal series of questions:

11d

Did your class write a report? An essay? A paragraph?

Use **exclamation marks** only to show strong exclamatory emphasis, especially in dialogue:

"All right! I found my notebook," Susan squealed.

It is best to avoid using exclamation marks in formal writing. Although the next sentence describes a crisis, there is no reason for making the statement sound like a scream of anguish:

The computer erased the data. The disk operating system may be defective.

11e PUNCTUATING A SERIES

Use commas between items in a series of three or more words or word groups:

I knew Mother would try a new recipe when I saw pineapples, oranges, apples, and kiwi on the kitchen counter.

You will always be correct if you include the comma before the *and* or *or* in a series, even if there are only three items in the series:

The storm blew noisily out of the northwest, rain drifted against the windows, and lightning flashed across the sky.

In less formal writing, you may omit *and* or *or* to speed up the reading and put less emphasis on each item in the series:

Visitors to the Culture Fair can enjoy a variety of activities--**old movies, jazz concerts, poetry readings, art displays**.

Conversely, you can use *and* or *or* between each item in a series, rather than commas, in order to slow down the reading and give emphasis to each idea:

In his poetry **and** his drama **and** his private correspondence, William Butler Yeats wrote endlessly of his love for Maud Gonne.

You must use commas between coordinate adjectives, which are adjectives that modify a noun equally and separately:

The coach favors **tall, strong, aggressive** players.

Each adjective in the sentence above modifies *players* separately. To determine if adjectives are coordinate, see if you can put the word *and* between them: tall *and* strong *and* aggressive. In addition, see if the adjectives make sense if you change the order: strong, aggressive, and tall. If the adjectives pass both tests, they are coordinate and must be separated by commas.

Adjectives that are not coordinate should not be separated by commas:

Sarah wore a shimmering black evening gown.

11e

In the sentence above, the adjectives build upon each other: *shimmering* modifies the three-word noun phrase *black evening gown*; *black* modifies the two-word noun phrase *evening gown*; and *evening* modifies *gown*. Again, use the two tests: (1) Can the word *and* fit between the adjectives (shimmering *and* black *and* evening gown)? (2) Can you scramble the order and still make sense (evening black shimmering gown)? Since the answer to both questions is no, the adjectives are not coordinate and should not be separated by commas.

When one or more items in a series already have commas, use **semicolons** between the major parts, instead of commas:

> The principal defended our school as one of the best in the state in order to promote its championship teams in football, women's basketball, and tennis; a musical program with band, choir, and orchestra; and, of course, a top-grade academic program.

You should use a **colon** to introduce a series of words, phrases, or clauses:

> When you write your essay, consider all of the following: line spacing, spelling, and punctuation.

Note: Do not use a colon after a linking verb, a preposition, or a relative pronoun:

delete this colon

/

When you leave for the pool, make sure you have: a
towel, sunscreen, and extra clothes.

11f USING PUNCTUATION TO CONNECT MAJOR SENTENCE PARTS

When you join two main clauses into a compound sentence, you must openly signal the
connection. There are several ways to make that
signal:

1. **Connecting main clauses with a comma
   and a coordinating conjunction.** A comma
   alone is insufficient for connecting main clauses; you must always use a coordinating conjunction (*and, but, for, nor, or, so, yet*) with
   the comma:

   I have met the new neighbors, **yet** my brother refuses
   to speak to them.

   You may be right, **but** I have serious doubts.

   You will always be correct if you use commas
   in these situations. You may omit the comma
   only in *short* compound sentences where the
   meaning is absolutely clear:

The storm blew noisily out of the northwest **and** rain drifted against the windows.

This sentence treats the weather in both clauses and the meaning is clear. However, the next sentence treats two different ideas: the weather and George's handling of the cattle. It needs the comma:

The wind blew noisily out of the northwest, so George brought the cattle into the barn.

2. **Connecting main clauses with a semicolon.** You can use a semicolon alone to separate main clauses that have two closely related thoughts. The semicolon below, for example, joins independent clauses that treat the same topic—the habits of students:

Some students procrastinate about exams until motivation disappears; others rush into the exam on the test day without careful study or preplanning.

3. **Connecting main clauses with a semicolon and a conjunctive adverb or a transitional phrase.** You can strengthen the connection between two main clauses by using both a semicolon and a conjunctive adverb (such as *moreover, therefore, then*) or a transitional phrase (such as *for example, in other words, on the contrary*). As shown below, the semicolon precedes the conjunctive adverb and a comma follows:

The poet Robert Burns wrote the lyrics to "Auld Lang Syne," the famous New Year's anthem; **however**, the music was borrowed from an old folk melody.

4. **Connecting main clauses with a semi-colon and a coordinating conjunction.**
   You should use a semicolon (rather than a comma) with a coordinating conjunction (*and, but, or*) only if one or both independent clauses contain internal punctuation:

   She was greatly excited, nervous, and irritable; but she grew calm after we administered the medication.

5. **Connecting main clauses with a colon.**
   While the semicolon separates two major ideas, a **colon** introduces further elaboration on what has been said in the first clause. You can use a colon to introduce material that extends or explains the idea of the first clause:

   Those who oppose sex education in public schools are ignoring one important fact: Acquired Immune Deficiency Syndrome (AIDS) lives in the hallways and classrooms.

   You should use a colon before, not after, phrases such as *for example, that is,* or *namely*:

   Flannery O'Connor's short stories and novels always contain unforgettable characters: for example, Hazel Motes in <u>Wise Blood</u> remains on your mind long after the novel is finished.

You should use a colon to introduce a formal quotation:

> Edward R. Murrow's words ring true today: "Our major obligation is not to mistake slogans for solutions."

Be careful not to confuse colons and semi-colons. A semicolon means *stop* while a colon means *go forward, there is more to come*:

> The drama teacher designed the perfect plan: a 10-foot screen would encircle the set.

In the sentence above, the phrase after the colon explains the plan. A semicolon is appropriate when the second clause does not explain the first:

> The drama teacher designed a 10-foot screen to encircle the set; all other set designers disliked the idea.

11g PUNCTUATING DIRECT QUOTATIONS

Quotation marks enclose direct quotations from printed sources and from direct speech. They enable a writer to reproduce another person's exact words. They appear always as a pair, one to open and one to close the featured element:

We might live in a self-centered "me" generation, but the Bible says, "Love thy neighbor as thyself."

If you interrupt a quotation with other words, put each quoted section in a pair of quotation marks:

"I only regret," stated Nathan Hale, "that I have but one life to lose for my country."

If you rewrite the words of another person, you are using indirect quotation, which does not require quotation marks:

I asked if she was all right, but she told me to mind my own business.

To show one quotation within another, first use double marks, then single:

Thomas Nelson says, "Shakespeare has few kind words for family relationships, as shown by his line: 'A little more than kin, and less than kind.'"

Note: Do not use quotation marks around quotations of four lines or more; instead, set off long quotations by indenting ten spaces from the left margin:

In Julius Caesar, Shakespeare uses Mark Antony to make this passionate plea:

> Friends, Romans, countrymen, lend me your ears;
> I come to bury Caesar, not to praise him.
> The evil that men do lives after them,
> The Good is oft interred with their bones;
> So let it be with Caesar.

11g

When you create dialogue, begin a new paragraph each time a new speaker speaks:

"The election rules are clear," argued Sam.

"Not so," countered Justin. "I have examined the by-laws and find no provision for absentee ballots."

Sam responded, "But the band and choir members have a right to vote, and they'll be out of town on election day."

"So change the day of the election," said Justin. "The by-laws permit a change of date but not the use of absentee ballots."

Be sure to use quotation marks correctly with other punctuation marks. Periods and commas always go inside both single and double quotation marks:

"Deceive boys with toys," Plutarch said, "but men with oaths."

Semicolons and colons always go outside the quotation marks:

Lincoln reflected about the past and spoke to the future when he talked about a government "of the people, by the people, for the people"; we still take these words to heart each time we hear them.

Question marks and exclamation points may go inside or outside the quotation marks—inside if they are part of the actual quotation, outside if they are not:

> "Did the counselor move you into geometry yet?" Simon asked.

The quotation above forms the question. Compare:

> Who wrote "The Rat Trap"? Wasn't it Selma Lagerlof?

In the following sentence, Sabrina's remark is the exclamation:

> Sabrina shouted, "You leave my purse alone!"

Dashes go outside quotation marks if they are not part of the quotation:

> Thomas Paine stated, "Give me liberty or give me death"—no, it was Patrick Henry.

If a line of dialogue ends with a dash, follow the dash with quotation marks:

> "What do you want?" Renee demanded. "Answer me, or----."

Finally, when you use words in a special or ironic sense, do not use quotation marks:

> delete the quotation marks
> /   /
> If you consider yourself to be "mature," then act your age.

EDITING CHECKLIST: UNNECESSARY COMMAS

1. Have you used a comma to separate a subject and a verb or a verb and its object or complement?

delete this comma
/

This week players in age groups 8-10 and 11-12, will practice during the afternoon.

The comma separates the subject *players* from its verb *will practice.*

2. Have you used a comma between compound elements that are not independent clauses?

delete this comma
/

Freshman members of the mathematics team, and a few eighth grade students will compete in a separate division.

The comma separates two parts of a compound subject, *members* and *students.*

3. Have you used a comma with a restrictive modifier?

delete these commas
/   /

Bikers, who do not stop at traffic signals, risk their lives.

The commas set off an essential clause that identifies which bikers will risk their lives.

4. Have you used a comma before the first word or after the last word in a series?

delete this comma
/

Several items that charities accept for resale are, books, appliances, tools, and even clothes.

The comma separates the verb are from its predicate nouns *books, appliances, tools,* and *even clothes.*

5. Have you used a comma before adverbial clauses that end sentences?

delete this comma

/

She was undecided about attending college, after she graduated.

The comma is inappropriate with a trailing adverb.

6. Have you used a comma between adjectives that cannot be separated with *and*?

delete this comma

/

The bright, red paint made the car sparkle in the sun.

The comma is unnecessary because the adjectives *bright* and *red* are not coordinate adjectives that modify paint equally and separately.

7. Have you used a comma before an opening parenthesis?

delete this comma

/

Senator Sam Nunn, (Georgia) is a powerful man on Capitol hill.

No comma is necessary before a parenthesis.

11g

12

CHAPTER

HANDLING TITLES, NAMES AND SPECIALTY WORDS

*S*ome titles must be underlined, some are enclosed within quotation marks, and most require some capital letters. This chapter will address the basic mechanics for naming titles and specialty words.

12a UNDERLINING TITLES

Use underlining for titles of books:

In <u>A Day No Pigs Would Die</u>, Robert Peck portrays the maturing of a boy into manhood.

If your computer can produce italics, use italics rather than underlining:

In *A Day No Pigs Would Die*, Robert Peck portrays the maturing of a boy into manhood.

TABLE 12.1   Titles That Require Underlining

The following list shows what kinds of major works require underlining:

Ballets: <u>The Nutcracker</u>

Books: <u>Life on Earth</u>

Bulletins (in book form): <u>1992 Financial Report</u>

Cassette tapes: <u>The Jefferson Bible</u>

Court cases: <u>Roe</u> v. <u>Wade</u>

    Note: Do not underline <u>v</u>. or <u>versus</u>.

Films: <u>Romancing the Stone</u>

Journals: <u>English Journal</u>

Magazines: <u>Sports Illustrated</u>

Newspapers: <u>The Atlanta Constitution</u>

Operas: <u>Aida</u>

Paintings: <u>American Gothic</u>

Plays: <u>The Miracle Worker</u>

Poems (in book form): <u>The Idylls of the King</u>

Radio series (but not one program): <u>The Prairie Home Companion</u>

Record albums (but not one song): <u>Hotel California</u>

Symphonies: <u>Eroica</u>

Sculptures: <u>Winged Victory</u>

Television series (but not one program): <u>Home Improvement</u>

Yearbooks: <u>The Equestrian</u>

Videocassette tapes: <u>Fievel Goes West</u>

12a

You should also underline the names of specially designed ships, aircraft, and other vehicles, but not the general names of a fleet.

T A B L E 1 2 . 2 Vehicles That Require Underlining

Aircraft: <u>Air Force One</u> (but Boeing 747)
Automobiles: the <u>Blue Flame</u> (but Ford Taurus)
Ships: <u>Titanic</u> (but not U.S.S. or H.M.S. before a ship's name:
      U.S.S. <u>Enterprise</u>)
Spacecraft: <u>Apollo II</u> (but space shuttle)
Trains: <u>The Zephyr</u> (but Burlington-Northern)

12b USING QUOTATION MARKS WITH TITLES

Enclose within quotation marks the titles of short works, those that are not book length. For example, if you mention a short paper in the body of your essay, place it within quotation marks:

> John Welter's essay, "My Store of Grievances," gives a humorous look at convenience stores.

TABLE 12.3 Titles That Require Quotation Marks

The following list shows works that you should enclose within quotation marks:

First lines of poem as title: "The grass so little has to do"
Journal, magazine, and newspaper articles: "The Lost Money"
Lectures and speeches: "The Gettysburg Address"
Short poems: "After Apple Picking"
Short stories and essays: "A & P"
Songs: "Amazing Grace"
Titles of sections and chapters of books: "The War Years"

12c LISTING TITLES WITH NO UNDERLINING AND NO QUOTATION MARKS

Certain titles do not require underlining, nor should they be enclosed within quotation marks. Most notable in this category are biblical works:

We read Genesis from the Old Testament.

TABLE 12.4 Titles That Require Neither Underlining Nor Quotations Marks

The following list shows titles that require neither underlining nor quotation marks:
Titles of sacred writings: Bible, Koran, New Testament, Exodus, I Timothy 2, Matthew 6:33
Government documents: Bill of Rights, Article 5 of the Constitution of the United States

Titles of editions or series: the Parrott Edition of Shakespeare's Plays, third edition of <u>The World Book Encyclopedia</u>
Parts of a book: Chapter Two, Appendix B, Preface, canto 4
Form, number, and key of musical works: Symphony No. 3 in E-flat (but, <u>Eroica</u> symphony)
The title on the opening page of your theme:

Butch Czwonski

11th grade English

November 12, 1993

   The Water Imagery in Two Frost Poems

12d USING CAPITAL LETTERS WITH TITLES AND NAMES

There are certain rules to follow in capitalizing titles of books, articles, and works of art. You should always capitalize the first and the last word of a work's title and subtitle:

<u>Letters from the Earth</u>

Capitalize all other words, with the following exceptions. Do not capitalize articles (*a, an, the*) unless they are the first word of the title:

<u>In **the** Middle</u>

<u>**A** Shakespeare Companion</u>

12d

Do not capitalize coordinate conjunctions:

<u>War **and** Peace</u>

Do not capitalize prepositions unless they are the first or last word:

"Caught **in** the Grasp of Greatness"

"A Lesson to Live **By**"

Do not capitalize the *to* of infinitives:

"Someone **to** Love"

Capitalize all other words, no matter how short:

"We Are Free"

When the first line of a poem serves as the title or part of the title of that poem, reproduce the line exactly as it appears in the original (and capitalize the author's name as he or she prefers):

"The Theme of Love in cummings's 'anyone lived in a pretty how town'"

Capitalize both parts of a compound word in a title:

<u>Grammar in the Spanish-Speaking World</u>

But use "a Spanish-speaking country" in your text.

Capitalize proper nouns—the names of specific people, places, and things—and any words that are derived from them. Do not capitalize common nouns.

TABLE 12.5 Capitalization of Nouns

Proper nouns	Derivative nouns	Common nouns
President Reagan	Reaganomics	a college president
God	Godspeed	god, godly, godless
Tennessee Volunteers	Vols	athletes

Capitalize titles, specific organizations, days, months, holidays, historical events, and geographic areas.

TABLE 12.6 Capitalization of Other Names or Titles

Days: Tuesday
Holidays or religious days: Hanukkah, Christmas
Historic events: Inauguration Day
Historic periods: Restoration
Months: October
Official documents: Magna Charta
Organizations and institutions: Sigma Chi, Folger Library
Political parties: Republican Party
Titles: Sergeant Rosso, King Henry V
Trade names: Microsoft, Pepsi

Geographic Names
Bodies of water: Pacific Ocean
Cities: San Francisco, Nashville
Continents: Europe, Africa
Counties: Franklin County

12d

Countries: Somalia, England
Landforms: Rocky Mountains
Planets and heavenly bodies: Venus, the Milky Way
Public parks and designated areas: Washington Square
Sections of the country: New England, the South
State nicknames: the Granite State
States: Vermont, Georgia
Streets and roads: Front Avenue, Interstate 15

A few guidelines may help you solve unusual capitalization problems:

1. Capitalize **nicknames** and **labels** that substitute for a proper noun:

   Tell **Mother** to light the candles when **Skipper** arrives.

   But: The **brothers** and their **nephews** arrived late.

2. Capitalize titles that precede names:

   Principal Ed Scott and **Superintendent** Robert Livingston

   But: Ed Scott, **principal** of Riverdale High School

3. Capitalize most words derived from proper nouns:

   Thoreau followed the basic **Emersonian** principles.

4. Capitalize articles or prepositions that are part of surnames only when they begin a sentence:

   De Gaulle's return to France signaled the beginning of a new era.

   But: The people celebrated **de Gaulle's** triumph.

5. Capitalize the proper names of countries, districts, regions, states, counties, cities, lakes, rivers, and so on:

   the High Plains
   the Southwest
   the Seine River
   Cape Fear

   But do not capitalize compass directions or regions, lakes, or rivers when they are used as common nouns:

   She drove **west** on Highway 61.

   The two **rivers** join near the state line.

6. Capitalize the names of nations, nationalities, races, tribes, languages, and persons identified by geographic locations:

   Our school has three **German** exchange students.

   Oklahoma is home to many members of the **Cherokee Nation.**

7. Capitalize names of religions and their members, their deities, and their sacred books:

   The accounts of the life of Abraham and his descendents are found in the book of **Genesis**.

   Many Americans are turning to Asian religions, including **Buddhism**.

However, do not capitalize the word *god* when using it generically:

The ancient Greeks had **gods** for all occasions.

For clear reference, capitalize pronouns that refer to a deity:

The **Lord** advised Luke of **His** higher mission.

Table 12.7 shows additional guidelines in a variety of areas.

TABLE 12.7 Capital Letters and No Capital Letters

Capitals	No Capitals
Mayor Nathan Boardman	Nathan Boardman, the mayor
Riverside High School	several Georgia high schools
January	winter
Advanced Physics	I skipped physics
the High Plains of Texas	the Texas plains
Jehovah	the Greek gods
Principal Ted Jones	Ted Jones, the principal
Here comes Brother Bob	Here comes my brother Bob

12d

13

HANDLING ABBREVIATIONS, NUMBERS AND CONTRACTIONS

On occasion, you can shorten words, phrases, and figures by using abbreviations, numbers, and apostrophes. It is quicker for you and the reader to use *AIDS* throughout a paper rather than the full title of the disease, *Acquired Immune Deficiency Syndrome.* In a paper full of facts and figures, it only makes good sense to use the figure *345* rather than *three hundred forty-five.*

13a USING ABBREVIATIONS, INITIALISMS, AND ACRONYMS

There are a number of ways to shorten words and titles in your text and documentation. **Abbreviations** are shortened forms of a word or words. Most good dictionaries provide a list of standard abbreviations:

no. (number)

lbs. (pounds)

St. (street)

Mr. (mister)

Oct. (October)

Initialisms are formed by using the initial letters of a group of words:

CBS (Columbia Broadcasting System)

NAACP (National Association for the
    Advancement of Colored People)

IRS (Internal Revenue Service)

MTV (Music Television)

Acronyms are initialisms that evolve into pronounceable words:

NATO (North Atlantic Treaty Organization)

PAC (Political Action Committee)

MADD (Mothers Against Drunk Drivers)

You should use initialisms and acronyms in your papers as long as you define them the first time you use them; thereafter, use the shortened form:

> Seasonal Affective Disorder (SAD) afflicts a small portion of the population. In some cases, SAD patients require heavy medication.

In general, you should avoid using abbreviations in your text, but use them often in documentation. Follow these guidelines:

1. In your text, abbreviate titles before and after proper names:

First use:	Thereafter:
Sen. Jim Sasser	Sasser or
	Senator Sasser
Ralph M. Hooper, Jr.	Hooper
Mrs. Jonathan B. Matthews	Matthews

Do not use abbreviations alone or with a surname alone:

> NEVER: The **Dr.** will begin physical examinations at 12:00 noon.

> CORRECT: The **doctor** will begin physical examinations at 12:00 noon.

In academic writing, use a person's full name without *Mr., Mrs., Ms.,* or *Miss* at first mention:

Walt Whitman

Jane Austen

William Shakespeare

13a

Thereafter, use the last name only: *Whitman, Austen, Shakespeare.*

When you refer to people by their initials, don't use periods or spaces between the letters:

Many reforms enacted by **FDR** (Franklin Delano Roosevelt) are still active today.

You should abbreviate academic degrees:

Lorenzo Lopez earned his **M.D.** in 1992.

Usage varies, but a period after each part of an academic degree is always correct: *B.A., M.A., B.S., J.D., LL.D., M.Ed., M.S., Ph.D.*

Do not use a title in front of a name and again at the end:

NEVER: Dr. Stimpson Smith, Ph.D.

CORRECT: Dr. Stimpson Smith *or* Stimpson Smith, Ph.D.

2. Use A.M. and P.M. (or a.m. and p.m.), B.C., A.D., $, and No. (or no.) only with specific times, dates, or figures:

Flight **No.** 87 departs at 8:30 **a.m.**, and the ticket price is $412.

Note: *B.C.* means "before Christ" and follows the number (*44 B.C.*); *A.D.* means "in the year of our Lord" and precedes the number (*A.D. 43*).

13a

3. Abbreviate as often as possible in documentation, addresses, and parenthetical matter. In your text write:

> The fifth book of Matthew records the Sermon on the Mount.

In your documentation write:

> To paraphrase the words of Jesus, we still need to let our light shine before our friends (**Matt. 5:16**).

The chart below shows how to use full words in your text and abbreviations in your documentation and notes.

TABLE 13.1 Abbreviations

Text	Documentation
Charles J. Ard	C. J. Ard
Avens and Son, Incorporated	Avens & Son, Inc.
Scott, Foresman and Company	Scott
Monday	Mon.
November	Nov.
California	CA
Germany, United States	Ger., U.S.
Allen Boulevard	Allen Blvd.
Independence Day	4 July 1993
physics, history	phy., hist.
chapter	ch. or chpt.
section	sec.
page, pages	p., pp.
pint, pound, quart	pt., lb., qt.

13a

13b USING NUMBERS

In your writing, you should spell out numbers in some cases, but not in others. In general, spell out numbers in formal writing, but use figures in technical and scientific writing. Follow these guidelines:

1. Spell out numbers that you can write in one or two words; use figures for other numbers:

   Six hundred people preregistered.

   The judge was surprised when **384** supporters honored him.

   The committee must examine **eighty-five** applications.

2. If the largest in a category of numbers contains three or more digits, use figures for all:

   We selected **3** of the **104** subjects. (not three of 104)

3. When one number immediately follows another, spell out the smaller number and use figures for the other:

   The architect plans to build **three 110-story** buildings.

   The architect plans to build **110 three-story** buildings

4. Write out all numbers at the beginning of a sentence or recast the sentence so it does not begin with a number:

Nine hundred and sixty-five people surprised us with contributions to the scholarship fund.

We were surprised when 965 people made contributions to the scholarship fund.

Note: newspapers and some publications use figures for all numbers ten and over.

As the following table shows, use numerals in your text for specific places and exact figures.

TABLE 13.2 Numbers

Addresses:

Mail it to 160 Roberts Dr., Riverdale, GA 30274.

Average ages:

The students averaged 15.5 years of age.

Dates:

School begins on August 26, 1993.

Shakespeare was born in A.D. 1564.

Decimals and percentages:

The average weight is 3.5468 grams.

The team shot only 23.5 percent.

Divisions of books:

The famous balcony scene in *Romeo and Juliet* is found in Act 2, Scene 2.

You will find the quotation in volume 3, chapter 6, pages 231-42.

Identification numbers:

My receipt numbered 5469000021 is enclosed.

The vial number 7836 is missing.

Money:

You owe parking fines of $43.65.

13b

Statistics:
> We recorded ACT scores from 14 to 27.
> Scores in the 890-1100 range appeared frequently.
> The first overtime finished in a 74-74 tie.
> Seven 4-year-olds scored 8 on a 12-point scale.

Time of day:
> The sunset will occur at 6:10 A.M.

Note: Use **Roman numerals** only for titles of persons (*King Henry V*), sections of an outline (*I., II., III.*), prefatory pages (*ii, iii, iv*), or established terminology (*Type II virus*). In all other cases use **Arabic numerals** (*3, 18, 345*).

13c USING APOSTROPHES AND FORMING CONTRACTIONS

The apostrophe has three main uses.

1. The apostrophe shows omission in contractions, enabling you to tighten the wording in order to duplicate speech sounds:

> We **aren't** ready for this type of examination.

> The '90s will be known as the Clinton years.

> Billy Joe shouted, "Well, I'm not **goin'**."

Note: You should avoid contractions in formal writing but use them often in the dialogue of short stories.

2. The apostrophe signals possession, giving you an abbreviated method for showing ownership:

> **Diane's purse** holds nearly everything she owns.

> **The Ford Escort's design** has won many awards.

> **Montana's climate** is not for the weak at heart.

For all **singular nouns**, even if the last letter is an *s*, use *'s*:

child's toy

NATO's peace plan

Japan's culture

fox's tail

actress's role

Yeats's poems

Dickens's novels

For **plural nouns** not ending in *s*, use *'s*:

people's shoes

mice's holes

deer's habitat

The men's tournament

For **plural nouns** ending in *s*, use an apostrophe only:

the teachers' lesson plans (several teachers have plans)

13c

actresses' script (the script for several actresses)

the students' study habits (the habits of
several students)

For **compound nouns**, use *'s* or *s'* after
the last word:

editor-in-chief's argument (one editor-in-chief)

father-in-laws' advice (more than one father-
in-law)

For **indefinite pronouns** (*everybody,
nobody, each other,* and so on), use *'s*:

somebody's book bag

nobody's books

another's boyfriend

To **show joint possession** by two or
more people, use *'s* after the last noun only:

Taylor and Murphy's science project [one project]

To show **separate possession**, use *'s* after
each noun:

Ron's and Cynthia's schedules (each has a separate
schedule)

13c

3. The apostrophe can be used to form plurals of some letters, words, and abbreviations:

> Mind your **p's** and **q's**.
> Dot your **i's** and cross your **t's**.
> He made all **A's**.
> **The's, and's**, and **be's** appear often in English prose.

In general, do not use *'s* to show the plural of numerals or abbreviations, though usage varies:

> We were at 5s and 6s.
> We were at sixes and sevens.

> The 1980s are the Reagan years.
> The SATs were in the 1000s.

4. Do not misuse the apostrophe. Do not use an apostrophe with the possessive pronouns *its, whose, ours, yours, theirs, his*, and *hers*. In particular, use *its* and *whose* to show posses-sion, and use *it's* and *who's* to mean *it is* and *who is*:

> The hamster stuffed its food into its mouth. It's incredible how much his mouth will hold.

> Whose article is this about the regional tournament?
> Who's the sports editor for the school newspaper?

13c

Do not use an apostrophe with plural nouns that are not possessive:

delete this apostrophe
/
Some of the apartment resident's have filed formal complaints against the owner of the property.

14

CHAPTER

HANDLING HYPHENS AND SPELLING

When you are faced with any question about the spelling of a word, your best friend will be a good dictionary. Use it often. This chapter discusses some guidelines for improving your spelling, but the English language is unconventional in many ways. The one vital technique for improving your spelling is to check any questionable word. Even the best spellers avoid making a guess. They keep a thesaurus and a dictionary handy; they also check spelling on a computer when they use one.

14aU S I N G   H Y P H E N S

The hyphen (-) is a useful stylistic tool. It joins words to make a single unit of two or more words, such as *hand-to-hand* or *forget-me-nots*. It also divides words to make right-hand margins uniform, although that practice no longer applies to handwritten or typed manuscripts.

When you are uncertain whether a term is one word, two words, or a hyphenated compound word, consult the dictionary. For instance, does a bank have a *driveup, drive-up*, or *drive up* window? In this case, the correct answer is *drive-up*.

Follow the guidelines below for the correct use of hyphens.

1. Hyphenating Compound Words and Numbers Correctly

You should hyphenate two or more words that function as one adjective in front of a noun (but not if the words follow the noun):

ultra-pasteurized whipping cream

a **well-known** television evangelist

But: He is an evangelist **well known** on television.

You should not hyphenate a compound adjective if one part is an adverb ending in *ly* or if a number or letter is part of the adjective:

a **poorly officiated** game

a **frequently asked** question

Grade A whipping cream

Use hyphens to show that each adjective in a series modifies a noun:

Faulkner's novels come in **two-, three-, and four-volume** sets.

The damaged trees are **four- and five-year-old red oaks**.

You should use hyphens to form compound nouns:

There is pressure placed on every **scholar-athlete**.

Working as **actor-director** divided his attention.

Hyphenate written fractions and compound numbers from twenty-one to ninety-nine:

The choir director is **thirty-seven** years old.

Thirty-nine dollars, which is **one-fifth** of my paycheck, went to pay the traffic ticket.

14a

You can also use the hyphen to create sound effects and unusual compound words:

> The tuba sounded **um-pa-pa-um-pa-pa** as it passed the reviewing stand.

Finally, you should use hyphens to join numbers:

> Read pages **79-82** and **149-64**.

> The years **1776-1812** were crucial to the formation of America's democracy.

2. Using Hyphens with Prefixes and Suffixes

Most words with prefixes and suffixes require no hyphen. For example, do not hyphenate most words formed with these prefixes:

co-	coed, cooperate
pre-	prefabricate, preholiday
post-	postgame, postwar
non-	nontoxic, nonsense
multi-	multiply, multifold
re-	rejoin, recount
un-	unruly, unmerciful

However, you should use a hyphen with a prefix or suffix when the second element of the word is capitalized or a figure:

14a

Latisha enjoys **after-Christmas** sales.

The **pre-1992** statistics offer misleading information.

You should also use a hyphen when one part of the word is a single capital letter:

The **I-shaped** beam was the main support for the roof.

Hyphens are also sometimes needed to distinguish a word from a homonym:

If you **re-cover** the chair, you will **re-create** the art of a master artist.

Words that begin with *ex-, self-,* or *all-* should be hyphenated:

Although he is only a freshman, Randy is an **all-star.**

Similarly, words that end with the suffix *-elect* should be hyphenated:

The **senator-elect** has plenty of money to pay for his political advertising on television.

It is also wise to hyphenate a word if leaving it unhyphenated would result in confusion:

The reading test included **five word-exercises**. (as distinct from **five-word exercises**)

3. Following Conventions for End-of-Line Hyphenation

Style guides for research papers now discourage any use of hyphens at the end of lines, even to the point of leaving one line extremely short. Therefore, **do not hyphenate any word at the end of a line in your compositions**.

That rule should solve many problems for you. Before, you were required to write a paragraph with hyphenation like this:

> Glucose provides plants with energy by using a process known as respiration. During respiration, the plant uses some of the oxygen produced by photosynthesis.

With today's convention, you need not worry about using the hyphen with *process* or with *photosynthesis*. Instead, break the end of each line with a full word, even if a line seems unusually short:

> Glucose provides plants with energy by using a process known as respiration. During respiration, the plant uses some of the oxygen produced by photosynthesis.

Note: if you write with a word processor, you should turn off the automatic hyphenation commands.

In rare instances, you may need right-hand justification (that is, a right margin with a uniform edge) for a locally produced newspaper, booklet, or pamphlet. If so, follow the general guidelines for hyphenation given below, but

14a

always use a dictionary to check hyphenation of compound words.

1. Hyphenate between syllables only:

   Ameri-can

   juve-nile

   Note: In general, hyphenate after a vowel, not before, as in Ameri-can, above.

2. Do not hyphenate one-syllable words:

   sweep, not swe-ep

   flash, not fla-sh

3. Break compound words between full words only:

   under-study

   book-keeper

4. Leave three or more letters at the end or beginning of a line:

   thank-fully, not thankful-ly

   embar-rass, not em-barrass

14b UNDERSTANDING SPELLING

Spelling is seldom a stylistic choice, so most writers dutifully learn to spell new words and use the dictionary regularly. Others, less diligent, panic in the face of the spelling demons. A strict regimen may be necessary.

1. Becoming a Better Speller

First, keep a dictionary handy and use it often. Use an authoritative reference, such as the *American Heritage Dictionary* or *Webster's New Collegiate Dictionary*. Use the first spelling listed: *bettor* not *better* for one who bets; *theater* not *theatre*; *laid* not *layed*.

Get into the habit of checking the spelling of plurals, especially words derived from foreign languages; for example, *thesauri* is giving way to *thesauruses*.

Call upon memorized words that you might have learned during spelling units at grammar school:

don't choose booze

sporty at forty

there's A RAT in sepARATe

there are LICE in LICEnse

I have a NIce NIece

If you write with a word processor, use it to check spelling. However, using a computer to check spelling has limitations. It cannot correct improper usage of correctly spelled words (*except* for *accept* or *altar* for *alter*), and it does

14b

not contain a complete inventory of words. However, the computer can help you track troublesome words with its SEARCH command. For example, if you have a history of misspelling *alot* for *a lot* or *seperate* for *separate*, SEARCH for the words and correct the text accordingly.

A good way to improve your spelling is to keep a personal spelling list. Change it constantly to cross out words you have learned to spell and to add difficult new ones. Table 14.2 demonstrates one student's list of troublesome words.

Pronouncing words correctly can contribute to correct spelling. Do not add syllables (*umb-e-rella* or *ath-e-lete*) or delete syllables (*libary, probly, sophmore*) when you are speaking. However, pronunciation offers little help with some words (*site, cite,* and *sight* are all pronounced the same). Consult the list of common homonyms in Table 14.1 for a clear understanding of homophones.

Proofread your papers for spelling errors. If you consider yourself a poor speller, reserve time at the end of every writing assignment to proofread the paper for spelling errors. Proofread one time, word by word, to check your spelling, nothing else. If you suspect a mis-

14b

spelling of any word, look it up, correct it, and then add it to your list of troublesome words.

2. Using Ei and Ie Correctly

The old rhyme about *i* before *e* and its exceptions still works well:

I before *e*
Except after *c*,
Or when sounded like *a*
As in *neighbor* and *weigh*

Here are some words with *ie*:

chief	niece
grief	relieve
pierce	yield
field	wield

Here are some words with *ei* after *c*:

ceiling	conceit
deceive	perceive

And here are some words with *ei* not after *c*:

sleigh	freight
height	neighbor
stein	weigh

Unfortunately, you need to memorize some important exceptions to the rule:

seize	weird
either	sheik
protein	science

financier   height

foreign   leisure

3. Adding Prefixes and Suffixes to a Root Word

Again, we encourage you to consult a dictionary for correct spelling of words with additions to the front (prefix) or to the back (suffix). Consider the following basic guidelines.

1. Prefixes attach to the root without doubling or dropping letters:

   dissatisfied   disappear

   unusual   unnoticed

   misquoted   misspent

   replay   reapply

2. Drop the final unpronounced *e* before suffixes beginning with vowels, but retain the *e* before suffixes beginning with consonants:

Root	Suffix begins with a vowel	Suffix begins with a consonant
care	caring	careful
desire	desiring	desireless
manage	managing	management

   There are exceptions, such as *mileage, argument, courageous, truly,* and *ninth.*

14b

3. Double the final consonant before a suffix beginning with a vowel if the final consonant is preceded by a single vowel and if it ends a one-syllable word or a stressed syllable:

One-syllable words		Stressed syllables	
keen	keenness	propel	propelling
bet	betting	forget	forgetting
drag	dragged	begin	beginning

4. Do not double the final consonant of most words (consult your dictionary as necessary):

cup	cupful
appear	appearance
sleep	sleepless
commit	commitment (**but** committed)
wet	wetly (**but** wetting and wettable)

5. Change *y* to *i* before adding a suffix when the *y* is preceded by a consonant:

dry	dried
salary	salaries
apply	applies
enemy	enemies

6. Do not change *y* to *i* when *y* is preceded by a vowel:

pray	prayed	prayer	praying
monkey	monkeys		

7. Do not change *y* to *i* when adding *ing*:

try   trying

copy   copying

8. Do not change *y* to *i* with any proper name ending in *y*:

the Oakley family   the Oakleys

9. When adding *ly*, do not drop a final *l* from a root word:

careful   carefully

hopeful   hopefully

unusual   unusually

4. Spelling Plurals Correctly

Spelling plurals is fairly straightforward if you pay attention to the following guidelines:

1. Add *s* to form the plural of most singular nouns:

three small girls

a pack of dogs

two brothers-in-law

the Millers

three 8s

the 1990s

2. For words ending in *o*, add *s* when a vowel precedes the *o*, but add *es* when a consonant precedes the *o*:

rodeos   videos

14b

radios   Oreos

tomatoes   echoes

potatoes   mosquitoes

Exceptions: shortened words (*memos, autos, pros*); plural words that use either spelling (*zeros* and *zeroes, mottos* and *mottoes,* and *nos* and *noes*); and words of Italian origin (*pianos, sopranos, solos*).

3. Add *es* to form the plural of nouns ending in *s, ch, sh,* or *x*:

cardboard **boxes**

the **Crosses** moved to Indiana

the boat has **hatches**

Sid **smashes** his opponents

4. For singular nouns ending in *y* preceded by a consonant, change the *y* to *i* and add *es*:

blueberry   blueberries

ninety   nineties

lady   ladies

5. For some singular nouns ending in *f* or *fe,* change the ending to *ves*:

knife   knives

leaf   leaves

calf   calves

6. Some nouns form plurals irregularly. Do not use *s* or *es* with these nouns:

man   men

goose   geese

mouse   mice

ox   oxen

child   children

7. Some words of foreign origin have unusual plural spellings. Do not add *s* or *es* to these words:

crisis   crises

datum   data

medium   media

criterion   criteria

5. Distinguishing Between Words That Sound Alike

Pronunciation will not always serve your spelling needs, especially with pairs of words that sound alike: *principle, principal; capital, capitol; hole, whole; passed, past*. Several troublesome areas are identified below.

1. Possessive pronouns do not have an apostrophe and *s*, but contractions do:

It's time to give the cheerleading team **its** due credit.

You're required to buy **your** own sports shoes.

There's a mistake in these exams: **theirs** are mixed with ours.

14b

You're never going to finish **your** homework.

2. There are several two-word phrases that sound similar to single words:

   You need to **allot** your time to **a lot** of activities.

   Nobody noticed that her hair had **no body.**

   What you say **may be** true, but **maybe** I refuse to accept it.

3. There are also singular nouns that end in *nce* that sound like certain plural nouns that end in *nts*:

   With too many **patients** to care for, the nurse lost **patience**.

   We felt fortunate that we could lend **assistance** to our **assistants**.

4. English is full of **homophones**, which are words that sound alike but have different meanings, different uses, and, especially, different spellings. See Table 14.1 for the most common.

TABLE 14.1 Common Homophones

---

all ready (adverb and adjective: completely prepared)
already (adverb: previously)

all together (noun and adverb: in one group and in agreement)
altogether (adverb: entirely)

bare (adjective: naked)
bear (noun: animal; verb: carry)

born (adjective: brought forth as in a birth)
borne (verb: carry or endure)

brake (noun: device for stopping movement)
break (verb: shatter and separate into parts)

capital (adjective: first in importance; noun: accumulated goods)
capitol (noun: building in which government meets)

cite (verb: to quote)
sight (noun: a spectacle; verb: to see)
site (noun: a place or piece of ground)

desert (noun: dry land; verb: to withdraw)
dessert (noun: a delicacy at the end of a meal)

fair (noun: exhibition; adverb: just)
fare (noun: money for travel; verb: succeed)

forth (adverb: forward)
fourth (noun: a number)

hear (verb: to perceive by the ear)
here (noun: this place; adverb: at this place)

hole (noun: an opening into or through a thing)
whole (adjective: sound condition; noun: complete amount)

its (possessive pronoun: of or relating to it)
it's (contraction: it is)

knew (verb: past tense of know)
new (adjective: for the first time)

14b

passed (verb: moved, proceeded, departed)
past (noun: a former time; adjective: elapsed; preposition: after)

principal (adjective: chief or leading; noun: head of a school)
principle (noun: rule, fundamental concept, basic truth)

sense (noun: awareness, consciousness; verb: to perceive)
since (conjunction: from past to present)

stationary (adjective: immobile and unchanging)
stationery (noun: material for writing or typing)

their (possessive pronoun: relating to them as possessors)
there (adverb: in or at that place)
they're (contraction: they are)

to (preposition: in the direction of)
too (adverb: also, besides, excessively)
two (adjective and noun: something that has two units)

threw (verb: to toss something)
through (preposition: into one side and out the other)

who's (contraction: who is)
whose (possessive adjective and pronoun: possessor or agent)

your (possessive pronoun: possessor or agent)
you're (contraction: you are)

6. Focusing on Troublesome Words

Table 14.2 shows one student's list of troublesome words. In your journal, keep your list of the words that you have trouble spelling.

TABLE 14.2 Troublesome Words

accommodate	embarrass	recede
accumulate	exaggerate	rhythm
bureau	hypocrisy	supersede
calendar	irrelevant	vacuum
cemetery	knowledge	
disastrous	mischievous	

7. Misspelling for a Purpose

Sometimes, writers use a purposeful misspelling for effect:

Slooowly, the cat crept up on the chattering bird.

Onomatopoeia, a sound that is written as a word, can be used to create sound effects. This may require creative spelling:

The old Plymouth gave out a **rumble-grumble** and a **whizzing whistle** as it came to a stop.

The reproduction of slang words may require unusual spelling, especially in its application of new meanings such as *zod* for a person who is out of style or *rad* for "radical." However, keep firmly in mind two principles. First, know and use the fundamental conventions correctly before you experiment with unusual spelling. Second, use unusual spelling with restraint and for a good reason.

14b

A CONCISE GRAMMAR

15

UNDERSTANDING THE PARTS OF SPEECH

The eight parts of speech are nouns, pronouns, verbs, adjectives, adverbs, prepositions, conjunctions, and interjections. A good dictionary will show these classifications and provide examples. In addition, as a dictionary will show you, many words can serve as several parts of speech.

15a UNDERSTANDING NOUNS

A **noun** names a person, place, thing, quality, or idea. Nouns have *class, form,* and *function.* Each of the following words can be used as a noun:

Martha	beauty
Jupiter	justice
automobile	

Understanding Noun Classes

Using proper and common nouns

Nouns can be classified as proper nouns and common nouns. **Proper nouns** name a particular person, place, or thing to add precision and interest:

Marty Thompson flew the **Cessna 172** to **St. Louis**.

Common nouns, on the other hand, name one or all members of a general class:

The **pilot** flew his **plane** from **coast to coast**.

Using abstract and concrete nouns

Proper and common nouns can be either abstract or concrete. **Concrete nouns** name tangible items (*desk, symphony, Charles Dickens, lemons, smoke*), as in the following sentence:

> **Mark Twain** served as a **pilot** on a **paddle-wheeler**.

Abstract nouns name intangible qualities, such as ideas, theories, conditions, and feelings:

> The **injustice** of your decision will cause **anger** and **anarchy**.

Using collective nouns

Collective nouns, whether proper or common, name a group or unit (*family, Kiwanis Club, jury*), as in the following sentence:

> Both the **faculty** and the **student body** sat enraptured by the singing of the **Bay Street Congregational Choir**.

Understanding Noun Forms

There are three noun forms that you need to be aware of as you write: *number, gender*, and *case*.

Understanding number

Most nouns change form to show **number** (which indicates whether they are singular or plural). **Singular nouns** name one place, one person, one thing, or one idea:

Garth Brooks sang only one **song** at the **concert**.

Plural nouns name two or more places, persons, things, or ideas:

> The **cheerleaders** will conduct three car **washes** on successive **Saturdays** in April.

Compound nouns can be singular (*baseball, ex-president, scholar-athlete*) or plural (*undergraduates, mothers-in-law, blacksmiths*):

> The **president-elect** of the French Club is also the **actor-playwright** of the Senior Follies.

Understanding case

Nouns change form (or **case**) to reflect a relationship with certain other words. The three case forms are *nominative, possessive,* and *objective*. Nouns change form only in the possessive case.

A noun in the **nominative case** functions as a subject or predicate complement:

> Gym **classes** begin tomorrow.

A noun in the **possessive case** shows ownership or possession:

> The **superintendent's** decision changed the **school's** schedule for spring break.

A noun in the **objective case** functions as a *direct object* (DO), *indirect object* (IO), *retained object* (RO), or *object of the preposition* (OP). (See Chapter 16, "Understanding the Parts of a Sentence," for additional details.)

Understanding gender

Nouns have four classifications according to **gender**:

Masculine: father, brother, nephew, stallion

Feminine: mother, sister, niece, filly

Indefinite (male or female): principal, teacher

Neuter (no gender identity): limb, lamp, dollar

Understanding Noun Functions

Nouns function as subjects, objects, complements, appositives, and modifiers.

A **subject** either acts, is acted upon, or is discussed:

The **teacher** ignored my waving hand.

An **object** will receive, either directly or indirectly, the action of the verb or it will complete a preposition:

The teacher gave honor **grades** to three **students**.

A **complement** completes a verb. A noun used as a **predicate complement**, best known as a **predicate noun** (PN), completes a linking verb and renames the subject:

   S LV   PN

Justin is the new class **president**.

An **objective complement** (OC) completes a direct object:

         V   DO OC

This powder makes the soup **chili**.

An **appositive** (A) is a noun, or noun phrase, placed immediately after another noun to rename and explain the first:

                    A

The new science teacher, my **uncle**, showed no favoritism.

15b UNDERSTANDING PRONOUNS

A **pronoun** is a word used in place of a noun. Pronouns are usually one word (*I, he, you, we, they, who*), but some are compound words (*somebody, myself*), and a few are phrases (*each other*).

Each pronoun has an **antecedent**, which is the noun to which the pronoun makes reference. For example, after naming Alexander Hamilton once in the following sentence, the writer can refer to *he, him,* or *his*:

> Alexander Hamilton loved to stir the political waters. **He** willingly defended **his** political judgment, which often placed **him** in conflict with Thomas Jefferson.

Pronouns must agree with their antecedents in gender, number, and person—in this case *masculine gender, singular number,* and *third person*. In addition, a pronoun can refer to an unknown or unspecified antecedent:

> **Someone** lost a wallet.

Pronouns have three primary uses:

1. To avoid repetition:

> WORDY: Roger gave Roger's textbook to Roger's sister.
> BETTER: Roger gave his textbook to his sister.

2. To intensify words:

> The queen **herself** presented the trophy.

3. To relate one item to another:

The gun **that** fired the fatal shot has disappeared.

Understanding Pronoun Form

The form of a pronoun is governed by four factors:

Number: singular or plural
Gender: masculine, feminine, or neuter
Person: first, second, third
Case: nominative, possessive, objective

Understanding number

The **number** of the pronoun signals that it is singular (*I, you, he, she, it*) or plural (*we, you, they*). *You* can be either singular or plural:

I want to give all of **you** [plural] special recognition.

Understanding gender

The **gender** of the pronoun signals its masculine, feminine, or neuter characteristics:

Masculine: *he, his, him*
Feminine: *she, her, hers, her*
Neuter: *it, its*

Understanding person

The point of view for the pronoun indicates three different categories of **person**. The **first person** pronoun names the speaker:

We want a recount of the ballots.

The **second person** pronoun names the person spoken to:

Mr. Peterson, we want **you** to recount the ballots.

The **third person** pronoun names the person or thing spoken about:

They called for a recount of the ballots.

TABLE 15.1   Person

	Singular	Plural
First person	I, me	we, us
Possessive	my, mine	our, ours
Second person	you	you
Possessive	yours	yours
Third person	he, she, it, him, her	they, them
Possessive	his, hers, its	theirs

Understanding case

The **case** of a pronoun shows its grammatical relationship with other words in the sentence. A pronoun in **nominative case** may serve as the subject of the sentence or as a *predicate noun*. Nominative forms are: *I, you, he, she, it, we,* and *they*:

> **You** will receive your SAT score by mail.

A pronoun in the **possessive case** demonstrates ownership or possession. Unlike nouns, a pronoun does *not* use an apostrophe to show possession; it changes to one of these forms: *my, mine, your, yours, his, her, hers, its, our, ours, their,* or *theirs*:

> **Our** pompons are gold and black; **theirs** are gold and navy.

A pronoun **determiner** limits or specifies the noun that follows it:

> **My** birthday is this Saturday.

A pronoun in the **objective case** may act as a *direct object*, an *indirect object*, or an *object of a preposition*. The objective pronouns are *me, you, him, her, it, us,* and *them*:

> Pizza Hut donated napkins to **us**. [object of preposition]
>
> Ronald brought **me** some flowers. [indirect object]
>
> I wore **them** to the dance. [direct object]

TABLE 15.2 Case

Singular pronouns

	Nominative Case	Possessive Case	Objective Case
First person	I	my, mine	me
Second person	you	your, yours	you
Third person	he	his	him
	she	her, hers	her
	it	its	it

Plural pronouns

	Nominative Case	Possessive Case	Objective Case
First person	we	our, ours	us
Second person	you	your, yours	you
Third person	they	their, theirs	them

Understanding Pronoun Classes

In addition to the personal pronouns, explained above, pronouns have five additional classes: *relative, interrogative, reflexive/intensive, demonstrative,* and *indefinite.*

Relative pronouns

Relative pronouns introduce subordinate clauses. They are *who, whose, whom, which, what,* and *that.* In the following sentence, *who will star in the film* describes *actress:*

The actress **who** will star in the film has won three Oscars.

Certain rules prevail with relative pronouns:

1. Refer to persons with *who, whoever, whom, whomever,* and *whose*:

   The violinist **who** played last night feels ill.

2. Refer to animals and things with *which, whichever,* and *what*:

   Do you know **which** files were erased from the computer?

3. Refer to animals and things with *that*:

   The course **that** frustrates me is calculus.

4. The adverbials *where, when,* and *why* sometimes function as relative pronouns:

   The curve **where** I had the wreck has been repaired.

Interrogative pronouns

Interrogative pronouns introduce a question; they are *who, whose, whom, what,* and *which*:

Who spoke at the lecture last evening?

Reflexive and intensive pronouns

Reflexive and **intensive pronouns** are the *self* pronouns: *myself, yourself, yourselves,*

himself, herself, itself, ourselves, and *themselves.*
Reflexive pronouns name the receiver of an action when that receiver is also the one doing the acting. **Intensive pronouns** emphasize and distinguish a noun:

> He submitted **himself** to authorities. (reflexive)

> He delivered the baby **himself**. (intensive)

Note: Never use *hisself* or *theirselves*; these are not standard English.

Demonstrative pronouns

Demonstrative pronouns show which nouns perform or receive the action. *This* and *these* refer to something close by; *that* and *those* refer to something farther away. When used as adjectives, these words will modify a noun:

> **This** switch has several functions.

When used as demonstrative pronouns, the words substitute for a noun:

> Keep these books but send **those** back to the library.

Indefinite pronouns

Indefinite pronouns stand for a vague or unspecified number of people or things.

> **Many** are called, but **few** are chosen.

TABLE 15.3   The Classes of Pronouns

Relative: who, whose, whom, which, what, that
Interrogative: who, whose, whom, which, what
Reflexive/Intensive: myself, himself, herself, yourself, themselves, ourselves
Demonstrative: this, that, these, those
Indefinite:

all	both	many	one
another	each	neither	several
any	either	nobody	some
anybody	everybody	no one	somebody
anyone	everyone	none	someone
anything	few	nothing	something

* See Tables 15.1 and 15.2 for a list of personal pronouns.

Understanding Pronoun Functions

Pronouns function like nouns, that is, as subjects, objects, complements, appositives, and modifiers:

She ignored my waving hand. [subject]

The teacher gave **them** high grades. [object]

The damaged computers are **those** stacked in the corner. [predicate nominative]

My photography and **your** editorials give the newspaper an extra spark. [adjectives]

15c UNDERSTANDING VERBS

Verbs have two functions—they show action or a state of being. They change **form** to show number, person, tense, voice, and mood; and they have five **classes**.

Understanding Verb Functions

Verbs shows action:

The hot air balloon **collapsed**.

Verbs can also show a state of being:

The Gulf Stream **is** nature's gift to Florida.

Understanding Verb Forms

Main verbs take several different forms:

Infinitive: She wants *to dance, to think, to rejoice*

Present tense -s form: She *dances, thinks, rejoices*

Present participle: She is *dancing, thinking, rejoicing*

Past tense form: She *danced, thought, rejoiced*

Past participle: She *has danced, has thought, has rejoiced*

Regular verbs (such as *dance* and *rejoice*) form the past tense and the past participle with *-ed, -d*, and sometimes *-t* (as in *dwelt*).

Irregular verbs form the past tense and the past participle in several ways, especially by changing an internal vowel.

	Infinitive	Past	Past Participle
Irregular	run	ran	run
Verb	think	thought	thought
	see	saw	seen
	write	wrote	written

A dictionary will help you identify the correct verb to use:

dragged
/
Someone **drug** a hose through the flower garden.

Verbs change **forms** to indicate:

person: first, second, third

number: singular or plural

tense: present, past, future, present perfect, past perfect, future perfect

voice: active or passive

mood: indicative, imperative, and subjunctive

Understanding person

Person affects the form of the verb usually in *third person singular* of the *present tense* only:

You drive a Corvette, I drive a Corvette, and he **drives** a Corvette.

TABLE 15.4	**Person**	
	Singular	**Plural**
First person	I speak	we speak
Second person	you speak	you speak
Third person	he/she/it speaks	they speak

Understanding number

A verb shows **number** (*singular* or *plural*) in order to agree with its subject; both must be singular or both must be plural. Examine Table 15.4 and you will find that a verb in third person singular requires an *s*:

The bell **rings** too early during exams and **rings** terribly late during lectures. [singular]

Understanding tense

Verb **tense** indicates the time of the action or condition. Editing for tense and tense sequence first requires a knowledge of simple present (he *laughs*) and simple past (he *laughed*).

Simple tenses show one action in a finite time frame. **Present tense** shows what happens or can happen now:

Jon **works** at the Taco Bell after school.

Past tense shows what did happen at one time in the past:

> I **worked** until ten o'clock.

Future tense shows what will happen at a particular time in the future:

> I **will work** on my report until it is finished.

A verb in **perfect tense** will refer not only to the time when the action started, but also to the time the action ends. The **present perfect tense** uses the auxiliary verb *have* with the past participle (see Table 15.5) and shows a past action that continues to the present:

> I **have worked** on my report for a week.

The **past perfect tense** uses *had* with the past participle and shows a past action that was completed before another past action:

> I **had worked** many months before I realized that the job stifled my creativity.

The **future perfect tense** is used to express action that will be completed in the future before some other future action or event; it is formed with *will have* or *shall have* and the past participle:

> I **will have worked** on this report for a month when I finally submit it.

Progressive tenses enable you to show a continuous action. The **present progressive** shows a continuous action that is occurring now:

I **am working** frantically to finish my report.

The **past progressive** shows a continuous action that occurred at the time of another past action:

I **was working** late at the library when the lights were suddenly turned off.

The **future progressive** shows a continuous action that will occur during another future action:

I **will be working** while you are on vacation.

The **historical present tense** enables you to write about universal truths and scientific principles:

On his historical journey in 1969, Neil Armstrong saw in person that the moon **has** an earthrise.

Though nobody is on the moon to see it now, the earthrise continues to occur. The historical present tense is also known as the **literary present tense** when it is used to refer to a work by a writer or artist, even one who is dead:

In his novel <u>Catch-22</u>, Joseph Heller **satirizes** the insanity of bureaucratic regulations.

TABLE 15.5 Tense and Voice

Active voice

Tense	Singular	Plural
Present	I paint	we paint
	you paint	you paint
	he/she/it paints	they paint
Past	I painted	we painted
	you painted	you painted
	she painted	they painted
Future	I will paint	we will paint
	you will paint	you will paint
	she will paint	they will paint
Present perfect	I have painted	we have painted
	you have painted	you have painted
	she has painted	they have painted
Past perfect	I had painted	we had painted
	you had painted	you had painted
	she had painted	they had painted
Future perfect	I will have painted	we will have painted
	you will have painted	you will have painted
	she will have painted	they will have painted

Passive voice

Tense	Singular	Plural
Present	I am painted	we are painted
	you are painted	you are painted
	she is painted	they are painted
Past	I was painted	we were painted
	you were painted	you were painted
	she was painted	they were painted
Future	I will be painted	we will be painted
	you will be painted	you will be painted
	she will be painted	they will be painted
Present perfect	I have been painted	we have been painted
	you have been painted	you have been painted
	she has been painted	they have been painted

15c

| Tense | Passive voice | |
	Singular	Plural
Past perfect	I had been painted	we had been painted
	you had been painted	you had been painted
	she had been painted	they had been painted
Future perfect	I will have been painted	we will have been painted
	you will have been painted	you will have been painted
	she will have been painted	they will have painted

Understanding voice

Verbs that can take a direct object have two **voices**: active and passive. In the **active voice**, the subject *performs* the action:

The columnist **questioned** the suspect aggressively.

In the **passive voice**, the subject *receives* the action:

The suspect **was questioned** by the columnist.

The active voice is more concise, vigorous, and emphatic than the passive voice, which can bury the actor in a phrase or omit the actor altogether:

The club's photograph **was deleted** from the yearbook.

Who deleted the photograph? The passive voice hides the actor.

The passive voice can be used appropriately to emphasize the receiver, especially when the actor is irrelevant:

Our new telephone system **will be installed** tomorrow.

Understanding mood

A verb changes form to show **mood**, which displays the speaker's attitude about the statement and indicates that the statement is factual, a request, or a wish. Verbs have three moods. The **indicative mood** makes a statement or asks a question:

Class **begins** at 8:30 A.M.

The **imperative mood** makes a command or a request:

Please **be** on time.

The **subjunctive mood** makes a wish, an indirect request, or a statement contrary to fact:

I wish I **were** still in bed.

The subjunctive mood uses only *were* (the plural past tense form of *be*) or the infinitive form of the verb:

The teacher's handbook stipulates that each teacher **attend** every meeting of the school P.T.A.

Understanding Verb Types

Verbs have two main types, **transitive** and **intransitive**, and two minor, but important, categories: **linking** and **auxiliary** verbs.

Transitive verbs

A **transitive verb** requires a direct object—a noun that completes the meaning of the verb by answering, in most cases, the question *What?*

> Straining to reach the ball, Jennifer **spiked** the winning point.

Jennifer spiked what? *The point.* The transitive verb *spiked*, in active voice, tells how the subject, *Jennifer*, completes an action that affects the direct object, *the point*.

However, a transitive verb in passive voice causes the subject, rather than the direct object, to receive the action of the transitive verb:

> The winning point **was spiked** by Jennifer, who strained to reach the ball.

Therefore, a transitive verb in active voice is the preferred form because it shows the actor *(subject)* and the receiver (*a direct object*):

> The angry **student tore** his **essay** to pieces.

An **indirect object** tells *to whom* or *for whom* something is done, especially with the verbs *ask, bring, find, give, pay, promise, send, teach,* and *throw*:

> Jennifer gave **me** the trophy.

If the sentence said, "Jennifer gave the trophy *to me*," the word *me* would be the object of the preposition *to*, not an indirect object.

Intransitive verbs

An **intransitive verb** indicates a completed action. There is no receiver, that is, no direct object, no indirect object, and no retained object:

> The teacher **laughed** at my joke, but the principal only **smiled**.

Although some verbs are transitive only, such as *ignore* and *complete*, or intransitive only, such as *arrive* and *sleep*, most verbs can be either:

> TRANSITIVE VERB: Jennifer **played** forward on the basketball team.

> INTRANSITIVE VERB: Jennifer **played** best when the game was on the line.

TABLE 15.7 *Transitive and Intransitive Verbs*

Intransitive: sit, lie, rise
Transitive: set, lay, raise
The verb forms *sit, lie*, and *rise* are intransitive and do not receive objects:

                          sat
                           /
How long have you ~~set~~ in the chair?

                                     lay
                                      /
After working the sheep, the dogs ~~laid~~ down to rest.

                          rises
                           /
When the dough ~~raises~~, put it in the oven.

The verb forms *set, lay*, and *raise* are transitive and do take objects:

        set
         /
We ~~sat~~ two chairs there this morning.
But:
The sun should **set** in about an hour. [no object]

Linking verbs

A **linking verb** is one type of intransitive
verb. Accordingly, it does not take a direct
object, but it does connect a subject to a word or
phrase that renames or describes it:

> The library **was** noisy yesterday. [*noisy* is the predi-
> cate adjective]

> Members of the basketball team **became** diplomats
> to promote the city as well as the school. [*diplomats*
> is a predicate noun]

The most common linking verbs derive from *be*
(*am, are, is, was, were, being, been*), but you
ought to replace them, if possible, with other

linking verbs that have more precision (*seem, become, appear, stand, taste, feel, smell, sound, look, turn, grow*):

appears
/

The substitute teacher ~~is~~ harried and increasingly nervous.

Auxiliary verbs

Auxiliary verbs often join the main verb to form verb phrases. The modals (*can, will, shall, should, could, would, may, might, must*) can act only as auxiliaries, not as main verbs:

Mason **should** pay for the damage.

A different set of auxiliary verbs may serve also as main verbs (*be, am, is, are, were, being, been, do, does, did, have, has, had*):

The clock **has been** reset twice this week. [auxiliary]

She **has** my money. [main verb]

An auxiliary verb is often a signal that you need the past participle form of the verb:

done
/

The players had all ~~did~~ their push-ups and wind sprints.

15d UNDERSTANDING ADJECTIVES

Adjectives modify nouns and pronouns. You can use adjectives in your writing to add colorful and interesting detail to describe, to limit, or to specify: *plaid* shirt, *heavy* traffic, the *first* person, my *only* child, *that* apple, his *favorite* uncle. Adjectives can be words, phrases, or clauses:

The students, **dazed and bewildered by a day of examinations**, walked slowly to the dining hall. [participial phrase used as an adjective]

The teacher **who issued the memorandum** remains anonymous. [clause used as an adjective]

The **indefinite articles** *a* and *an* and the **definite article** *the* are classified as adjectives. Standard English uses *an* before all vowel sounds, even those words that begin with a silent consonant (*an hour*):

$$\overset{\text{an}}{\diagup}$$

The golfer suddenly encountered ~~a~~ alligator in the fairway.

A **predicate adjective** completes a linking verb and describes the subject of the clause:

The water felt **cold**.

In general, use the adjectives *good* and *bad* after linking verbs to modify the subject:

She felt **bad** about the trouble she had caused.

An adjective may serve as an **object complement**. Below, the adjective *foolish* describes the program, which is the direct object:

The dean thought the program **foolish**.

Three adjective groups have the same form as pronouns; however, they modify a following noun rather than replace a noun.
Demonstrative adjectives (*this, that, these, those*) indicate which object is being talked about:

This plan needs more refinement.

Possessive adjectives (*her, his, your, its, our, their*) indicate who owns the object being talked about:

Your plan needs more work.

Indefinite adjectives (*any, each, every, some*) indicate an unknown number of objects:

Every plan submitted today has several flaws.

15e UNDERSTANDING ADVERBS

Adverbs modify verbs (and verbals), adjectives, and other adverbs. You can use adverbs to show or clarify time, place, manner, and degree; they can also be used to affirm or deny:

When? again, always, early, never, forever, often

Where? above, below, up, down, here, there

Why? why, therefore, wherefore, then

How? badly, easily, foolishly, how, not, no, surely

To what degree? almost, much, more, most

To affirm or deny: yes, no, maybe, perhaps

Adverbs that modify adjectives or other adverbs must precede the word modified because they intensify or limit that one word:

She gave an **extremely** short performance.

Adverbs that modify a verb can appear in any position in the sentence:

Secretly he laughed.

He **secretly** laughed.

He laughed **secretly**.

An adverb can be a word, phrase, or clause:

He **always** finishes his work **when he has a vacation planned**.

Adverbs sometimes modify an entire clause:

Unbelievably, she jumped from the edge of the cliff.

Adverbs modify some prepositional phrases:

Your work is **seldom** on time.

No and *not* are adverbs, even when they appear with a helping verb:

You can**not** understand my position.

Mom would**n't** let me drive to the game.

Try to understand the differences between adjectives and adverbs in order to distinguish between such words as *sure* and *surely, real* and *really, easy* and *easily*, and *certain* and *certainly*:

Surely and **easily** the burros walk down the trails in Grand Canyon. [adverbs modifying *walk*]

The footsteps of the burros in Grand Canyon are **sure** and **easy**. [adjectives modifying *footsteps*]

Some words that can function as both adjectives and adverbs are *hard, little, slow, straight, early*, and *fast*:

The teacher can't draw **straight** lines on the chalkboard. [adjective]

I walked **straight** into the door because I wasn't looking. [adverb]

Some adverbs have two forms, such as *slow* and *slowly*, *hard* and *hardly*:

adverb
/

It rained **hard**.

adverb
/

I **hardly** recognized you.

Note: *slow* and *hard* are also adjectives:

Take the **slow** train.

Ms. Lesley gives **hard** exams.

Use the adverbs *well* and *badly* after action verbs:

He played **well** in the game yesterday.

Make sure you use adverbs, not adjectives, to modify verbs, adjectives, and other adverbs:

The bolt slid into place **easily**. [adverb modifying verb]

Members of the class were **awfully** worried that the fire had destroyed the grade book. [adverb modifying adjective]

Adjectives and adverbs have three forms: positive, comparative, and superlative. Use the

positive form to modify one item (a *soft* pillow), the **comparative** form to compare two items (yours is *softer* than mine), and the **superlative** form to distinguish one item from two or more other items (Tammy's is the *softest* of all).

The following list gives examples of the three forms:

Positive	Comparative	Superlative
sweet	sweeter	sweetest
fast	faster	fastest
good	better	best
bad	worse	worst

Do not use **double comparatives** or **double superlatives**, which usually combine *-er* or *-est* with *more* or *most*. Avoid using *more deeper, most deadliest, more funnier.*

Note: **Absolute modifiers** cannot have comparatives or superlatives. Words such as *unique, perfect, dead, square, circular,* and *singular* describe absolute concepts: something is either unique (which means *the only one*) or it is not. Try to avoid phrases like *most unique.*

Double Negatives

A double negative is a nonstandard sentence pattern in which two negative words are used when one is adequate:

NONSTANDARD: I **can't hardly** hear what you are saying.

STANDARD: I **can hardly** hear what you are saying.

In certain uses *but* and *only* are negatives. Avoid using them with *not*:

NONSTANDARD: I can't help **but** admire her bravery.

STANDARD: I cannot help **admiring** her bravery.

No, nothing, and *none* should not be used with another negative word:

NONSTANDARD: We don't have **none**.

STANDARD: We have **none**.

A double negative is acceptable when a positive meaning is intended:

The runners were **not unhappy** with their performance.

15f UNDERSTANDING PREPOSITIONS

Prepositions are words used with a noun or pronoun (and their modifiers, if any) to form a phrase that shows place, position, time, or means: *at college, in the city, on Monday, by the first available taxi*:

```
       prep.    adj.  obj. of prep.
        /        /      /
```
The defendants stood **before** a stern judge.

A prepositional phrase used as an adverb elaborates upon the verb of the sentence and tells *when, where, why, how,* or *under what circumstances.* A prepositional phrase used as an adjective elaborates upon the nouns of the sentence and tells *which one* and *what kind of:*

```
         adjective         adverb
            /                 /
```
Three members **of the team** left early **for the airport.**

It is generally permissible to end a sentence with a preposition, although some instructors may object. In the following sentence, *what* is the object of the preposition *about:*

What was he arguing **about**?

Prepositions can be single words, compound words, or phrases:

above	beyond	of
across	by	on
after	down	out
among	for	over
at	from	to
below	in	under
beneath	in front of	with
between	into	without

15g UNDERSTANDING CONJUNCTIONS

Conjunctions connect words, phrases, and clauses to show order and to relate two or more ideas. The three classifications of conjunctions are *coordinating, correlative*, and *subordinating*.

Coordinating Conjunctions

Coordinating conjunctions—*and, but, for, nor, or, so,* and *yet*—join equal items:

Bob **and** Betty syndicated their talk show. [joins two words]

We will have the prom in the school's gym **or** at a hotel downtown. [joins two phrases]

We left the party early, **but** everyone else stayed late. [joins two independent clauses so it must be preceded by a comma]

Correlative Conjunctions

Correlative conjunctions also join items of equal grammatical rank, but they always function as a pair:

The best jobs promise **both** financial rewards **and** exciting challenges.

Joey Martinez is **not only** captain of the football team **but** he is **also** president of the Student Council.

Other correlative conjunctions are *either . . . or,*
neither . . . nor, not only . . . but [also], and
whether . . . or.

Subordinating Conjunctions

A **subordinating conjunction** connects a
subordinate clause to an independent clause to
show that the clauses are *not* equal. The subordinate clause cannot stand alone and depends
on the main clause to complete its meaning.

TABLE 15.7   Subordinating Conjunctions

after	even though	though
although	if	unless
as	in order that	until
as soon as	provided that	when
as though	since	whenever
because	so that	where
before	then	wherever
even if	that	while

Subordinating conjunctions show relationships of cause, time, location, degree, and
manner:

Unless the committee acts quickly, the president will
disband it.

A **conjunctive adverb** (such as *however,*
finally, furthermore) sometimes joins indepen-

dent clauses as does a **relative pronoun**, such as *who*:

> The apostles are any of the twelve original disciples of Christ; **however**, the Apostolic Fathers were contemporaries **who** were not part of the original twelve.

15h UNDERSTANDING INTERJECTIONS

Interjections show surprise or emotion. They are short outbursts—a sound, a word, a phrase, or even a sentence—that serve no special grammatical function. Therefore, set off interjections from the rest of the sentence by a comma, an exclamation mark, or a period. Most interjections are informal or colloquial; hence, they are appropriate only in speech and dialogue and in some informal essays:

> **Oh no**, we've lost the game.
>
> **Glory be!** We won!
>
> **Hurry!** We'll miss the bus!

16

CHAPTER

UNDERSTANDING THE PARTS OF A SENTENCE

A sentence is a complete thought that contains a subject and a predicate. The subject names the performer or the receiver of the action, and the predicate expresses the action of the sentence. A sentence begins with a capital letter and ends with a period, question mark, or exclamation point:

The experiment failed.

Sentences can assert, question, command, make a wish, or exclaim:

The scientist discovered a new species. [assertion]

Is the species rare? [question]

We hope to complete the experiment today. [wish]

Oh no, I dropped the slide! [exclamation]

Be careful. [command with an implied subject—*you*]

16a UNDERSTANDING SUBJECTS

The **subject** of a sentence acts, is acted upon, or is discussed. A **simple subject** is a noun or pronoun without its modifiers:

Classes start tomorrow. **I** can hardly wait.

The **complete subject** is the simple subject plus any modifiers:

Adult education classes at the museum start tomorrow.

In most cases, you can find the subject by asking *who* or *what* about the verb: *What* starts? *Classes* start.

A **compound subject** has two or more simple subjects joined by a coordinating conjunction, such as *and, or,* or *but,* or by a correlative conjunction, such as *either . . . or* or *neither . . . nor*:

> **Neither Ford, Chrysler, nor General Motors** has dominated the domestic automobile market.

Noun phrases and clauses also function as subjects:

> **To live each day fully** is my credo.

16b UNDERSTANDING PREDICATES

All sentences have a predicate, which tells what the subject is doing, indicates what is being done to the subject, or expresses something about the subject. A simple predicate consists of the verb alone:

> Mary Ann **cringed**.

A **complete predicate** consists of the simple predicate and all modifiers, objects, and complements that complete the meaning of the verb:

> The unscrupulous clerk **sold Ted an overpriced stereo**.

A **compound predicate** has two or more simple predicates joined by a coordinating conjunction, plus all the modifiers, objects, and complements:

> Ted **collects old records** and **plays them in a jazz club on Saturday nights**.

A predicate with a **linking verb** will include a word or word group that (1) describes the subject with a **predicate adjective** or (2) renames the subject with a **predicate noun**:

> predicate adjective
> /
> This set of blood samples may be **contaminated**.

> predicate noun
> /
> The Pied Piper of Hamelin is **a mythical character**.

A predicate with a **transitive verb** includes a direct object that names the receiver of the action:

> transitive verb
> /
> Francisco Pizarro **founded** the city of Lima.

The sentence above has the transitive verb *founded* in active voice, which means the subject (*Pizarro*) acts and the direct object (*Lima*) receives the action. Transitive verbs in passive voice reverse the order so that the subject receives the action:

The city of Lima **was founded by** Francisco Pizarro.

A sentence with an **intransitive verb** cannot take direct or indirect objects, nor can it take predicate nouns or predicate adjectives. The intransitive verb may be followed by an adverb or adverbial word group:

intransitive verb
/
My teacher **disagrees** completely with orthodox teaching.

16c UNDERSTANDING OBJECTS

There are basically four kinds of objects to be aware of as you write: direct objects, retained objects, indirect objects, and object complements.

Direct Objects

A **direct object** receives the action expressed by a transitive active verb:

Sarah bought **flowers**.

You can usually identify direct objects by asking *who, whom,* or *what* about the subject and verb: Sarah bought *what?* Sarah bought *flowers.*

Retained Objects

A **retained object** receives the action of a verb in the passive voice. Below, *first place* is the object of *was awarded,* a verb in the passive voice:

The speech was awarded **first place** by the judges.

In contrast, note how the transitive active verb takes the direct object:

The judges awarded **first place** to John's speech.

Indirect Objects

The **indirect object** receives the action of the verb indirectly; it tells *to whom* or *for whom* something is done:

I.O.   D.O.
/   /

Sarah bought her **mother flowers**.

Indirect objects occur often with the transitive verbs *ask, bring, find, give, pay, promise, send, teach,* and *throw*:

The Lipinskis gave the **library** their collection of rare books.

Object Complements

An **object complement** is either a noun that renames the direct object or an adjective that describes the direct object:

The new chemist calls a test tube a **vial.** [noun]

The players all consider the new offense **inferior** to the old wishbone attack. [adjective]

16d UNDERSTANDING SUBJECT COMPLEMENTS

Subject complements complete a linking verb by renaming or describing the subject. Thus, they form part of the predicate. There are two kinds of subject complements: predicate nouns and predicate adjectives. A **predicate noun** renames the subject:

Milt Campbell is the **coach** of the debate team.

Note: a predicate noun is also known as a **predicate nominative**.

A **predicate adjective** describes or modifies:

Mr. Patrick appears to be totally **humorless**.

You should edit your sentences to add any missing verbs needed to connect a subject with its complement:

is
/
Professor Adams ∧ an excellent teacher and artist.

16e UNDERSTANDING PHRASES

A **phrase** is a group of related words used as a single part of speech. A phrase cannot be a sentence because it lacks a subject, a predicate, or both:

in the morning

to cook a pot of chili on an open campfire

running across the concourse to catch a flight to Denver

Verb Phrases

Verb phrases consist of the main verb, any auxiliary verbs, and modifiers:

The crew **had been working all day to control the fire**.

Note: A **phrasal verb** is a verb joined by *across,*

down, for, in, off, out, to, up, or *with* to create a new meaning:

> She **turned out** the lights. [phrasal verb]

> She **turned to the left**. [verb phrase]

Noun Phrases

Noun phrases consist of a main noun and modifying words:

> **The canvas tent flapping in the breeze** awakened the campers.

Gerund phrases and appositive phrases always function as nouns:

> **My screaming into the darkness** attracted the rescue squad. [noun phrase used as a gerund that serves as the subject of the sentence]

> Weather conditions, **subfreezing temperatures and strong winds**, can numb both body and brain. [noun phrase used as an appositive to rename the subject]

Infinitive Phrases

An **infinitive phrase** may also serve as a noun:

> Several men tried **to build a fire**. [noun phrase used as an infinitive; the infinitive serves as a direct object]

Adjective Phrases

Adjective phrases tell *which one* or *what kind* about an attached noun:

The smile **on Jack's face** faded at the news. [prepositional phrase used as an adjective to modify *smile*]

Smiling for the photographer, the children anticipated the flash of strobe lights. [participial phrase used as an adjective to modify *the children*]

Adverb Phrases

Adverb phrases tell *why, where, when, how, under what conditions*, and *to what degree* to describe a verb, adjective, or another adverb. They need not appear next to the word they modify:

Work **with extreme caution** when you set the fuse. [prepositional phrase used as an adverb to modify the verb *work*]

The crew used dynamite **to demolish the building quickly**. [infinitive phrase used as an adverb to modify the verb used]

Prepositional Phrases

A **prepositional phrase** consists of a preposition and its object. When used as an **adjective**, the prepositional phrase modifies the noun or the pronoun next to it:

> Consumers admired the new cars **in the dealer's showroom.** [*in the dealer's showroom* modifies *cars*]

When used as an **adverb**, the prepositional phrase tells *how? why? where? when? under what conditions?* It need not appear next to the word modified:

> **On Tuesday,** all workers must report at 7:00 a.m.

On rare occasions prepositions serve as **nouns**, as in the following sentence:

> Old age for some people means **over the hill**.

Verbal Phrases

A **verbal phrase** is a group of words that contains a verb form and that functions as a noun, adjective, or adverb, not as a verb. The three types of verbal phrases are the gerunds, participles, and infinitives.

A **gerund phrase** is always a noun, and it serves primarily as a subject or an object in sentences. The gerund always ends in *-ing*:

> **Watching television** can numb your brain. [gerund phrase as subject]

Many people continue **drinking and driving** despite strict laws. [gerund phrase as direct object]

A **participial phrase** functions as an adjective, so it must be connected to the word it modifies:

Defeated by his Republican opponent, the mayor withdrew to his coastal retreat.

Most participles end in *-ing* or *-ed,* but some have irregular forms:

Some of the mourners, **overcome by grief**, fainted at the funeral service.

An **infinitive phrase** can serve as a noun, adjective, or adverb. It combines *to* with the base form of a verb (*to see, to have, to excite*) and usually takes an object (*to have money*) or an adverb (*to arrive safely*). The *to* is implied in certain phrases: "He helped me [to] wash the car."

Infinitive phrases can serve as any noun, especially as subject, predicate noun, or direct object:

To practice patience and forethought is the mark of a wise person. [infinitive phrase used as subject]

The scientists tried **to isolate another strain of bacteria**. [infinitive phrase used as direct object]

In some circumstances, a noun may be the subject of an infinitive:

The coach wanted his **players to learn patience.**
[the noun *players* serves as the subject of the infinitive]

When used as adverbs, infinitive phrases indicate *when, where, why,* and *how* and show *conditions* and *degree*:

> She bought a gun **to protect herself and her children**. [infinitive phrase used as adverb to explain *why*]

When used as adjectives, infinitive phrases usually appear immediately after the noun they modify:

> With a final chance **to win the debate trophy**, we stepped nervously to the stage.

Absolute Phrases

An **absolute phrase** consists of a noun followed by a participle, and it usually contains additional modifiers:

> **Heads bowed**, the men silently mourned.

As shown above and below, an absolute phrase should be set off by commas:

> The general paced the room, **voice pitched with passion, eyes darting from one person to another, hands gesturing wildly**.

Note: absolute phrases are always adverb phrases.

Appositive Phrases

Appositive phrases rename or give additional information about a noun:

Roger Bannister, **one of the most famous Olympic runner**s, was the first to run the mile in under four minutes.

They appear next to the noun that they modify, and they usually are set off by commas. One-word appositives that identify the subject do not need commas:

My brother **Mark** works at a boot store.

16f UNDERSTANDING CLAUSES

Clauses, like phrases, are grammatically related word groups. Unlike phrases, however, clauses have both a subject and a predicate. They can be independent clauses or subordinate clauses.

Independent and Subordinate Clauses

An **independent clause** is a complete sentence:

The hawk flew into the woods.

Although it contains a subject and a predicate, a **subordinate clause** cannot stand alone as a complete sentence because it contains a subordinating conjunction or a relative pronoun. Subordinate clauses can serve as adverbs, adjectives, or nouns:

> Robert is confident **when his parents attend the games.** [adverb clause]

> The man **who came to dinner** stayed forever. [adjective clause]

> **Whoever comes for dinner** will get leftovers. [noun clause]

Subordinate Noun Clauses

Subordinate noun clauses do not modify, but neither can they stand alone:

> **Why he forgot his appointment** is a mystery. [noun clause as the subject]

> The Chicago *Tribune* reported **that Dewey defeated Truman.** [noun clause as the direct object]

Adjective Clauses

Adjective clauses modify nouns and pronouns. Usually, they follow directly after the word they modify:

The athlete **who distinguishes himself on the field** can also win lucrative endorsement contracts.

Your men installed new lights **that are too bright.**

Honeysuckle, **which attracts hummingbirds**, is orange and trumpet-shaped.

Note: Remember to set off nonrestrictive subordinate clauses with commas, but do not set off restrictive modifiers. *That are too bright* tells *which* lights, so it is not set off by a comma. However, *which attracts hummingbirds* does not restrict the sentence to one type of honeysuckle, so it must be set off with commas.

Adjective clauses usually begin with relative pronouns (*who, whom, whose, which,* or *that*), although they can begin with words such as *when, where,* or *why*:

Days **when we have no chores to do** are as rare as winning lottery tickets.

Adverb Clauses

Adverb clauses tell *when, where, why, under what conditions,* or *to what degree.* Usually, they modify the verb and may appear anywhere in the sentence. They begin with subordinate conjunctions such as *when, if, unless,* or *where*:

I will starve **unless I get a job.**

16g UNDERSTANDING SENTENCE CONSTRUCTION

There are four types of sentences: simple, compound, complex, and compound-complex.

Simple Sentences

Sentences with one clause are called **simple sentences**. They may be short or long:

> We cried.

> Standing in the silent stadium long after the game ended, **the coach and his wife cried** about the end of a long, illustrious career. [phrases before and after the main clause]

Compound Sentences

Compound sentences have two or more independent clauses, but no dependent clause:

> Some journalists travel all over the world for their stories, but most spend their time on the telephone.

Complex Sentences

Complex sentences contain one independent clause and one or more dependent clause(s):

dependent adverb clause
/
Although television journalism looks glamorous,

independent clause
/
reporters work long hours behind the cameras.

Compound-Complex Sentences

Compound-complex sentences contain at least two independent clauses and at least one dependent clause:

Many television reporters majored in broadcast journalism and started their careers in radio or television, but others moved to television from newspapers, where the emphasis is on investigation and good writing.

16h UNDERSTANDING SENTENCE PATTERNS

Sentences contain a **subject** and a **predicate** and may include **objects, subject complements**, or **object complements**. These parts of the sentence can form five basic sentence patterns.

1. Subject-verb

   S V
   I went to Detroit on a midnight flight.

2. Subject-verb-object

   S V O
   I left Detroit at 6 p.m. the next day.

3. Subject-verb-subject complement

   S   V   SC
   The entire trip was a hectic, eye-opening experience.

4. Subject-verb-indirect object-object

   S V   IO   DO
   I gave the executives the advertising proposal.

5. Subject-verb-direct object-object complement

   S   V   DO   OC
   The executives considered the proposal premature.

Familiarity with these patterns will add richness
and variety to your compositions.

DOCUMENTING YOUR SOURCE MATERIALS MLA STYLE

APPENDIX

Some of your papers will be drawn from source materials, perhaps a book, an encyclopedia article, or a magazine article. Every time you *borrow* from a source, you must show the source both in your text and in a "Works Cited" page at the end of your composition. This fact is true whether you are writing a short paper or a formal research paper.

USING IN-TEXT CITATIONS

In the past, researchers used footnotes or endnotes to document sources, but current practice requires what is called an *in-text citation* of each source used in the paper. The MLA style, established by the Modern Language Association, requires you to list an author and a page number in your text, usually within parentheses, and then to provide a full bibliography entry on a "Works Cited" page at the end of your paper. Notice how this next passage uses names and page numbers to cite two direct quotations:

> The <u>cell theory</u> was developed in the late 19th century. According to John Hartley, "Scientists discovered single cells that divided into two identical offspring cells" (56). Another scientist explains the two parts of the cell theory: "All organisms are composed of cells and all cells derive from other living cells" (Justice 431).

This passage accomplishes several necessary tasks:

1. It credits the sources properly and honestly, naming the author and the page number.
2. It correctly uses quotations marks to enclose both instances of direct quotation.
3. It demonstrates the student's research into the subject.

Similarly, you should introduce a paraphrase with the author's name and close it with a page number, placed inside the parentheses. A **paraphrase** is a passage that you put into your own words, so it does not require quotation marks:

> Herbert Norfleet states that the use of video games by children improves their hand and eye coordination (45).

This paraphrase makes absolutely clear to the reader when the borrowed idea begins and when it ends. Note: if you do not provide the name of the source with a page number, you will be guilty of plagiarism. Plagiarism is theft of another's ideas presented as your own (see Figure A.1 below). Here is another example to show how to cite the author of borrowed materials:

> Herbert Norfleet defends the use of video games by children. He says it improves their hand and eye coordination and that it exercises their minds as they work their way through various puzzles and barriers. Norfleet states, "The mental gymnastics of video games and the competition with fellow players are important to young children and their physical, social, and mental development" (45).

You can, if you like, put the authority's name and the page number at the end of a quotation or paraphrase, but give your reader a signal to show when the borrowing begins:

> One source explains that the DNA in the chromosomes must be copied perfectly during cell reproduction: "Each DNA strand provides the pattern of bases for a new strand to form, resulting in two complete molecules" (Justice, Moody, and Graves 462).

By opening with *One source explains*, the writer signals when the borrowing begins.

FIGURE A.1   PLAGIARISM

Plagiarism violates the academic code of conduct, which demands that you must give credit to others for their words and ideas when you use them in your own work. Plagiarism occurs when you purposely and knowingly commit one of these errors:

- You turn in another student's paper as your own.
- You copy portions of another student's paper into your own.
- You copy source material into your paper without quotation marks.
- You provide a direct quotation but omit the in-text citation to author and page.
- You change a source into your own words (paraphrase) without providing an in-text citation to author and page.

Granted, there are exceptions for common knowledge. Most people know that George Washington was our first president and that he lived at Mount Vernon. However, if one source says Washington often ignored his Secretary of State, Thomas Jefferson, to seek the wisdom of Alexander Hamilton, his Secretary of the Treasury, then a citation to the source would be in order.

Therefore, make it a regular habit to identify the source within your text. When you do, you are demonstrating your scholarship and adding credibility to your paper.

CITING UNUSUAL SOURCE MATERIAL

Some sources will raise questions in your mind about citation rules; there will be no author, several authors, no title, or extra information. The following rules apply.

Citing a Source When No Author Is Listed

When no author is shown on a title page, cite the title of an article, the name of the magazine, the name of a bulletin or book, or the name of the publishing organization:

"In one sense toys serve as a child's tools, and by learning to use the toys the child stimulates physical and mental development" ("Selling" 37). [a shortened magazine title]

The report by the school board endorsed the use of Channel One in the school system and said that "students will benefit by the news reports more than they will be adversely affected by advertising" (Clarion County School Board 3-4).

Identifying Nonprint Sources

On occasion you may need to identify nonprint sources, such as a speech, the song lyrics from a compact disk, an interview, or something you have heard on television. In these cases, there will be no page number, so you can omit the parenthetical citation. Instead, introduce the nature of the source so that your reader (especially your teacher) will not expect a page number:

Thompson's lecture defined <u>impulse</u> as "an action triggered by the nerves without thought for the consequences."

Peggy Meacham said in her phone interview that prejudice against young black women is not as severe as that against young black males.

Citing Somebody Who Has Been Quoted in a Book or Article

Sometimes the writer of a magazine article will quote another person, and you will want to use that same quotation. For example, in a newspaper article in *USA Today*, page 9A, Karen S. Peterson writes this passage in which she quotes two other people:

Sexuality, popularity, and athletic competition will create anxiety for junior high kids and high schoolers, Eileen Shiff says. "Bring up the topics. Don't wait for them to do it; they are nervous and they want to appear cool." Monitor the amount of time high schoolers spend working for money, she suggests. "Work is important, but school must be the priority."

Parental intervention in a child's school career that worked in junior high may not work in high school, psychiatrist Martin Greenburg adds. "The interventions can be construed by the adolescent as negative, overburdening and interfering with the child's ability to care for himself."

He adds, "Be encouraging, not critical. Criticism can be devastating for the teen-ager."

Suppose that you want to use the quotation above by Martin Greenburg. You will need to cite both Greenburg, the speaker, and Peterson, the person who wrote the article. Note: Peterson's name will appear on a bibliography entry on your "Works Cited" page, but Greenburg's will not because Greenburg is not the author of the article:

After students get beyond middle school, they begin to resent interference by their parents, especially in school activities. They need some space from Mom and Dad. Martin Greenburg says, "The interventions can be construed by the adolescent as negative, overburdening and interfering with the child's ability to care for himself" (qtd. in Peterson 9A).

As shown above, you need a double reference that introduces the speaker but that also includes a clear reference to the book or article where you found the quotation or the paraphrased material. Without the reference to

Peterson, nobody could find the article. Without the reference to Greenburg, readers would assume that Peterson spoke the words.

Citing Material from Textbooks and Large Anthologies

Reproduced below is a small portion of a textbook:

METAPHOR

The Skaters

Black swallows swooping or gliding
In a flurry of entangled loops and curves;
The skaters skim over the frozen river.
And the grinding click of their skates as they impinge
        upon the surface,
Is like the brushing together of thin wing-tips of silver.
—John Gould Fletcher

—From *Patterns in Literature*, edited by Edmund J. Farrell, Ouida H. Clapp, and Karen Kuehner, page 814.

If you quote from Fletcher's poem, and if that is all you quote from *Patterns in Literature*, you should write two pieces of documentation. First, cite the author and the page in your text:

In "The Skaters," John Gould Fletcher compares "the grinding click" of ice skates to "the brushing together of thin wing-tips of silver" (814).

Second, write a comprehensive entry for the "Works Cited" list:

Fletcher, John Gould. "The Skaters." <u>Patterns in Literature</u>.
Ed. Edmund J. Farrell, Ouida H. Clapp, and Karen
Kuehner. Glenview: Scott, 1991.

Suppose, however, that you want to quote not only from Fletcher but also from the authors of the textbook (Farrell, Clapp, and Kuehner) and from a second poem in the book. You should make three in-text citations to names and pages. Your "Works Cited" page would then feature a primary entry to the textbook and various cross references to it. In the text, you would write something like this:

> In "The Skaters" John Gould Fletcher compares "the grinding click" of ice skates to "the brushing together of thin wing-tips of silver" (814). The use of metaphor is central to his poetic efforts. One source emphasizes Fletcher's use of metaphor, especially his comparison of "the silhouettes of a group of graceful skaters to a flock of black swallows" (Farrell, Clapp, and Kuehner 814).
>
> Metaphor gives us a fresh look, as when Lew Sarett in his "Requiem for a Modern Croesus" uses coins to make his ironic statement about the wealthy king of sixth century Lydia:
>
> > To him the moon was a silver dollar, spun
> > Into the sky by some mysterious hand; the sun
> > Was a gleaming golden coin—
> > His to purloin;
> > The freshly minted stars were dimes of delight
> > Flung out upon the counter of the night.
> > In yonder room he lies,
> > With pennies in his eyes. (814)

Adding Extra Information to In-Text Citations

As a courtesy to your reader, you should occasionally add extra information within the citation so they can be sure which work you are citing. Show parts of books, different titles by the same writer, or several works by different writers:

> In a letter to his Tennessee Volunteers in 1812, General Jackson chastised the "mutinous and disorderly conduct" of some of his troops (Papers 2: 348-49).

The citation above gives an abbreviation for the title (*The Papers of Andrew Jackson*), the volume used, and the page numbers.

> Thomas Hardy reminds readers in his prefaces that "a novel is an impression, not an argument" and that a novel should be read as "a study of man's deeds and character" (Tess xxii; Mayor 1).

The writer above makes reference to two different novels, both abbreviated. Full titles are *Tess of the D'Urbervilles* and *The Mayor of Casterbridge*.

> Several sources have addressed this aspect of gang warfare as a fight for survival, not just for turf (Rollins 34; Templass 561-65; Robertson 98-134).

The citation above refers to three different writers who treat the same topic.

PUNCTUATING CITATIONS PROPERLY AND WITH CONSISTENCY

Keep page citations outside quotation marks but inside the final period (with the exception of long indented quotations, as shown below). Use no comma between name and page within the citation (Jones 16-17 *not* Jones, 16-17). Do not use *p.* or *pp.* or *page* with the number(s).

Place commas and periods inside quotation marks unless the page citation intervenes. Place semicolons and colons outside the quotation marks:

> "Modern advertising," says Rachel Murphy, "not only creates a marketplace, it determines values." She adds, "I resist the advertiser's argument that they 'awaken, not create desires'" (192).

The example above shows (1) how to interrupt a quotation to insert the speaker, (2) how to put the comma inside the quotation marks, (3) how to use single quotation marks within the regular quotation marks, and (4) how to place the period after a page citation.

When a question mark or an exclamation mark comes at the end of a quotation, keep it inside the quotation mark. Place the page number after the authority's name so that your citation does not interfere with a final question mark:

> Scientist Jonathan Roberts (54) asks, "Why do we always assume that bacteria are bad for us?"

The following example shows you how to place the page citation after a quotation and before a semicolon:

Brian Sutton-Smith says, "Adults don't worry whether <u>their</u> toys are educational" (64); he adds, "Why should we always put that burden on the children?"

Indenting Long Quotations

Set off long quotations of four or more lines by indenting ten (10) spaces. Do not use quotation marks around the indented material. Place the parenthetical citation *after* the final period of the quotation, not inside the period:

> In his book <u>A Time to Heal</u>, Gerald Ford, who replaced Richard Nixon in the White House, says he was angry and hurt that Nixon had lied to him, but he was also bothered deeply about Nixon's effect on the status of the presidency:
>
> > What bothered me most was the nature of Nixon's departure. In the 198 years of the Republic, no President had ever resigned, and only one other Chief Executive—Andrew Johnson—had ever been the target of an impeachment effort in the Congress. But Nixon, I had to conclude, had brought his troubles upon himself. (Ford 5)

WRITING ENTRIES FOR THE "WORKS CITED" PAGE

A "Works Cited" page lists the books and articles used to develop a research paper. This list of sources, also called a *bibliography*, serves others who might wish to read further in the literature.

You should provide an entry for each source that you have cited in your paper. Do not list sources that you skimmed but did not use in the paper. Place the first line of each source flush with the left margin and indent succeeding lines five spaces. Double-space throughout. Conform to the following standards of MLA style.

Books

Use this order: author(s), title, a specific volume number, editor(s), edition other than the first, number of volumes if more than one, place of publication, publisher (abbreviated), date, section, and page. List the items that your reader might need to find the source:

Book: One Author

Zindel, Paul. <u>The Pigman</u>. New York: Bantam, 1978.

Book: Two Authors, edition

Bining, Arthur C., and Thomas C. Cochran. <u>The Rise of American Economic Life</u>. 4th ed. New York: Scribner's, 1964.

Book: Anthology, Textbook, Other Edited Works

Magill, Frank N., ed. <u>Masterpieces of World Literature</u>. New York: Harper, 1989.

Farrell, Edmund J., Ouida H. Clapp, and Karen J. Kuehner, eds. <u>Patterns in Literature</u>. Glenview: Scott, 1991.

If you cite one work from an anthology, use this form:

Keats, John. "Ode to a Nightingale." <u>Literature of the Western World</u>. Ed. Brian Wilkie and James Hurt. 2nd ed. 2 vols. New York: Macmillan, 1988. II: 797-99.

However, if you cite several individual authors from one anthology, you will need a primary reference to the text and several cross references to it:

Keats, John. "Ode to a Nightingale." Wilkie and Hurt, II: 797-99.

Homer. <u>The Odyssey</u>. Wilkie and Hurt, I: 254-573.

Wilkie, Brian, and James Hurt, eds. <u>Literature of the Western World</u>. 2nd ed. 2 vols. New York: Macmillan, 1988.

Wolfe, Thomas. "An Angel on the Porch." Wilkie and Hurt, II: 1291-96.

Book: Part of One Volume with Page Numbers

Seale, William. <u>The President's House: A History</u>. 2 vols. Washington: White House Historical Assoc.: 1986. II: 915-1001.

Book: One Volume of Several Volumes

Jackson, Andrew. <u>The Papers of Andrew Jackson: 1770-1803</u>. Vol. 1. Ed. Sam B. Smith and Harriet C. Owsley. 4 vols. Knoxville: U of Tennessee P, 1980.

TABLE A.1   Publishers' Names

In your "Works Cited" list, abbreviate the names of publishers. Use this list as a guide

- Scott (Scott, Foresman and Company)
- Norton (W. W. Norton and Company)
- Allyn (Allyn and Bacon, Inc.)
- Bobbs (Bobbs-Merrill Co., Inc.)
- Holt (Holt, Rinehart, and Winston, Inc.)
- Oxford UP (Oxford University Press)
- U of Chicago P (University of Chicago Press)

Book: A Novel in a Special Edition

Hardy, Thomas. The Mayor of Casterbridge. A Norton
    Critical Edition. Ed. James K. Robinson. New York:
    Norton, 1977.

Book: Two Works by the Same Author

Dickens, Charles. David Copperfield. A Norton Critical
    Edition. Ed. James K. Robinson. New York: Norton,
    1977.

---. Hard Times. New York: Macmillan, 1962.

In the example above, note the use three dashes, not three
underline marks, to represent the name of the preceding
author.

Magazines

In citing magazines, use this order: author(s), title of
the article within quotation marks, name of the magazine

underlined, specific date, inclusive page numbers (but use a "+" with the opening page (14+) if advertising pages intervene or if the article skips to the back pages of the magazine):

Magazine: One Author

Schneider, Susan. "The Trade in Sticky Fingers." <u>Lear's</u> September 1990: 38+.

Magazine: Two Authors

Johnson, Lorenzo, and Peggy L. Forrester. "Toys That Teach." <u>Games</u> 16 April 1990: 34-37.

Magazine: No Author Listed

"Selling to Children." <u>Consumer Reports</u> 55 (Aug. 1990): 518-21.

Note: This magazine publishes with continuous pagination for the whole year; it requires a volume number, like a journal article.

Journals

Most journals page continuously through all issues of an entire year. Thus the volume number, year, and pages are sufficient for locating a journal article. If a journal does page anew each issue, provide the issue number (for example, *66.2* would indicated the second issue of the sixty-sixth volume):

Tegano, Deborah, Janet K. Sawyers, and James D. Moran. "Problem-Finding and Solving in Play: The Teacher's Role." <u>Child Education</u> 66 (1989): 92-97.

Review Articles

For review articles, provide reviewer and title of the review as well as the work and author under review:

Beeston, Richard. "Book Reviews." Rev. of <u>A Touch of Genius: The Life of T. E. Lawrence</u>, by Malcolm Brown and Julia Cave. <u>Smithsonian</u> July 1990: 132-33.

Newspapers

For citations to newspapers, include the section with the page number as it appears in the newspaper (D1, D-1, or 1D):

Hellmich, Nanci. "College Studies Are Often a Full-time Job." <u>USA Today</u> 11 Sept. 1990: 1D.

Government Documents

In citing government documents, provide government, body, subsidiary body, title, identifying number, and publication facts:

United States. Cong. Senate. <u>Anti-Flag Desecration</u>. S 607 to accompany S.R. 412. 93rd Cong., 2nd sess. Washington: GPO, 1990.

Other Sources

Conform to the examples below for bulletin, cassette tape, computer data, film, interview, letter, microfilm, music, television, videotape, and so forth. Provide enough information so that readers can understand exactly the nature of the source:

Bulletin

Alexander, Ralph. <u>Sports and Steroids</u>. Bulletin 24A. Washington, DC: GPO, 1989.

Cassette Tape

Burney, Elizabeth C. "Comic Women in Shakespeare." Lecture on cassette tape. Nashville: Vanderbilt U., 1991.

Magazine Advertising

"Mexico World Environment Day." Advertising page. <u>Smithsonian</u> July 1990: 143.

Computer Handbook

<u>Wordstar Reference</u>. Computer software. Novato, CA: Wordstar International, 1990.

Database File

"Alexander Hamilton." Database file. <u>Academic American Encyclopedia</u>. 1981 ed. CompuServe, 1983, record no. 1816.

Interview

Norfleet, Joe Eddie. Interview with the county historian. Dalton, 6 July 1990.

Letter

Wilfong, Richard, and Wynona Wilfong. Letter to the author. 14 March 1990.

Map

<u>Clayton County Topography</u>. United States Base Map GA-56, No. 19. Washington: GPO, 1985.

FORMATTING THE "WORKS CITED" PAGE

A final "Works Cited" page must list each source that you cite in your text, and only those sources. If you list sources that you did not cite in the text, call the list "References." If you use nonprint sources, label the list "Sources Cited." Arrange the list in alphabetical order by the last name of the author. Double-space throughout. If no author is listed, alphabetize by the first important word of the title. If an author has two works, substitute three dashes for the second listed name (see below). If you make cross references to an anthology, mingle the references alphabetically with the other entries.

Works Cited

Allison, John. "The Mero District." American Historical Magazine 50.2 (1896): n.p.

Curtis, James C. Andrew Jackson and the Search for Vindication. Boston: Little, 1976.

Durham, Walter T. The Great Leap Westward: A History of Sumner County, Tennessee. Gallatin, TN: Sumner County Public Library Board, 1969.

---. James Winchester: Tennessee Pioneer. Gallatin, TN: Sumner County Public Library Board, 1979.

Dykeman, Wilma. Tennessee: A History. New York: Norton, 1984.

Fisk, Moses. Unpublished Papers. Tennessee State Library and Archives, Nashville.

Hays, Stockley Donelson. Letter. Jackson, Papers, II: 211.

"Jackson, Andrew." Encyclopedia Americana. 1986 ed.

Jackson, Andrew. The Papers of Andrew Jackson. Ed. Sam B. Smith and Harriet C. Owsley (Vol. 1); Harold D. Moser and Sharon MacPherson (Vol. 2). 4 vols. Knoxville: U of Tennessee P, 1980, 1984.

---. Misc. Papers. <u>The Messages and Papers of the Presidents</u>. Ed. Richardson, James D. 10 vols. Washington: n.p., 1900.

U.S. Congress. <u>American Archives</u>. Fourth series. Vol. 1. Washington, DC: United States Congress.

Williams, Sampson. Letter. Jackson, <u>Papers</u>, II: 195.

SAMPLE RESEARCH PAPER

The composition that follows demonstrates the style and format for the research paper.

Elysia Emsweller

Mr. Lester

December 1, 1992

"The Masque of the Red Death"

Edgar Allan Poe's "The Masque of the Red
Death" discusses a plague, the Red Death, that
seems destined to kill all people. He published
the short story in 1842 (Wilson xxi), and,
ironically, that year his wife contracted
tuberculosis. Five years later, in 1847, she
died (Ljungquist 591). In "The Masque of the
Red Death," Poe seems to predict that certain
diseases, like the Red Death, would eventually
diminish humanity.

He could not predict a specific disease,
but Poe's story suggests the ravaging dangers
of AIDS in today's society. Richard Slick makes
this very assertion, saying, "'The Masque of
the Red Death' is a provocative tale and would
be effective in generating and opening discussion
with young people in an instructional unit on
AIDS" (26). Slick also asks:

> Is it so far-fetched to hypothesize
> that he [Poe] could have been
> predicting in this fabulous allegory
> "The Masque of the Red Death"
> something like the terrible AIDS
> virus that seems to appear more and
> more in human communities across
> the world? (24)

Every age, perhaps, has its own devastating disease. In Poe's time it was tuberculosis; in our time it is AIDS. Poe gives us the allegory that fits any life-threatening disease.

The castle is society, and the various rooms show stages of physical (or moral) decay. The first room, blue, symbolizes sadness or birth--the birth of the disease. Purple represents royalty, saying that diseases do not discriminate and that they strike the noble as well as the commoner. Serenity characterizes the green room (perhaps a remission occurs); the orange room emits light that suggests hope; purity characterizes the white room (again, diseases do not discriminate between innocent and experienced persons); and violet shows the bloodiness and pain of the disease. The seventh

room, black, symbolizes the death of the victim.
The ebony clock stands in this room, and it counts
the minutes of life (beginning at birth and ending
at death).

Life is like a confusing maze. Accordingly,
the rooms in the castle are not lined straight
with the hallways. Instead, there exist several
sharp turns, probably explaining that the course
of a disease always changes. These twists and blind
corners also point to the fact that no one knows
what lies ahead.

The idea that the Red Death does not
discriminate proves true because Prospero
contracted the disease, and he possessed royalty.
Once again, this contagious illness is comparable
to AIDS. Prospero tried to "shut out" the disease
by throwing a party and having this attitude:
"The external world could take care of itself.
In the meantime it was folly to grieve or to think"
(Poe 123). Ignoring the disease, however, does not
make it disappear.

Poe, referring to the Red Death, says, "He
had come like a thief in the night" (129). Indeed,
the statistics on prevention show that experts are

still not completely sure as to how to prevent

the virus and thereby avoid "the thief in the

night." Abstaining from sex or having monogamous

relationships and abstaining from drugs (needles)

reduce the risks, but, like Prospero, most young

people feel they are invincible.

Poe's wife died of tuberculosis, anyone

contracting AIDS dies, and anyone that gets the

Red Death dies. Basically, these diseases kill, and

the diseases spreads quickly. (Tuberculosis is rare

now, but during the 1800s it killed.) Even though

AIDS spread quickly and has infected thousands of

people, let us hope that this next quotation never

occurs: "And Darkness and Decay and the Red Death

held illimitable dominion over all" (Poe 129).

Works Cited

Ljungquist, Kent. "Edgar Allan Poe." <u>World Book</u>
        <u>Encyclopedia</u>. 1990 ed.

Poe, Edgar Allan. "The Masque of the Red
        Death." Wilson 122-29.

Slick, Richard D. "Poe's the Masque of the Red
        Death." <u>The Explicator</u> 47.2 (1989): 24-26.

Wilson, James Southall, ed. <u>Tales of Edgar</u>
        <u>Allan Poe</u>. New York: Scribner's, 1927.

COMMON USAGE PROBLEMS

The guidelines below indicate the current preferences of editors, teachers, rhetoricians, and writers, as given by authorities such as *The American Heritage Dictionary* and *The New York Times Manual of Style and Usage*. Pairs of additional words that cause confusion will be found in the list of homophones in Chapter 14.

a, an Indefinite articles. Use *a* before words that begin with a consonant sound: *a book, a computer*. Use *an* before words beginning with a vowel sound: *an orphan, an example*. Note: *an honor* (*h* is not voiced) but *a history book* (*h* is voiced). He left *an* hour ago. This has been *a* hot, muggy day.

accept, except The verb *accept* means "receive." *Except* can be a verb or a preposition and means "omitting or leaving out": I cannot *accept* this expensive gift. Everyone *except* Marsha finished the test.

adapt, adopt To *adapt* means "to make modifications or to become adjusted to new conditions." To *adopt* means "to accept or choose": The committee *adapted* the recommendation in expectations that the full board would *adopt* it. Note: *adopt* takes a direct object while *adapt* is usually followed by *to, for*, or a *self* pronoun.

advice, advise *Advice* is a noun that means "a recommendation." *Advise* is a verb that means "to recommend": Your *advice* saved me money. I *advise* you to give up smoking.

affect, effect *Affect* is a verb that means "to influence" and *effect* is a noun that means "result": The new rules did not *affect* the old players. The *effect* of the part was to increase speed. *Effect* is also a verb meaning "to bring about": Your alcohol *effected* blood sugar in the sample.

all, all of Use *all* to modify a noun: We ate *all* the spaghetti. Use *all of* only before a pronoun or proper noun: *All of* us must read by Friday all of Shakespeare's *Hamlet*.

all ready, already *All ready* means "to be completely prepared and ready for action"; the adverb *all* modifies the adjective *ready:* We shall be *all ready* very soon. *Already* means "previously," "before now," or "just now": It is *already* two o'clock.

all together, altogether *Altogether* is an adverb that means "entirely"; the phrase *all together* means "assembled together in one place": We were *altogether* dumbfounded that the choir was *all together* and ready to board the bus.

allusion, illusion An *allusion* is an indirect reference, but an *illusion* is a strange or deceptive appearance: He opened the speech with an *allusion* to Homer's *The Odyssey*. The *illusion* in the rearview mirror seemed real.

almost, most *Almost* is an adverb that means "nearly" (*almost* ready); *most* is an adjective that means "a large part of" (*most* students): *Almost* [not *most*] all the delegates are seated now.

alot A nonstandard word that is often incorrectly substituted for *a lot* (two words): We cared *a lot* about the outcome of the game.

alright A nonstandard word that is often incorrectly substituted for *all right* (two words): The collision was severe, but everyone is *all right*.

among, between Both of these words are prepositions. *Among* is used when referring to three or more people or things. *Between* is usually used when referring to two people or things: I divided the prize money *among* my friends. Keep the secret just *between* you and me.

amount, number *Amount* is a singular noun that refers to large, uncountable quantities; *number* is a plural noun used with specific, countable quantities: The *amount of* support for this proposal will depend heavily upon the *number of* teachers who voice support. Note: follow *amount of* with a singular noun and follow *number of* with a plural noun or nouns.

and etc. *Et cetera* (*etc.*) means "and others"; *and etc.* is therefore redundant. It is best to use "and so forth" or "and so on" in your writing.

anybody, any body, anyone, any one (*everyone, every one*) These look-alikes differ. *Anybody, anyone,* and *everyone* are indefinite pronouns that mean "any or every person at all": Can *anybody* help me with this problem? *Any body, any one,* and *every one* refer to specific persons or groups: *Any one* of you might win the scholarship.

anymore, any more In negative constructions, *any more* means "no more": The SGA president doesn't want *any more* debate on this piece of legislation. The adverb *anymore,* meaning "from now on," also has negative connotations: The council will not meet *anymore* this semester.

anyway, any way, anyways *Anyways* is not a word. *Anyway* is an an adverb that means "in any case" or "nevertheless: He will hold band practice *anyway. Any way* is a noun phrase meaning "in any manner": He will waste his talent *any way* he pleases.

as *As* may cause confusion if used to mean *when, because, since, when* or *while:* As the candidate was arriving, we hurried to put up all the campaign posters. Does this mean *while* or *because* or maybe both? Replace as with an exact term.

as, like Use *like* only as a preposition meaning "similar to," "characteristic of," or "inclined to": works *like* magic, feel *like* sleeping. Use *as* as a conjunction, not *like:* She takes to mathematics *as* a duck takes to water.

awful, awfully Do not use *awfully* as an intensifier; instead, use *very, exceedingly,* or a precise word: an *extremely* (not *awfully*) hard exam. Especially avoid *awful* as an adverb in writing: a *very* [not an *awful*] hard practice session.

awhile, a while *Awhile* is an adverb that means "for a short period of time": Stay *awhile. A while* is a noun preceded by the article a; it usually serves as the object of a preposition: Stay for *a while.*

bad, badly *Bad* is an adjective: I felt *bad*. *Badly* is the adverb: We played *badly* tonight.

because, cause The subordinate conjunction *because* means "due to" or "as a result of." When joining ideas, use the complete word *because:* We hurried home *because* it started to rain. *Cause* is usually a noun that denotes "an issue" or "reason," but it can also be a verb meaning "to move" or "invoke action": The *cause* of the leak is unknown. Steve *caused* an outburst of laughter.

beside, besides *Beside* is always a preposition that means "by the side of": The dog sat *beside* the large tree. As a preposition, *besides* means "in addition to": *Besides* books, magazines are good reading. As an adverb, *besides* means "also" or "moreover": *Besides,* you owe me money.

breath, breathe *Breath* is a noun that means "the air we inhale and exhale": I'm out of *breath*. *Breathe* is a verb that mean "to inhale and exhale": If you will *breathe* deeply, the dizziness will diminish.

bring, take *Bring* indicates motion toward a speaker or writer: Please *bring* the plant inside. *Take* indicates motion away from the speaker: *Take* the trash out.

burst, bust, busted The verb *burst* means "to blow up" or "fly to pieces." Its principal parts are *burst, burst, burst*: We *burst* the air balloon, and the owner then *burst* into tears. There is no such word as *bursted*. Avoid the use of the slang words *bust* and *busted*.

can, may *Can* shows the ability to accomplish something: Mike *can* whistle loudly. *May* asks or indicates permission or shows chance: *May* I have another slice of pie?

capital, capitol *Capitol* is a building (*the state capitol building*) or the hill on which it sits. Use *capital* in all other occasions (*capital* offense, *capital* city, *capital* letter).

censor, censure *Censor* means "to audit and stop questionable material"; *censor* can also refer to the person who *censors:* Mrs. Minter, the newspaper sponsor, *censored* several paragraphs from my article. *Censure* means "to condemn, blame, or criticize": Mrs. Minter *censured* our lack of correct spelling.

climactic, climatic *Climactic,* the adjective form of *climax,* refers to "a culmination" or "moment of great intensity": The *climactic* moment of the game had arrived. *Climatic,* the adjective form of *climate,* refers to the weather: The *climatic* extremes destroyed his love for Alaska.

compare, contrast To *compare* means "to show resemblance"; to *contrast* means "to show differences." *Compare* can be used to show both similarities and differences.

compare to, compare with. Use *compare to* to demonstrate that one item is like another: He *compared* the crowd to a swarm of bees. Use *compare with* to show similarities between items: The class discussion *compared* President Clinton *with* former President Bush.

complement, compliment To *complement* means "to make whole" or "bring to perfection": A bouquet on each table *complemented* the delicate china. To *compliment* means "to admire or praise": Rufus *complimented* my new hair style.

compose, comprise A whole *comprises* the individual parts: The test *comprises* four units of study. The individual parts *compose* the whole: Punctuation, mechanics, word usage, and spelling *compose* the exam.

conscious, conscience *Conscious,* an adjective, means "aware of" or "capable of thought." *Conscience,* a noun, means "a sense of right and wrong": Although *conscious* of your presence, I left anyway. Later, my guilt affected my *conscience.*

continual, continuous *Continual* means "constantly recurring" and should be used for events (*continual* battles, *continual* mistakes). *Continuous* means "unceasing" and should be used for an uninterrupted flow (*continuous* pain in my ear).

council, counsel A *council* is a group: The Student *Council* meets on the last Wednesday of each month. *Counsel* is both a noun and a verb. The noun means "advice": I sought *counsel* from Mrs. Welker. As a verb it means "advise": Mrs. Welker *counseled* me after my test scores were returned.

criteria, criterion *Criterion* is singular and means one "standard for making a judgment." *Criteria* is the plural form of *criterion:* All three *criteria* will be used.

data, datum *Data* is the plural form of *datum* in academic, scientific, and other formal writing: The *data* show three areas of heat exchange. Use *datum* for the singular noun.

different from, different than *Different from* is the preferred usage: The agenda for this band festival is *different from* the one for the regional contest.

differ from, differ with *Differ from* means to be "unlike" and *differ with* means "to disagree": Your opinion may *differ with* mine. This half-time program *differs from* the one used last year.

discreet, discrete *Discreet* means "tactful," "judicious," or "modest": The lady's *discreet* behavior made her the confidant of many people. *Discrete* means "distinct" or "separate": The thesaurus and spelling checker are *discrete* items in separate files.

disinterested, uninterested *Disinterested* means "uninvolved": Teachers and students need a *disinterested* person to resolve the conflict. *Uninterested* means "unconcerned": Most student appear *uninterested* in the charity ball.

doesn't, don't *Doesn't,* the contraction for *does not* is singular: He *doesn't* try anymore. *Don't,* the contraction for *do not,* is plural: We *don't* care who wins the contest.

dreamed, dreamt *Dreamed* is the preferred past tense form of dream.

due to, because of *Because of* is a preposition: *Because of* the fight (not *due to*), the referee stopped the game. *Due to* is a predicate adjective following a linking verb: His success was *due to* his persistent practice.

each other, one another *Each other* refers to two, *one another* refers to more than two: My boyfriend and I love *each other.* The English department exchanged gifts with *one another.*

elicit, illicit *Elicit* means "to derive or get information"; *illicit* is something illegal: The principal *elicited* the confession about the gangs use of *illicit* drugs.

emigrate, immigrate Both of these words are verbs. *Emigrate* means "to leave a country to settle elsewhere." *Immigrate* means "to enter a foreign country to live there." A person *emigrates* from a country and *immigrates* to another country: Ellen's parents *emigrated* from Poland. Gustavo *immigrated* to the United States.

everyday, every day *Everyday,* an adjective, means "ordinary" or "commonplace": The *everyday* dishes will be fine for this dinner. *Every day* is a modifier and noun meaning "each day": He needs tutoring for 30 minutes *every day.*

everyone, every one, everybody *Everyone* and *everybody* are relative pronouns that mean "every person": *Everybody* helped make the carnival a success. *Every one* is a modifier and noun that means "each single person or thing": Did *every one* of the clowns get to perform?

expect, suspect Expect means "to look forward to": We *expect* opposition at the meeting tonight. Avoid using *expect* for *suppose* or *think:* Do you *suppose* [not *expect*] that coach will use the flea-flicker play tonight?

farther, further *Farther* refers to distance: How much *farther* do we have to go? *Further* means "additional" or "to a greater degree or extent": *Further* information was not available.

fewer, less *Fewer* refers to a countable number: *fewer* dollars, *fewer* cheerleaders. *Less* refers to an uncountable amount: *less* money, *less* motivation.

figuratively, literally *Figuratively* means "in terms of another thing": *Figuratively,* this team plays like lambs, not lions. *Literally* means "actually": The gang *literally* denied any responsibility for the damage.

first, firstly Use *first* (*second, third*).

formerly, formally *Formerly* is an adverb the means "at an earlier time": We *formerly* lived in the Flint Hills region of central Kansas. *Formally* is an adverb that means "in a conventional manner": We dressed *formally* for the Christmas ball.

good, well *Good,* an adjective, often follows a linking verb: Your performance was very *good. Well,* an adverb, usually follows an action verb: This team works *well* together.

hanged, hung *Hung* means "suspended": The posters are *hung* on most bulletin boards. Reserve *hanged* for an execution: The sheriff *hanged* the prisoner immediately after the trial.

hardly, scarcely *Hardly* and *scarcely* should be used alone, without the help of *not* or *can't:* I can hardly [not *can't hardly*] hear the announcements.

have, of Do not use the preposition *of* as a substitute for the verb *have*. Nonstandard: He should *of* started on time. Standard: He should *have* started on time.

imply, infer Speaker's *imply* to the reader or listener, who *infers*. That is, speakers and writers *imply,* which means "to suggest by word or actions": The dean *implied* that he would reconsider the resolution. Listeners and readers *infer,* which means "to draw conclusions": After listening to the principal, one could easily *infer* that he would not fund the proposal under any circumstances.

in, into Use *in* for location or condition: Your wallet is *in* your jacket. Use *into* for movement or a change in condition: Three actors dressed *in* black suddenly walked *into* the audience.

incredible, incredulous *Incredible* means "unbelievable": Your attitude in this matter is *incredible. Incredulous* means "to be skeptical, doubting, unbelieving": Your behavior left the entire faculty *incredulous* and dismayed.

ingenious, ingenuous *Ingenious* means "clever": Your *ingenious* methods enabled the committee to salvage the resolution. *Ingenuous* means "naive": Your *ingenuous* smile has won my heart.

instance, instant, incident An *instance* is "an example": Sue's actions are an *instance* of caution. An *instant* is "a moment of time": He was gone in an *instant.* An *incident* is "an event or an occurrence": The *incident* frightened the little girl.

irregardless Nonstandard because it is a double negative. Both *ir* and *less* mean "not." Always use *regardless:* We plan to pass this resolution *regardless* [not *irregardless*] of its cost.

is when, is where Avoid these phrases that complete the linking verb with an adverb rather than a noun or adjective: The enrollment period is the *time* [not *is when*] to change your class schedule.

its, it's *Its* without the apostrophe serves as a possessive pronoun: The cat licked *its* fur. *It's* is the contraction for *it is*: *It's* too late to get to the movie on time.

-ize Avoid this suffix; it creates awkward verbs such as *fraternalize, finalize, budgetize,* and *racialize*.

lay, lie *Lay,* a transitive verb means "to put or place" and takes a direct object: Please *lay* the report cards on my desk. *Lie,* an intransitive verb, means "to recline": The report card *lay* on Mother's table, where it has *lain* since Tuesday.

learn, teach To *learn* is "to gain awareness": We *learned* to play Nintendo. To *teach* is "to convey knowledge": Maybe my brother can *teach* me new techniques.

lend, loan *Lend* is a verb: Check with Amy—she might *lend* you some money. *Loan* is the noun: Thanks for the *loan* of the pen.

liable, likely *Liable* means "to be responsible for": The freshman class is *liable* for damages to the gym floor. *Likely* refers to "probability": The punishment will *likely* be severe.

loose, lose *Loose,* an adjective, means "not fastened" or "not tight": The stage rigging was *loose*. As a verb, *loose* means "to untighten": *Loosen* this knot for me. *Lose* is a verb meaning "to misplace" or "be defeated": Don't *lose* the tickets for Disney World.

lot, lot of, lots of Colloquial usage. Instead, use *many, much, a lot, a great deal*.

mankind Sexist usage. Instead, use *human beings, humankind,* or *people*.

may be, maybe *May be* serves as a verb phrase: You *may be* the winner, but let's wait for the final results. *Maybe,* an adverb, means "perhaps": *Maybe* I can win the butterfly face.

may of, might of, must of Nonstandard phrases. Instead use *may have, might have,* or *must have.*

media, medium *Media,* the plural form of *medium,* refers to "agents of mass communication": When choosing from local advertising *media,* the best two *are* the local newspaper and the radio station. The best *medium* for print ads is the newspaper.

most Do not substitute *most* for *almost: Almost* [not *most*] every teacher will give a mid-term examination.

myself Do not use *myself* as a substitute for *I* or me: Sandra and I [not *myself*] will co-chair the committee.

nauseated, nauseous *Nauseated* means "sick or queasy": Three students became *nauseated* after eating the pizza. *Nauseous* is an adjective meaning "sickening and disgusting": The *nauseous* odor swept across the dining hall.

notable, noticeable *Notable* means "remarkable": a *notable* performance or a *notable* speech. *Noticeable* means "perceptible or observable": a *noticeable* scar.

nowhere, nowheres *No where* is the correct usage. *Nowheres* is nonstandard and should be avoided.

off of *Off* is sufficient.

ok, o.k., okay Appropriate in conversational usage only. In composition, use *all right, correct, approval,* or other similar terms: The drama teacher gave the set design his *approval.*

per In writing, use **per** only with Latin phrases (*per capita, per se, per diem, per annum*). Otherwise, use the appropriate article or the preposition *according to*: $2.50 *a* [not *per*] person.

percent, percentage Use *percent* with numbers: Only 20 *percent* of the registered voters cast ballots. Use *percentage* without numbers: A large *percentage* failed the exam. Use *part,* not *percentage,* when you do not mean a specific portion or share: A large *part* [not *percentage*] of the set construction is finished.

phenomena, phenomenon A *phenomenon* is one happening. Several such happenings are *phenomena* or *phenomenons.* Do not use *phenomenas:* The strange lights in the sky were a *phenomenon* to us all.

precede, proceed *Precede* means "to come before another in time, order, or rank": Security officers *precede* the president into press conferences. *Proceed* means "to go forward or to carry on": You may *proceed* with your writing.

proved, proven Use either *proved* or *proven* as a past participle: He *has proved* [or *has proven*] his value to the track team several times.

quote, quotation Avoid the use of *quote* as a short form of *quotation:* Each section opens with a *quotation* [not *quote*] from Charles Dickens.

quiet, quite *Quiet* means "to be in a state of calm or free from noise": The librarian asked us to be *quiet. Quite* means "completely," "wholly," or "to a considerable degree": He was *quite* ill after the operation.

raise, rise *Raise,* meaning "to lift or to increase", requires a direct object: The conductor *raised* the baton into position. *Rise,* meaning "to get up or to ascend," does *not* take an object: The sun will *rise* at 6:05 a.m.

real, really Avoid using *real* for *really:* We were *really* [not *real*] happy. Note: another adverb (or none at all) might be more precise: The exam was *extremely* difficult.

reason . . . is because Avoid this nonstandard phrase by using *that* rather than *because:* The *reason* we forfeited *is that* one player was ineligible. Or say: We forfeited *because* one player was ineligible.

respectively, respectfully *Respectively* means "in order": We honored *respectively* the teacher, the coach, and the principal. *Respectfully* means "with respect": The board considered our proposals *respectfully*.

sensual, sensuous *Sensuous* means "to appeal to the senses": Enjoy the *sensuous* pleasure of our Florida beaches. *Sensual* means "sexually attractive": The actor's voice grew more *sensual* as the plot thickened.

set, sit *Set*, a transitive verb, means "to put," and it requires a direct object: I *set* the coffeepot on his desk. *Sit*, an intransitive verb, means "to be seated". It does *not* take an object: Please *sit* on the sofa.

shall, will Use *shall* for asking formal questions: *Shall* we eat at home or go out to dinner? Use *will* in other circumstances: I *will* join the club, so maybe our friends *will* also join the club.

since, because *Since* signals time: The coaches have waited *since* Tuesday for your decision. Use *because* in most other situations: We need your help *because* the senior play requires many dancers.

sometime, some time, sometimes *Sometime,* an adverb, means "at some indefinite time": Let's meet for lunch *sometime. Some time*—two words—is an adjective modifying a noun that means "a period of time": We haven't seen each other for *some time. Sometimes,* an adverb, means "occasionally": We meet for lunch *sometimes*.

sure, surely Use *sure* only as an adjective meaning "certain" (a *sure* winner). Use *surely* as an adverb: He is *surely* [not *sure*] confused by this software program. Use *sure to* not *sure and*: Be *sure to* lock the door.

Than, then *Than* is a conjunction for comparisons: Dora is taller *than* her older brother. *Then*, an adverb, shows time: Thomas *then* began his solo.

their, there, they're *Their* is a possessive pronoun: Have you seen *their* cluttered locker? *There* is an adverb of place: Your shoes are over *there*. *They're* is a contraction of *they are*: *They're* arriving backstage right now.

till, until Neither *till* or *until* should be used as a substitute for when. *Till* should be used to refer to what one does to the soil or ground: The farmer *tilled* the 40 acres he owned. *Until* is a preposition and must have an object: You may keep the book *until* Friday.

toward, towards *Toward* is preferred, but both are acceptable.

try and, try to Avoid *try and*; use *try to*: Most distance runners *try to* win the Boston Marathon.

usage, use, utilize The word *use* means "to put a thing or person to a given purpose to accomplish a task": The *use* [not *usage*] of the cellular phone will speed your work. Can we *use* [not *utilize*] the yearbook staff to write copy? *Usage* means "the act or method of using": The computer was damaged by rough *usage*. *Utilize* implies putting something to a profitable or a practical use: We can *utilize* these waste products.

use to, used to Avoid *use to*; *used to* is always past tense, so always retain the *-d*: The school *used to* have an indoor swimming pool.

want, won't *Want* is a verb that implies desire or a need to have something: I *want* you to clean your room immediately. *Won't* is a contraction that means *will not*: We *won't* be attending the banquet.

which, who Use *who* to refer to people and *which* or *that* to refer to things: One of the people *who* spoke left his pipe, *which* I found beside the lectern.

while *While* can suggest a period of time or mean "although". Be sure your meaning is clear: *While* most of the stage crew worked on the flats, we painted the floor. *Although* some wanted to wait, we painted the floor that night.

who, whom *Who* is a pronoun in the nominative case. It is used as a subject or predicate nominative: *Who* nominated you for class secretary? *Whom* is a pronoun in the objective case and is used mainly as a direct object, an indirect object, or the object of a preposition: To *whom* are you speaking?

who's, whose *Who's* is the contraction of *who is*: Who's arriving next? *Whose* is the possessive form of *who*: *Whose* recipe will we follow?

-wise Some *-wise* words are standard: *clockwise, likewise, otherwise*. However, do not add this suffix in order to coin new words, such as *campuswise, weatherwise, jobwise,* or *computerwise*.

your, you're *Your* is the possessive form of *you*: *Your* basket at the bell won the game. *You're* is the contraction of *you are*: *You're* the champion.

INDEX

Decimals, using numbers in, 261
Declarative sentence, 231
Definite articles, 249, 315
Definitions, writing with, 95
Demonstrative adjectives, 316
Demonstrative pronouns, 301, 302
Denotation, 190
Dependent clause, 140
Description, writing with, 93–95
Detailed description, 129
Details, concrete, 129
Determiner, 298
Dialogue, 129
    emphasizing key ideas in, 115
    in expressive writing, 27
    punctuating, 240
Dictionary
    improving spelling with, 274
    finding appropriate words in,
        163–165
Direct objects, 293, 331–332.
    See also Object complement
Direct quotations
    ellipsis in, 229
    punctuating, 238–241
Districts, capitalizing proper
    names of, 253
Documentation, abbreviations in,
    257, 259
Double comparatives, 320
Double negatives, 320–321
Double superlatives, 320
Draft
    answering questions about, 40–41
    outlining rough, 42–43
    writing second, 51–54
Drafting
    methods in, 35–38
    selecting form for, 26–35

E

Editing
    for clarity, 147
    for coherence, 58–60
    eliminating wordiness, 65–66
    for preciseness, 62–64, 152–155
    for unity, 56–58
    using computer for, 69–73
    verbs, 60–61
Ellipsis, 229
Endnotes, replacement of, by in-text
    citations, 345
English
    conversational, 176, 180

formal, 178, 179, 181–182, 183
informal, 178–179, 180–181
standard, 176–178
Euphemisms, 183–184
Examples, writing with, 95–96
Exclamations, mild, 231
Exclamation mark, 232, 327
    to set off interjections, 325
    using with quotation marks,
        240–241, 356
Explanatory writing, 27–29, 33–34,
    96–99
Expressive writing, 26–27, 31–33

F

Facts, getting right, 154–157
Figures of speech
    creating original, 209–213
    hyperbole, 209
    metaphors, 206–211, 212–213
    onomatopoeia, 190, 199
    personification, 208, 211–212
    similes, 206–211
    synecdoche, 208, 211–212
First person pronoun, 297
Flashbacks, 30
Footnotes, replacement of, by in-text
    citations, 345
Formal English, 178, 179, 181–182, 183
Fragments, sentence, 67–68, 143–146
Freewriting, 13–14
Future perfect tense, 306
Future progressive tense, 307
Future tense, 306

G

Gender
    for nouns, 293
    for pronoun, 296
General words versus specific
    words, 62–64
Generating ideas, 6–7
    asking questions, 11–12
    clippings, 15–16
    clustering, 9–11
    freewriting, 13–14
    listing key words in, 7–9
    other strategies for, 16
Gerund phrases, 335, 337–338
Government documents, citing,
    on works cited page, 362
Grammar, correcting, 67–69

H

Historical present tense, 307
Homophones, 282–284

N

Names, using capital letters with, 249–254

Narration
    in expressive writing, 26–27
    writing with, 92–93

Narrator, in creative writing, 30

Narrowing the topic, 17–20

Nationalities, capitalizing names of, 253

Nations, capitalizing names of, 253

Negatives, double, 320–321

Newspapers, citing, on works cited page, 362

Nicknames, capitalization of, 252

Nominative, predicate, 333

Nominative case, 292, 298

Nonessential elements, using commas to set off, 223–224

Nonprint sources, identifying, 351

Nonrestrictive subordinate clauses, commas to set off, 342

Noun(s), 186–192, 290–294
    abstract, 187, 291
    case in, 292–293
    changing weak, to action verbs, 197–198
    collective, 291
    common, 290
    compound, 264, 292
    concrete, 186–187, 290–291
    connotations of, 190–192
    definition of, 290
    functions of, 293–294
    gender in, 293
    as metaphors, 212–213
    nominative case for, 292
    number in, 291–292
    objective case for, 293
    as object complements, 333
    plural, 292
    possessive case for, 292
    predicate, 330, 333
    prepositional phrase as, 337
    proper, 253, 290
    in series, 189–190
    singular, 291–292
    using forceful, 186–192
    with sound effects, 190

Noun clauses
    as subjects, 329
    subordinate, 341

Noun phrases, 335
    as subjects, 329

Number
    of noun, 291–292
    of pronoun, 296
    of verb, 305

Numbers, 260–262

O

Objects, 293, 331–333
    direct, 331–333
    indirect, 293, 311–312, 332–333
    retained, 293, 332

Object complement, 294, 316, 333

Objective case, 293, 298

Object of the preposition, 293

Onomatopoeia, 190, 199

Originality, 118–119
    problems with, 119–120

Outlining rough draft, 42–43

P

Paragraph, 83–85
    coherence of, 58–60, 84
    developing, to meet the demands of form and structure, 90–106
    matching point of view to purpose, 114–115
    placement of topic sentences in, 112–114
    pronouns in, 111–112
    repeating key words and phrases in, 110–111
    transitional words and phrases in, 106–110
    unity in, 56–58, 84, 85–89
    using dialogue to emphasize key issues in, 115

Parallelism, 124–127

Paraphrasing, 345–349

Parentheses, 227–228

Participial phrases, 221, 338

Passive voice, 131–133, 309, 330–331

Past participle, 303

Past perfect tense, 306

Past progressive tense, 307

Past tense, 303, 306

Percentages, using numbers in, 261

Perfect tense, 306

Period
    in abbreviations, 258–259
    to end sentences, 230, 327
    to set off interjections, 325
    with quotation marks, 240, 356

Period faults, 136–137

Recalling, 16
Reflecting, 16
Reflexive pronouns, 300–301, 302
Regions, capitalizing proper
  names of, 253
Regular verbs, 303
Relative pronouns, 299–300, 302, 325,
  341, 342
Religions, capitalizing names of, 253
Repetition, of key words and phrases,
  110–111, 123–124
Request, 231
Research paper, sample, 366–371
Retained object, 293, 332
Review articles, citing, on works cited
  page, 362
Revising
  answering questions about your
    first draft, 40–41
  body, 46–49
  conclusion, 49–50
  introduction, 44–46
  outlining the rough draft, 42–43
Roman numerals, 262

S

Second person pronoun, 297
Semicolons
  to connect main clauses, 236–237
  in series, 234
  with quotation marks, 240, 356
Sentence fragments, 67–68, 143–146
Sentences
  complete, 143–146
  complex, 138–139, 343–344
  compound, 137–138, 343
  compound-complex, 139–140, 344
  declarative, 231
  definition of, 327–328
  originality in, 118–120
  position of adjectives and adverbs
    in, 201–202, 317–318
  preciseness in, 62–64, 151–155
  punctuating end of, 231–232
  punctuating interruptions within,
    222–229
  simple, 136–137, 343
  word order patterns in, 344–345
Sentence interrupter, 135, 144
Sentence modifiers, 134–135
Series
  adjectives in, 204–205
  adverbs in, 204–205
  nouns in, 189–190

punctuating, 232–235
verbs in, 198–199
Showing versus telling, 128–129
Similes, 130–131, 207–209
Simple predicate, 329
Simple sentences, 136–137, 343
Simple subject, 328
Simple tenses, 305–306
Single quotation marks, 239
Singular nouns, 291–292
Slang, 214–215
Sound effects
  nouns with, 190
  verbs with, 199
Source material, citing unusual,
  350–355
Specific words, using, 62–64
Spelling, 273–285
  plurals, 279–281
  adding prefixes and suffixes to
    root word, 277–279
  troublesome words, 284–285,
    373–388
  using *ei* and *ie* correctly, 276–277
Spontaneous writing, 35
Standard English, 176–178
States, capitalizing proper
  names of, 253
Statistics, using numbers in, 261
Step-by-step writing, 35–38
Subject(s), 293, 328–329
  complete, 328
  compound, 329
  simple, 328
Subject complements, 333–334
Subjunctive mood, 310
Subordinate clauses, 341
Subordinate noun clauses, 341
Subordinating conjunctions, 324–325,
  341, 342
Suffixes
  adding, to root word, 277–279
  using hyphens with, 270–271
Superlative form, 320
Supplemental information, enclosing,
  in parentheses, 227–228
Synecdoche, 209, 211–212
Synonyms, 162–163
  on computer software, 167–169
  in dictionary, 163–165
  in thesaurus, 165–166

"You want me to babysit?" Mike knew *that* wasn't in his job description.

"This kid was in an accident. I need you to keep him away from his mother until she's stabilized," Dr. Ana Ramírez said.

Mike gulped as Ana walked away. Saying no wasn't an option. He was going to look after the little boy even though he knew nothing about children.

The boy gripped the gurney that held his mother. The sight of the child broke Mike's heart.

"The doctors need to take care of your mom, buddy," Mike explained calmly. "Will you come with me?" When the boy nodded, Mike put him in bed in another room.

"Will you stay with me?" the kid whispered.

"As long as I can." Mike took the child's hand. For the first time since he'd started work at the hospital, he felt like he belonged here.

Books by Jane Myers Perrine

Love Inspired

The Path to Love #310
Love's Healing Touch #414

JANE MYERS PERRINE

grew up in Kansas City, Missouri, has a B.A. from Kansas State University and has an M.Ed. in Spanish from the University of Louisville. She has taught high school Spanish in five states and now she teaches in the beautiful hill country of Texas. Her husband is minister of a Christian church in Central Texas where Jane teaches an adult Sunday school class.

Jane was a finalist in the Regency category for a Golden Heart Award. Her short pieces have appeared in the *Houston Chronicle, Woman's World* and other publications. The Perrines share their home with two spoiled cats and an arthritic cocker spaniel. Readers can visit her Web site www.janemyersperrine.com.

Love's Healing Touch
Jane Myers Perrine

Steeple
Hill®

Published by Steeple Hill Books™

STEEPLE HILL BOOKS

Steeple
Hill®

ISBN-13: 978-0-373-87450-7
ISBN-10:   0-373-87450-2

LOVE'S HEALING TOUCH

Copyright © 2007 by Jane Myers Perrine

www.SteepleHill.com

Printed in U.S.A.

Come to me, all you that are weary and are carrying heavy burdens, and I will give you rest. Take my yoke upon you, and learn from me; for I am gentle and humble in heart, and you will find rest for your souls. For my yoke is easy, and my burden is light.

—*Matthew* 11:28-30

This book is dedicated to my family:

My parents, "Dr. Bob" and Martha Myers,
who took me to church, to Sunday school,
to youth group, to choir, to camp…

My big brother, Mike Myers, and my sister,
Patricia Myers Norton, who were such wonderful
Christian examples as I was growing up and are
wonderful friends now. Thank you.

And, as always, to my husband, George,
for his love and support—and for forty-one years
of inspirational sermons. I only slept
through a few, honey.

Chapter One

"Coming through," a nurse shouted as she pushed a crash cart down the hall of the emergency room.

Mike Fuller leaped away and landed in the path of a gurney being moved at breakneck speed. "Hey, you," shouted the orderly as he swerved around Mike, "grab the door to the elevator and keep it open."

Mike dashed toward the closing door and held it open until the orderly and his patient arrived. After the doors shut behind them, Mike again entered the E.R. and navigated through a hallway so crowded with patients on gurneys that there was only a narrow pathway between them. Ahead was the central desk where he'd been told to check in with the nursing staff.

No one was there.

A glance through the window on his right showed a waiting room filled with people. From outside the building, the siren of an approaching ambulance wailed, a sound which warred with the sounds inside the building—shouts of medical personnel and the bellow of the loudspeaker calling doctors and spewing forth codes. Amid the noise, medical staff hurried past, stopping in one cubicle or another.

Mike inhaled the stifling scent of disinfectant and looked around him. Even if he was only an orderly—well, *clinical assistant,* but everyone knew that meant *orderly—* he was here, in Austin University Hospital during the late shift. The commotion made him feel alive and want to be part of it. Unfortunately, he had no idea what he should do. Whether he was an orderly or a CA, he could do only what he was told. That had been pounded into him during his training and three-day orientation.

"Orderly."

He turned to see a beautiful woman watching him. She was short, but beneath her open lab coat—which meant she was a doctor so he shouldn't be noticing how attractive she was—were curves, delightful curves. Right now, he had too much going on in his life to even look at a woman, but only a dead man wouldn't check out this one. She was exactly the kind of woman he'd always liked in the past—except for that one mistake with tall, blond Cynthia.

This doctor's dark hair was pulled back in a round little knot. She had beautiful golden-brown skin and brown eyes, which, he realized, were glaring at him. In addition, her lovely pink lips were forming words. "I need you," she said as she pointed at him, "to check the vitals of the patients in the hall. Then get gloves and a bucket and start cleaning Exam 6."

"But—" Mike started.

"I know, that's housekeeping's job but with the mess

tonight, we're all going to have to pitch in on everything." Then she walked away, saying, "Thank you," over her shoulder as she entered one of the cubicles.

"I see you've met Dr. Ramírez, the head resident in the E.R.," said a nurse as she returned to her desk. "She can be demanding at times, but she's a great doctor." She glanced at Mike's name tag. "Welcome, Fuller. I'm Pat. We can really use you tonight."

"Is it always this busy?"

"Depends. Tonight there was a chemical spill south of town." She picked up a marker and started writing names on the dry-erase board. "We've got injuries from three traffic accidents and a gunshot wound in Trauma 1. And a family in a house fire." She shook her head. "A lot of other injuries I can't remember. A fairly normal night here."

Then she sat. "Might as well get you started. I'll have Williams show you around." Her gaze scanned the area. "Williams, come on over here."

When the brawny orderly arrived, he smiled to expose a gold front tooth. "Glad to see you, man. We're two orderlies short so I'm working too hard."

"Mike Fuller." He held out his hand.

"No time for that." Williams slapped Mike on the back. "Come with me."

"Dr. Ramírez wanted me to—"

"Check the vitals on the patients in the hall. Let's get going." The other orderly handed Mike a stethoscope. "You'll be supervised by the head nurse, but everyone in this place will give you orders. Just do anything anyone tells you to do, and you'll be fine."

The rest of the shift was spent in hard work, eight solid hours with only a few minutes break here and there.

Once he found himself whispering, "Dear Lord, please get me through this." The prayer surprised him because, right now, he and God weren't on the best of terms.

Once, as he pushed a gurney toward the elevator, he passed Dr. Ramírez making notes in a chart at the nurses' station.

"Look but don't touch," Williams warned him. "Yes, she's pretty but she's a doctor. She makes sure we all know that. Her body language says, 'Keep away.'"

Mike didn't read it that way exactly, but staying away from Dr. Ramírez was good advice, both personally and professionally.

After the first wave of those who'd been affected by the chemical spill had been taken care of, two ambulances arrived from a gang shooting. The vitals of the first kid to come in had dropped and the EMTs couldn't get the wounds to stop bleeding.

While everyone hovered around the gangbanger, Dr. Ramírez looked at a tiny Hispanic woman on another gurney who'd been an unlucky bystander, the EMT had said.

The doctor picked up the paramedic's notes and read them. Finished, she said, "I want that woman in there." She pointed at Mike then at Trauma 2.

He nodded, grabbed the gurney and pushed it into the cubicle Dr. Ramírez had indicated. On the count of three, he and a nurse's aide named Gracie moved the woman to the trauma bed. Gracie cut and peeled off the woman's blood-soaked clothing, then put her in a gown.

The patient closed her eyes, whimpered a little and bit her lower lip.

"Get a drip started," Dr. Ramírez told a nurse. Then, her voice soft and low, she said to the patient, *"¿Le duele mucho,* Señora Sánchez?"

Mike remembered enough of his college Spanish to know that she'd asked the elderly woman if she hurt. The patient nodded.

The doctor pulled the blanket and gown down to study the area on the patient's right shoulder the paramedics had treated. *"¿Aquí?"* She gently pressed on the area around the wound which had begun to seep blood.

"Ay, me duele mucho."

He could tell from her expression that the pressure had hurt the woman, a lot.

"Help me turn her on the left side," Dr. Ramírez said to Mike. "Slowly and carefully." Once Mrs. Sánchez was turned, Dr. Ramírez ran her hand over the patient's shoulder and back. "No exit wound," she said.

"Okay." Dr. Ramírez glanced up at Mike. "After the IV is going, take her to the OR. I'll call the surgeon."

Before Mike could transfer Mrs. Sánchez to a gurney, the doctor took Mrs. Sánchez's hand and said, *"Señora, todo va a estar bien. Cálmese. El cirujano es buena gente."*

Something about everything being okay, to calm down because the surgeon was a good guy, Mike translated for himself. The elderly woman took a deep breath and unclenched her fists as Mike rolled the gurney away.

Seemed Dr. Ramírez was more than a tough professional. She cared for her patients, understood what they needed. That was the kind of doctor he wanted to be, the kind he would be if he could get the money together to go back to med school.

Because he'd been in foster care, the state had paid college and medical school tuition. During four years of college and one of medical school, he'd roomed with four guys in a cheap apartment and worked part-time to make it through. But with the extra money he needed to rent the house, buy food and cover whatever expenses came up until his mother and little brother could get on their feet, he had to work full-time. No way he could go to medical school and support them, which he had to do. After his father had deserted them almost twenty years earlier, Mike was pretty much the head of the family.

He'd considered other options but couldn't afford the time off and the seven-hundred-dollar fee for paramedic training. With overtime, he'd make more as an orderly than teaching high school, plus he'd be in a hospital. All that made the decision to be an orderly easy.

By seven the next morning, he was so worn-out he moved in a fog. This was hard work, but he loved the feel of the hospital, the certainty that amid the commotion, all the patients would be helped, that he was doing good, meaningful, healing work.

The sight of Dr. Ramírez added a lot to that positive feeling. After all, he could appreciate the view, if only from a distance. At this moment and maybe for several years, with the mess that was his life, all he could enjoy was the view.

A week after his first day in the E.R., the phone rang in the small house Mike rented. When he answered, his younger brother, Tim, said in a shaky voice, "I had an accident, but it wasn't my fault."

Mike held the telephone tightly. "Are you all right?"

Tim cleared his throat and spoke without the quiver. "Yeah, I'm fine. It was minor."

Knowing Tim, a minor accident meant the car still had most of the tires and not *all* the glass was broken. "And you're really okay?"

"The paramedics checked me over. No problems."

"Where are you? How will you get home?"

"The cops'll bring me. Talk to you then." Tim hung up.

Mike disconnected the phone, put it on the end table, and dropped onto the sofa. He was glad Tim was okay. Mike whispered a quick, "Thank you, God, for taking care of Tim."

Sometimes Mike wondered if God ever got anything done while watching over Tim.

Even with a minor accident, the insurance company would total the car which meant he wouldn't get enough money to buy another anytime soon.

Mike hadn't been in a fix like this since he was eighteen. Of course, this time he wouldn't take a gun and hold up a convenience store, which showed he had learned something over the past six years. And this time most of the problems weren't his. He'd inherited them from other people.

Thank goodness the wreck hadn't happened last week when he'd moved from his apartment to this rental house. Now, for the first time in eight years, he'd be living with his family: his eighteen-year-old brother, who'd just been released from the state foster care system, and their mother, who was getting out of prison where she'd served time for fraud. He wouldn't want the living arrangements any other way, but it was still a big change.

He leaned back and put his feet up on a cardboard box marked Kitchen. He was supposed to take his cousin Francie to the doctor in an hour and the hospital had called and asked him to come in early for his shift. In a few days, he had to meet his mother's bus and get her settled in the house.

But he had no car.

No, he hadn't caused most of these problems, but he couldn't shift them to his much-loved but equally scatterbrained mother or his absentminded and immature younger brother.

He couldn't lean on Francie. She had enough to deal with, what with the baby coming, fixing up her house and finding time to be with her husband. Besides, he owed her big-time. She'd put her life on hold for him, taken the rap for him when he'd been young and almost irredeemably stupid.

No, he couldn't toss this on Francie, which left *him* in charge. Not a prospect that filled him with joy.

When the phone rang again, he picked it up and hoped it wasn't more bad news. "Hey."

"How's it going?" Francie asked.

"Tim wrecked my car."

"How is he?"

"He says he's fine, but I can't take you to the doctor's office. No car."

"I'll pick you up. After you bring me home, you can use my car as long as you need it."

"Francie, should you be driving? Didn't you say your doctor had some concerns?"

"The doctor hasn't told me to stop driving. Besides, if you have my car, I can't drive."

"But…"

Ignoring the interruption, Francie said, "You have to have a car. Brandon will agree with me. If it makes you feel better, you can be my chauffeur, take me anywhere I want to go," she said in her don't-argue voice. "See you in twenty minutes."

After Mike hung up the phone, he went to the window to watch for the cop car bringing Tim home.

When the police arrived, he moved to the front door and held it open for Tim. "Let me look at you," Mike said as his brother sauntered inside, bravado showing in his swagger.

"This time it wasn't my fault." When Tim stumbled a little and put his hand on the wall to steady himself, he lost a lot of his macho attitude. "It really wasn't, Mike."

Tim was tall with dark hair pulled back in a ponytail. Two years of lifting weights had put some muscle on him. Now he had wide shoulders with an even wider chip perched there.

As he scrutinized Tim, Mike saw several facial lacerations and a couple of bruises beginning to form. "Let me check you out."

"The paramedics cleared me. Why do you have to, Mike? You're not a doctor."

Mike drew in a breath at the painful reminder that no, he wasn't a doctor and wasn't likely to be one. "Just go along with me. Let me practice on you."

Tim shrugged then winced at the pain the movement brought. "Well, okay. If it makes you happy." With a grimace, he pulled the T-shirt over his head.

"How did it happen?" Mike ran his fingers down Tim's ribs, feeling for any knots or abnormalities and watching his brother's reaction.

"I was driving along Guadalupe and this other car didn't even slow down, ran right into the front of your car. The police said it was the other guy's fault. Ouch. What are you doing?"

"Almost through." Mike's hands brushed over a discolored diagonal line across Tim's chest. "Glad you were wearing your seat belt."

"For once." Tim nodded. "Guess I must have been listening to you."

"Also, for once." Mike looked into Tim's eyes. "You look okay, but you're going to be sore. Put some ice on your face."

"Yeah, sure." He limped off.

Mike shook his head and hoped Tim would grow up before he did any real damage to himself or someone else.

"Thanks for loaning me your car." Mike backed Francie's little red Focus out of the drive and turned south. He glanced at his cousin, taking warmth from her smile. Dark curls surrounded her face, a little fuller now in pregnancy.

As he stopped at a light, he noticed the worried frown on her face. "So how's little Ebenezer doing?"

"I wish you wouldn't call the baby that." She

laughed, the lovely, happy sound that always made Mike feel great. "A girl named Ebenezer? It would be terrible enough for a boy." She paused before adding in a worried voice, "As I said, I'm having a few physical problems. I'm pretty sure the doctor will tell me to cut down my activities until I deliver."

"What's going on?"

"Unless you're the father or the grandparents of this baby, you don't want to know." Her voice trembled a little.

"Francie, I took a course in genetics, embryology and reproduction my first and only year of medical school."

"Well, then I'd prefer not to tell you. It's kind of personal." She softened the words with a smile. "Anyway, that's why Brandon wanted you to drive me since he couldn't get off today. We're not sure what the doctor's going to say." Tears shimmered in her eyes. "We first-time parents worry a lot."

He signaled and turned on the ramp to Loop 1 or the MoPac as everyone in Travis County called the highway. "Take care of yourself, okay?"

"I do. And I will." She sighed. "So you might as well drive the car. Brandon or his family will drive me anywhere so I won't need it. If using my car makes you feel guilty, bring me some of Manny's good soup from the diner every week or two."

"Fine with me." He stopped at a light and turned toward her. "Mom's coming home next week. I'll be able to pick her up at the bus station."

"Are you excited to see her after—how long has it been? Seven, eight years?"

"Eight." He considered the question. "Hard to say. I'm excited *and* worried both. The three of us haven't lived together since she left. We'll be crowded in that tiny house." He stepped on the gas as the light changed. "Tim and I have to share the second bedroom. The owner has bunk beds in there." Mike grimaced. "Fortunately, Tim's still enough of a kid to like sleeping in the top bunk."

"Oh, and you're such an old man you couldn't get up there?"

"I don't want to get up there." He turned off on the Thirty-fourth Street exit and drove a block before he said, "There's another reason I'm worried." His hands beat out a rhythm on the steering wheel. "You know how much I love her, but how's Mom going to move on from prison life? She's never worked. What if she wants to forge paintings again?"

"That's hard, Mike." She shook her head. "I don't know. Guess you'll have to lay down the law, which is *not* something this family is good about accepting. I'll pray for you. You might do some praying for yourself."

He nodded. No use telling the woman who'd introduced him to church and helped him develop his faith that prayer had become only habit. It didn't work for him anymore.

Francie folded her hands over the roundness of her stomach and struggled to find a comfortable position. "How's Cynthia?"

"Don't know. Haven't seen her for a while." He signaled for a turn, carefully kept his gaze on the road and refused to meet her eyes. "Not a lot of traffic. We should get to the doctor's office in plenty of time."

"Don't change the subject." She pushed herself around in the seat to look at him. "What happened with Cynthia? I thought you two were made for each other."

"I thought so, too." He clenched his jaw, not wanting to say more, but he knew Francie wouldn't leave him alone until he explained. "When I told her I had to quit medical school to work, that we couldn't get married for two or three years, not until Mom and Tim are on their own, she said she wouldn't wait."

"Oh, I'm sorry."

"She wants to marry a doctor, not an orderly who lives with his mother and brother." Her departure had filled him with an emptiness it would take time to fill, so at least he wouldn't hurt every time he thought about her. "I don't blame her."

"You should blame her. She's a shallow ninny."

He didn't feel like it, but he had to laugh.

"Why aren't you angry? You should be furious," she said.

"I thought Christians didn't get angry."

"Well, in some situations, like when your former fiancée is being a shallow ninny, I think it's okay. For a while."

Well, then, yes, he'd been angry when he realized Cynthia hadn't wanted *him.* How could he have misjudged her feelings and character? How could she have fooled him so completely? Maybe he was the idiot for believing she loved him. It would be a long time before he opened himself to that kind of hurt again.

"When did this happen?" she asked.

"About a month ago. When I made the decision for

Mom to live with me instead of going to a halfway house, I told Cynthia."

"Well, I'm put out with her. I'd like to talk to that girl, set her straight about what's important in life."

"There's nothing you can do." He shook his head. "But Brandon and little Ebenezer are blessed to have you watching over them."

"I'm the one who's blessed. I have a wonderful husband whose family loves me and this baby coming. I have you and Tim and Aunt Tessie will be home soon. What more could I want?"

Ana Dolores Ramírez—Ana Dolores Ramírez, *M.D.*—tossed a newspaper off the only comfortable chair in the gray, dingy break room and fell into it. After taking a drink of her cold coffee, she leaned back, almost asleep.

What an evening: a terrible accident on I-35, and a fire in a crowded restaurant, all that in addition to the normal everyday emergencies like broken bones, ODs and injuries from gang and domestic violence. Why had she ever thought she wanted to work in an emergency room?

Well, yes, she knew. She loved the excitement, the challenge, the urgency to save people, the fight against death, bringing healing from tumult and despair.

Another reason was the memory of the doctors who had worked so hard to save her leg and the staff in the E.R. who had saved her mother's life.

"It's harder than it looks, isn't it?" Dr. Leslie Harmon, the Director of Emergency Services, entered the lounge.

Ana yawned. "Why are you here so late?"

"I was called in when the cases started to back up. I wanted to come in during a busy stretch on this shift to evaluate how the E.R. staff handles a heavy load."

"How'd we do?"

"Very well." Dr. Harmon rubbed her neck and rotated her shoulders. "I was particularly impressed with one of the CAs. The new guy—dark-haired, handsome kid—seemed really sharp. Who is he?"

Before she could reply, Ana's pager went off. Checking the message, she pulled herself up with a groan. "Not a very long break, but I've got to go." She gulped the last of her coffee and tossed the paper cup in the overflowing trash can as she headed back to the emergency room.

"What's coming in?" Ana pushed through the swinging doors, instantly alert. Paramedics pushed gurneys into the hallway while a clerk wrote the names of the incoming patients on the large white board at the central desk and nurses began to take vitals. Instant activity and a huge increase in the noise level.

"Another traffic accident," the new orderly said.

What *was* his name? She took a peek at his ID tag as she picked up a chart to make notes in. "Thanks, Fuller." As Dr. Harmon had said, he seemed pretty bright. More than just a strong body to lift and position patients. Earlier tonight, he'd recognized the signs of shock and taken quick action, more like a paramedic. He'd also helped with triage, stepping in when he saw how thin the staff was stretched. His assessments hadn't been perfect, but he'd done well enough with those minor cases. After she'd quickly doubled-checked his decisions, she'd been able to concentrate on major traumas.

As the injured were quickly evaluated and moved to treatment rooms, to surgery or to wait in the hall, Ana noticed a boy about six years old standing by one of the gurneys. The woman on the gurney was pale, her eyes closed. Blood stained the bandages the EMTs had applied to her forehead and chest.

When his mother's gurney was pulled into a cubicle, the boy grabbed the side of it and ran to keep up. "Mama," he sobbed.

"Fuller," Ana called.

After he pushed a gurney against the wall, Mike hurried over to where Dr. Ramírez stood next a gurney with a little boy hanging on to it.

"This kid came in with a family from an accident. Please take care of him."

"What? Babysit?" He didn't remember that on the job description. His duties were all medical and nursing.

"We need to keep him away from his mother until we can stabilize her. Find the paramedics. Ask them if he has family here or if there's someone coming to pick him."

"Shouldn't social services—"

"Yes, they should and they usually do take care of the children of our patients, but they're backed up and short-handed. Can't be here for a couple of hours. I need to treat his mother now. I'd appreciate your handling this."

While Mike watched and wondered what he should do next, she bent her knees to be on the child's level. "My name's Ana. What's your name?"

The child studied her solemnly. "Stevie."

"Well, Stevie, because your mommy was in an

accident, we need to patch her up a little. I promise we'll take very good care of her." Gesturing toward Mike, she added, "This young man is going to keep you company while we do that. Okay?"

Then she stood and turned back toward the trauma room.

What was he going to do? Mike gulped as he watched her walk away. Saying "no" wasn't an option. "But, Dr. Ramírez, I don't know anything about children," he protested.

"Do it," she said in the clear, firm voice Mike figured no one ignored. "Please."

He turned and started toward the boy as Dr. Ramírez entered a cubicle.

No one, not even lowly orderlies, ignored Dr. Ramírez's voice when it got that certain tone. For that reason, yes, he was going to look after the boy even though, no, he didn't know anything about children.

The boy slumped, his spine curved in exhaustion, but still he kept a tight hold on the gurney that held his mother.

The sight of the child broke Mike's heart. Even worse, he had no idea of what to do. Mike squatted so he was on the same level as the boy's sad eyes. "Hi, Stevie. Where's your family?"

The child shook with sobs and clung more tightly to the gurney.

That had gone really well. Trying again, Mike took the child's hand from the rail and held it although the boy fought to put it back. Was this the right thing to do?

"The doctors need to take care of your mother,

buddy," Mike explained calmly. "They can't get around very well with you here."

The child looked at his hand in Mike's then glanced up. "Is she going to be okay?"

"These are the best doctors in the world. They're going to do everything they can to make sure she's all right, but they need enough room to do that."

The boy nodded and stopped his efforts to pull his hand from Mike's.

Mike wiped the child's eyes and nose as he stuffed a handful of tissues in the kid's free hand. "Well, Stevie, do you want to thank the paramedics who helped you? They're really cool guys." When the boy didn't resist, Mike led him into the hall.

"The paramedics are down there." When Mike pointed the boy nodded. "I'm going to talk to them now."

Yawning, Stevie pulled away to wiggle onto a chair. He leaned back and closed his eyes as Mike walked toward the emergency entrance. The flashing red lights of ambulances pulling up outside lit up the area in flickering streaks of red.

"Hey, guys," Mike greeted the paramedics, keeping his voice low. "Did you bring that kid in?" He gestured toward Stevie.

"Yeah, an accident on MLK. The family in a van was hit when a drunk ran a light."

"What are the kid's injuries?"

"Didn't find anything serious. Probably should have that cut on his forehead checked later, but that's it."

"Do you have a last name? Any identification? Is there family around?"

"The family members who came in with him are all in the E.R., pretty badly injured. The cops are running the name down and getting in touch with relatives," the older paramedic said.

"Thanks."

As he walked back down the corridor, he saw Stevie had fallen asleep. Mike picked him up and carried him to the E.R.

"Orderly," Dr. Yamaguchi, the on-call orthopedic surgeon, said as Mike entered the department. "Now."

Mike nodded at Stevie. "Dr. Ramírez wants me to take care of this kid. His mother's in the E.R. and we can't find a family member."

Dr. Yamaguchi glanced at the kid. "Put him in the emergency bed on the end and check on him when you can, but you have to transport patients."

"Yes, sir."

For the next few hours, Mike checked on Stevie whenever he wasn't pushing gurneys or following the instructions from the medical staff.

Once when Mike entered the cubicle where Stevie had been sleeping, Dr. Ramírez was trying to examine him. Stevie had pulled away from her and cowered as far away from the doctor as possible.

"Hey, buddy, it's okay. Remember those great doctors I told you about?" Mike asked. Stevie nodded. "This is one of them."

"Will you stay?" the kid whispered.

"As long as I can." Mike took Stevie's hand.

"Guess you're here for a while," Dr. Ramírez said.

"Guess so." The prospect would have alarmed Mike

a few hours ago but not now. For the first time since he started work, he felt as if he belonged here, as if he had an important role to play and this was part of it.

"Orderly," came a shout from another exam room. "Transport to X-ray."

Then again, maybe not.

Chapter Two

"Good job, Fuller." Dr. Ramírez's voice echoed through the now-empty hall in front of the curtained cubicles of the E.R.

Her voice wasn't exactly friendly, but she didn't sound as if she were ready to chew him out.

"I appreciate the way you pitched in tonight, picking up wherever you were needed." She pulled off her latex gloves, tossed them in the hazardous-waste bin and said, "Thanks for taking care of the boy until his uncle showed up."

Then she smiled at him. Not a big smile. Just a slight turning up of her lips. Still, it was a great look compared to her usual serious expression. Now her eyes sparkled a bit and a dimple appeared on her cheek. For an instant, she assumed the appearance of a human being, a real person, not a doctor.

Probably noticing his confused look, she allowed her usual professional expression to slide across her features again. Then she said in a voice bit softer than her usual this-is-what-you-have-to-do tone, "Fuller, let me buy you a cup of coffee. There's something I want to discuss with you. Purely professional. Nothing personal."

He wondered what *purely professional* meant and why she had given him that smile. Probably didn't mean a thing to her but it was the first almost-full smile he'd ever seen from her. It was a dazzler.

If he wanted to keep things professional, he shouldn't join Dr. Ramírez for coffee. Meeting Dr. Ramírez outside the E.R. seemed odd to him, but he deserved a little bit of the good stuff—and Dr. Ramírez was really good stuff.

"Yes, ma'am, um, Doctor…Ramírez." He hadn't babbled like that since he'd asked Maribel Suárez out when he was a shrimp in the tenth grade. He cleared his throat and said, "I have to restock a room. Meet you in the cafeteria."

When she left, he checked cabinets in Exam 1, made sure equipment had been replaced in the correct cabinets, and replaced gauze, tape and other supplies that were low. As he worked, he replayed the incident with Dr. Ramírez and felt like an idiot. Since Cynthia broke up with him, he'd been questioning everything in his life, but there was nothing unusual here. The idea she might put a move on him in the middle of a hospital cafeteria was crazy…but very appealing.

He almost slapped himself for that last thought.

Finished, he stripped off his gloves, washed his hands and splashed water on his face. Then he ran damp fingers through his hair as he attempted to make out his reflection in the paper towel holder.

"Hot date, Fuller?" the tall, balding RN asked him

as he came through the curtains. What was his name? Oh, yeah, Sam Mitchelson. "Couldn't help but hear the invitation from back there."

"Just a cup of coffee. Like she said, 'Nothing personal.'" Mike tossed the towel away and moved toward the door.

"That's more than any of us, including doctors, have been asked to share. You must possess something special to rate that."

Mike grinned. "Only good looks, high intelligence and great charm."

"Don't forget she's a doctor, Fuller," he said to Mike's back. "If you want to keep your job, never disagree with a doctor."

Mike left the E.R. and headed toward the cafeteria, passing a row of wheelchairs outside X-ray and dodging a crowd getting off the elevator as he walked down the main corridor.

Macho posturing aside, Mike reminded himself again she'd asked him for coffee, only coffee, not a date. As he'd told himself a million times, he had no interest in a relationship and no time, but his response showed he found Dr. Ramírez very attractive. His reaction to her had him thinking that Cynthia hadn't completely killed his interest in women.

Just past the hallway to ICU, he turned to open the door to the cafeteria. The usual mix of medical personnel and family members of patients sat at the square tables. Straight ahead by the windows was Dr. Ramírez with another doctor.

Maybe this wasn't a good idea.

* * *

From her table, Ana watched Fuller enter the cafeteria. Tall and handsome with broad shoulders, he looked great in scrubs. That was pure observation, not attraction, she told herself. His height and those broad shoulders made it easier for him to move and transport patients.

When he saw her, he paused and looked a little uncertain. His confusion was probably because Dr. Craddock, the chief of staff, sat next to her, flirting with her. At least thirty years older than she and married, the fool was flirting.

The closer the orderly got to the table, the more obvious Craddock's attention became. Thank goodness they would soon be interrupted.

Fuller stopped when he saw Craddock still talking. He backed away, but she beckoned him forward with a wave.

As he reached the table, Fuller said, "Hello, Dr. Craddock." At her gesture, he dropped into the chair next to Craddock. She pushed a cup of coffee closer to Fuller.

"Hello." Dr. Craddock studied the orderly with one eyebrow raised. "And you are?"

"Mike Fuller. I'm a CA in the E.R." He poured cream in his coffee and stirred it.

"Oh? An orderly?" Craddock's voice and that still-raised brow left no doubt he felt the orderly shouldn't be sitting with two doctors.

"I asked Mr. Fuller to join me. I need to discuss something with him." She smiled at Craddock and gave his hand a sisterly pat. That should put him in his place.

Craddock stood. "I see that I'm the one who's not needed here."

"Dr. Craddock doesn't approve of your ignoring the hospital social order." Fuller watched the older man move away to join a table of doctors.

"Doctors can be a rigid bunch." She picked up her coffee and took a sip. "But that's not what I wanted to talk to you about." She rubbed her thumb along the side of the cup before she looked up at him. "Fuller, I've watched how you handle situations. You're intelligent and capable."

"Thank you."

He must wonder where this conversation was going. Had she thoughtlessly put him in an awkward situation? Probably so. That's what she got for pushing herself into other people's lives. They weren't always grateful.

"You're an excellent clinical assistant."

He nodded.

"You must have a high-school diploma or a GED or you wouldn't be working here."

He nodded again and gazed over her shoulder toward something behind her.

"Do you have any college hours?"

He scrutinized her face for a moment. "I'm not comfortable with this conversation, Dr. Ramírez. Is there a reason for your questions?" he said, politely but clearly setting boundaries.

"Yes, there is, and, honestly, I want to encourage you."

He took a gulp of coffee.

"Do you have any college hours?" The question sounded rude. She really needed to work on her delivery.

He paused before nodding, again not meeting her eyes.

She was stymied. He clearly wasn't going to give her

any more information than he had to, and he didn't have to give her any. "I know I have no right to ask you, but I'd really appreciate it if you'd answer a question or two." After a pause when the orderly didn't say a word, she added, "Please."

When he raised an eyebrow but didn't say no, she asked, "How many college hours?"

"I have a degree." He drank the rest of his coffee, placed the cup on the table and pushed the chair back.

"Please don't go." She put her hand on his.

The touch was *not* the friendly pat she'd intended. As she pulled her hand away, she glanced up to gauge his reaction. His eyes held a spark of interest before he looked down at his empty cup. The man had gorgeous brown eyes, a slight stubble on his cheeks and a square chin. A pleasant glow spread through her. Obviously, more was involved in her feelings for Fuller than mentor for student. Why hadn't she noticed that before she asked him to meet her for coffee?

"Dr. Ramírez, I prefer not to continue this discussion." His words were polite but, when he stood, he glared at her, as much of a glare as an orderly dared give a doctor. She couldn't blame him.

"I'm sorry, Fuller. I don't mean to make you feel uneasy." She forced her attitude back to the purely professional. "I don't have a gift for subtlety, and I know I don't have the right to expect you to sit down and talk to me, but I'd really be grateful if you would."

At least he didn't bolt for the door. Instead, he pulled his chair back to the table, sat and asked in a voice that showed more than a little exasperation, "Why?"

"Fuller, I'm impressed with you."

She tapped on her cup. When she looked into his eyes, he immediately lowered them. "You are intelligent and have so much ability. I'd like to encourage you to go back to school, to pursue a career in medicine or science."

"Thank you." He fiddled with the handle of the cup.

A lot of playing with their cups, Ana noted. Obviously neither of them felt comfortable with the exchange.

"Have you thought about being a doctor?" she asked bluntly in an effort to hurry the conversation along.

"Tried med school. One year. Didn't work out."

"It didn't work out?" she repeated.

Ignoring her question, he said, "Thank you for the coffee, Dr. Ramírez," placing great emphasis on *doctor.*

"You're welcome."

This time he did bolt for the door.

The conversation had not gone the way she'd planned it. She'd acted pushy and nosy. She'd sounded like a superior expecting the orderly to comply with whatever she demanded.

Obviously he had no desire to discuss this or anything with her. Why should he? He seemed like a very private person, just like her father.

No matter. She wasn't about to give up on Fuller. He should be a doctor or a nurse or a medical technician, not an orderly, and she was going to help him see that.

As *her* mother had said, Ana always had to have a project. Fuller seemed to be her latest one.

She'd find out what he meant by, "Didn't work out," another time.

* * *

Mike strode back to the E.R. to finish his shift.

What right did the woman have to interrogate him? To expect him to sit there while she dug for personal information? Why hadn't he left earlier?

He threw a swinging door open with one hand and watched it hit the wall with a satisfying smack. But when he got to the E.R., an RN shouted, "Fuller, transfer."

He didn't have time to think about Dr. Ramírez's prying now. Maybe he should remember the other parts, the good parts: he'd had coffee with a beautiful woman and all the male staff was jealous. In addition, Dr. Ramírez had complimented him on his intelligence and how well he was doing. After the recent problems in his life, it made him feel a lot better.

Only two hours later, Mike was asleep at home when the phone rang. He pulled himself out of bed and dragged his tired body into the living room. Light filtered through curtains, which made it possible for him to find the phone on the coffee table but not before he narrowly avoided falling over a box of clothes.

"Good morning," Francie said. "Will you please drive me to church this morning? Wake your brother up and bring him, too."

Mike glanced at his watch through eyes still blurry with sleep. He groaned. "I've only been asleep for an hour. Why don't you let me sleep a few more?"

"Because church will be over by then. You can take a long nap when you get home. Or you can sleep through the sermon."

"Reverend Miller won't like that."

"But God will be glad you're there. Besides, you said you'd take me wherever I need to go."

"Aren't you supposed to be taking it easy?"

"The doctor said church is fine as long as I don't drive."

"What about Brandon?" Could he think of any more reasons to go back to bed? If this one didn't work, he'd have to go, because he could never tell Francie no.

"He's at a training session in Dallas," she explained patiently. "Well?"

"Okay, I'll pick you up at ten."

"Thanks. Bring Tim."

Driving her to church was the least he could do. When he was eighteen, he'd held up a convenience store. He groaned, hating to relive that act and its consequences. To save him, so he could be a doctor, Francie had confessed and was serving time before he could take the blame himself. They were the same height and he'd worn a ski mask and jacket so she looked like the person in the surveillance tape.

He'd made a terrible, stupid mistake, and she'd paid for it. He still struggled to figure out why he'd done it—heredity, Francie would say—and to make it up to her somehow.

Yes, he owed her everything. He could never turn her down.

After a shower, he shook Tim awake. "We're going to church."

Tim threw back the sheet. "Terrific," Tim said as he sat up on the bed, dropped to the floor and stood to stretch. "I've missed church."

"Why didn't you say something?" Mike never knew what his brother was thinking. Of course, Tim never talked about stuff that was important to him. They were a lot alike that way.

"I like sleeping in, too."

At ten forty-five, the cousins were seated together in the sanctuary. Bowing his head, Mike hoped to be filled with the peace this time of silent meditation used to bring him, but it still eluded him. Maybe he was out of practice. Maybe he'd missed too many services. Whatever the reason, the Spirit didn't fill him. He had a feeling it wasn't the Spirit's fault.

He prayed for his family and patients. He knew those requests had been heard, but when he prayed for guidance for himself he felt cold and alone.

Where was God when he needed him so much?

After church, Mike pulled the car into the drive of Francie's house and stopped.

"Why don't you come in?" Francie said as Tim got out of the backseat. "You can make some sandwiches and bring me one." She took Tim's extended hand to get out of the car. Once standing, she went around to the driver's side, opened the door, grabbed Mike's arm and pulled him toward the house.

Once inside, she yawned and said, "I'm going to bed. Would you fix us lunch?" She'd taken a few steps down the hall when she turned to say to Mike, "Before you do that, come with me to look at the baby's room. Brandon painted it last week, and I added a few touches."

Mike followed her down the hall and stopped to look into the bright yellow nursery. On the walls, Francie had hung pictures of whimsical animals in both brilliant and pastel hues. His mother would love this, would want to add a few fanciful ideas of her own.

For a minute, Mike was overwhelmed by the memory of how he and Cynthia had planned to have three children. Their babies could have had a room like this. Well, knowing Cynthia, she wouldn't have liked purple dragons or turquoise birds, but they would have had a nursery. When he noticed Francie studying him, he said, "It's great."

"Hey, Mike, how do you turn on a gas stove?" Tim called.

"Don't do a thing. I'll be right there." Mike pulled himself from his reverie to hustle to the kitchen. If he allowed Tim to light the stove, he might have to explain to Brandon where he'd been when Tim blew up the house.

After he took a tray back to Francie, Mike settled in Brandon's chair in the living room. In no time, he was asleep.

"Hey, Fuller." Dr. Ramírez caught him in the hall outside the E.R. the next evening. "Sorry if I intruded yesterday. I didn't mean to invade your privacy, but…" She bit her lip. "Anyway, I'm sorry."

"Thank you." It was hard to hold a grudge against her. Mike figured she'd be angry if he told her she was so attractive any man would forgive her for anything. And that lip-biting part was distracting. Very distracting.

When Mike moved back toward Trauma 3, he saw Mitchelson watching Dr. Ramírez as she walked away.

"How'd the cup of coffee go?" the nurse asked with a grin. "Was that all? Just a cup of coffee?"

"Just a cup of coffee. She wanted to talk about my work as an orderly."

"Did she tell you that you should be a doctor or nurse?"

Mike glared at Mitchelson. "How did you know she said that?"

"Because we all think so. Can't figure out why you're not in med school, but we're glad we got you in the E.R. and hope you won't leave anytime soon." When his beeper went off, Mitchelson hurried away before Mike could say a word.

"Thank you," he shouted down the hall. Mitchelson waved back.

"Fuller," Dr. Ramírez called in her doctor voice. "Transfer, please."

Back to normal. No more compliments, only a lot of lifting and hard work.

Three days later his mother's bus arrived at 10:00 a.m. which gave Mike plenty of time to clean up after his shift and drive to the bus station.

Before she went to prison, Mom had looked like her paintings: full of life and sparkle, happiness shining from her. She'd changed during those years. Hard to remain vibrant in prison, she'd explained on his frequent visits, as if he couldn't guess that.

He waited on the platform, surrounded by the noise and the strong fumes from diesel engines.

When she got off the bus, he hugged her, noticing she was thinner than he'd remembered.

She pulled away to study him and put her hand on his cheek. "It's so good, so absolutely marvelous to be here," she whispered. "I can't believe I'm out of prison and back with my boys."

"I'm glad, too, Mom."

She still had an innocent face, which had helped her market her forgeries but hadn't fooled the judge. Now her skin bore lines and wrinkles, but the beauty remained.

After she pointed out her one shabby suitcase, Mike handed the baggage claim to the bus driver and carried it to the car.

"I'm so tired of wearing trousers." His mother smoothed her jeans. "Boring, boring, boring, my dear, and not at all feminine." She glared at her white shirt. "Do you still have my dresses?"

"Yes, Francie stored everything while you were gone." Mike started the car and backed out of the parking place. "But it's been eight years. They're probably out of style."

"Good clothing never goes out of style."

He grinned as her sudden air of certainty and confidence. Yes, it was great to have her home.

After he stopped at several lights, she said, "My, my, the traffic is even worse than before." She chattered on about how things had changed in Austin while he drove.

When he pulled up in front of the small house, she said, "What's this? We aren't living here, are we?"

"I know it's not very big, but it's what I can afford."

The shrubbery needed to be trimmed, but the house appeared neat enough on the outside. With white paint that flaked only in a few areas, black shutters, and a porch the size of a postage stamp, it had a homey aspect. But it was small, a fact even more evident when his mother opened the front door and stepped inside.

The living room held a short sofa, two folding chairs and a television on an ugly metal stand. "It came furnished," he explained.

But she didn't notice the furniture when she saw the paintings she'd forged, the ones Francie had saved for her, covering the walls. His mother had loved the impressionists and these glowed with the brilliance of color and light, illuminating the room. She turned to take them in, reaching out her arms to bathe in the beauty. Then she walked slowly toward one and touched her fingers to the rough surface.

"Oh, thank you," she said. "I'd forgotten how much I love these."

After a few minutes, she shook herself and walked through the rest of the house. First, she wandered back to the kitchen which had maybe five feet of counter space, a few cabinets and a card table with three wobbly chairs.

"I fix most of the meals in the microwave," Mike said.

"Then I'll do the cooking," Mom said.

"I gave you the master—well, the larger—bedroom." He led her toward the door, shoved it open and followed her in to put the suitcase on the bed.

She turned to consider the double bed, one dresser and bare walls. "White," she said. "All the walls are white."

"Tim and I can paint them. You choose the color."

"Thank you. I'd like that." She left the room and

looked into the bathroom and the other bedroom. "You and Mike both sleep in here?"

"We'll be fine, Mom. We're brothers. We'll get to know each other better after the years apart."

She nodded again as he followed her back to her bedroom.

"This is a nice part of town. There's an H-E-B grocery store only a block from here. It's an easy walk. And there's a park nearby."

She placed her hand on his arm and patted it. "Mike, this is fine. I appreciate you opening your house to us. We've been apart so long. I'm glad we're together." She smiled and for a moment it was her old smile. "You're a good brother and a fine son." She dropped her hand. Opening the suitcase, she placed her things in a small pile on the bed before she opened the closet.

When she saw what was inside, she pulled out one dress, sat on the end of the bed and stared into the closet. In her lap she held a gown of brilliant green with a shimmering pattern of gold. Tears streamed down her cheeks.

"My clothes," she said. "All of my favorite things are here. Thank you." She stood and embraced Mike.

When Mike opened a drawer in the dresser to show her the jewelry Francie had kept and a small bottle of his mother's favorite perfume he'd bought for her, she cried harder.

"Thank you, son. You've given me a wonderful homecoming."

Oh, boy. Too much emotion for him. When the phone rang, he gave his mother an awkward pat on her back. "I'll get that." He pulled away but touched her shoulder, which seemed to satisfy her. Then he ran into the living room and grabbed the receiver.

"Yes, I can come in early today," he said as he checked his watch. "I'll be in by three."

He hung up the phone, placed his hand on one of the paintings and closed his eyes. With his mother here, the house was filled with turbulence. He could feel it—the tingle of her strong personality, the scent of her musky perfume, the rough swipes of paint in the painting under his fingers.

Yes, Hurricane Tessie had hit. As calm as she seemed today, his mother was always a force to be reckoned with.

He'd let her settle in today, but tomorrow he'd have to talk to her about getting a job to satisfy the conditions of her parole and because they just plain needed that income.

He thought how tired and how much older she'd looked when she got off the bus, about her joy at seeing her clothes and her art. Then he shook his head as he remembered her tears. His mother never cried.

Maybe he'd wait a few days before he suggested she find work.

Chapter Three

Almost midnight a few days later, and a moment of quiet during a long shift in the E.R.

Mike headed outside and leaned back against the wall of the hospital. He took a deep breath, held it and let it out. Sometimes he was overwhelmed by the smell and the stress of the E.R. Tonight it was more than he could handle. After a few minutes and more cleansing breaths, he turned to go inside, walking back through the waiting room and the door into the E.R.

"When did you come in today?" Williams, the big orderly, asked as he pushed an empty gurney.

Stretching, Mike answered, "Three."

"Double shift, huh? You must need the money."

"Don't we all?" He covered a yawn before he went back into Exam 5 to clean the empty room.

"Why are you doing that?" Williams said. "House-keeping's supposed to do that."

"Because they're running behind and I don't have anything else to do."

"You make us all look bad." Williams headed toward the central desk.

As he dumped the paper bed cover in the trash, Mike realized how beat he was after nine hours of the double shift. With his mother back home, Mike could work longer hours because he didn't have to worry about Tim. Before her arrival, Mike had covered only the night shift, eleven to seven. That way he could get his brother dinner, make sure Tim got up in the morning, and push him out to look for a job. Hard to do all that between a couple of naps.

Now Mike could work more hours to cover his mother's expenses until she got work. Maybe earn enough to catch up with the bills.

"You said last week your mother was coming back to Austin. How's that going?" Mitchelson came into the room.

"Okay. She got here Wednesday and is settling in." He pulled on a new pair of gloves and began disinfecting the counters.

"Where was she?"

"The women's prison in Burnet." When he turned to throw a paper towel into the bin, he saw Dr. Ramírez standing next to the curtain. Her mouth was open a little. She had obviously heard what he'd said.

Actually, it was a good thing she'd caught the conversation. She might as well know he wasn't the man she thought he was. Maybe she'd stop nagging him and leave him alone. A mother in prison wouldn't fit into her idea of what a doctor should be or the kind of man she'd date.

A man she'd date? Where had that thought come

from? The one cup of coffee last week hadn't been an invitation, wasn't meant to be a date of any kind. No, there wasn't any chance of a relationship between them other than doctor-orderly. But, even if the smallest possibility of that existed, the information about his mother would completely scuttle it. An ex-con in the family tended to do that.

"Transfer, Fuller." Dr. Ramírez moved back to the other operating room.

Five minutes later, the injured from an automobile accident and two gunshot victims came in. All needed immediate stabilization and surgery.

He was working calmly until he saw one of the injured was a four-year-old girl, her pink T-shirt smeared with blood and her leg at an angle he didn't like. He forced himself to grin at her as he untied her little sneakers. They had kittens on them, kittens covered with blood.

"Hey, kid," he said. "My name's Mike. Your shirt says you're Naomi."

"My leg," she whispered. "Hurts. A lot."

"I bet it does, buddy. The doctor will be out in a few minutes. She'll help you."

"Fuller," Dr. Ramírez called.

Mike started to move away when Naomi grabbed his hand. "Don't go," she said.

"I'll be back as soon as I can." He wished he had something to give Naomi to keep her company. He took a clean towel, tied it in a knot and handed it to Naomi. "This is Whitey, the friendly polar bear who lives in the hospital and keeps little girls company."

Naomi took the towel and hugged it.

"Nicely done, Fuller," Dr. Ramírez said from the doorway. "Have you thought about working in pedes?"

He faced her. "Need a transfer?"

"Yes." Dr. Ramírez strode toward Naomi then gently pushed the hair from the child's forehead. "Move this gurney into Exam 4 and take her mother upstairs."

By 5:00 a.m., the hospital had quieted again. He'd transferred four victims to the operating room then to their rooms once they came out of recovery. And he'd taken one body to the morgue. His least favorite transport.

Not a hard night in the E.R., but two shifts added up to a backache and the need to relax for a few minutes. He wished he had time for a nap, but when he got to the break room, another orderly snored on the sofa.

He took a thermos from his locker and poured the last of the coffee into his cup. With a groan, he settled down in the only comfortable chair in the room and leaned his head back.

Barely a few breaths short of falling asleep, he opened his eyes to see Dr. Ramírez put a can of soda on the table and drop in the chair across from him. She seemed to be favoring her right leg and was rubbing her thigh almost surreptitiously.

"Old football injury," she said with a slight smile before she nodded at his thermos and asked, "Saving money?"

"I can't take the coffee someone makes in the E.R."

"I know." She held up her Coke. "Tastes like it's spiked with old motor oil."

"My mother makes terrific coffee. I'd rather have it than pay for it in the cafeteria."

"I heard you say your mother is home from prison."

He nodded and shifted in the chair.

"What was she in for?"

"Forgery."

"Checks?"

"Paintings."

"Oh, an artist." She took a drink of Coke. As she lifted her chin, Mike watched a wisp of hair that had come loose to curl on her neck. He'd never thought of Dr. Ramírez as having curls or long hair…and he'd better *not* think about that.

She put the can down and licked her top lip with the tip of her tongue. The motion wasn't meant to be seductive, just cleaning up after the last drop, but all Mike could think of for a few seconds was her lips, round and soft and pink. She'd spoken for several seconds before Mike realized she'd said something.

"I'm sorry. I'm falling asleep. What did you say?"

"My uncle was in prison." She stood and put the can in the recycle bin.

"Oh?" He swiveled to look at her.

"It was really hard on his family."

That was all she said. She didn't offer sympathy or platitudes or advice or dig further into his life. She only commented on a shared experience. And she didn't say, "I know how you feel." Because no one really did.

"Thank you."

"Fuller," came a male voice from the hall. "Transfer."

"And the fun keeps on coming," Dr. Ramírez said. She gave Mike a smile, that little smile that was only a curving of her lips. It made the long shift seem not nearly as bad.

* * *

Ana stretched and massaged the muscles in her neck. She hated the night shift, but that was what she had to cover if she wanted to learn everything she could about emergency medicine.

Besides, her schedule wasn't all that bad: on twenty-four hours, off twenty-four, with no more than seventy hours a week. It allowed her time with her family, time to study and a few hours to rest.

The pain in her thigh was worse than it had been for years. She must have twisted her leg. Now all she wanted to do was elevate it for a few hours. Not an easy thing to do in the E.R.

In the long run, she was sorry she'd heard the conversation between Fuller and the other orderly. Better for her not to know about the private lives of anyone she worked with.

So why *was* she interested in Fuller? Had she made him her project of the year? Usually her projects were easier to handle, more open and not nearly as attractive as Fuller. Wait. When had she started to think of Fuller as attractive?

Well, what woman wouldn't? He had great longish dark hair and a terrific smile, although few people over the age of ten saw it. What she usually saw was a face clear of expression with a hint of anger in the depths of his dark eyes. The charm and the anger made him, well, interesting, as if he had dimensions he never shared.

Add to that his broad shoulders, great build and the black stubble that covered his chin and cheeks by the end of the shift, and—¡caramba!—what's not to like?

Which meant it was time to get back to the E.R. before she had any more completely unprofessional thoughts about a man with no ambition. Maybe in other people's minds, Fuller wouldn't be seen as lacking in ambition. He worked hard, made good decisions, was great with kids. On the other hand, as an orderly he wasn't using every bit of his ability. Why wasn't he in school? Her brothers always told her she was an education snob, and maybe she was, but she hated it when people didn't push themselves to live up to their potential.

Besides that, he was a man who had clearly but politely told her to leave him alone, a man she had absolutely no interest in.

None at all.

"Hey, *chica,*" Enrique, Ana's sixteen-year-old brother, said as she entered her family's home that evening. "What's for dinner?"

"What does it matter, Quique? You eat everything I put on the table. You'd eat lizards if I could catch enough to fill you up." She grabbed him in a hug that became a wrestling match when he tried to slip away.

"Sounds good."

"And you never put on a pound." Ana glanced at his skinny body then down at her rounder hips. "I don't think we come from the same family."

She headed for the kitchen and glanced back at him. "Where are you going?" As if she didn't know. He was wearing baggy shorts, a Spurs T-shirt and his favorite Nike runners.

"Pickup game at Rolando's."

"Dinner is at seven. Be home." She glared at him, well aware that he'd probably grab a bite with Rolando's family before he meandered home in a few hours. "I'd like to see you sometime."

"Mira." He held out his arms and rotated slowly in front of her. "Look, here I am."

"Just go." She waved as he ducked out the door.

"Ana, is that you?"

Hearing her father's voice from the kitchen, she hurried toward it. "Hi, Papi."

Her father sat at the table doing a crossword puzzle. He and Enrique looked so much alike. Both six feet tall and slender. Her father had streaks of white in his still-full, dark hair. Before her mother's death almost a year ago, he'd been a quiet and often moody man. Since then, he'd retreated deeper, lost any spring in his step and his shoulders were more rounded. He was still a handsome man but not a happy one, as much as he tried to hide it.

"What's a five-letter word for *hackneyed?* Ends in an *E.*"

"How 'bout *stale* or *trite?*"

"Those might fit." His pen hovered over the folded newspaper.

She pulled an apron from the pantry, tied it around her, and continued to watch her father. He was always doing puzzles. Crossword and Sudoku and anagrams. He had a basket by his chair with puzzle books in it and spent most of his time at home solving those puzzles. He'd become a hermit.

"Papi, you have to get out more." She picked up a

dishrag and squirted detergent on it. "Let's go to a movie next Saturday."

He didn't answer, just stared at the crossword clues.

The kitchen cabinets were dark walnut; the linoleum floor that was supposed to look like bricks was well-worn. This place felt a lot more like home than the tiny efficiency she'd recently rented a few blocks from the hospital and spent so little time in. She squeezed out the dishrag and started cleaning the white tile counters.

When she finished, she said, "I thought I'd fix enchiladas tonight." She pulled down a jar of tomato sauce. Her mother had always made her sauce from scratch, with real tomatoes, but this would just have to do. Except for her father, no one could tell the difference. After eating his wife's cooking for thirty-five years, he knew homemade sauce from canned.

Ana's philosophy about cooking was if she covered every dish with cheese and onion, they tasted great. Well, not flan, of course. Because her father was diabetic, she used low fat cheese and watched his portions although he did pretty well keeping track himself.

"Who's going to be here tonight?"

Her father stood, held on to the back of the chair before he walked across the room. He was only sixty-one but appeared much older. A day at the store wore him out now. She'd made him go to the doctor but he said nothing was wrong with her father, not physically. How long did it take to recover from the death of a wife? Obviously, a year wasn't enough.

"Robbie and Martita are coming with Tonito and the baby. She said she'd bring a cake," he said.

"Luz, Quique and Raúl also?" Ana listed the other siblings who lived in Austin. Her brother Robbie, his wife and their small family were fun to be around, and Martita made wonderful cakes. "I want to be sure so I can make enough enchiladas for everyone and still leave some for your lunch Saturday." If Quique didn't eat them when he went through the refrigerator later.

"Well, Raúl will probably stop by. He's between gigs."

Raúl was always between gigs. Fortunately, he had a steady job at the family's furniture store Robbie managed. "Is he between girlfriends?"

"I'm never between girlfriends," Raúl said as he came in from the garage.

"Oh, yes, I know. Women always throw themselves at you. Poor dears." Ana pulled tortillas from the fridge. Store-bought tortillas, another shortcut her mother would never have considered.

"*¿Cómo no?* Why not? They can't resist my smile or my guitar."

What was he going to do in the future? Raúl floated through life, making it on his dark good looks, great smile and personality, plus a dab of talent.

"Hey, Ana, *no te preocupes.* Don't worry."

"Why would I worry about you?" She took out a slab of white cheese and began to grate it.

"Because you always worry about me and Luz and Quique. We're all young." He pulled one of his guitars from the hall closet and came into the kitchen. "We'll grow up someday."

Ana rolled her eyes. "I hope so."

"We'll never be as responsible as you are." He ran

his fingers over the strings. "After all, you were born responsible, but you don't *always* have to worry about us."

"Yes, she does, Raúl." Her brother Robbie followed his five-year-old son, Tonito, into the kitchen and placed a cake on the counter. "That's what Ana does. Worries about her family. She's a rescuer."

"Someone has to do it," Robbie's wife, Martita, said. "It's a full-time job. I refuse to take it on." She handed Marisol, the baby, to Robbie and sat at the kitchen table. "But sometime, *chica,* you are going to have to stop taking care of your family and find a life of your own."

A life of her own? An interesting concept. Taking care of her family was, well, habit—one she'd never tried to break until she realized how dependent her father was getting on her. That, and the short drive from her little efficiency to the hospital were the reasons she'd moved. Not one to make changes easily, she felt this one was enough for now.

"You want a date?" Raúl said. "I could fix you up with some guys."

"Thank you," Ana said politely, but she'd never take him up on that. Although she was only twenty-eight, all his friends were *years* younger than she in both age and maturity.

"Don't ever go out with any of his friends," Robbie said. "None of them are serious about anything."

"Why don't you come to church with us?" Martita said. "There's a big singles' group there."

Ana smiled but didn't answer. Other than weddings and funerals, she'd seldom been to church, although Martita had often invited her to the community chapel her family attended. Ana'd never consider going to church only to find a date. It didn't seem quite right to her.

After dinner, they gathered in the family room to sing "Adelita" and "De colores" and other family favorites. Raúl and Quique sat on the bench by the fireplace and strummed their guitars. Her father leaned back in his blue recliner while Martita held her kids on the other recliner, the one Ana's mother had always sat in. Everyone else relaxed on the sofa while Tonito played with his trucks on the floor.

As she watched, Ana was filled with love and with a terrible feeling that this was to be her life: to watch while her brothers and sister married and had babies and the babies grew up and married. And through those years, she'd worry about them, every one of them, exactly as Raúl and Robbie said she would. Forever. She knew that about herself, too.

Sometimes, like now, she wanted more. Now that she'd reached her professional goal, she needed to look ahead. What she wanted now was a family of her own.

Odd—she hadn't thought about marriage for a long time, not since high school when Tommy Schmidt had wanted to marry her after graduation. Her drive to be a doctor had broken up their relationship. There hadn't been anything serious since. Oh, she'd dated, but she'd been so wrapped up in her family, in her push to finish medical school and her need to learn everything she could, to be the best doctor possible, to finish the residency, that she'd never found time for a relationship. Hadn't really wanted one.

Now that she was almost there, what would she do?

Was it too late for her to have a life and family of her own? If she did, she was going to have to leave the warm, comfortable circle of her family and enter the world of dating. The whole idea bothered her. She wasn't good at flirtation or chatter, and her intensity frightened men.

Then the image of Mike Fuller's unsmiling face danced in her brain. As much as she tried to force his image away, she couldn't. As far as she could tell, she didn't intimidate him.

She could not, would not even consider him. How many times did she need to remind herself he was too young for her? No, that was an excuse. How old was he? Twenty-two, twenty-three? Six or seven years wasn't that much of an age difference.

But there were other reasons. To her, he seemed un-motivated and that bothered her, a lot. And he was so guarded, so wary and uncommunicative.

No, Fuller wasn't the man for her, but, well, other than Raul's friends he was the only unmarried man under fifty she knew.

Chapter Four

What really scared Mike was that he could always tell when Dr. Ramírez was in the hospital. He knew when he walked into the E.R.—without even seeing her—if she was there. He didn't understand how this happened. It couldn't be the scent of her perfume because she didn't wear any.

So how did he know?

He refused to believe in psychic phenomena, but every time he spotted her in the E.R. for the first time in a shift, it didn't surprise him.

If he wanted to know for sure, her schedule wasn't hard to figure out. She worked three of seven nights each week. Sometimes he thought about going to the nurses' station and trying to glance at her schedule. Inconspicuously of course because staff was always around.

Besides, the idea of actually planning this and carrying it out felt a little strange, as if there was actually something between the two of them, a relationship of some kind. He shuddered. After Cynthia and with the uncertainty of his life now, even the word scared him. No, there wasn't a relationship between him and Dr. Ramírez, and he could never consider the possibility.

Nevertheless, when he walked in that day at 3:00 p.m. for a double shift, he knew she was there.

Ana gently probed the leg of the crash victim. She couldn't feel anything odd. Of course, the swelling didn't allow for a complete manual examination. "X-ray," she shouted and turned to glance over her shoulder.

He was there. Fuller. Getting ready to transfer the victim to a gurney so the other orderly could push the gurney of another patient into its place.

His presence made her feel a little giddy.

Get a grip, she lectured herself.

"Dr. Ramírez," said an RN. "You have another patient."

"Thanks, Olivia." She dried her hands and held them out for the nurse to slide the clean gloves on her.

The entire night passed in the same way, patient after patient rolling in, being attended to, then moving on. Between those emergencies, she enjoyed the tantalizing glimpses of Fuller transporting patients or checking with an EMT or picking up a patient's chart. As she did with everyone, she nodded to him or thanked him or got out of his way so he could take the gurney to surgery or a room. At midnight, her aching back forced her to lean against the wall and stretch her muscles. Fuller hurried past, this time giving her a smile, much to her surprise.

He had a great smile. Too bad she didn't see it more. Or, maybe it was a good thing. If he smiled more often, she might behave more foolishly, if that were possible.

During a lull a few hours later, she decided to take a nap. She had two choices. The first: she could hurry over to the on-call rooms on the fifth floor of the east wing. Narrow little places, each with a bed and little else. The problem was, every time she took off her shoes, settled in the bed and pulled the covers over her, her cell rang. Walking all the way over there wasn't worth the trouble.

So she decided on the second choice. She headed for the sofa in the break room and hoped she didn't have to pull rank to get it. Fortunately, she got there first. When she was almost asleep, the door swung open. She knew it was Fuller. How? She still couldn't figure it out.

She opened her eyes a slit to see if she was right. She was.

As she watched, he stepped into the room and watched her with a gentle expression, one that didn't fit the Fuller she knew, the Fuller who seldom spoke to her. It must be the dim light that allowed the deviant thought that Fuller might look at her in that way, caring and—oh, certainly not—tender.

After a few seconds, he backed out and closed the door silently. She sat up. What had just happened? Quickly she halted the absurd tangent her brain had taken off on. Tenderness in Fuller's eyes? Ridiculous.

She had to stop thinking about the orderly. It was not professional. He was not the man for her.

But something inside her didn't agree, and she was left to wonder why he'd looked at her like that.

Driving home, Mike could barely keep his eyes open. Not the safest thing to do when he was driving, but the extra money from those long double shifts allowed him to breathe more easily. For the first time since college, he had a small savings account. For the first time in weeks, he felt there might be better times ahead that didn't consist of constant work, that held the promise he might be a doctor someday.

Not that doctors had easy lives, but they had partners to trade off with, got paid a good bit more and didn't have to do the scut work.

"Orderly," he imagined himself saying in some far-off day when he was Michael Robert Fuller, M.D. "Transport this patient to X-ray, then check on the woman bleeding in Trauma 8. And while you're there—" He almost smiled. Life was getting better when he could see a little humor in the situation, when he felt there might be a future for him in medicine.

He turned onto his street in time to see Tim ride away in his friend's car. Where were they going? He didn't have a job yet. He'd ask Tim later where he'd gone, if he remembered, but he wasn't worried. This was too early in the day to get in trouble, even for Tim.

Pulling Francie's car into the drive, he got out and stretched. He waved down the street toward the neighborhood kids waiting for the school bus as he walked across the lawn and onto the porch. It was hot already, even though it was only late May. That was central Texas.

He unlocked the front door, shoved it open and took a step inside. Silence surrounded him, the usual situation with Tim gone except normally his mother was drinking coffee and reading the paper in the kitchen when he got home. Today the door of her bedroom was shut and a line of light glowed from beneath it. Was she sick?

He knocked and said, "Mom, are you okay?"

When she threw the door open, the dazzling light from her smile and several lamps made him blink.

"I'm magnificent, dear. Look at this." She swirled and gestured around her.

The blast of brilliance made him stand still for a moment. Then he took three steps inside and blinked in an effort to take the scene in.

On the wall to his left, his mother had painted a view of a meadow with two women walking through it. Vibrant green grass and a dazzling sky filled the entire area. On the wall in front of him, she'd begun to paint a pond with gauzy water lilies floating on its shimmering surface.

Wearing one of his shirts and old jeans smeared with paint, his mother stood in the middle of an amazing blaze of beauty.

"I see you're Claude Monet today," he said stunned by the joy in his mother's face and the glow of the painting on the walls. Mixed with all this was the realization this was a rental house for which he'd signed an agreement: all plans to paint had to be approved by the landlord. He didn't think the landlord would appreciate the swirling glory on the walls, but it was too late to worry now. He and Tim could paint over it before they moved out.

Walking to the center of the room, he allowed the paintings to fill him with joy. "When did you decide to do this?"

"After you left yesterday afternoon, I took a walk." While she talked, she picked up a paper towel and wiped the plate she'd used as a palette. "There's a wonderful art store only three block from here. Did you know that?" She glanced up at him with a smile, the kind he remembered from when he was a kid.

He dropped on the bed to listen.

"They had a bin of old paint really cheap, so I bought some and a few brushes, and, well, everything I needed. It cost almost nothing." She turned in a slow circle to study her creations. "Once I got started, I couldn't stop. I painted the rest of the day and all night, stopped to feed Tim dinner and breakfast then came back here." With a sigh, she put the plate down and sat next to him on the bed.

"I didn't know how much I missed it. The painting." Her eyes shone. "Not until I put the first stroke of color on the wall and inspiration flowed through me. It kept coming and coming, like it had been locked up inside me all these years."

"You painted for twenty hours?"

"Almost." She smiled. "It was wonderful. It was like coming home, coming home to you and Tim and my painting." She stood to twirl in the middle of the room.

Mike pulled himself off the bed. "I'm glad, Mom. It's great."

"Thank you, dear." She patted his cheek. "Now, let me get you some breakfast. We can eat together. Then I have to take a nap. Although," she said, "my brain is so filled with images, I don't know if I can sleep."

"Mom, it's beautiful. What's next? Another Monet? Degas's dancers? Seurat?"

"Never Seurat. I find painting all those little dots so tedious."

She was happy. He'd let her finish her bedroom, which wouldn't take long at the speed she was going. *Then* he'd help her find a job.

Almost a week later, his mom still hadn't found work although she'd made several calls and filled out lots of applications. On the other hand, a Degas dancer stretched her long right leg across one corner in the kitchen. In the hall, the start of his mother's interpretation of a Pisarro view of a street made Mike feel as if he were walking through Paris. The landlord might be able to use the house as a gallery or charge higher rent with all the art filling it.

"Fuller, there's a kid in the E.R. who needs you," Dr. Armstrong said, interrupting Mike's thoughts.

In the past few weeks, Mike had gotten a reputation for being good with kids. This was good because he liked children, but bad because he really hated to see a kid hurt.

After finding the child, comforting her and getting her prepped for surgery, he transported her to the OR and promised he'd be there when she got out of surgery.

A few hours later, Mike glanced at his watch. Almost 6:00 a.m. His mother would be picking him up after the shift change. She'd needed the car to go to the doctor yesterday afternoon, only a routine visit, she'd said. He hoped everything had gone well.

Because he'd expected her to arrive an hour later, seeing her in the E.R. hallway surprised him. Even more amazing, she supported a gray-haired man with one hand and tried to staunch the blood dripping from the towels wrapped around the man's arm with the other.

"Mom?"

"Hello, dear." She gave him a quick smile. "I met Mr. Ramírez in the parking lot and helped him in." She lowered the man into a chair. "He says his daughter works here. Do you know her?"

"Yeah." Mike pulled gloves from his pockets, slipping them on as he ran to the nurses' station. "Page Dr. Ramírez, please." Then he grabbed a couple of towels from a hall cabinet, dropped the blood-soaked towels from Mr. Ramírez's arm on the tile floor and wrapped the clean ones around it. Before he could do more, Dr. Ramírez rushed toward her father.

"Papi, what is it?" She kneeled in front of him and glanced at the already-bloody towels. "Fuller, get a wheelchair and take my father to—" she checked the whiteboard "—Trauma 2."

"I don't need a wheelchair." Mr. Ramírez pulled himself to his feet and took a step.

Dr. Ramírez didn't say a word, just gave her father the look that stopped orderlies in their tracks or had them leaping to do what she expected. He sat.

"Marvin," she said to the clerk, "check my father in and get housekeeping here stat to clean the area and get rid of the towels."

Mike pulled his gloves off and dropped them in a closed bin. "Mom, get some soap from Marv and wash your hands and arms and face really well. Scrub hard."

Then he helped Dr. Ramírez's father into the wheelchair and pushed him to the desk where the older man handed his insurance information to Marvin.

"Marv, I'll get you the rest of the info in a minute. I

need to check on my father." Dr. Ramírez grabbed the chair and wheeled it into the cubicle. "Fuller, transfer."

Once her father was lying on the examining table, Dr. Ramírez started to unwrap the arm. "How did you do this, Papi?"

"I was trimming the hedge—"

Mike took the wheelchair away as nurses and an intern and other personnel crowded into the trauma bay.

"Papi, you know you should leave those jobs for one of the boys to do," Mike heard her say as he left.

"I'm not a baby, Ana. I can do this."

"Papi," Dr. Ramírez said. "You always think you're so macho, invincible."

When Mike left the wheelchair in the corridor, he reminded himself to have housekeeping clean it well. He entered the waiting room, and his mother looked up at him.

"How is he? Will he be all right?"

"I don't know, but he has the best doctor in the place taking care of him. I'll check in with her later and let you know." He sat in the green plastic chair next to her and took a hand that was still a little damp. "Why are you here so early?"

"I was going to eat breakfast in the cafeteria and be here when you got off."

"Well, go ahead." He reached into a pocket for a bill. "Get some breakfast."

"No, no. I don't feel like it now. I'll wait here."

"Then tell me what happened. You found him in the parking lot?"

"Yes. Poor man, he drove himself here. I saw him getting out of the car. He almost fell and his face was white." She fanned out the skirt of her long, gauzy mauve dress before she stared at the dark smears on it. "I didn't realize I was getting bloody. What should I do?" She glanced up at Mike. "I should change clothes."

"I'm worried. I'm sure he's a nice man, but blood can carry infections like hepatitis, which would be dangerous for you."

"I know, Mike, but I couldn't leave the poor man to lie on the pavement."

Of course she couldn't, despite the risk. "I'll get you a set of scrubs."

She straightened. "Scrubs?" She bit the words off with obvious distaste.

"I know they aren't your usual style, but scrubs are all we have. They're better than what you're wearing."

She nodded. "All right. I'll try scrubs."

"You'll make them look good."

As he stood, Dr. Ramírez entered the waiting room. Approaching his mother, she reached out her hand. "I'm Dr. Ramírez. I can't thank you enough for helping my father."

"I'm Tessie Fuller, Mike's mother." She got up. "I was glad to help. I can't believe your father drove himself here."

"What can I say?" Dr. Ramírez shrugged. "He thinks he can do anything."

"How is he?" His mother grabbed Dr. Ramírez's arm as she spoke.

"Dr. Price, a surgeon, is stitching up the arm. That won't take long, but we're going to keep him overnight. He lost a lot of blood and would have lost more if you hadn't helped." She nodded at his mother and smiled. "We want to make sure everything is okay before we release him."

"Oh, my, yes. I understand."

"I'm glad to meet you. Thank you again." Then she dropped the smile and said. "Fuller, transfer."

Before he could follow Dr. Ramírez into the E.R., his mother pulled on his hand. "She's a pretty young woman *and* a doctor." She studied Mike's face. "Nice smile. And you work together."

"Yes, Mother." He knew what was coming and tried to pull away.

"She could be the right one."

"Mom, she's a doctor. I'm a med-school dropout which makes her the absolutely wrong one." He pried her hand off his arm and said, "I've got to go back to the E.R., but I'll get you the scrubs when I can."

A long shift change ended at seven-thirty. Wearily, Mike walked into the waiting room carrying a set of scrubs. His mother wasn't there.

Great.

He asked the clerk if she'd seen his mother but she'd just replaced Marv and didn't know her. Maybe Mom had decided to eat breakfast. He'd taken a step toward the hallway when Dr. Ramírez called him from the door to the E.R.

"Fuller."

He turned back.

"Guess who was visiting my father when I checked on him at seven?" She shook her head and smiled.

"My mother?" His stomach tightened. Please, no.

She nodded. "Yep. If you're looking for her, you might try there."

Great. He jogged down the hall, pushed the elevator call button impatiently until the door finally swished open and he got on. His mother collected strays. That was how Francie had come to live with them when her father went to prison, but this stray happened to be Dr. Ramírez's father. The complications of a friendship between them overwhelmed him.

He got off the elevator on the fifth floor and walked down the hall looking for the room number the clerk had given him. When he got there, the door was open. Inside, his mother buttered a piece of toast and held it out for Mr. Ramírez to take a bite. The patient had his arm wrapped and elevated. A monitor was attached while an IV dripped. He had some color back in his face and gazed at his mother with all the interest a man in pain could.

Well, well, well.

After watching for a minute, Mike entered the room. "Mom, do you want these scrubs?"

"Oh, yes, dear." She wiped her hand on a napkin and stood. "I'm sorry, Antonio, but I need to go change now and go home. I'll call to check on you tomorrow." She put a sheet of paper in her pocket. "I have your number."

"Thank you, Tessie." Mr. Ramírez smiled at her. "Thank you for helping me into the hospital and for feeding me breakfast. Please call."

"Of course, but you take a nap." She followed her son from the room.

"You fed him breakfast?" Mike smiled at her while they waited for the elevator.

"Poor man. He couldn't feed himself with only one arm, now could he? And the aides couldn't help him until much later. His food would have been cold." She put her hand on his arm and nodded, her dangling earrings bouncing with the movement of her head. "I believe it's so important to help others, don't you?"

Just terrific.

Chapter Five

When Ana walked into her father's kitchen the next day, Mrs. Fuller sat at the table with her dad. Ana paused for a minute and tried to think of any reason Mike's mother would be there.

In spite of what her family might say about her, Ana wasn't nosy. At least, not today. She'd dropped by to check on her father and start dinner, but he didn't look as if he needed her care. Which was fine, but she wondered what was going on. After all, the charming widow had spent time with her father while he was in the hospital. Now he'd been home for only a day and here she was again.

Her father held the business section of the newspaper—odd because recently he was only reading the sports page and doing the crossword puzzles. But when she saw the pen in Mrs. Fuller's hand and the pad of yellow paper in front of her, the reason for the rendezvous made sense.

With her nice, conservative black slacks, with a plain

black cotton sweater, it was an outfit that looked like something Ana's mother might have worn with a pair of tiny gold earrings and the cross Papi had given her when they married. But Mrs. Fuller accessorized her outfit with a huge red scarf covered in gold swirls tossed around her shoulders. Her gold sandals with red bangles matched it. In greater contrast to Ana's mother, when Mrs. Fuller spoke she waved her hands and light flashed off the jewels of her many rings. The bangles on her wrists jangled and reflected the light coming in the window.

Flamboyant was the word that came to mind. Oh, Mrs. Fuller was lovely, full of energy but so very different from Mama. Sweet, loving, *quiet* Mama.

For a minute she watched them: Mrs. Fuller tapped her pen on the table, which caused her bracelets to clank together. Then she looked at Papi with a smile he returned. He said something to her, and Mrs. Fuller leaned toward him and laughed.

And so, in spite of the differences, Ana couldn't be unhappy. For the first time in over a year, her father was smiling. Mrs. Fuller seemed to pump him up, to delight him, to make him happy, all of which were good. He needed company during the few days Ana had made him stay home from the store. However, there was still the problem with Mrs. Fuller's criminal past, but this was hardly the place to discuss that.

"Hello, Mrs. Fuller. It's nice to see you again," Ana said.

Fuller's mother glanced up at her. "Hello, Doctor. Your father is helping me find a job." She scowled and tapped a pen in frustration. "I'm afraid I have no employable skills."

"Hello, Ana," Papi greeted her. "I was thinking when I go back to the store next week, Tessie could work for me and help with some of the little things. Answer the phone. Take messages."

"Oh, Antonio, really?" Mrs. Fuller's rings glittered when she clapped her hands. "At your store?"

"Sure, I can use the help for a while."

"I could be a gofer, too." Mrs. Fuller clapped, her bangles shimmering in the light from the window. Then she bit her lower lip. "But I don't want to take advantage of your good nature."

"It's a good idea." Ana slid past the table. "I don't want my father to overdo it."

"And it will give you some experience and a reference," Papi said.

"I don't have much experience," Mrs. Fuller said to Ana. "And no references." She sighed. "I've called fifteen places today, and they aren't interested. Even if I didn't have a record, they wouldn't be interested."

"We'll keep searching," Papi said.

"Oh, thank you, Antonio. I don't know what I'd do without your encouragement."

"Would you like to stay for dinner, Mrs. Fuller?" Ana opened the freezer to pull out a casserole. "We always have plenty of food."

"Please, call me Tessie." She glanced at the kitchen clock. "I didn't realize it was so late. I have to catch a bus and get home in time to fix dinner for the boys." She stood. "But thank you. Please ask me again."

"Has Tim found a job yet?" Papi asked.

"Yes, he's working at Burger Heaven a few blocks

from where we live. He started last week." She picked up her tapestry purse and said, "Goodbye, Antonio. Goodbye, Doctor." With a swirl and to the jingling of her bangles, she dashed from the kitchen.

After she heard the front door shut, Ana said, "Papi, are you sure you should be going back to the store so soon?"

He gave her the don't-contradict-me expression he'd perfected years ago and didn't answer. She'd known he wouldn't.

Ana scrutinized the gunshot wound in the young man's thigh. Not much bleeding because the EMT had cut the trouser leg off and done a good job stanching the flow, but it hurt the patient on the gurney.

"What's your name?" Ana asked.

"Julio Rivera," he said through clenched teeth.

"How did this happen, Mr. Rivera?" Ana asked.

"A car drove by and someone inside shot me."

Ana observed the young man. His light brown complexion was dry, no sweating, no sign of shock, although pain was obvious in his dark eyes. "They're holding an operating suite for you. We'll take you there in a few minutes and will get you pain medication while you're in recovery." She shone her light in his eyes. The pupils were fine. No drugs, no concussion. Not that there would be with a leg wound, but it never hurt to check. Patients didn't always tell doctors everything.

"I don't understand." He shook his head. "I didn't recognize anyone." He closed his eyes. "I was waiting for the bus to go to work, not doing a thing to anyone, when they shot me."

"Gang initiation?" Mike spoke softly from behind her.

Startled by his closeness, Ana looked over her shoulder. To hide the pleasant flutter seeing him gave her, she said in her professional voice, "Maybe, but now he needs a transfer."

"Yes, Doctor." He moved the gurney around her leaving her to stare at his back as he moved farther away.

"Doctor," Olivia, the nurse, called. "Patient in Trauma 1."

A few hours later, Ana leaned against the wall around the corner from the emergency entrance. Despite the howling of ambulances and the shouts of the medical personnel, it was a peaceful place. At least as peaceful as it got around the hospital with maybe the exception of the chapel. She didn't know because she'd never felt like visiting the place.

Across the lawn was a small garden outside the west wing. If she ignored the noise and focused on the greenery, she could calm herself.

Feeling the approach of Mike, as she was beginning to think of him, she turned toward him. Yes, it was Mike Fuller. How amazing that she knew that. Not wanting to examine the phenomenon that made her a little breathless, she said as she watched his approach, "I didn't know you came here."

"Yeah," he said with no explanation.

"Did you know your mother visited my father at our home?"

"No." He frowned. "I slept most of the day and came in early."

"When I went to my father's house last night, she

was there. He was helping her look for a job. What do you think?"

Mike nodded and leaned against the wall next to her. "What do you think?"

Just like Fuller to answer her question with one of his own. She watched his face but it was blank, no emotion showed anyplace. Here she was with her heart beating faster and longing to get some reaction from him, but the man never gave anything away.

"He hasn't smiled so much since my mother died last year."

"That's not what I meant." He dropped his gaze to his feet. "I mean how do you feel about your father seeing an ex-con?"

"I don't know." She considered her words. "Actually, I do. It bothers me because I don't know your mother, but this is my father's decision. I know better than to interfere in what my father does." She sighed. "If she makes him happy, I'll accept it. I'll be glad for both of them."

For almost a minute she watched Mike's hands on the top of the wall, powerful hands with thick, strong fingers. Finally she looked up to meet his glance. "What do *you* think of your mother's keeping company with my father?"

He shoved his hands in his pocket. "It's okay."

"They are, after all, adults who have raised families and can make their own decisions." When he didn't answer, she said, "Right?"

He nodded.

She shouldn't care if Mike communicated with her or not. They worked together. There was no reason for her to say much more to him than, "Transfer" and "Thank you" and "Fuller." He did respond well to those, transferring when asked, coming when needed, but not a lot else. She had no right to expect or demand more.

As he moved away, she said, "Let's not allow anything between our parents to affect our work situation."

"Doctor, orderly. Got it." Without another word, he headed back to the E.R.

"That's not—" she started to say but he was already around the corner. Taking a deep breath and attempting to gather enough calm to last the rest of her shift, she followed him into the building a minute later.

Mike strode inside when the automatic doors opened.

What was his mother doing? Keeping company with Dr. Ramírez's father would make life difficult. It would make *Mike's* life difficult.

When he heard, "Transfer" from the E.R., he hurried down the hall to answer the call, but his mind continued to consider the situation between his mom and Mr. Ramírez.

He could handle being attracted to Dr. Ramírez. He'd deny it, ignore it and work through the situation. That's all there was to it. The buzz he felt when she was around was extremely pleasant but couldn't—wouldn't—lead anywhere. If he allowed it to be any more than that, he was setting himself up for trouble, for a complication he didn't need.

If their families became close, the line between doctor and clinical assistant might blur or even be erased. The thought scared him, a lot.

At the direction of the attending physician, he grabbed a gurney with a patient to transfer to the OR, pushed it toward the elevator and pressed the call button.

As the elevator door opened, he could hear calls of "Transfer" and there were only two orderlies on tonight. Better get moving.

Almost a week later, Mike dropped on the sofa as soon as he got home and fell asleep immediately.

"Antonio has invited us to dinner tonight." His mother's voice filtered through the shroud of sleep, seeping into his brain, slowly. After trying to make sense of the syllables, their meaning came together. He opened his eyes and muttered, "What? Who? When?" sounding like a high-school journalism teacher. Then he blinked several times, rotated his shoulders, and swung his feet around to sit up. "You're going to Mr. Ramírez's house for dinner?"

Not good. He'd hoped any attraction between his mother and Mr. Ramírez would slowly go away. He'd wished they were just friends, but what he'd seen sparkling between the two of them at the hospital, added to the fact she'd visited Mr. Ramírez in his home and now planned to go to his house for dinner—that added up to more than just the beginning of a friendship.

She sat on the sofa next to him. "We're all going to their house for dinner. You, Tim and I."

He stretched and yawned, trying to think of an excuse.

"I'm sorry I woke you up, but I was so excited."

"I have to work tonight." Work was a terrific reason not to go.

"Not until eleven, right?"

He nodded reluctantly. Could he call now and get on an earlier shift? "Mom, I don't feel comfortable. Dr. Ramírez is my supervisor."

"They're going to have Mexican food." She smoothed his hair away from his face and attempted to pat down his cowlick. "Everyone is bringing a dish. You love enchiladas."

"I don't think mixing work with…"

The smile on her face disappeared. She slumped and bit her lip. "I understand," she said. "I thought how nice it would be for Antonio's family to meet mine, but if you can't make it, I understand. You work very hard for us."

As he watched her, Mike realized how brave his mother had been, flitting around the house as if she had no cares, painting the wonderful scenes, which brightened the entire house, taking care of her sons. All her activity hid the fact she'd only recently been released from eight hard years in prison. She was almost sixty and sometimes looked every day of it and more. As she bent her head, he could see silver streaks threaded through her red hair. She was no longer Hurricane Tessie. She wasn't even Light Breeze Tessie.

Certainly he could do one thing for her.

"All right, Mom. I'll go this time, but don't ask me again, okay?"

"Oh, thank you." She smiled at him, the sparkle returning to her eyes and taking ten years from her age. "Just this one time." She nodded and stood. Glancing at her watch, she said, "It's barely noon. We need to be there at six, so you have plenty of time to get a nice rest. Go back to sleep."

As if there were any possibility of his getting any more sleep now. He lay on the couch for fifteen minutes, eyes wide-open and staring at the ceiling before he got up and took a shower.

When she'd gotten off her shift the morning of the dinner, Ana had stopped at the grocery store on the way back to her apartment. Only a few blocks from the hospital, her place cost more in rent than an apartment so small should, but she was earning more now and the proximity to the hospital was worth the cost.

She parked her car, got out and took the elevator to the third floor. Once there, she unlocked the door to go inside, dropped her purse on the table in the entry, walked across the tiny patch of beige carpet that was her living room and into the narrow galley kitchen. There, she pulled out the ingredients for the dish she was taking to the dinner.

First she cut the *menudo* into small pieces, put it in a pot with a calf's foot, chilies, bay leaf and garlic, leaving them to simmer while she slept.

When she awakened six hours later, she checked the *menudo,* added a few more ingredients, then took a shower.

How should she dress tonight? she wondered while she dried her hair.

For goodness' sake, why was she acting all girlie? Tonight was a family dinner, only with a few extra guests. She'd dress as she always did for family dinners: jeans and a T-shirt.

But one of those extra guests was Mike Fuller and, for a reason she refused to admit, she wanted to look better than "okay." She hated the fact he only saw her as a doctor with her funny little bun, lab coat and comfortable shoes. She wanted to break free of the image tonight, to be a real person.

On the other hand, their relationship was doctor-CA so she should choose her clothing accordingly. Having made the decision not to dress in any special or unusual or totally different way for the additional guests, she pulled her hair in a ponytail, slipped into her jeans, shirt and athletic shoes, and studied herself in the mirror.

Plain. Exactly what she looked like. Her younger sister and friends wore makeup, but with her schedule, Ana stayed with a fluff of powder and swipe of lip gloss which was usually gone after a few hours. Did she have anything more in the drawer?

A touch of blush and a dab of mascara made her appear a little prettier. Next she pulled her hair from the scrunchie and brushed it. She liked it curling down her back. Finally, she changed into a yellow cotton blouse with ruffles around the neck and put on matching sandals.

This time when she studied her reflection, she had to admit she looked good, really good. She shook her head to allow the curls to swish across her shoulders.

She was no longer Dr. Ramírez. She was Ana Ramírez, and she was all female.

In the entire city of Austin, how had he ended up in front of *this* house, with Dr. Ramírez inside? His mother would, of course, expect him to enter it. He would have banged his head against the steering wheel in frustration if having to explain the injuries didn't present such difficulty. So instead, he sat in the car with its engine still running in front of the Ramírez's house and thought, *She's in there.*

"Are you getting out?" Tim asked from the backseat. "I don't how you feel about it, but we've been promised Mexican food. I'm not going to miss any of it." He leaped out and loped toward the house.

"Mike," his mother said with concern in her voice, "you don't have to go in if you're uncomfortable."

Uncomfortable wasn't the word he'd use to describe the reluctance he felt.

"Thanks, Mom." But it would be worse if he sat in a car in the drive all evening. They'd think he was more of an idiot than he actually was. He turned off the ignition, got out of the car and went to the other side to help his mother out. Before Mike could reach her, Mr. Ramírez hurried from the house and opened the car door.

"Bienvenida, querida mía," the widower said with a big smile and stretched his arm out for Tessie to take. After she turned in the seat and stood, he kissed her on the cheek.

Dr. Ramírez's father was kissing his mother. That stomach-tightening thing hit him again. Oh, sure, it was on the cheek, but it was a kiss.

How was a son supposed to respond to seeing his mother embraced by a man? Mike had no idea. He'd never thought of Mom as, well, a woman who would be attractive to a man, as a woman a man would want to kiss. Only Tim's running out of the house seconds later saved Mike from standing by the car with his mouth hanging open and looking like a fool.

"Hey, Mike, wanna play some roundball?"

Mike closed his mouth and nodded. He probably would have agreed if Tim had said, "Wanna jump into a pit of cobras?"

"This is Quique," Tim said, pointing to the wiry, good-looking kid holding a basketball who'd followed him. "He says there're some kids down the block always ready for a pickup game." His mother and Mr. Ramírez moved on to the lawn as Tim grabbed the ball from Quique and dribbled it down the sidewalk.

"What about dinner?" Mike asked.

"Ana said I was in the way and kicked me out," Quique shouted as he ran after Tim. "Told us to come back in an hour."

After his brain reminded him Ana equaled Dr. Ramírez, he realized that playing ball would get him out of a situation that could be potentially embarrassing, uncomfortable, better avoided for as long as possible, *or* all of the above.

He slammed the car door on the passenger side, pretended not to notice his mother and Mr. Ramírez holding hands as they strolled toward the house, and followed Tim and Quique down the street.

Ana surveyed the kitchen table in her father's house. The chorizo Martita brought was on the table next to Ana's *menudo*. Rice and *frijoles refritos* flanked those dishes. Her father had made his delicious enchiladas, everything from scratch, the old Mexican way. Her younger sister, Luz, would bring *pan dulce* and salad from the H-E-B where she worked. Even Raúl had brought something, tacos from a Mexican food place. For drinks there were *yerba verde* and soda. Ana would fix the sopaipillas for dessert later.

"What can I do to help?" Mrs. Fuller asked.

"Nothing, thank you. Everything's as ready as possible until Luz gets here." Ana tugged at the corner of the tablecloth to square it.

"Please tell me about Luz. From what Antonio says, she seems like a lovely young woman."

"Yes, she is. She's nineteen. She graduated from high school last year and has been working. A month ago, she decided she'd like to join the army to learn a skill and get financial help for college."

"Sounds like a determined young lady."

"Yes, everyone in our family is determined to reach their goals." She thought of Raúl and Quique. "Well," she added, "almost everyone is."

As she watched Mrs. Fuller sit by her father, Ana wondered where Mike was. She'd seen Tim dash by with Quique, but where was his older brother?

Not that she really cared where he was, but she needed to know so she'd have the correct number of plates set out, enough glasses.

Maybe he'd weaseled out of dinner. *Weaseled,* not an attractive word, but she would've done the same thing if she hadn't promised her father she'd help set up a dinner for friends. Next time, she'd get more information about the guests before agreeing.

Finally, Luz arrived, her dark hair coming loose from

the ponytail she wore to work. "Sorry, I had to stay a few minutes late," she said. "Go call Quique and I'll finish setting up. I saw them playing basketball at the Parker's when I drove past."

Ana should have refused the request because when she got to the door, the three guys were heading up the drive. They were all sweaty and their T-shirts clung to their chests. Tim and Quique were skinny and didn't look all that great.

But Mike. Oh, yeah. She had to stop herself from saying, "Wow," as he walked toward her. His shirt stuck to broad shoulders and a muscular torso. Powerful legs showed beneath khaki shorts. Perspiration trickled down his smiling face. He was breathing a little heavily but still laughing and bickering with the two younger guys.

All in all, he looked absolutely spectacular. She'd never seen him look happy and so masculine and would prefer *never* to see him look that great again.

When Mike saw her, he stopped talking. For an instant admiration shone in his eyes as he studied her hair and the ruffled blouse. Then the usual Mike Fuller unemotional face covered his features again.

After the three reached the door, Mike said, "Go on in, guys. I'll follow in a minute." Once the boys shut the door behind them, Mike dropped on the porch bench, leaned over and took deep breaths.

Ana had planned to follow the young men in but his respiration bothered her. She sat next to him, grabbed his wrist and began counting his pulse as she checked her watch. "What's wrong?" she asked. "Do you have any chest pain?"

He tugged his wrist from her hand. "I'm fine." After a few more deep breaths, he added, "Just the idiocy of trying to keep up with kids."

"You're okay?" She sat back. "I thought you were dying." Now that she knew he was fine, Ana attempted not to laugh.

"I did, too, for the last fifteen minutes." He groaned and shook his head. "I haven't played basketball so hard in years."

He sat next to her struggling to breathe with perspiration pouring off him. All in all, he looked better than a man had the right to. She couldn't take her eyes off him.

"Why didn't you stop if you were so tired?" she asked.

"And let the kids win?" He stared at her with an expression that said women just didn't get it. "Besides, it was a lot of fun."

He was right. She didn't get it. How could he think pushing himself to the point of exhaustion was a lot of fun?

She'd never understand men.

Chapter Six

From the swing in the side yard, Ana watched her family and the Fullers. The younger group laughed together in wicker chairs pulled into a semicircle. Martita and Robbie pulled the last of the patio chairs around the big table and talked to Raúl, Papi and Tessie, who sat across from them.

Ana could hear the "rrr" noises Tonito made as he rolled his toy cars across the patio. Baby Marisol played with her toes on a blanket next to her mother.

Mike, the last one out of the house with his plate, stood on the back steps and searched for a place to sit. Glancing at Tim, then away, made it clear he didn't want to sit with the youngsters. Too old for their antics? A glance told him the round table was full and there were no more chairs on the patio.

"There's a seat on the swing." Tessie pointed behind her. Mike smiled at his mother and started in that direction.

At that moment, Ana realized something frightening:

Mike was no longer *her* project. She and Mike were their *families'* project. Even worse, she guessed Mike's mother was as persistent as her family. They'd never escape.

As she watched Mike approach her, Ana knew exactly when he realized the seat on the swing, the place his mother had indicated, was next to her, the dreaded Dr. Ramírez. After two steps, his smile slipped and he hesitated. Only for a second, a pause imperceptible to anyone who hadn't been watching him as closely as she had. Almost immediately, he took another step and another until he stood only a few feet from her.

"May I join you?"

At her nod, he put his drink on the table next to the swing and held on to the arm to lower himself onto the cushioned seat. Neither said a word, not a single word, while chatter and laughter from the others floated across the lawn toward them. The fun everyone else was having made their silence even more awkward.

She searched for something to say to fill the quiet that became more uncomfortable by the second. Then her gaze landed on the plate in his lap. "Do you like Mexican food?"

"Yes." He took another bite of the chicken enchilada.

Great conversation.

When he swallowed, she said. "What's your favorite?"

Before she finished her question, he took another bite. Not to let him off the hook, she continued to watch him until he swallowed and said, "Tacos."

"I mean, *real* Mexican food."

"What?" He turned toward her, his forehead creased in confusion. "Tacos are Mexican food."

Success. The response was five words long, and he'd

made eye contract. "And you know that because they serve them at Taco Bell?"

He laughed. "Okay, tell me why tacos aren't Mexican food."

Wonder of wonders. A laugh and another complete sentence.

"In Mexico, tacos are like sandwiches," she said. "You put whatever leftovers you have around the house into the taco shell. Fish, vegetables, anything handy."

He shook his head. "I can't imagine eating a fish taco so I'll say my favorite food is this chorizo. I love the spicy sausage."

She was feeling good about the conversation until he added, "Is that answer acceptable, Dr. Ramírez?"

"I didn't mean to sound so much like Dr. Ramírez." She could kick herself for the pedantic streak that showed up at the worst times. "Tonight, while we're all family, why don't you call me Ana. It's more comfortable."

He cleared his throat and glanced away, not acting a bit comfortable.

She'd guess he wouldn't call her anything tonight, most certainly not Ana.

He took a forkful of another food. "Now this is good. It might be my new favorite." He studied the serving on his plate. "What is it?"

"Menudo."

"What's *menudo?*" He took another bite.

"Tripe." When he raised an eyebrow, she said, "That's intestine, beef intestine."

He stopped chewing and looked as if he wanted to spit it out but was too polite.

"If it tastes good, it doesn't matter what it is," she said.

He swallowed and nodded. "I guess so, in theory, at least to a certain extent." He shook his head. "But intestine?"

After a few more minutes of chatter about the food and their families, she decided to try something more risky—digging for information she'd like to know while he was more talkative. "So, Mike, why did you decide to become a doctor?"

He didn't answer. Instead, he gazed at their families and down at his plate until he responded. "All the wrong reasons."

At least he'd answered. She'd figured he'd put up his barrier again. "What are the wrong reasons?"

"Money," he said. "Big house, country club membership so I could play golf on Thursday afternoons. Everything a kid with my background dreams of but doesn't have a chance at."

She pushed the swing slowly, watching the pinks and yellows of the sunset streak the sky before she asked, "So why didn't it work out?"

Ana couldn't believe how quickly his eyes lost every sparkle of interest and became bleak, how his lips thinned and his posture became rigid. He'd thrown up a barrier and glared at her from behind it.

Back to the old Fuller. How frustrating.

"Why did you become a doctor, Dr. Ramírez?" he asked in a voice devoid of interest.

His choice of "Dr. Ramírez" and his asking her the question showed how far she'd trespassed into his territory.

Should she tell him that after the traffic accident her mother was involved in that had nearly take Mama's life, Ana had admired the skill of the doctors so much she'd vowed to be one? Or should she give him the expanded, emotional reason?

After her mother's accident when Ana was eight years old, she and her father had raced to the hospital, terrified that her mother would die. Ana'd stood on tiptoe to look through the glass into the emergency room. It had been calming to know all the people on the other side of the window were caring for Mama. When Papi had found her, he tried to carry her back to the waiting room, but she'd insisted on staying.

After they'd wheeled her mother to the operating room, she put her arms around his neck and kissed his cheeks. *"No llores,* Papi. *Los doctores le van a salvar la vida."*

He'd quit crying and the doctors had saved her mother's life, but she was *really* sure Mike wouldn't want to hear all the touching details.

"When I was a kid, emergency room doctors saved my mother's life."

He nodded. "That's a good reason." Then he stood. "Coffee?"

"Oh, no." She jumped to her feet. "I have to make the sopaipillas for dessert."

They both went in different directions. Actually, Ana thought they'd fled in different directions because the sharing was more than Mike could handle and she was beginning to feel embarrassed about pushing him to talk.

But no one else would see that. The Ramírezes and the Fullers would feel this had been a successful blending of the families. Only she knew that Mike wasn't ready for the sharing and kidding the Ramírez family did every time they came together.

Because Martita had said her family had to leave early to get the children home and to bed, Mike was driving the family home from the Ramírez home at nine.

"What did you think?" his mother said. He tried to read her expression but she'd turned toward the window.

Had she noticed that he and Dr. Ramírez—he could *never* call her Ana—had been talking? Of course she had. She'd planned that. Had she noticed how abruptly he'd moved away from the swing to stand and talk with Tim, Luz and Quique? Yes, she saw that, also. She probably thought it showed a strong attraction between him and Dr. Ramírez. Again, she was right, but nothing was going to come of it no matter what his mother's creative brain came up with. He didn't have the time, money or resiliency for a relationship. He might consider that once his family was taken care of.

"Nice family." Mike turned onto I-35.

"That Luz is great." Tim spoke from the backseat. "Did you know she's going into the army in a few months? She's got her whole life mapped out."

"What's she going to do?" Mom put her hand on the back of her seat and turned to watch her younger son.

"After she gets out, she wants to be an architect."

In the rearview mirror, Mike saw Tim shake his head as if in wonder. Tim had never been drawn to smart girls with plans for the future.

"Are you interested in her?" Mike asked to get the spotlight off himself.

"No," Tim denied strongly. "She's way too focused on her future, but she said she'll get out of the army with enough money for college." Tim paused. "Maybe I should do that."

"If you want to go to college, you don't have to join the army," Mike said. "The state pays for college for foster kids. I wouldn't have made it through without that."

Tim shrugged, which meant the end of the conversation. From now on, Mike would leave any vocational considerations up to Luz. Tim accepted ideas from a pretty young woman better than advice from an older brother. No surprise about that.

When he'd parked the car and all three had entered the house, his mother took Mike's arm in the dark living room before he could follow Tim to their bedroom. "Did you like Antonio?" she asked softly.

"He seemed very nice." He smiled down at his mother. "And quite interested in you."

The hand on his arm relaxed. "What did Tim think about him?" he asked.

"Oh." She waved her hand. "I didn't ask Tim. He likes everyone." With a kiss on his cheek, she switched on a light in the kitchen.

What did that say about Mike? That he didn't get along with everyone?

He saw the glow of the hall light. "Are you going to bed?" she asked from there.

"In a minute."

He'd always thought he got along with people, but

as he watched her go into the kitchen, Mike had to recognize that since the breakup with Cynthia and with the addition of other responsibilities, he *had* changed, reverted to earlier behavior, silent and closed up. Not that he'd ever had the happy-go-lucky attitude Tim had. If he had, they wouldn't have a place to live.

Heading toward the bathroom and turning the kitchen and hall lights out behind him, he had to admit that, yes, he'd always been different from Tim. Maybe part of that was because he'd been too hurt by their father's second abandonment after Tim's birth.

For years before Mom was incarcerated, he'd been a pretty happy kid, a lot like Tim. He had changed, become less trusting after Mom went to prison and he'd been shuffled from foster home to foster home. No one wanted or put up long with a sullen teenager.

He thanked God for his cousin Francie's support and encouragement. Without that, he didn't know how he would have ended up. Certainly in prison, probably likely to return.

Mike went into his bedroom where Tim was already snoring in his upper bunk. Mike watched him and wondered why they were so different now.

Most likely because Tim had lived with the Montoyas for eight years. They were a great foster family. They'd truly been Tim's family and kept up with him still.

Mike undressed, entered the bathroom and took a shower. As the water slammed down on him, he remembered the terrible emptiness inside him when his mother had gone to prison and the family had been separated. He'd been too masculine, too embarrassed to mention it. Instead, he pretended he didn't care when it had torn him up inside. So no one would know how he felt, he closed in on himself. He bluffed his way through the concerns of teachers and school counselors, keeping his grades up, playing basketball, looking great on the outside. That was how he'd coped then. That was how he was coping now.

Why had it been so important not to allow anyone to see the inside?

Why was it still so important to keep people out?

After getting out of the shower, drying off and brushing his teeth, he went back to the bedroom.

"G'night, Mike," Tim mumbled when Mike came in.

"'Night," Mike said, but the light snores told him Tim had already fallen asleep.

He got dressed before looking at the clock. Only a little after nine-thirty. He was due at work in an hour, so Mike picked up his anatomy book and lay down to read it after he set the alarm. In spite of an interesting section on the ulna, thoughts from the past still bombarded him.

When he got to college, the first year was hard. He didn't know how to make friends, to build a relationship. Then he began to succeed and the shell had begun to crack bit by bit. It split open when he got to medical school. He'd believed his outer shell had disappeared when he and Cynthia were engaged.

After almost half an hour, Tim turned his light on and hopped from the top bunk. When he came back a few minutes later he had a handful of cookies and a glass of milk. The kid ate even in the middle of the night. Tim finished the snack, put the glass on the floor and got back in bed.

"What do you think about the Ramírez family?" Tim's voice filtered down.

"Seems nice." He shut the book, turned to pull his shoes on then stood to leave the room in the hope he could avoid what he figured would be Tim's next remark.

"Yeah."

Mike thought his brother had dozed off, but as he reached the door Tim said, "Ana's pretty, too. And a doctor. What do you think of her?"

He ignored the question. After grabbing his keys and leaving the house, he got in the car and headed to the hospital.

Yes, Ana, Dr. Ramírez to him no matter what she said, had looked great. Her hair was as long and wavy, as beautiful as he'd imagined. He'd had to clench his fists to keep from touching it, from filling his hand with the mass of dark curls. She was wearing a frilly blouse and seemed very feminine and soft, not a word he'd ever associated with her in the past. Sitting next to her on the swing, he smelled her perfume, something flowery and light, felt her warmth, felt himself being drawn to her. Because he couldn't allow that to happen, he'd leaped to his feet and run.

Pretty bad when the pleasure of sitting next to a beautiful woman frightened him, when it seemed like the worst thing that could happen.

What kind of idiot felt that way? Obviously, he was exactly that kind of idiot.

For a moment, he thought about praying. That's what

he'd have done a year ago, even a few months ago, but he didn't. He couldn't figure out what to say to God, what to pray for.

Chapter Seven

Two days later, during the next shift Ana and Mike worked together, she could tell his barriers were up and he'd posted guards on every entrance and tower. When she passed him in the hall, he gave her a polite nod. No more Mr. Let's-Have-a-Chat. If she called for transfer, he'd hurry in, move the gurney and leave without a word. The few times she talked to him, he answered, "Yes, Dr. Ramírez," or "Of course, Dr. Ramírez," or "Right away, Dr. Ramírez."

All of those responses, every one of them, were proper ways for a CA to answer a doctor. Why did they upset her so much?

She hit the roof when she looked down the hall and saw Mike and Mitchelson joking and laughing. Why couldn't Mike do that with her? They'd had a nice time at the family gathering a few days earlier. She thought they'd gotten to know each other, but he was more distant than ever.

That was the reason she lost it when she asked him

to check on the trache tubes in OR 3 and, again, he'd answered oh so politely, "Right away, Dr. Ramírez."

"All right, Fuller," she'd said in the voice she'd practiced since med school to be as intimidating as possible.

He stared at her in surprise. The staff of the E.R. looked at her amazed. She didn't care. At least this time he had noticed her, really noticed her, but he only said, "Dr. Ramírez?"

"I need to talk to you. Privately." She turned to the clerk and said, "I'm going to use the empty office on E wing."

She stalked off. Once she got to the door, she looked over her shoulder to make sure Mike was following. He'd better be.

"Okay," she said once they were inside and she'd slammed the door behind them. "What's going on?"

He blinked. "What do you mean, Dr. Ramírez?"

"Why are you behaving this way?"

"What way?"

Now she felt foolish and a little embarrassed. She seldom allowed her temper to take over. Now she was in a mess, acting both unprofessional and resentful. How could she accuse him of being too courteous? "So…so cold?" In an instant she realized her mistake. She'd showed him how vulnerable she was, revealing much more about herself and her feelings than she'd meant to. This man muddled her brain and made her forget how she should behave.

"Dr. Ramírez," he said slowly and with great emphasis on the word *doctor*. "If you have a complaint about my work, please discuss that with me in detail and put a note in my employment record."

"I'm sorry. This is so unprofessional." She dug her hands in the pockets of her lab coat. "But you're really confusing me," she whispered.

She caught a glimpse of uncertainty in his expression before he cleared all emotion from his face. He turned to leave without saying a word.

"I need you to…I don't know." She studied his back but his rigid stance wasn't encouraging. "Just don't be so cold. Everyone's thinking something's going on between us. They believe you're angry with me for some personal reason."

He turned back to her with an eyebrow raised. "They are?" He considered that. "No one's mentioned it to me."

Well, of course not. Only *she* thought he was angry with her for a personal reason.

"I don't understand," she said, "We had such a nice evening together, I thought maybe we'd—" She bit her lip to stop the revealing words. "We have to be professional but you're more than that. You're overly polite, and it drives me nuts."

"Dr. Ramírez." He used the same courteous tone he'd used before. "I have two choices in the way I act around you—cold and professional or…something else."

"Something else?"

"Yes." He searched her face. "Like this." He took her by the shoulders, moved her to the corner, away from the window in the door, and pulled her against him to rub his cheek on hers.

The feel of his breath on her neck, the warmth of his embrace filled her with longing and almost made her toes curl up. Confused, she looked up into his face. "What do you mean?"

"If I allowed myself to do what I want to do, I'd kiss you, now."

That sounded terrific.

Ana wound her arms behind his neck. His nearness and his scent—a mixture of man, musky aftershave and disinfectant—jolted her both physically and mentally. She should pull away but was completely thrown off balance by Mike's closeness and, when she glanced up at him, the need in his eyes. She refused to give it up, to shorten the time of this amazing connection.

When at last Mike stepped away, he rubbed his index finger down her cheek. "Dr. Ramírez," he spoke softly but firmly, "your choices for my behavior around you are cold and polite or what just happened between us. I don't know how we could handle this attraction without people starting to talk."

She yearned to return to the circle of his arms but he'd crossed them firmly on his chest. She shook her head in an effort to kick-start her brain, to understand what had happened.

What had happened was that Mike had embraced her, and she'd folded herself in his arms with great delight and enthusiasm. "Could we ignore this? Could we go back to working together in a friendly way?"

He ignored that suggestion. "Coldness or this." He waved his hand as if to encompass what had just happened in this office. When he looked at her, she saw the same confusion she felt. "I've already passed friendship."

"I prefer the second choice." She blinked. "Very much, but you're right. This." She waved her hand around the office as she spoke. "This isn't the best way to act in the hospital or for either of us professionally."

The focus that had guided her for twenty years came back to clear her head. Being found in the embrace of another staff member in a hidden corner of an unused office was not how she wanted to be remembered, was not what she'd worked for all these years.

And yet, how could she forget that moment? Maybe whatever was between them might be better than what she'd prepared for all her life.

She took a step closer and rubbed her fingers along the stubble on his cheeks. When she paused, he moved her hand to his lips, kissed the palm and held it.

With a sigh of resignation, she tugged her hand away. "You're right. As wonderful as this was, it can't happen again."

He nodded, attempting to look cool and distant. It didn't work. The tautness of his expression told her the attraction between the two of them bothered him as much as it did her and that he had made the same decision.

"Let's go back to how we were before—staff members, people who work together," she said.

He nodded again. "Yes, Dr. Ramírez."

"Fuller." The voice of Olivia, the RN on duty, filtered through the thick door. "Transfer."

Ignoring the voice for a second, he kept his eyes on her.

"Fuller, we've got a lot of patients backed up out here. We need you. Now!" Olivia shouted.

Without a word, he strode toward the door, opened it and left the room.

Ana moved to look in the mirror. Light whisker burns colored her neck and right cheek. That was going to be hard to hide and harder still to explain. Her makeup bag was in her locker, but she did have the small tube of lotion she carried in her pocket to keep her hands soft after so many washings. She took it out, squirted a bead into the palm Mike had so recently touched and rubbed it on her reddened skin. That would have to do.

"Dr. Ramírez?" Olivia's voice came from the open door.

"Yes?" She turned.

"I'm sorry I bothered you and Fuller."

What? Did the entire E.R. know what had happened between them? How embarrassing. There hadn't been time for him to tell anyone. Also, she was sure he wouldn't have, so how did Olivia know? Had she been able to see them in the corner? She glanced in that direction.

"I think Fuller is a great CA," Olivia said. "But if you had to call him down, I'm sorry I interrupted. I wouldn't have if we didn't have an emergency."

"No, that's not what I had to talk to him about." Not that she was about to say what the topic had been.

"I know how much you hate to counsel employees on behavior." Olivia nodded sympathetically. "I hope you got your business finished."

"It wasn't—" She stopped midsentence. "Yes, we completed our business." Remembering their business, she grinned. Very inappropriate.

Olivia stepped back into the hall. "You're needed in Trauma 3. Possible broken back from a swimming accident."

"Thanks, Olivia. What are the vitals?" She hurried out of the office and toward the trauma room.

She'd figure out some way Mike wouldn't take the fall for their disappearance, but not now. At the moment, she had a patient and she'd better focus on that, not the touch of that gorgeous but elusive man.

Besides, after a few hours of the rush and stress of emergency room life, maybe everyone would forget about the incident. Almost everyone, but not her and, she felt certain, not Mike.

What had he been thinking? Mike pushed a gurney into the elevator. Obviously, he hadn't been thinking at all.

An orderly didn't go around holding head residents during working hours, no matter how much the head resident had liked it. There could *not* be anything between them. He was in no position, either financially or mentally, to consider having a relationship with anyone.

Maybe when he finished medical school, they could pursue this.

Oh, sure. *If* he finished med school. By then she'd be married and have a couple of kids.

Why couldn't he get it through his head that a man who'd quit school and was trying to support his mother and brother wasn't exactly a prize? Better to treat Dr. Ramírez with the respect and courtesy she deserved, to pretend he'd never held her against him, that she hadn't leaned into his arms. He had to remember where he was in his life. On top of the emotional turmoil the incident had awakened, he needed this job too much to behave unprofessionally.

* * *

How much he needed the job was reinforced when he leafed through the mail on the kitchen table a week later. The electric bill was higher than he'd budgeted. In the credit card statement, he found a charge no one had told him about. Where would he find an extra ninety-eight dollars to cover it?

"I bought some delicious Canadian bacon for you." His mother put a plate on the table in front of him and he began to eat. "It was a little expensive, but I know how much you loved it when you were little." She sat next to him and sipped her coffee. "And I found some wonderful fresh orange juice at the grocery store. I had to get that for your breakfast."

"Mom." He put down his fork. "Thanks for thinking about me. I appreciate it."

"You're welcome, Mike. You take such good care of Tim and me. I want to spoil you a little."

"But we don't have money for extras like freshly squeezed orange juice."

"Oh, dear, but it's not all that expensive. Only about a dollar more a bottle."

"We don't have that extra dollar. I don't know how we're going to pay the credit card bill."

"I had to buy a pair of jeans and some shirts for Tim." She bit her lip. "His were in such bad shape."

"I know, but you need to tell me so I can plan to work more shifts."

"Oh." She nodded. "I promise."

He took a drink of the delicious freshly squeezed orange juice that was worth every penny it had cost. He might as well drink it since they had it. "How's the job hunt going?"

"Not well. Not at all well. I've found nothing since I helped Antonio for a week." She shook her head. "Too bad he doesn't need me anymore, although I'm delighted he's feeling so strong." She sighed. "Employers are so closed-minded about ex-cons, Mike. Almost no one will give me a chance."

He glanced up from his breakfast. "You said *almost* no one. Were there any who would hire you?"

"Yes, but I don't think I would enjoy doing the kind of work they wanted." She fluttered her hands.

"What were they?"

"One was working in a cleaners." She counted off on her fingers. "That would be such hot work. I did that for a year in prison, and it's not pleasant. Another was working in a fast-food place like Tim. I'm his mother. I should have a better job than my son has. One was in a restaurant, washing dishes, I believe."

"I hope you can find a job you'll enjoy, but right now, I need you to get a job. Any job. We need more money and you have to consider your parole status."

She frowned. "Darling, I didn't realize we were in such dire straits."

"Until I got these bills, I thought we were doing better. I haven't had to take money out of the savings account until now."

"I guess I could take one of those jobs."

"Mom, we're going to run out of money soon. After I pay the rent, we might not have enough for other necessities."

"Why didn't you tell me before?" She reached out to pat his hand. "When you don't communicate, no one knows what you want. I'll take the next job I find, even if it's cleaning out a horse stable."

The vision of his mother mucking out a stall in one of her long, spangled dresses and her jingling bracelets made him smile. "Thanks, Mom. You should be able to find something better than that."

"And I'll talk to Tim about what he's doing with the money he's earning. More of that should go into house-hold expenses."

"Great. Tim gets upset when I tell him that. He says it's his money, and I can't tell him what to do because I'm not his father."

"Tim doesn't behave like an adult sometimes."

"No, he doesn't. I bet you can get him to put some in the pot and to buy his own clothes."

"I'll talk to him." She patted Mike's hand. "If you wouldn't hold everything inside, life wouldn't be so hard for you."

As if he didn't know that already, but the habit of a lifetime was hard to break.

When she stood and waved her hand, her bracelets clinked together. "I'll get the want ads and make some phone calls now." She'd almost reached the arch to the living room when she turned back. "By the way, I've invited Antonio and his family to dinner Thursday."

Antonio and his family to dinner Thursday? Where would he find money to buy food to feed that many people?

"Tim said he'll help buy groceries. Antonio's going to bring the meat so I only have to provide the rest."

That helped on the cost.

She looked at him and bit her lip. "I'd really like you to be here."

Which brought up the more important question: where could he hide from Dr. Ramírez? After what happened in the empty office, the idea of seeing her outside of the hospital, probably dressed like a normal person and with her beautiful hair down, filled him with panic. He opened his mouth to say he was working the afternoon shift when his mother cut him off.

"Don't try to get out of it. I checked your schedule. You don't go in until eleven that night."

"Okay, I'll be here." In a real party mood, he added to himself.

She put her hands on her hips and glared at him. "I don't know why you don't want to flirt with that darling Ana. You seem to ignore her, and she's such a pretty, smart young woman."

"I'll be nice to everyone, Mother," he said. "I always am."

But he was *not* going to flirt with that darling Ana no matter how much she begged.

"Thank you, dear."

Trapped again.

Chapter Eight

Before the guests arrived Thursday evening, Mom said, "Why won't you take the money when it's offered to you? You know Brandon can afford it." She shook her head before she dashed off to wipe the counters again and check on the food in the oven.

Mike looked up from the kitchen table where he was studying an anatomy text book. "I know Brandon can afford it. I know he wants to help Francie's family, but I want to do this myself."

"Stubborn," she mumbled.

"Yeah, it runs in the family." The scent of garlic bread filled the room and made it hard for him to concentrate. He closed the book.

"You and Francie have always been so close. You know she wants you to take the money and go back to med school."

"Mom, it's because I *do* owe Francie so much that I can't take the money. I owe her everything, but I want to do this on my own."

"That makes no sense at all."

"It does to me. I can't take more from her even if it's Brandon's money. I have to take responsibility for my life, and this is one way I can. This is a start."

"Well, you're going to have to explain that to Francie because I can't." His mother put the teakettle on the burner and leaned over to pick up a dust bunny on the floor, her silver bracelets and earrings swinging with the motion. When she turned to toss the offending particle in the trash, her scarlet dress swung with her.

"She'll understand."

What *he* understood was why Mom had invited Brandon and Francie to the dinner tonight. She'd said it was because she wanted them to meet Antonio. Mike figured that was one reason. The other was in the hope Francie could convince him to take the money.

"You know, even with help, I'd have to work at least forty hours a week to rent the house and buy food. I couldn't do that and go to medical school." And, yes, he could take out a loan, but with his future looking so dim, he hated to owe more money than he already did from the first year of med school. He stood and headed out of the kitchen, the anatomy book in his hand, then dropped it on the sofa. "Looks like you need to get the table ready for the party tonight. I'll set the table, then I'll study in the living room."

"That's another thing," she said as he took the plates from the cupboard and placed them in a stack on the table. "Why are you studying if you aren't going back to school?"

"Because I like it, because I can use it at work. It's

exciting to see what I'm reading about happening right there in the E.R."

But she wasn't listening. The Ramírez family would be here in a few hours and that's what she was concentrating on. The house looked good because she'd forced Tim, who'd complained every minute, to pick up his stuff. Now she was brewing tea and checking the vegetable casserole and a dozen other little chores while he placed a pile of napkins next to the plates.

He was glad his mother was so happy, but Mike dreaded the evening. Being with Dr. Ramírez—because that was what he had to call her in his mind to keep his distance—outside the E.R. made his life complicated and uncomfortable. How could he keep his distance with his mother shoving them together? How could he resist Dr. Ramírez when she had her hair down, wore civilian clothes and smiled? No man could.

At a few minutes after six, Raúl, Luz and Mr. Ramírez knocked. Hearing Mike's shout of, "Come in," they entered the house. Raúl carried a large glass casserole dish while his sister Luz closed the door behind them.

"We're here, Tessie," Mr. Ramírez said.

Mom turned her cheek for a kiss. She glowed with happiness.

"Ana's parking her car. She'll be right in."

"My niece Francie and her husband, Brandon, will be here in a few minutes, too. You'll like them. Plus, she's bringing a wonderful dessert, something chocolate and filled with whipped cream."

"It sounds delicious," Dr. Ramírez said as she entered.

* * *

As she entered, Ana glanced at Mike. As usual, he looked terrific. He sat on the sofa, a book in his hands, pretending he hadn't seen her come in. But she'd seen his eyes lift toward her for a nanosecond before he'd begun to read again.

Tonight he wore khaki slacks with a gold shirt that fit his shoulders marvelously and probably made his eyes look great, which she couldn't see because he'd buried them in his book. Probably the nice clothes meant no pickup basketball game with the neighborhood kids this evening.

"Papi made his wonderful brisket," she said to Mrs. Fuller.

"Brisket? I didn't realize that was a Mexican dish."

"We don't always eat tacos, *querida*." Papi's eyes crinkled in amusement. "Sometimes we eat hamburgers and hot dogs, although we prefer them with hot sauce."

"We have an uncle that carries his hot sauce with him," Raúl said. "Uses it even on chicken tetrazzini, but the rest of us eat almost anything, sometimes without salsa."

"Especially this one." Papi waved toward his son.

"Let's put your lovely brisket in the oven to keep it warm." She walked through the arch into the living room, and the Ramírez family followed her, chatting with each other.

After she entered the kitchen, Ana stopped and looked around her at the art on the walls. She was so engrossed, she barely noticed Raúl place the meat on the butcher-block counter.

A Degas ballerina painted on the wall framed the

table, her long right leg stretched across the corner, "This is beautiful. Was it here when you moved in?"

"I told you about Mom, didn't I?" Mike spoke from only a few inches behind her, so close his breath tickled her neck.

When had he put down his book and come in the kitchen? She didn't care. He was here, and he was close. Very nice. She looked at him over her shoulder. "Art forgery?" she whispered. His proximity made her fluttery and a little breathless. The feeling was so unlike her, she wanted to move away from his warmth but with Luz, Papi and Mrs. Fuller sharing the tiny space, she couldn't move. Unless she shoved hard, like a tackle through the offensive line, she was stuck close to him.

He nodded and took a step back. The movement should have been a relief to Ana but didn't turn out that way. Perversely, she missed his warmth and longed to step back with him.

Mike's mother stood in the middle of the kitchen with everyone studying the beautiful artwork. She looked worried about their opinions, wiping her hands on a towel she'd picked up and trying to read their faces.

"Tessie," Ana said as she slid between Luz and Papi to stand in front of the mural and feel the power of the art, "this is one of the most beautiful paintings I've ever seen. It's absolutely marvelous." She reached out to touch it. "The color, the texture, the use of light, all are amazing."

Tessie stopped twisting the towel, relaxed and smiled.

"*Querida,* I knew about your painting but had no idea how very talented you are," Papi said.

"Let me take you into the hall and her bedroom," Mike said. "You aren't going to believe these paintings, either."

And they couldn't. After many "oohs" and "aahs," several soft strokes across the colors and textures, they returned to the kitchen, overwhelmed.

"These are all lovely." Papi kissed Tessie's cheek. "I'm proud to know a woman with the ability to bring such joy into the world."

She blushed. "Oh, Antonio."

Ana watched her father in amazement. Around Tessie, he was different. She slanted a glance at Mike to see if he was as amazed and amused as she at the relationship between their parents. He didn't seem to have a problem with it at all. Did she? She'd thought she would. With his mother's criminal record, she hadn't been too excited about Tessie, but she made his father happy. He hadn't smiled for such a long time, but he did around Tessie.

Was Tessie a widow? What had happened to his father? From the way they never talked about him, he must have been gone or dead for a long time. What had Mike done when his mother was in prison if his father was gone?

None of your business, Miss Nosy, she lectured herself.

"I brought dinner," Quique called from the living room. He entered the kitchen and dropped a bag of chips on the table.

"Thank you, Quique," Tessie said politely.

"Nice thought, *mano.*" Raúl laughed.

"Quique knows only three food groups," Ana said. "Fat, carbs and sugar."

"Hey." Quique held his hand up. "I was being

thoughtful. I could have just brought myself, which you would also enjoy greatly."

"You're a perfect guest," Tessie said. "I appreciate the addition. Thank you, again." She opened the sack and poured the chips into a bowl.

"De nada," he said with a bow. "You're very welcome."

When Francie and Brandon arrived a few minutes later, Tessie introduced them. Francie seemed interested to meet Ana, smiled and asked her a few questions. Brandon, who was tall, blond and very handsome, hovered around his pregnant wife.

"Why don't you sit here?" He took his Francie's hand, led her to the sofa and helped her get settled. "I'll bring you something to drink."

"He spoils me." Francie grinned as she watched her husband go into the kitchen.

After Luz arrived, everyone grabbed a plate and walked around the kitchen table to load them up. They could chose from the tender brisket, Mike's favorite corn pudding, green bean casserole bubbling under onion rings, bread, tortillas, guacamole, biscuits, salad, and more.

Plates filled, they crowded into the living room to eat. When Ana entered, she saw the four younger ones on the floor, legs crossed, chatting and joking. She was too old to sit that way and much to old for their conversation. Tessie and Francie sat on the sofa with a space between them. Thinking if she sat there, she could get to know both women better, Ana headed in that direction. Before she could sit, Francie scooted into the empty space faster than Ana had ever seen a woman that pregnant move.

Ana turned toward the now-empty place on Francie's left.

"That's for Brandon," Mike's cousin said with a sweet smile.

"Okay." Ana turned toward the folding chair next to Tessie.

"That's for your father." Tessie smiled, also.

Very suspicious, all this smiling and scooting. The only other seats were the two folding chairs in the corner. With a sigh, she gave up and took one of those. This reminded her of the time everyone had pushed her and Mike together on the swing at her family's house. Here, the room was so small they wouldn't be isolated, just extremely close together.

Brandon left the kitchen, handed Francie her drink and plate before he went back to get his own. As he did, Papi sat next to Tessie.

Almost last to come into the living room was Mike. He saw the place next to Francie and headed toward it, but his cousin said, "It's for Brandon. Sorry."

"You might as well give up," Ana said. "They want us to sit together."

Mike stiffened and turned toward the only empty chair before he walked across the room to sit next to her.

"Sometimes," he mumbled, "they are so obvious. I'm sorry."

He was embarrassed and had become Mr. Closed-In again. She hated all this prickliness and careful stepping around his ego. Not that it made a difference. No matter how their families pushed them together, no matter how much she'd enjoyed the interlude in the office, she wasn't sure she wanted attention from a man so much like her father—well, like the way her father used to be. If she were looking for a relationship, a man who smiled and shared more seemed like a better choice.

So why was she so pleased he was sitting next to her? She had to stop kidding herself. As much as she'd tried to forget what had happened there, the interlude in the office showed the tantalizing promise of what could develop between them.

"Francie's your cousin?" Ana asked after a few minutes of silence under the watchful eyes of both families.

As she'd expected, he only nodded.

She'd known better than to ask a yes or no question. She made another effort but missed again. "Are you two close?"

"Yes." The monosyllable fell into the sudden silence of the room.

She glared at her father and brothers. Immediately everyone started loud discussions.

"Why?" There, she'd finally gotten to an information question. Would he answer it?

"When Francie's father went to jail, she went to live with our Uncle Lou. When Uncle Lou went to jail, she came to live with us."

She almost dropped her fork at the information but forced herself to respond calmly, "I didn't realize so much of your family has served time."

"Francie's certain there's a faulty gene involved." He smiled at his cousin fondly.

"But you and your brother?"

"Haven't been in jail, though neither of us have been

immune to the call of the wild side." His smile vanished and he stared back at his plate as if he'd said something he wished he hadn't. "Francie pretty much kept me on the straight and narrow."

"What happened when your mother went to jail? Did you live with Francie?" He was silent. For a few seconds, she didn't think he was going to answer. Was she getting too close to him?

"No, Tim and I both went to live in foster families. Tim's was great. They still keep up with him, have him over for meals. None of mine were great." Before she could ask more about Mike's foster families he hurried on, "Francie was eighteen and living on her own, but she wasn't settled enough to take us in."

It felt as if he were speaking, adding facts, to keep her away from what he didn't want to talk about. She'd like to ask him more: Where was his father? What had his foster homes been like? But she didn't. Miss Nosy did have some boundaries, even if her family teased her about never recognizing one.

"The brisket is good," he said after a few minutes of silence. "It has an interesting taste, sort of spicy."

"It's my father's special recipe. I think he puts peppers and chili sauce in before he cooks it, but he won't share it with us. Says it goes to the first son."

"Is Robbie the oldest?"

"No, my oldest brother, Martín, lives in Houston. Also there's Hector who lives in San Marcos and Laura who's a lawyer San Antonio. They're all older than I am. You've met the rest of us."

"Big family."

"You should see it when everyone comes home. We're really packed in with all the spouses and kids."

They ate in silence until Tim said in a voice loud enough to stop the other conversations, "I think I'd like to snowboard."

"Oh?" Tessie tilted her head to try to grasp what he was saying. "Have you ever been on a snowboard before?"

"No, but professional snowboarders make a lot of money," he continued. "Endorsements and stuff."

In silence, they all stared at him.

"Umm, Tim." Mike paused and looked at Ana. "Help me," he whispered. "What can I say to convince him this is a stupid idea?"

"I don't think there are any words to persuade him of that," Ana whispered back.

He nodded and didn't say anything.

"Hey, way cool," Quique said.

"There aren't a lot of snowboarding sites in Texas," Francie said.

"There's not, like, a lot of snow in Texas, period," Raúl added.

"I'd have to go to Colorado." Tim nodded and took another bite of brisket.

"When did you decide this?" Brandon asked.

"Saw it on television, extreme sports. Think I could do it."

By now, everyone was struggling to keep from smiling, but it didn't work. They all started laughing, even Quique and Raúl who were just as likely to go off on such a crazy tangent.

"What?" Tim wailed. "No one ever takes me seriously."

"And you wonder why?" Mike teased his brother.

Ana watched the family chemistry and had to laugh again. It was hard to believe with all the Fuller family had been through, but right now they seemed like any normal family, joking and teasing. A moody Mike looked fine and almost too tempting with his smoldering eyes, but a smiling Mike took her breath away.

Once the room had quieted, Tessie said, "I need your help, everyone. I have to get a job. If you know of any leads, please let me know."

"Tessie." Papi took her hand. "You can always come back to the store."

"Thank you, Antonio, but you don't need me any longer. That would be charity and I want to work, to help Mike support us." She looked back at the room. "So, if anything turns up?"

"We'll let you know," Francie said.

Mike and Ana didn't have a minute alone for most of the evening. Although Tessie suggested they take a walk through the neighborhood, Mike refused. Oh, he refused politely, in a way that didn't hurt his mom's feelings, but, still, it was a refusal and probably the right decision.

After dinner, the two of them ended up washing dishes together, trapped into it when everyone left the kitchen.

By accident, he flipped soap bubbles out of the sink. When they hit her in the face, he looked stricken, realizing what he'd done to the head resident. As a reprisal, she picked up a handful of suds and tossed them on his head, which led, of course, to his slapping the water in the sink, which soaked them both. She squealed when the foam started down her neck.

"What's going on in there?" Quique shouted, followed by low chorus of "shhs" from the others in the living room. "Do I have to come in there?"

That question was followed by whispers of, "No."

"Lot of good your coming in here would do," Ana called back to her brother.

Then she looked into Mike's face. His smile had slipped as he ran his gaze over her wet hair, the drips sliding down her face and neck. Finally, he studied her with eyes dark with longing. Reaching out a finger, he slowly and gently traced a soap bubble that rolled down her neck.

She knew, if they were alone, he would kiss her. For a moment she lost herself in the warmth of his gaze, savoring the attraction that zinged between them. She placed her hand on his arms and leaned toward him, yearning to be closer.

Hearing a movement, she glanced toward the arch to see everyone's eyes, sixteen in all, glued on the scene. She jumped back from Mike. When the families realized she was staring at them, they quickly turned away and began a loud conversation while they returned to their seats.

After he dropped his hand to his side, he looked away from the crowd at the door and finished cleaning up, keeping his eyes firmly fixed on the sink. That done, he shouted to those in the living room, "Is everyone ready for dessert?"

Ana moved toward the fridge to take Francie's concoction out but stepped into a small splash of water left over from their horseplay. Her foot slipped from under her, and a searing pain ripped through her right thigh. Biting her lip to cut off the scream, she reached toward

Mike as she crumpled. He grabbed her and wrapped his arms around her to keep her upright before she could hit the floor.

"What happened? Did you break something?" He held her tense body against him as she balanced on her left leg.

"It's her thigh." Papi ran to his daughter. "An old injury." He took Ana's left arm. "Help me get her to a chair."

Once she was seated, Ana leaned back and forced her body to relax in an effort to relieve the pain. Deep breaths usually helped. She was aware Mike had pulled a chair next to her and had put his arm around her shoulders, but she ignored his closeness and massaged the muscles to alleviate the throbbing.

"Do you want a cold pack?" Mike whispered.

She nodded, and he went to the refrigerator. While she rubbed her thigh, she heard the expressions of worry around her and the start of her father's explanation.

"When Ana was about five," Papi told everyone gathered in the kitchen, "my oldest son Martín was helping me paint the house. Ana wanted to help. No matter how many times I told her, 'No,' she kept asking."

"You know what she's like," Raúl said. "Once she decides on something, she doesn't give up."

Everyone murmured agreement.

"What's wrong with that?" she asked through gritted teeth. She took the cold pack from Mike and laid it carefully on her throbbing thigh.

As if he hadn't heard the question, her father continued. "When Martín and I went into the house for a drink, she got a paintbrush and climbed the ladder. I should have known she would. I should have put the ladder away."

Ana heard the guilt in her father's voice. "Papi, you can't blame yourself. It was all my fault," she said as the pain lessened.

"When she got to the roof," Papi said, "the ladder tipped and she fell, all the way to the ground and onto a storm window we'd taken off."

"Oh, no," Tessie whispered. "What happened?"

"The glass broke and shards tore up the muscles and a lot of other stuff in her thigh. The doctors thought she'd never be able to use that leg again. Even then, Ana refused to give up. She exercised, did physical therapy four times a day, suffered a lot to be able to use the leg."

"But when she twists it, it hurts." Raúl put his hand on his sister's shoulder. "She's the toughest, most tenacious person I know. Nothing stops her from getting what she wants, except that leg."

"But I don't let that happen," Ana said.

"Let's go back to the living room," Francie pulled on Brandon's hand. "It can't be fun for Ana to have everyone watching her."

They left her alone with Mike again. He still had his arm around her shoulder. Now, as the pain began to diminish, she could enjoy his comforting closeness.

"I remember once when I first started work you were in the break room rubbing your thigh." He began moving his fingers up and down her neck in a gentle caress.

"Sometimes if I move awkwardly or stand too long, it begins to ache, but this is the worst it's felt in a long time." She shook her head. "I'm sorry I ruined the party."

"Don't worry." He leaned closer and rubbed his cheek against her hair.

Had he placed a light kiss there, against her curls? She couldn't tell because it happened so quickly, but the thought he might have warmed her.

"I'm better." She looked into his face. Upset because of his worried expression, she rubbed her palm across his cheek. "I'll be okay."

"Take care of yourself, Doctor."

The soft tone of his voice and the concern in his eyes filled her with immeasurable joy.

The party broke up immediately. When Mike took her arm to help her off the porch and to her car, Ana protested. "I can walk fine. I'm fine."

"Just give it up, Doctor. I'm going to help you whether you want it or not." Actually it was a great excuse to hold and support her.

In spite of her continued objections, when they reached the car, he opened the door and carefully handed her inside.

"I can do this." She pulled her legs inside and turned in the seat.

"I know." Once she was settled in her car and had the key in the ignition, he waved and walked back inside the house.

That may have been a mistake. Maybe he should have waited outside until everyone left, because Francie waylaid him immediately.

"What about the money for school?" she asked.

"Thanks, but I can't accept it. I have to take responsibility for my life and my future."

With a sigh, she nodded. "I knew you wouldn't take it, but I want you to know the offer's always open."

"I know." He hugged her.

Francie squeezed him back then whispered, "Ana's better for you than Cynthia. I really like her. Smart, pretty, nice and just right for you."

"Why does everyone assume Dr. Ramírez and I should be together?" he muttered.

"Because you *are,* silly. We all know that. You two just haven't admitted it yet."

He hoped she was wrong—and that she was right. "I don't have time for anything else in my life, not now."

"Love never comes at the most convenient time." She looked out the open front door at her husband, who waited on the porch for her. "Who could have believed a parolee would fall in love with her parole officer? Or that he'd love her—that's me—too?"

"But you're special."

"Mike, you're special, too." She kissed him on the cheek then turned to leave.

With the guests gone, Mike headed back to the bathroom. Before he got there, he saw his mother on the sofa, her hand over her eyes.

"What's the matter, Mom?" He fell into the seat next to her.

"Oh." She started and glanced up at him. "How's Ana going to be? I hated to see her in so much pain."

"Fine. She says she knows how to handle this." Mike waited a few seconds as his mother put her hand over her eyes again. "Mom, what's really bothering you? I know it's not Ana."

"It's nothing." But she didn't look up.

"Mom, what is it?"

"Oh, Mike." She looked up at him, blinking back tears. "What if I can't find a job?"

"Mom, you'll find a job. It may take a while, but you'll find one." He patted her shoulder.

"But if I don't, how are you and Tim going to eat? He's still growing. He needs clothes and new shoes, and money to go to a movie every now and then."

"Mom, he's working. He has money to do that. I can work more overtime."

"You know I have to find a job to satisfy the terms of my parole." She sniffed. "I've looked all over. Doors close fast when you're my age, have no skills and a criminal record."

Mike squeezed her.

"They put my name on the list at the Biggy-Mart, but people only get jobs as greeter when one of them dies." She took a tissue and wiped her eyes. "And all the fast-food restaurants have enough kids off for the summer to fill every position." She gulped. "I don't know what I'm going to do."

"You tell your parole officer how hard you've looked for work." He squeezed her hand. "We'll make it. We'll be fine."

She stopped crying and wadded up the tissue. "Maybe I'll have to go back to forging paintings again."

He dropped her hand and sat straight. "What?"

"Dear," she said with a pitiful shrug, "forging is the only skill I have."

"No, Mother, you are not going to go back to forgery.

No, no, no!" When she didn't say anything, he added, "Your parole officer isn't going to like that."

"What do I care?" She stretched her arms out, the bangles on her wrists sparkling in the light. "I have to take care of my boys."

"No." Mike took both of her hands and turned her to face him. "Listen to me carefully. You're not going to go back to forging. Do you understand?"

She dropped her hands into her lap and the bracelets gave a light jingle. "But I have to help you somehow. Forging is the only—"

"I know you think it's the only skill you have, but it isn't true. You're friendly and good-looking. I say that even though you're my mother. You might be able to be a hostess in a restaurant or something."

"I'd like that." She looked down at her finger, at the short but nicely manicured nails. "I don't want to go back to forging, but it's the only job I've ever made money at. My pictures were so lovely."

"Yes, but you're not going to do that. You're not going back to that life." She still didn't respond. "And Mr. Ramírez would miss you."

"Oh." She bit her lip. "That's true. Antonio would miss me if I went back to prison."

"We all would." He spoke slowly. "And he would not like you to return to a life of crime."

"I know."

"Promise me you won't think about this anymore."

"All right." She sighed. "It's so very discouraging not to be able to find a job when we need the money. I guess I fell back into old habits."

"Old, bad habits."

The conversation might have been funny if she hadn't been so serious. Had he convinced her to stay straight?

So here he was, thirty minutes later, without a shower, driving to work at ten-fifteen, headed toward a job he both loved and hated.

What was happening in that little house? His mother had considered returning to a life of crime. They had deep financial problems and his brother wanted to be a professional snowboarder.

"Oh, God." The words left his mouth to his surprise. A prayer he hadn't planned to say had popped out.

"Oh, God," he repeated. "Where are You when I need You?" He stopped at a light and watched for a sign that God was listening. He didn't know what he expected: A sudden strike of lightning? A small voice? Perhaps a wind or a shimmer of light? He looked for any response, but none appeared. Inside, he didn't experience the assurance of God's presence that used to be such an anchor in his life. "Oh, God," he whispered. "I'm worried about Tim, and my mom's unhappy. I'm working hard to live a good life. We all really need You now." He paused again. "Are You listening?"

Again, no answer came.

He'd gone to God in prayer at his lowest time but had received no reply.

Well, that was it. If God wanted to talk with him, God was going to have to start the conversation.

Chapter Nine

A typical Friday night in the emergency room—sliding from busy to hectic and headed straight toward chaotic. About 3:00 a.m., staff was pulled from other floors to pitch in.

It had started with fifty guests at a banquet with food poisoning. Ten were admitted.

If that wasn't enough of a mess, fifteen coeds from a college dorm came in suffering from exposure to an unidentified poisonous gas. Follow that with several car wrecks, a Harley accident, a couple of gang shoot-outs, miscellaneous chest pain, appendicitis and other cases Mike could no longer remember, and the staff was exhausted and drawn thin trying to cover it all.

Still the ambulances came. Several were loaded with victims from a bar brawl while those in the waiting room filled that area and spilled onto the sidewalk.

With the shrieks and roars of the ambulances, the shouts of vitals from paramedics, the moans of patients and the urgent questions of the families, the noise level intensified. Mike leaned against a wall outside Trauma 3 for a quick vertical nap, a talent he was perfecting, when another sound grabbed his attention.

"Security," Dr. Ramírez yelled from Trauma 4. Shoving himself away from the wall, Mike ran into the cubicle just after the nurse ran out.

Inside stood a man six inches taller than Mike and a hundred pounds heavier. Worse, he waved a long knife aimlessly around the cubicle.

On the other side of the exam table, her escape route cut off by the man, Dr. Ramírez leaned against the wall of cabinets, her eyes wide and frightened. The man on the trauma bed had blood across the front of his T-shirt. From an earlier event or a wound from the armed guy? With his fingers curled around the railing of the bed, the patient looked terrified.

Fear hit Mike hard, almost paralyzing him until a jolt of adrenaline kicked in. With that, he focused, first glancing at Ana then scrutinizing the room to get an idea of the layout and what was going on.

"I'm gonna kill you, Benton." The guy with the knife kept shaking his head as if trying to clear it while the weapon shook in his hand.

"Security," Mike called. Outside he heard people running around, the sound of panicked voices, but no help came. He moved around the room stealthily, shortening the distance been him and Ana while he tried not to alert the man of his progress.

"Thought you'd get away with taking my girl, huh?" the man bellowed at the patient.

"Leave it alone, Jimmy."

The patient tried to speak calmly. Hard to do with a knife inches from his face Mike guessed. "It's over. Barb doesn't want to see you again. She's afraid of you."

Jimmy growled as his lips became taut and misshapen in a chilling grin. As the big man moved around the bed and swiped the knife through the air, his face got even redder, so bright Mike wondered if he were going to have a stroke.

Mike was only a few feet from Dr. Ramírez when she again shouted, "Security."

Jimmy looked up at her as if he'd forgotten she was there. "Why are you staring, lady?"

He turned toward her, raised his left hand—the one without the knife—and backhanded her hard across the face before Mike could move. By the time Jimmy could raise his fist to punch her again, Mike closed the last steps between them. With more strength than he believed he possessed, he sprang away from the wall and threw himself on the man's back. Once there, he reached over the man's shoulders with both arms, trying to keep his balance and to stop Jimmy before he could hurt Dr. Ramírez again.

"Dear Lord, help us," Mike whispered. He kept his balance with his legs scissored around Jimmy's hips and battled for the weapon as the man twisted and twirled around the room in an effort to dislodge him. He prayed constantly for strength and courage, prayed he could distract Jimmy from Dr. Ramírez and the patient.

"Security." Mike held on with a hammerlock, his left arm around the man's neck.

Dr. Ramírez picked up an emesis basin and struck Jimmy on the arms with it, careful to miss Mike and leaping away from Jimmy's reach. As he fought, Jimmy swung his free hand and smashed into one of the large lights over the trauma bed, breaking the glass and cutting his hand. The crystals showered down on the patient and the floor while blood spouted and flowed down Jimmy's arm.

Mike knew he couldn't hold out much longer against such a powerful opponent. Dr. Ramírez's efforts and the wound in Jimmy's hand seemed to make him even stronger, more violent, almost as if his anger fed off the battle.

"Get off," Jimmy shouted. He shuffled backward and fell against the wall in an effort to smash Mike against it. Air shot out of Mike's lungs but he held on. He had to. At least he'd distracted Jimmy. At least the man had stopped threatening Dr. Ramírez.

"Get out," Mike shouted to her as Jimmy moved away from the exit.

But she ignored him. Instead she replaced the basin with a crutch and began to punch at Jimmy's body.

Still Mike whispered a prayer with every breath. "Please, God. Please, God."

"Security," she called as she landed a good blow in Jimmy's abdomen. It didn't seem to faze the man.

"Shut up, everyone!" Jimmy brandished the knife and methodically beat his back against the wall, attempting to crush Mike with each slam.

Even as Mike softened the blows by bending his knees and pushing away from the wall with his feet, it felt as if his legs were breaking. He didn't know how long they'd last under the bombardment.

Then Mitchelson, the nurse, silently entered the small space. In a second, he grabbed the trauma bed with the patient on it, unlocked the brakes with his foot and shoved it outside. After that, he returned, moving around the edge of the room to take the crutch from Dr. Ramírez and stand in front of her.

"What's the problem, buddy?" the RN asked in a soothing voice.

"He's angry and high on something, maybe meth," Benton shouted from the hall.

Which explained the man's incredible strength, Mike thought as he pulled himself higher on the man's back.

"His name is Jimmy," Dr. Ramírez picked up another crutch and tried to push around Mitchelson.

"Jimmy, you don't want to hurt anyone here," Mitchelson counseled.

In response, Jimmy attempted to scrape Mike off again while he swung the knife toward Mitchelson.

Just as Mike thought he'd have to let go, three security guards and Williams, the big orderly, hurtled through the open door. Seeing them, Jimmy grabbed the crutch Mitchelson held, swung it and hit one of the guards in the head, knocking him down and out.

"You got his arms?" one of the guards asked Mike.

"Not really." Wasn't the swinging crutch evidence of that? With his last bit of strength, he reached over Jimmy's shoulders and grabbed the crutch as Mitchelson took hold of the other end.

"Hold on. We'll try to get his legs."

After scuffling for a minute, the two guards, Mike and Mitchelson each had a limb while Williams had knocked the knife to the floor and held one of Jimmy's wrists in each of his beefy hands. A guard cuffed Jimmy, which took a lot of the fight out of him. Security hustled him from the cubicle and toward the outer door while Williams followed. Mike bent his knees and flexed them up and down to relieve the knotted muscles in his legs.

"Cops are here," said a nurse to the medical team. "They'll want to talk to you."

Mike and Dr. Ramírez stood against the cabinets, breathing deeply, her face mottled red and white where the man had hit her. "I was really scared," she said in a shaky voice and swallowed hard. "Really scared."

"You were great." He opened him arms and pulled her into them while she shook. With one hand, he rubbed her back; with the other, he held her close, to keep her safe although the danger was over, but more to assure himself she was alive and pretty much unhurt. The fact that he held Ana, breathing, and thoroughly alive in his arms calmed him. He was not about to let go of her.

"Um, Fuller, I hate to interrupt but he cut you," Mitchelson said. "Better let the doctor examine it."

"He cut me?" Mike asked matter-of-factly as he reluctantly let go of Dr. Ramírez and stared at the blood dripping from a wound in his right arm. "I hadn't noticed."

Immediately Dr. Ramírez became a doctor again. "On the trauma bed, Fuller." She looked around before realizing there was no bed and the room was covered with broken glass while the floor was littered with instruments. The knife shone silver and crimson against the white tile floor.

"Guess this is a crime scene now," Mike said.

"Okay, let's go to Exam 1." She pushed Mike ahead of her. "Mitchelson," she asked, once they were in the new room and Mike was on the trauma bed, "what happened to the patient who was in there before this started?"

"Dr. Patel took him to Trauma 3. He's working on him while the police question him."

"I don't even remember what was wrong with the man." Dr. Ramírez shook her head. "Let's get you taken care of, Fuller."

"The police'll need a statement from us, too." Mitchelson got a suture tray while Dr. Ramírez cleaned the cut.

"Your wound is long but not deep," she said as she examined Mike's arm. "Won't take much to hold it."

By the time Dr. Ramírez had finished cleaning and closing the cut, Dr. Harmon, the Director of Emergency Services, bustled into the cubicle.

"Is everyone all right?" She glanced from the gauze on Mike's arm to the bruise beginning to show around Dr. Ramírez's eye. "Guess not."

"We're okay," Dr. Ramírez said. "Minor injuries. Fuller's arm will heal fine."

Dr. Harmon strode toward Dr. Ramírez and studied the redness and start of swelling on her left cheek. "You're going to have a beautiful shiner there. Better put some ice on it. Olivia," she shouted. "Get an ice pack in here, stat." Then she pulled out a small flashlight to examine Dr. Ramírez's pupils. "They're okay, but go home and get some rest." She pointed a finger toward the door when no one moved. "Everyone, home!"

"I can't." Dr. Ramírez moved away from the counter but had to lean against the trauma bed after her second step.

"Doctor, you are in no condition to care for patients." Dr. Harmon squinted at her. Mike thought she might shake her finger if Dr. Ramírez kept disagreeing with her. "You're unsteady, and you won't be able to see out of that eye in a few hours."

Although she kept her hand on the bed, Dr. Ramírez straightened and lifted her chin. "I'm not used to giving up. I can do this."

"No, Doctor, you cannot. Go home and stay there for a few days. If not for yourself, think of your patients. Remember the damage you could do and the hospital's insurance rates."

"I can't leave, not when we're so busy."

"Yes, you can, Doctor." Her tone of voice became more authoritative. "When your boss tells you to, you'd better do exactly what she says." She turned toward Mitchelson and Mike. "How are the two of you?"

Mike held up his bandaged arm. "Fine. A little cut."

"No injuries." Mitchelson put his arms out to show her.

"All right, you two gentlemen go home, too."

"I can't leave. I need the money," Mike said.

"You'll be paid for two shifts. I'll see to that. Don't forget to go to the business office and fill out the paperwork on worker's comp for an injury caused on the job." She waved them out of the exam room. "Get out, all of you. Just to be safe."

Mike tried to support Dr. Ramírez as she left the trauma room, but she shook his hand off.

"Thanks, but I can do this myself."

"Are you sure?" Although he was worried about her balance, Mike recognized her mood and was careful not to take Dr. Ramírez's arm as they walked down the corridor.

She nodded. Color had returned to her face and she'd stopped shaking and swaying, always a good sign. She held the ice bag Olivia had given her against her eye. "It hurts some, but I'm fine. I'm going to change clothes." She gestured to the lab coat smeared with Mike's blood. "Check in the business office then go home." She put her hand on his arm. "Thank you, Mike. You saved my life."

Sometimes all her determination drove him crazy. He watched her walk down the hallway, ambling more than striding but she didn't put her hand against the wall so he guessed she felt steadier. He would have admired her display of self-sufficiency and grit if the whole experience hadn't been so frightening.

Following instructions from security, Mike gave a statement to the police before he went to the business office to fill out forms. Focusing on the forms and his statement, the easy stuff, kept him from reacting to what had just happened.

When he could no longer hide behind routine, when he had to face the attack and the danger to all of them, anxiety filled him. He relived the moment Jimmy hit Dr. Ramírez, and he'd been powerless to stop it. She could have been killed or badly hurt. So could he or Mitchelson. Considering what a crazy man with a knife could do, they'd been fortunate. More than fortunate. They'd been protected and blessed.

"Thank you, God," he whispered.

He looked down at his watch. Almost 7:00 a.m., time to leave, but he had someplace to go before he went home.

* * *

In the chapel, three pews lined each side of an aisle wide enough for wheelchairs. On the walls were beautiful stained-glass windows backlit to show scenes of Jesus healing the blind and lame, welcoming the children, curing the leper. A gold cross dominated a Communion table covered in rich green cloth.

Alone in the chapel, Mike sank into a seat in the last row. Although he'd meant to kneel on the step in the front, his legs had turned so weak he couldn't walk farther. Back here, he sat in silence for a moment, eyes on the cross until the scene in the trauma room forced itself into his thoughts.

Over and over again, he saw Jimmy with the knife, hovering over the patient; Jimmy slapping Dr. Ramírez; and Dr. Ramírez hitting him with the basin and crutch. Didn't she realize the danger she'd been in? He could feel himself, dizzily whirling around the room on Jimmy's back, certain the out-of-control man would crush him then go after the doctor with his knife.

He shook all over as if he were chilling. Grasping his hands in an attempt to regain control, he sucked in huge gulps of air as he repeated, "The Lord is my shepherd," over and over. After what must have been at least ten minutes of those terrifying visions flickering through his brain, the shaking slowed and his breathing became close to normal.

Little by little, he realized he wasn't alone. The chapel was filled by a presence. He could feel the Holy Spirit surrounding him, here to enfold and comfort him, to bring him courage and peace.

"Thank you, God," he whispered, aware he and the

Lord were communicating again, at last. What else was there to say? Because he didn't want to break this sense of closeness, he added, "For watching over us all, for keeping us safe." He paused because the last prayer was hard. "Please help Jimmy find his way."

As he meditated, tears began to fall, but he didn't try to stop them. Instead, he reached for the box of tissue at the end of the pew to blot his cheeks while he allowed the tension and fear to flow from him. The disappointments and doubts of the past year poured out with them and he turned them over to God. In that moment of gratitude, he recognized God had always been near. God had listened to him every time, every second.

Twenty minutes later, he said another, "Thank you, God," wiped his face and stood to go, renewed. The few minutes had changed him. At the door, he turned toward the chapel again, hating to leave, then he headed to his locker.

He worried about Dr. Ramírez and Mitchelson and everyone who'd gone through the siege. Although still shaky from the experience, inside he was different. Within he felt strong and at peace, finally. He knew he could get through the next few years as he searched for God's will for his life.

How? He didn't know, but now he would listen.

His arm had started to hurt and he felt completely exhausted. Ready to drive home and crash for the rest of the day, Mike pushed through the doors into the E.R.

"Fuller," one of the morning shift nurses said, "there's a message for a Dr. Fuller on the E.R. bulletin board. Guess that means you." She pointed across the hall.

Why would anyone think he was Dr. Fuller? He took down the pink slip and read it.

"Seems you worked with this kid in the E.R. yesterday and her parents want to thank you." The nurse passed him with her arms full of supplies.

"How do you know?" But he knew how. Privacy was nonexistent in the E.R. He guessed everyone had read the note.

With a groan, he turned toward the elevators. He didn't feel like talking to anyone, not now. He wanted to go home and sleep for two or three days. The delayed reaction to the scene in the trauma room punched him in the stomach and neck and sapped his physical strength.

Maybe he'd go home now and come in to see the kid tomorrow, but returning would mean waking up and getting dressed to drive here. Of course, the kid might be discharged by then. Might as well go now. The parents wanted to thank him. That was nice and seldom happened to an orderly. Shouldn't take too long.

While the elevator ascended, he tried to figure out which patient this could be. He'd worked a double shift and seen at least three or four children. When the elevator stopped at the third floor, he got out and headed toward room 323.

Once there, he glanced inside. The room was filled with balloons and stuffed animals. In the bed, he saw the little redheaded girl who'd come in the previous evening with asthma. She'd been struggling to breathe but had calmed down when Mike talked to her and gave her the polar bear he'd made from a towel.

Leaning over the bed was the child's mother who'd

been so worried yesterday. "Dr. Fuller." She smiled and walked toward him. "I'm Julie Andres. I can't tell you how much my husband and I appreciate your care for Sarah."

"Yes, Dr. Fuller. We were so worried." Mr. Andres rose from the chair next to the bed and walked toward Mike with his hand out. "This was the worst attack Sarah has had. We're glad she stabilized. She's going home after a few more tests."

Mike took the hand Mr. Andres extended. "I'm glad I could help, but I'm not a doctor."

"You aren't?" The parents glanced at each other.

"We were sure you were a pediatrician." Mr. Andres let go of Mike's hand.

"No, I'm a CA, clinical assistant." Mike moved to the bed and smiled at Sarah who, although surrounded by plush animals, still held the towel bear tightly.

"Thank you," she said. "You were so nice to me."

"How are you feeling?"

She took a breath. "See, I can breathe now."

"And her blood gasses are good," Mrs. Andres said.

"I'm glad I was able to help."

Mrs. Andres caressed her daughter's arm. "You're great with children."

"I agree with my wife about that." Mr. Andres sat again and smiled at Sarah. "Thank you."

Mike patted the child's hand before he went to the door and turned to wave at her. When he left the room, he walked down the hall with an unexpected burst of energy. Heading toward the elevator, he passed a big window on the right, the window to the pediatric playroom. He stopped, took a few steps backward and looked inside.

At a table sat a little girl with an IV in her arm and on oxygen. She looked up and smiled. Close to the back wall, a child—he didn't know if this was a girl or boy because the head was shaved—sat in a wagon, reading and pointing out pictures to a woman. An older boy played with cars on another table while a pale little girl relaxed on a window seat and looked out at the view of the capital rotunda.

Children in pain.

Sick children.

Children he could help.

Children God wanted him to help.

He struggled to grasp this concept. God wanted Mike in pediatrics. The revelation hit him hard. He leaned against a wall and thought about it, filled with that certainty that, of course God wanted him in pediatrics. Why should the knowledge surprise him? God had been telling him that since Mike got here. So had most of the staff in the E.R.

God had been leading him, but Mike had resisted almost every step of the way.

He laughed. He didn't stop until he realized the children were staring at him. With another wave, he walked down the hall, confident *this* was where he belonged. This was his future. If it took him years and even more hard work, if it meant waiting until his mother and brother could support themselves, he knew he'd be here someday as a doctor, as a pediatrician: Michael Robert Fuller, M.D.

God had been speaking to him all along, but he'd been too stupid to hear Him, too filled with pain to pay attention, too angry to acknowledge God's voice and leading.

It seemed that, for him, the hardest part of praying was listening.

Smiling, he pushed away from the wall, dodged around the gurney, and ran toward the elevator.

He had to tell Ana what had happened.

Chapter Ten

Mike had to see Ana. Because the scene of her being attacked was still clear in his mind, he needed to touch her, to make sure she was all right. And he had to share with her what had happened in the chapel.

It was only as he left the hospital and headed toward his car that he realized he'd called Dr. Ramírez by her first name. *Ana.* On top of that, he'd decided to share this experience with her before he'd considered telling his mother.

Of course, when Mike tried to find someone he'd attempted to ignore for weeks, he couldn't. Her car was no longer in the parking lot. He had no idea of where her apartment was other than "only a few minutes" from the hospital.

He looked in the telephone directory but she wasn't listed. No way was he going to ask the E.R. clerk for the phone number or address. In the first place, due to privacy issues, the clerk couldn't give him either one.

Besides, Mike didn't want anyone to know he wanted to get in touch with her.

His mother would know how to get Ana's number. Did he want his mother to know he planned to talk to Ana? Didn't matter. If things worked out as Mike hoped, she'd know soon enough and be happy about it. She'd probably believe Ana and Mike were together because she'd maneuvered things so cleverly. If they ever got together.

Then he stopped in the middle of the parking lot, as he was putting the key into the lock on his car. What was all this about him and Ana being together?

Slow down, he told himself. He should not rush into anything. Probably better to go home, sleep for a few hours, take tonight off with pay and decide what to do tomorrow. As much as he'd like to talk to Ana tonight, acting impetuously always got him in trouble. Another family trait.

He unlocked the door, got into the car and started the engine.

If he waited until tomorrow or the next day or next week to talk to Ana, he could spend the time until then rejoicing, knowing God had always heard him and that he had a future, that God was leading him.

Would Ana be part of that? Putting the car in gear, he headed out of the lot and turned left.

What an idiot he was. He had a problem with acting recklessly. Actually, that wasn't the problem. He acted recklessly very well. His problem was in slowing down, thinking things through. He knew that, but his mind kept going full speed into fantasyland. It was way too early to consider Ana's place in his life. He shouldn't even think of Ana's sharing his future. Not yet, but he could feel that impulsiveness attempting to take over again.

And yet the entire experience—from the peril in the trauma room to his prayers in the chapel—had clarified his feelings. He couldn't ignore the fact that Ana or he could have been killed. What was the use of putting life on hold when it could have ended in the flash of a knife?

He didn't have to run to her immediately. He shouldn't. That would probably scare her anyway. If the strength of his feelings frightened him, imagine what a shock this would be to her.

He needed to slow down, rein in his rash nature.

What he *could* do was talk to her, just talk to her, tell her what had happened in the chapel, in Sarah's hospital room. She'd like to hear that. After all, nothing was going on between them. Nothing. They weren't dating. They worked together and were friends, nothing more than friends, through their families. He had no desire to take it further.

Oh, sure.

The truth was, he really wanted to be with Ana, but right now, his life was too crazy for a relationship. He was in no position to consider marriage.

Marriage? Where in the world had that idea come from? Marriage was not a possibility. What was he thinking? Was he thinking at all? He pulled off the road and into a parking lot to contemplate the situation. His mind and thoughts were going around in circles at a thousand miles an hour, headed for a serious crash if he didn't gain control.

Slowing his brain, he attempted to consider the situation, all that he'd gone through that night, and put it into a reasonable, rational order. First, he knew how hard it would be to talk to Ana as a friend and a colleague after he'd held her in his arms again, after she'd clung to him.

Second, he was aware that his family also got in trouble by not only conning others but themselves. It was important that he *not* lie to himself about Ana. The truth was, no matter how hard he tried to deny or ignore it, he wanted more than friendship.

Trying to be reasonable and not to lie to himself, he wondered if it was impetuous to want to be with a woman he cared about more than he should, a woman who'd been the length of a knife blade away from death.

He didn't think so, but he'd made a lot of poor choices during his life.

He didn't need to call her today. Not really. Today he'd sleep and think about things, and life and priorities. He could wait until the next day to come to a decision.

A good plan but a doomed one.

After he got home, he'd slept from eight in the morning to six that evening when he'd gotten up to make a couple of sandwiches. He was a little stiff from riding Jimmy's back and being banged into the wall, but rest and a soak in the tub would take care of that. No big deal.

While he ate, he kept glancing at the phone, almost calling Ana until he realized that he couldn't call her. He didn't have her number and was not going to call Mr. Ramírez to get it. The best thing to do was to watch a little television with his mother, read and go to bed early.

His determination failed. That impulsiveness again.

"Mr. Ramírez," he said when he called at seven-thirty after holding out for an excruciating ninety minutes. "This is Mike Fuller. Could you please give me Ana's phone number?"

"I could, but she's right here. Do you want to talk to her?"

"Sure." The decision of when to call her had been taken out of his hands, hands which at this moment were a little clammy.

He could hear muffled voices, then Ana said, "Hey, Mike. How are you? Have you recovered from last night?"

She thought he was calling to check on her. That was okay, a good start for the conversation. "I'm fine. My arm doesn't hurt much, but I don't mind not working tonight. How are you?"

"Okay. My eye hurts a little. It looks pretty ugly and will get worse. Maybe it's a good thing I'm not going in. I'd probably scare the patients." She paused. "Mike, thank you for coming into the trauma room. You probably saved the lives of both the patient and me."

"Glad to do it." Mike looked around the living room. On the sofa, his mother was sketching and Tim was flipping through a magazine next to her. Tim reading on a Saturday evening? No way. The kid was trying to listen to his call.

"I'm taking the phone outside. Give me a minute." Once on the porch, he sat on the front step. "I'd like to see you sometime."

"Okay." Her voice sounded pleased. "We can sympathize about our aches and pains. When?"

"Could I pick you up for breakfast Monday?" Breakfast seemed like a good choice. Not a real date like lunch or dinner. That would work until they decided where they were going, if they discovered anything between them. He knew how he felt. Was she interested in anything beyond comparing injuries?

"Breakfast? Sounds nice. Do you know where I live?"

He took down her address and phone number. "Is eight o'clock okay? That's early on a day off."

"Sounds fine. I can never sleep late. I'll see you then."

After they said goodbye, Mike turned off the cell and walked back into the house. Both his mother and brother glanced at him then back at their sketching and reading without saying a word. He picked up the remote and turned on the television.

"Mike," Tim said. "Are you going to use the car tonight?"

"Nope." He searched for a ball game.

"Could I borrow it? I told Luz and Quique I'd try to get the car and take them to a movie."

Luz, Quique and Tim as friends. That was good. Tim hadn't had a chance to make friends in the neighborhood.

"Sure." Mike tossed him the keys.

"What about you and Ana?" his mother asked as Tim hurried into his room to get ready.

"We're going to have breakfast together on Monday." Before his mother could begin to celebrate, he added, "Only breakfast, Mom. That's all. Don't get excited."

He shouldn't have wasted the warning. His mother tried to hide a smile but he knew she was humming "Here Comes the Bride" inside her head.

"I'm going to church tomorrow morning." Mike sat down and turned on the television to watch the Astros. "I'd like you to come with Tim and me."

"To church?" She stopped humming and gazed at Mike with a blank expression. "Why would I go to church? I mean, really, why would I want to?"

Putting the remote down, Mike said, "Francie took me to worship a couple of years ago. I really liked it. I stopped going for a while, but that was a mistake. Francie took me back to church just a few weeks ago. I've missed it. Church helps me. God gives me strength to live the way I believe I should. I'd like to share that with you."

"Sunday at church?" She glanced at her lap and smoothed the gauzy material of her mauve skirt, her bracelets jingling with each movement. Then she looked at him. He thought he could see terror and sadness in her eyes. "Mike, I'm not good enough to go to church. I'm not one of those churchy-type people."

"Mom, you'll be accepted and loved at this church. Francie goes there. If you're uncomfortable at any time, we'll leave, but I'd like to share this with you."

"I don't know." When he didn't push anymore, she nodded. "All right." She sighed. "If it makes you happy. What time do I need to get up?"

"We'll leave at ten."

She fidgeted a little more. "I dress funny." The panic was back in her eyes. "Not like those churchwomen in their expensive, fashionable clothes and purses and matching high heels. What should I wear?"

"Mom, Francie started going to church there only a few months after she got out of prison. She wore old jeans, but neither her clothes nor her past made any difference with the church members. They'll love you. They want you there. God wants you there and doesn't care what you're wearing."

"Oh." She nodded. "I'll try it once."

"Once," he agreed.

Sunday morning went well. They sat with Tim, a very pregnant Francie and her husband, Brandon. His mother had stayed through the service and had charmed everyone who introduced themselves to her, including the minister.

After the service, his mother agreed that she might try it again. After all, she got to see Francie and Brandon and the songs were pretty, too. The preaching she wasn't as sure about. "The man surely hit a lot of tough places in my life. Felt sort of like meddling to me."

"That's one ugly shiner." Ana studied herself in the mirror. Her eye, surrounded by deep purple bruises, was almost swollen shut. The ice packs she'd used probably helped some, but her face would be a multicolored splendor for days.

What should she do about it? This girlie stuff was as new to her as were all the bruises. Should she cover them? No way. Although she might be able to even out the skin tone, nothing would hide the swelling. And to cover the purple would take more concealer than Wal-Mart carried.

With a sponge, she patted on a little liquid foundation and puffed on a light dusting of powder. That was the best she could do. If she turned her head to the side, she looked okay: khaki slacks, nice makeup, a pink cotton tee that flattered her complexion. Pretty good except for the really ugly part around the other eye, which nothing could help.

She picked up a pair of sunglasses and slid them on. Better. She wouldn't scare people on the street.

But should she wear them in the restaurant? Would it be impolite to sit across from Mike in sunglasses?

"Stop being such a girl," she told her reflection. "This is just breakfast. Nothing big. When did you get to be so wishy-washy? So anxious to please?"

Since she saw Mike the first time, she answered herself.

Whirling away from the mirror, she left the room, grabbed her purse and headed downstairs to meet him. After all, this wasn't a date. No reason he should come up to her apartment when this wasn't a date.

Odd, but she felt as though it was one.

As she was getting off the elevator, she saw Mike standing in front of the other one. How embarrassing it would've been if he'd gone up in one elevator while she'd come down in the other. They could have played that game for hours.

She might as well give up. She'd never been cool and felt fairly certain she never would be.

"Hey." She grabbed his arm. "I decided to meet you down here."

He didn't seem to notice she was uncool. Instead he scrutinized the bruises he could see, then reached out to take off her glasses. He gently touched the corner of her eye.

"How does it feel?"

"Do you want a medical or a personal description?"

"Personal."

Something about his being so close and the gentleness of his touch made it hard for her to speak and think. With a concerted effort, she cleared both her throat and her befuddled brain. Neither effort was completely effective.

"It aches, exactly the way someone like you with a year of medical school would know." She blinked. "I'd be no good in the E.R. because I can't see out of that eye. I have no depth perception."

He handed back her glasses. Then, being careful not to touch the bruised area, he put his palm on her cheek.

"How's your arm?" she asked. Oh, the man was potent. It was hard for her to put a few coherent words together with him watching her and so close.

He rolled up the sleeve on his blue plaid shirt. "Under the bandage, it looks fine. I had good medical care."

"Did you change the dressing?"

"Yes, Doctor. Twice a day as instructed."

She nodded at the same time she realized she'd certainly started their time together off on the wrong foot, more like a medical consult. "I want to thank you again. I was never happier to see anyone than I was to see you."

Holding the door open, Mike allowed her to precede him then moved to the street side of the walk. A gentleman. She slipped her glasses back on.

"There's a diner a few blocks down that has great food. It's an easy walk."

"I've always thought I could do anything I wanted by willing myself to do it." She matched his steps. "But when I saw that man swinging the knife—" she shook her head "—I knew I wasn't going to get out of it alone."

"You were holding your own. If you'd had better weapons you'd have taken him out."

"Possibly, but the emesis basin wasn't doing much damage."

"I've never seen anyone use a crutch as a weapon like a samurai warrior."

"Only not as successful." She shook her head.

The thought made both of them smile. "I didn't think I'd ever find the experience funny," she said. "I guess humor is one way to cope."

As they waited for the light, Ana asked, "What did you want to talk about?"

He didn't answer, just kept walking. She knew his ability to duck a question. Behind those beautiful dark eyes lived a man as uncommunicative as her father.

Thank goodness Mike did have such beautiful dark eyes or she might not put up with that.

"The Best Diner," Ana read the name over the door. "It looks nice." She waved at the big plate glass windows with red-and-white checked curtains.

"It's my favorite place." Once inside, Mike waved at the cook. "Hey, Manny, why are you cooking breakfast? I thought you only did lunch and dinner."

"Morning cook got sick." The man Mike had called Manny wiped his hand on his apron and came out of the kitchen. "Good to see you, kid."

The two men shook hands and hit each other on the shoulder before Mike led Ana to a booth and slid in across from her.

"Who's this lovely young lady?" An attractive dark-haired waitress dropped two menus on the table.

"This is Ana Ramírez. She's a doctor at the hospital." He waved a hand at the two who were studying Ana. "Ana, these are two of my best friends, Julie and Manny Trujillo. They're almost like family."

"What do you mean *almost?*" Julie said. "We are family." She pointed at Mike. "This is the greatest kid in the world. You be nice to him."

Ana smiled. "Yes, ma'am."

"Nice girl," Julie said. "Pretty, too."

"Come on, Julie. Don't embarrass them." Manny waved toward his wife. "She's always butting into other people's business. Ignore her."

"Only for their own good," Julie said. She flipped her order pad open while Manny hurried back to the kitchen.

"Why are you here so early?" Mike asked the waitress.

"When Manny gets up this early, I can't go back to sleep." She pulled out her pencil. "Talked to your cousin Francie yesterday. She said she's taking it easy but doing okay."

"She's doing great." He leaned toward Ana. "My cousin used to work as a waitress here."

"We love her." Julie smiled at Mike. "You want a number four?"

Mike nodded. "The usual."

"Don't even write that down," Manny said from the kitchen. "The kid wants orange juice, two eggs, sunny-side up, bacon and a stack."

"They know you pretty well here." Ana laughed as she studied the menu. "I'd like Fruity Fiber cereal and a cup of coffee. Black."

"That's all?" Mike asked.

"Not everyone can eat like you and not put on weight." Julie handed the order to the cook and brought them water and coffee before she moved to wait on another table.

"Tell me about your name," Mike said. "I know Manny has two. He's Manuel Trujillo Rivera."

"I use my father's last name, Ramírez, and my mother's last name, Gutiérrez. My full name is Ana Dolores Ramírez Gutiérrez." She took a sip of coffee. "We used to put *y* meaning *and* between the names, but no longer."

He nodded and repeated, "Ana Dolores Ramírez Gutiérrez. Very pretty name."

"Thank you. *Muchísimas gracias.*" Ana put her cup down before she asked again, "So, what did you want to talk about?"

He grinned. "You always go right to the problem don't you, Ana?"

She raised a brow but made no comment when he called her Ana. Of course, she'd told him to, but he hadn't before. He seemed to feel more comfortable with the name now. She guessed saving another person's life did that.

"I had a great experience the other night." He drummed his fingers on the table. "I want to tell you about it, but this isn't easy for me to share." He stopped for a few seconds. "After the fight in the E.R., I went to the chapel and prayed."

"I didn't realize you're a religious person." She studied him seriously. Sharing religious experiences had always made her more than a little nervous.

"For a few months I haven't been. I haven't felt the Holy Spirit in my life."

"Oh?" She leaned back and bit her lower lip. "Mike, I'm not comfortable discussing religion."

"I understand. I used to feel that way, too, but I'd like to share what happened."

Sharing was good. She nodded uncertainly.

"I prayed for you, Mitchelson, Williams and everyone in the emergency room."

"Thank you. We can all use that."

"Here's your juice." Julie set the glass down and topped off the coffee cups before she moved away.

"Then I prayed for strength and guidance. For myself." Mike took a drink of the juice. "Francie says her faith changed her life, helped her change. I started going to church with her a couple of years ago." He looked up at the ceiling for a few seconds. "This is hard for me to explain."

"Go on," Ana encouraged. "This conversation makes me feel a little weird, but I know it's important to you."

"Like I said, I used to feel uneasy about discussing another person's faith, too." He paused and took a drink of water. "Okay. Here's what I wanted to talk about."

He still didn't say anything so Ana sipped her juice and waited, as hard as that was for her.

"A few months ago, I went through some hard times. I had to quit med school because my brother and mother came to live with me. I had to work to support us. On top of that, there were some other things going on, too. All that stress and change hurt my faith. I began to believe God wasn't around."

"And now?" She'd begun to find this interesting. Mike's face no longer looked like stone, as if he couldn't communicate. Now his eyes sparkled with excitement, and he spoke with emotion and conviction. He reached over to take her hand. It felt nice in his, warm.

"When I was in the chapel, I knew the Holy Spirit was there," he continued. "I prayed and knew my prayers were heard. It's hard to believe, but it happened. I felt it." When she squeezed his hand, he said, "After I left the chapel, I went up to pediatrics because the parents of a patient wanted to thank me for helping their daughter in the E.R." He shook his head. "They both assumed I was a pediatrician."

When he didn't speak, she said, "What happened after that?"

"I walked down the hallway and saw the children in the pediatric playroom." He held her hand more tightly. "I believe I can help children. I know that's where I belong."

"Okay." She nodded again and waited for him to go on.

"That's it?" he sounded more than a little disappointed when she didn't share his happiness. "I thought you'd be surprised or excited."

"Mike." She looked down at their linked hands. "We all know that pediatrics is where you belong. I've told you that. Everyone in the E.R. has told you that."

Hé blinked. "Oh, yeah. I forgot, but this time God told me that."

"Yes, and He is higher on the chain of command. If it took God to knock some sense into you, I'm very happy God took over." She leaned forward. "What does this mean in your life? Will you go back to med school?"

"I haven't worked the details out, but now I have hope. When everything crashed in on me, it was too much. Now I realize eventually Tim will move out, Mom will find a job, and I won't have to support them for the rest of my life."

"Did you really think you'd have to?"

"You've met Tim, right? Didn't that professional snowboarding idea give you some insight into him?"

"Yes, a little. I can see why you'd thought Tim would be around for a while."

"It's more like I'm afraid Tim would never grow up."

"He's always been a little, um, different?"

"Immature."

"Well, then, how did you get so responsible while Tim is immature?"

"Okay, here it is." But he didn't say another word for several seconds. "He's had a rough life. Never knew his father. Dad disappeared after I was born, came back for a year, just long enough for Tim's birth, then left again. When Mom went to prison, we both went into foster care. He drives me nuts sometimes." He fiddled with his napkin. "But I understand why he's the way he is."

"You went through the same things."

"Yeah, and at eighteen, I was pretty messed up, too."

"Is that why you didn't get Tim from foster care?"

"You know, you don't have to push me all the time." He looked into her eyes. "Right now, I'm willing to communicate without your help."

"Sorry." She put her hand over her mouth.

"Anyway, his foster family, the Montoyas, was great. They loved Tim and really helped him. All of us—the social worker, the Montoyas, Tim and I—felt it was better for him to grow up in a strong family because I couldn't take on a twelve-year-old boy with 'attachment issues' then." He shook his head. "I felt guilty about that decision, but I've prayed about it. This was best for Tim."

She bit her lip. "I don't know much about faith and religion, and I really don't understand prayer, but I'm glad you've made the decision to be a pediatrician."

As Ana spoke, Julie placed Ana's breakfast in front of her.

"Thank you," Ana said. "It looks wonderful."

"Hey, this girl is nice." Julie put Mike's breakfast down and scrutinized Ana for a few seconds.

Mike wanted to leap to his feet, grab Julie and hustle her back in the kitchen. He knew what she was fixin' to do. Exactly as Manny had warned, Julie couldn't stay out of other people's lives. Why hadn't he remembered that before he brought Ana here?

"You know," Julie nibbled the end of her pencil, "I like her a lot better than I did Cynthia."

Chapter Eleven

❧

Who was Cynthia?

Ana became even more curious about the identity of this Cynthia when Mike dropped his gaze to the plate piled high with food, picked up a fork and began to eat with great pleasure.

She knew that trick, doing something else when he didn't want to talk and hoping no one would notice. That was a tactic her father used when he didn't want to talk about—well, about anything.

Ana poured milk on her cereal and examined Mike's expression, which showed only enjoyment of his breakfast. "So, who's Cynthia?"

He took another bite and chewed. When he swallowed, he used his fork to pick up another bite of egg.

Putting her hand on his wrist to keep the fork on the plate and away from his mouth, she repeated, "Who's Cynthia, and why does the mention of her name make you so nervous?"

He looked at her then at his fork.

"I'm not going to stop asking so you might as well answer," she said.

"Sometimes you're very pushy."

"I don't consider it a bad quality. Don't try to change the subject. Who's Cynthia?"

"An old girlfriend."

"What's so bad about that? I'd expect you to have dated lots of women. You're a very good-looking man."

He nodded stiffly. "Thank you."

How cute that he was so uncomfortable. Maybe as attractive as he was, he wasn't the Mr. Cool around women she expected him to be. "Were you serious?"

He started to pick up the syrup but glanced at her, knowing she wouldn't back down. "We were engaged."

"What happened?"

His eyes lifted to her face again before he grabbed the pitcher and poured the syrup over his pancakes. "You're not going to give up?"

Ana shook her head.

"Even if it's personal and I'd rather not talk about it?"

"If it's personal, and you'd rather not talk about it, just say, 'It's personal, and I'd rather not talk about it.'"

As she'd hoped, the whole thing sounded so foolish that he gave up and said, "She broke the engagement when she found out I couldn't get married for a while."

"Because of your mother and brother?"

He nodded. "And because I had to quit med school."

"Julie's right. I am nicer than Cynthia."

The words brought a smile to Mike's lips.

So he'd had to quit med school to support his family and because of that his fiancée had broken up with him.

She'd really misjudged him. He wasn't lazy and unmotivated. Just the opposite. Hardworking and determined were very attractive traits to Ana.

After another sip of coffee, she noticed Manny and Julie watching them, whispering and grinning. Why? Those two were acting as if they thought Mike and she were on a date.

She blinked. Were they on a date? She really didn't know. She'd thought Mike had asked her for breakfast to discuss how they felt about surviving their shared experience, the terror they'd gone through together in the E.R. less than forty-eight hours ago. Maybe to debrief, to get better acquainted with each other because the incident had brought them closer.

Perhaps that wasn't the reason.

He *had* brought her to a special place, introduced her to friends, held her hand. He'd shared but been embarrassed about his ex-fiancée whom he'd also brought here and probably held *her* hand, as well.

This breakfast was beginning to feel like a date the longer they sat together, and a quick glance at his face didn't give her any clues. He was enjoying his pancakes. That was all.

She really needed to know. If this *wasn't* a date, she should force herself not to notice how handsome he was or how beautiful his eyes were. But here she was: drooling over his looks, mentally noting his good qualities. She acted as if this were the beginning of, if not a serious relationship, at least some kind of relationship when she had absolutely nothing to go on.

Yes, it was nice he wanted to share the answer to

his prayer and the renewal of his faith. As she took a bite of her cereal, he smiled at her. His eyes showed interest in her.

Of course, she wasn't very good at interpreting the message found in the eyes of attractive men. Maybe he was smiling because he'd just finished a mouthful of Manny's pancakes. She didn't know, and she'd better find out before she became too infatuated with him.

A little infatuation she could handle. That was the sort of thing that sent out sparks of happiness and enjoyment and made life more fun, but that wasn't where this train was heading. Her destination looked to be a Big Infatuation. She didn't want to arrive at that junction alone. She wasn't sure she was willing to risk following that track no matter who was on the ride with her.

All of which was far more railroad imagery than anyone needed. Right now, she had to find out the reason for this…um, this meeting.

Date or no date?

"Why are we here, Mike?"

Still chewing, he looked up, surprised. When he swallowed, he said, "Don't you like Manny's cooking? Well, probably not because you're eating cereal, but just try a bite of these pancakes." He cut off a small piece with his fork, dipped it in a little syrup, and held it out. "You're going to love this."

Eating pancakes from Mike's fork seemed a little, um, intimate, but what could she do? It would be rude to allow him to sit there, fork extended and dripping syrup on the table. She leaned across, took the morsel between her lips, chewed and swallowed. He was right.

"That is good."

"Yeah, Manny's a great cook. Francie loves his soup, any kind. I promised I'd get her some next time I was here." He checked the large red clock on the wall. "I wonder if he has anything ready this early."

"Did you eat here a lot when your cousin worked at the diner?"

He nodded. "Yeah, she…um…started working here after she got out of jail. Julie hired her. We've all been grateful for that."

What? "Francie was in jail, too?" She attempted to keep the shock out of her voice.

He nodded again. "Actually, a lot of my family has been, except Tim and me."

She sat back. Why had Francie been in jail? How did she feel about so many members of his family serving time? Surprised, yes, because Mike didn't look or act like someone from a family of criminals. Francie was doing so well now, and his mother was trying hard to make a new life. Her father had told her that. Her father wouldn't be interested in a criminal.

But Tessie had just gotten out of prison. She was a criminal. At least, a former criminal.

"I don't have the best family background, Ana. Francie worked really hard to break us of the family propensity toward crime. I'm determined to make a good life, too, for me and Tim and our mother."

"What was Francie in prison for?"

"I'd…I'd rather not say." The closed-off look fell across his face.

She could understand his reticence. Pushy as she

was, she occasionally did understand and recognize limits. "Okay, I do have a question I hope you'll answer," she said, returning to her earlier concern.

He looked at her, uncertainty showing in his expression.

"What is this?" She tapped the table with her index finger.

"You mean your cereal bowl?"

"No, what I mean is…" She hesitated. What had happened to that pushy person who never was embarrassed and *used* to inhabit her body? "Is this a date? What we're doing this morning, is it a date?"

"I think so." His puzzled eyes looked into hers as if trying to read her thoughts. "Isn't it?"

She sighed in relief. "I just wondered. I didn't know if we were friends discussing life or if this were a date."

"Do you mind if it's a date?"

"Not a bit. I just wanted to know." Realizing she wasn't going to eat any more of the cereal that had turned into mush while they talked, she put her spoon down and pushed the bowl away as she leaned forward. "Have you considered the consequences of our dating? There are people at the hospital who will gossip about us. Others will see anything I do for you as the result of our being close, not because you deserve it."

"None of that bothers me, but I didn't stop to consider how you might feel." He smiled. "I was so relieved when you weren't hurt Saturday night and so excited about God's leading, I wanted to see you, to tell you." He reached his hand across the table toward her. "I want to be with you because when you were fighting that guy off…" He paused, shook his head. "After that, after knowing he could have killed any of us, I realized how hard it is to foresee what life will bring."

"That's true."

"After that, I knew I had to see you now, to tell you…" He didn't finish the sentence but studied her face. "I want to be with you. Now. I don't want to put off being with you until I have enough money or I'm a doctor." He took her hand.

Grasping his fingers, she said, "I'd like that, to be with you." They gazed at each other. She could hear Manny and Julie chattering in the background but ignored them.

After a few minutes of mindless bliss, her expression turned into a frown. "The problem is this religion thing. I didn't grow up in the church. My parents never took us. It's something I've never even thought about for myself. I sleep, work or study on Sunday mornings."

"I used to be that way, but my faith changed that. Oh, I've been off and on, but no more. God's always been there when I listen. After the experience in the chapel, I'm really paying attention to God's way now."

As she scrutinized him, she could see that change. Overnight, the edge was gone. He wasn't as nervous and worried as he'd been when they first met. A feeling of calm and restfulness flowed from him now. "I'm impressed by the difference I see in you, but for me?" She shrugged. "I don't think that's me."

"I'm not going to push you, but I would like you to come to church with me on the Sunday mornings we're not working."

"I don't know if that's really for me. It's not my kind of thing."

"It won't hurt, I promise. We can spend time together, go to lunch, eat with your family or mine. We can be together." He rubbed the palm of her hand with his thumb. "I won't push, but I'd like to be with you whenever possible, and I'm going to be in church every Sunday I can."

She'd like to spend time with Mike, lots of time, but the idea of going to church tossed up warning signals. In this, she and Mike were different. Although they had lots of things in common, religion wasn't one of them. She'd lived almost thirty years and her father had lived his entire life fine without church.

But she also liked the feel of his hand in hers, his touch against her palm and the look of joy in his eyes.

"All right. I'll try it, but I'm not going back if I don't like it."

"That's all I ask. Try it."

After she put her hand on Mike's, a thought struck her. "Your mother. Does she go to church?"

"She didn't want to. I had to work on her, but she went with Tim and me yesterday and liked it."

Her father's life was about to change, too. It would probably be good for him because he needed to get out more, but for her?

"Maybe we could do some other things besides church. Do you think we could go to a movie sometime? Take a walk? You and your family could come to my apartment for dinner if we'd all fit," she suggested.

He dropped his hand to finish the last of his breakfast. "I don't have much money so we have to do inexpensive things, but I want to see you, spend time with you. Maybe we can go to some of the free events at Zilker."

For the next minute, the silence was filled with the comfortable sounds of Mike dragging his final bites of pancakes through the syrup and eating them.

"You need another stack?" Manny shouted from the kitchen.

"No, I'm finished." He held his empty plate toward Julie, who picked it up and cleared the table. "But I'd like some of Manny's good vegetable soup for Francie."

"I'll get it for you." Julie turned and carried the dishes into the kitchen.

"What about the check?" Mike said.

"We'll put it on your tab." Manny smiled and waved from the kitchen.

"Which means they won't accept my money." Mike shook his head. "I love these people and would like to eat here more often, but I wish they'd let me pay."

"They love you. Accept it."

"I should." As he stood and reached his hand out to help Ana slide from the booth, Julie put a carton down on the table.

"There's Francie's soup." She grabbed Mike in another embrace. "Give her a hug from us."

"How's your Mom's job hunt coming?" Ana asked after they left the restaurant and ambled toward her apartment. "Has she found anything?"

He stuffed his hands in his trouser pockets. "No. She doesn't like what's available but has agreed to consider any job. Her parole officer is getting concerned, although he's happy she's still looking."

"I'll check around, talk to some friends. Maybe there's something at the hospital."

"With her past? The conviction and prison time?" He held the front door of the building open for her. "Would they hire her?"

"The conviction wasn't for violent crime or drugs, right?" When he nodded, she said, "If it had been, there wouldn't be a chance. I'll look into it."

"I'd appreciate it." He shook his head. "I hate to ask you to do this."

"You didn't. I like your mother." She smiled at him. "And my father likes your mother."

Once inside the lobby, Ana pushed the elevator button. "Thanks for breakfast." She touched the puffy bruised area around her eye. "I'm going back to work Wednesday morning. Guess I'll see you on the late shift."

"I'm walking you to your apartment."

The elevator door opened.

"You don't have to."

"I know. I'm going to anyway."

When they got off on the third floor, she pulled the key from her purse and put it in the door. "Thank you again," she turned to say.

Setting down the bag with the soup in it, Mike reached out and put his arm around her shoulders to pull her into an embrace. He held her for a few seconds, his cheek resting against her hair. Then, with a smile, he stepped back, picked up the soup and turned toward the elevator.

Nice, very nice. Ana watched him go before she unlocked the door and went inside.

He hadn't kissed her. Probably too soon for that but she knew he liked her, liked her enough to take her on a date to a diner to meet friends, liked her enough to cuddle for an instant in the hallway.

All in all, with the exception of learning about his religious faith, this had been a great morning. She should be grateful. His faith had made him more open and willing to share with her. He'd spoken about something important to him, a breakthrough for Mr. Stone-face. It might mean they had a future, if he were willing to keep communicating.

Idiot! She was acting like a love-struck teenager with a big crush on the quarterback of the football team. No matter how smart and handsome Mike was, there were problems between them, a whole lot of problems.

A chasm separated Mike's relatives from her law-abiding family, although her father was attempting to bridge that. Her worry that Mike had been lazy had disappeared when she discovered everything he was coping with. She wondered if that Cynthia hadn't caused real damage when she broke up with Mike. What had that done to his self-esteem and ability to trust?

In addition to those family differences, the rigid hospital hierarchy made a relationship between a doctor and an orderly difficult. And there was that religion thing. This morning, they'd addressed a few of these issues. With further communication, they could probably handle anything that stood between them.

Did she really believe that or was she allowing his gorgeous eyes and beautiful smile to convince her?

* * *

"Hey." That afternoon, Tim sat next to Mike on the couch and shook his older brother to wake him up.

"Yeah?" Mike stretched and yawned. He must've fallen asleep watching baseball, a great sport to nap through.

"Did I wake you up?"

Mike stifled a sarcastic response. "What do you want?"

"Well, the other day I talked to Luz about the army. I think I'm going to join."

"Terrific." Mike sat up and swung his feet to the floor. "I really think it's a good idea, but you know you don't have to if you want funds for college."

He nodded. "I know the state will help me, but, you know, I'm a little immature."

Mike again bit back another insult. Instead, he nodded and said, "We all are, from time to time."

"Yeah, but with me it's sort of a lifestyle." Tim stared at his hands before he looked at his brother. "You've always taken the load in this family. Mom tells me you're having trouble with the bills."

"You've been putting in money. That's helped."

"But I'm not going to make much if I stay at the restaurant. If I go into the service, you won't have to feed me, and I can send some money home."

This was getting emotionally deep again, but it was one conversation he couldn't run from. "Tim, you don't have to move away. If you want to stay in Austin, we'll handle the finances somehow."

Tim nodded.

"Don't go into the army unless you want to. It's a long commitment."

"I'm ready for it. I really think I am." Then Tim stood quickly, patted his brother on the shoulder, said, "You're a great brother," and hurried out of the room.

Mike smiled. They were more alike than he'd thought, both hating to show emotion, hating to express or be part of it. Kind of a male-Fuller thing.

Chapter Twelve

On Friday evening almost two weeks later, the break room was packed with staff members who'd headed there to sample the Texas pecan cake Olivia made for Mitchelson's birthday.

Mike caught a glimpse of Ana across the room. During those weeks, they'd gone out a few times since the breakfast at the diner. Late one evening, he'd taken her for a hamburger before they both worked the late shift. He'd rented a movie and they'd watched it with Tim and Quique. Once they played miniature golf and often grabbed a sandwich together during their dinner breaks.

He smiled at the memories. Now, as the staff gathered, he watched her pick up a candied cherry from her napkin and pop it in her mouth. She grinned when she noticed his scrutiny.

"One of the patients today said this hospital sure could use some brightening up," Olivia said as she cut herself a piece of cake. "What do y'all think?"

"My first day here, I was surprised how gloomy it looked," a new orderly said.

"And the floors are gray," Ana agreed. "It's depressing. I know we work in a hospital, but does it have to look like a hospital?"

"Every room should be bright, should make people feel better." Mike licked a smear of the sticky glaze from his fingers.

"Didn't I hear once that the hospital was going to have an artist do some paintings after the renovation?" Ana nibbled on another cherry.

"I heard that, too," Olivia said. "But I haven't seen any paintings."

"Murals. I think they were supposed to be murals," the respiratory therapist added.

"Well, I sure would like something cheerful in the waiting room," Maybelle, the receptionist said. "It would make my job a lot easier if it cooled some of those patients off."

Mike watched Ana savor the cake. He liked her enjoyment of the taste, the way her nose crinkled a little when she bit into a tart piece of pineapple. He liked how she relaxed with the staff. He liked the quick, almost secret smiles she gave him. Actually, he liked pretty much everything about her and the knowledge concerned him. Was he rushing into this? Getting in too deep and too fast? Probably so.

Why couldn't he be like most guys, just relax and enjoy what was going on? One reason was because he was an idiot who couldn't forget rejections—from his father's on—which meant he was living in the past. *That* made him really stupid.

"I know there's research about colors and mood," the psych resident said. "I think the right colors would help *my* mood."

"As I remember, they didn't pay enough to interest a good artist," Olivia said. "I think that was the problem."

"Hey, what's going on?" Mitchelson strode into the room. "I'm out there doing all the work myself while you guys are in here eating my birthday cake?" He looked at the one-inch square and the couple of pecans that were left. "You devoured almost the whole thing. I haven't even had a bite."

"Okay." Ana stepped in. "Let's get back to work and let Mitchelson finish his cake."

They all groaned but immediately tossed their plates in the trash and left, everyone except Ana, who grabbed Mike's arm at the doorway.

"What do you think, Mike?" she whispered.

"What do I think about what? About how pretty you are?"

"No." She slapped his hand. "About the mural painting."

What was she talking about? He shook his head.

"As a job for your mother. Do you think she'd like to paint murals at the hospital?"

"I hadn't even connected the two. Probably concentrating too much on you." He took her hand. "You're a very nice person."

"Well, I've been thinking about her. I know it would make everyone's life better if she had a job."

"You've been thinking about me, too?"

"Fuller." She ignored his question, looking confused and cute. "Why don't you check into this? I'll give her a recommendation."

"Yes, Dr. Ramírez. I'll get right on that." He glanced around. When he saw no one in the hall, he took her hand. "Do you want to go out for dinner before my shift tomorrow?"

"Love to." That terrific smile appeared. "Why don't I pack some sandwiches? We can go to Zilker Park." She turned away and said, "See you later," over her shoulder.

While he watched her walk down the hall, a hand landed on his shoulder. Oh, yeah. Mitchelson. Too bad Mike hadn't remembered the big man was finishing off the cake, but when he was with Ana, he wasn't aware of anything or anyone else.

"Is the picnic in the park completely professional, too? Like the cup of coffee?" Mitchelson dropped his hand as Mike turned toward him.

"Not exactly," Mike said. "But keep it quiet, would you? I don't want this to end up as hospital gossip."

"I promise I will, but, from the way the two of you look at each other, even if I don't say anything, the grapevine will pick it up in a day or two." Mitchelson ran his hand along the cake plate for the last bit of glaze. "That smiling thing between you two gives everything away."

Yeah, that smiling thing did give them away, but Mike was so happy he couldn't help it.

When Mike picked Ana up in the lobby of her building, he gave her a quick hug. He looked great in khaki slacks and a blue shirt. She leaned into him, feeling his warmth and the strength of his arms. He smelled like mint toothpaste, that musky aftershave and chicken.

No, the chicken scent was coming from the picnic basket.

"I'm pretty sure I can guess, but what are we having?" he asked as he took the food from her.

"I picked up some fried chicken and potato salad at Randalls grocery."

"We can get cold drinks at the park. We should be set."

Once settled in the car, she said, "Did you get a chance to go to the employment office today?"

He grinned as he turned toward the Mo-Pac. "Uh-huh. Imagine my surprise when I discovered someone else had been there before me."

Oops.

"You know, there are some things I can take care of myself," he said.

Busted. She thought she'd been so inconspicuous, so devious. "I didn't even ask anyone. Much. I looked at the board, but the job to paint the murals wasn't posted so I asked the clerk if it was still open. That's all."

"Yes, but when two people on the same day ask the same clerk about a job that's been open for almost a year, she's bound to notice."

"I'm sorry, Mike. I wanted to find out. I was curious."

"You did it because you care. I appreciate that, but you don't have to do everything for everyone."

She sighed. "It's a bad habit of mine."

"Yes, but it's one of the reasons I l— like you."

What had he meant to say? Certainly not, "I love

you." They'd only been together for a few weeks, hardly enough time to be sure of such an emotion.

"What did you find out?" she asked, still wondering about his words but deciding she didn't need to follow up, not now. "About the job."

"It was never filled because, like Olivia remembered, it pays only $6.50 an hour for twenty-five hours a week. It's short-term and has no benefits. That's about $160 a week minus taxes. The clerk said they'd hoped maybe it would appeal to a student."

She turned to study his profile. "What do you think about this job for your mother? Would the salary be enough?"

"I picked up an application. If they'd hire her, I think it would work." He took the Barton Springs exit and stopped at a light. "She'd get a work history and bring in some money. One hundred dollars a week would help a lot, and she'd enjoy it. Right now, that's really important to me."

"Mike." This was not going to be an easy question to ask, but she needed to know this, both for recommending his mother to the personnel office and because of her father's interest in Tessie. "I don't know how to ask this, but how in the world did your mother end up painting forgeries? She seems so nice."

"That's exactly the reason. She's a nice person and a great mom." He started forward with the traffic as the light changed. "I told you my family has a bad history. My uncles both served time." He drove a block without speaking.

"My father left us after Tim was born," he said.

"Mom had no work skills. She lost every job because one of us got sick and she had to stay home or because she was so scatterbrained." He turned toward Ana. "I love her, but Mom has no common sense. I think Tim inherited that gene, too."

"Those years must have been hard, on all of you."

"Yeah."

He didn't elaborate but she hardly expected him to.

"Her original paintings didn't sell so she started forging to bring in money. After a few years, she got caught." He shrugged. "She really is a great person. I don't want her to go back to crime or jail." He pulled into a parking space near the trail next to the soccer fields. "Now, tell me about your family."

"We're really pretty ordinary." She got out of the car when he opened her door. "My father's family came to Texas about seventy years ago. Dad and Mom were both born here and are both citizens. They met in high school and got married when they graduated. Nothing exciting."

He bought them a drink to share at a concession booth and headed toward the picnic tables with the basket.

"You all speak Spanish." When they reached a table in the shade, he placed the food and the soft drink there.

"Yes, we're very lucky. We were brought up speaking both English and Spanish. That was a wonderful gift."

After eating and watching the soccer game between two teams of ten-year-old boys and girls, Mike suggested they walk to the botanical gardens.

"I don't like to walk that far," she protested.

"Your leg?"

"It's fine. That's not the reason. I'm tired. I work too

hard to wander around in the wilderness. It's hot." She grimaced. "I'm not an athlete."

"No excuses, Doctor. You know the importance of exercise, and you don't have to be an athlete to walk through the gardens." When he teased her and smiled, she couldn't resist him. Well, she couldn't resist much about him except that Leave-me-alone-I-don't-want-to-talk-about-it mood, but she saw much less of it now.

"Oh, all right." When she put her hand in his, he pulled her to her feet.

Crossing Stratford Drive and walking along the road, they strolled through the nearly empty parking lot to the entrance. After checking the map at the information kiosk, Mike asked, "Do you want to visit the dinosaur garden?"

"I loved it when I was a kid. We came here every summer because it was cheap."

"Free is always good," Mike said.

"But I'd like to see some of the other gardens. Let's start with the rose garden."

They wandered down a path surrounded by lush vegetation; the delicious scent of spice drifted to them on the breeze.

"Basil." Ana read the sign in the bed of plants.

As they strolled down steps at the entrance to the rose garden, they stood under the trellis covered with luxurious climbers of white and brilliant pink. Down a few more steps, they entered the garden and were surrounded by pink tea roses, multicolored blooms of apricot and gold, soft pink, yellow and deep lavender. Bushes showed brilliant coral and creamy white flowers. Ana reached down to rub the velvety petal of a dark orange tea rose.

"It smells wonderful." She lifted her head. "If I didn't know better, I'd think there were fruit trees in here."

"And tea." Mike put his arm around her. "Do you smell a strong tea scent?"

Another couple, the only people Ana had seen so far, sat on the other side of the garden. She and Mike ambled across a bridge and into the Oriental Garden, past ponds with golden koi flashing deep in the water and through the carefully laid out paths, small pagodas, large ferns and flowering plants.

After a few minutes of wandering, Mike pointed to the west. "There's a little path," he said. "Let's see where it goes. I don't remember. It's been so long since I've been here."

With his arm comfortably settled around her shoulders, they sauntered past beds of trailing lantana and up the path to a sign that pointed toward the Pioneer Village.

They walked by a red barn, blacksmith's shop, the school and the wishing well until, immediately ahead of them was a small gazebo. The lattice walls were pristinely white, its roof showing red through the trees.

"Let's go inside and rest," Mike suggested. "There's a bench here, too, around the inside. Years ago, Tim and I used to run around in there. Come on." He tugged her toward the gazebo. "I want to show you something inside."

"Oh?" Ana asked curiously. She didn't remember anything inside the gazebo. Of course, she hadn't been there for years, either. He pulled her along the trail and into the summerhouse.

"What did you want to show me?" she asked.

"This." He turned her to face him, keeping his arm

around her shoulder, and studied her face for a few seconds. The tenderness in his eyes made her breathless.

"What?" she whispered.

"This." He leaned forward, very slowly, and placed his lips against hers, then put his other arm around her and pulled her into the embrace.

It started as a gentle coming together, his lips soft against hers. Slowly, it became a wow of a kiss when he shifted a little so they were even closer. She felt his warmth where she fit into his arms, surrounded by the fragrant air and the promise of his kiss.

She was lost in his loving touch. Around them, leaves whispered in the wind. For a while she was aware of the floral scents of roses and spice heavy in the air and the sound of birds singing. While she was wrapped in his embrace, all that disappeared until she felt only his arms holding her and his lips against hers.

When he heard the sound of other visitors on the path down the hillside, Mike pulled away, although they stood only inches apart. Smiling down at her, he took a tendril of her hair and curled it around his finger. "That was nice." Then he smiled and took her hand.

On her part, Ana wasn't sure she could say a co-herent—or incoherent—word or walk next to him on legs made wobbly by that embrace. However, not a woman to give in to weakness, she took the hand he held out, stiffened her spine and forced herself up the path with Mike. After only a few steps, she felt her brain restart after she'd feared it might have ceased to function forever.

"Nice," she said, "doesn't begin to describe that."

"No, it doesn't, but that was the only word I could

think of at the time." He turned to look at her. "You dazzle me, Ana."

She couldn't believe Mike Fuller was talking like that. He dazzled her, too.

After another enchanted hour during which they'd strolled through the rest of the gardens with kisses stolen by a pagoda or a bench overlooking the rose garden or in the butterfly center, he took her home. Once they reached the door to her apartment, Mike put his hand high on the wall and leaned above her. "Go to church with me Sunday?"

The question easily shook Ana out of her infatuated state. "Mike, I prefer not to talk about church. I'm happy as I am."

He took his hand from the wall and cupped it under her chin, lifting her face to look into his. "Ana, I have a gift of great worth I want to share with you. I hope you'll come with me."

"Mike, I—"

He leaned forward to kiss her tenderly. "Please, Ana."

"Okay," she murmured against his lips.

When he gave her a final hug and turned to catch the elevator, she shouted, "Fuller, you don't play fair."

He didn't, not at all, but she didn't hold that against him. How could she when he made her so happy in every other way?

Once inside her apartment, she tossed her purse on the entrance table and threw herself on the sofa. Was she falling in love with him? Yes, she was.

He was gorgeous. His good looks had drawn her first: the rare smile, the broad shoulders, the great hair. Then she'd seen him with children, a real eye-opener. Mike cared so deeply for them and the affection was returned. When she'd found out about how he gave up his dream to take in his family, she recognized what a fine person he was. Now she knew he was a really great kisser.

She wasn't falling in love. She'd already landed there and was happier than she'd ever thought she could be.

Mike decided to stop at home to see his mother before he headed to work. He was in a great mood. He'd kissed Ana, the best kisses ever. And, oh, yes, he had a work application for his mother. Before he went into the house, he tried to look not quite so dazzled. Had he really told Ana she dazzled him? He never talked about his feelings and not in words like that.

Once he had settled his features to show a glimmer of intelligence instead of the absolute goofiness that had covered his features when he'd looked in the rearview mirror, he entered the house. Inside, his mother was seated on the sofa and sketching with pastels. He sat down next to her. "Mom, there may be a job at the hospital for you."

"For me?" She dropped her chalk. "In the hospital? A job?"

He nodded.

"Tell me."

"Painting murals."

"Painting murals? Painting?" Tears gathered in her eyes. "Oh, Mike, I'd love that."

"It doesn't pay much."

"Would it bring in enough money to help? You must think so or we wouldn't be talking about it."

"Yes, Mom, I think it might work. With taxes and withholding, you'd bring home over a hundred dollars a week. That would help a lot."

"Go on." She took his arm and held tightly.

"It's also short-term."

"That would give me some experience to list for another job." She nodded. "What do you think?"

"It would be perfect for you."

"Oh, Mike, I agree." The smile faded. "But I'm an ex-con."

"Dr. Ramírez says she doesn't think it would be a problem. You should call your parole officer to discuss it, then he can talk to the human resources office."

She put her hands over her face and began to sob, her shoulders shaking. He hugged her, handed her a tissue, then stood and started out of the room.

"I never thought I could make honest money painting. I'm so happy."

Why in the world did women cry when they were happy?

After getting off her next twenty-four-hour shift which had turned into a thirty-hour shift due to a three-car pileup on I-35, Ana got in her car and headed toward her father's house.

What did Papi want to talk to her about? She'd asked when he called this morning, but he wouldn't say more than, "Would you come home to talk to me after work?"

Why would he want to talk to her on this bright Saturday morning when she'd fixed him dinner just a few days earlier? Not that she'd really expected him to tell her. Although he was different around Tessie, he was pretty much the same as usual with his family, not communicating unless absolutely necessary. Had he gone to the doctor and gotten some bad news? Maybe something had happened to Martín or one of her other older siblings, something Papi needed to pass on.

"Hola, querida." He kissed her when she came in. With his back straight and a buoyant stride that was new to him, he led her to the family room. Once she was seated on the sofa, he settled in his recliner.

For a few minutes, they didn't talk. She glanced around the familiar room, every bit of which brought back strong memories of Mama and the family: the worn rug where Quique had played with his toy race cars; the ragged side of the sofa damaged by generations of stray cats Mama had taken in; the pictures Luz had drawn on the wall in crayon, painted over but still showing a little to anyone who knew they were there.

"What's up, Papi?" she asked when he didn't say anything. She studied his face. He looked years younger than he had only a few months earlier.

"You know how much I loved your mother, don't you? You know when she died, I thought my life was over."

"Of course I do. She was the center of our family." She felt a pang of sorrow. "We all loved her. It was hard for all of us, but much more difficult for you and the younger children."

"She was the love of my youth. I remember when I first saw her, sitting in algebra class, her hand up, always wanting to answer the questions." He smiled at the memory. "You were so alike, both so smart."

"Yes, Papi." With that beginning, Ana decided this conversation wouldn't be about anyone's health. She could relax.

"I never thought I'd love anyone again, but I do, Ana. I've fallen in love with Mrs. Fuller, with Tessie, and I wanted to tell you that."

She sat back in the seat. Oh, she'd known Papi found Tessie attractive. That he had fallen in love surprised her although she could see why he had. Tessie was a lovely, vibrant woman. Still, this was a shock. "She's so different from Mama."

"I know. Your mother was quiet and shy. You may have noticed, Tessie isn't like that." He laughed. "Even though she's had difficult times, Tessie's exciting and very special. She brought me back to life."

"I'm glad. I worried about you after Mama died."

He smiled sadly. "I worried about myself, too, but no longer."

She waited, allowing her father to bring up whatever it was he wanted to say.

After a false start, Papi said, "I had trouble at first because of Tessie's record. I'd never met anyone who'd been to prison, except your uncle."

"That's hard. I mean, in a relative, it's one thing, but to choose to care for someone with a criminal past, to accept it, must be difficult."

"It has been. I had to think it through very carefully. I was attracted to Tessie before I knew about her past, but it still threw me when she told me. I thought about what her record meant for me and you children and the grandchildren."

"What did she think of that?"

"Fortunately, she understood my hesitation and gave me time. As I thought about her, I realized she was a woman who struggled her whole life, who grew up in a family where honesty wasn't a value. In the end, she made a bad choice to earn money to care for her family."

"And now?"

"Now that I understand her better, I decided to look at the woman she is becoming instead of the person she was." He leaned forward. "I love her, Ana. I accept her completely. I hope you can, as well."

She had no choice. Her father had made that clear so she nodded. "Of course. What does the rest of the family think?"

"I haven't talked to them yet. I wanted to start with you because you were so close to your mother."

"But I'd never want you to be unhappy and lonely because Mama and I were close." She stood and walked across the room to sit on the arm of his chair. "I love you."

She hugged him and felt the tension leave his body.

"Thank you for understanding," he said.

"Are you going to get married?"

He smiled, a really happy smile. "That question, *mija,* is much too nosy."

Chapter Thirteen

No, Ana hadn't wanted to come to church; however, the service wasn't too bad after all. She sat next to Mike, which was worth the trip. Down the pew were Julie from the diner, Francie and Brandon, Tim, Tessie, in a dark blue and much more conservative but still-spangled dress, and Ana's father. Quite a group.

The music was nice, the sanctuary had lovely windows, and, well, she was with Mike.

Those qualities she'd noticed about him when they first met—the edge to his personality, a nervousness which made him a little intimidating, and, of course, that closed-off expression—had disappeared in this place. He was at peace. A changed Mike, but still as attractive.

Not that she should notice the magnetism between them at church. At church, she should follow his example, and he was completely involved in the service. So she stood with him for the opening chorus, bowed her head during the prayer, met and chatted with others during the greeting time and smiled when the children sang.

To her surprise, the sermon was thoughtful and interesting. She'd always thought they'd be long and boring with little substance. Probably the prejudice of a person who didn't go to church. Even in the large sanctuary, she felt an intimacy, as if the minister were talking to her, which she found a completely comfortable situation.

At the end of the service, many members of the congregation stopped to talk to Mike's family and introduced themselves to her. Everyone was friendly and invited her to return.

All in all, the morning was not horrible. If Mike asked her, she'd come back with him. If she came back to church just to be with Mike, did that make her attendance a sin? Perhaps God would like her to come back to church whatever the reason.

After Tessie had been painting for two weeks, the murals were the talk of the hospital. Patients and staff gathered to watch Tessie paint and to praise what she'd finished. She'd completed one with dogs and cats playing on a vibrant green background in pediatrics.

In the E.R. waiting room, using soothing colors, she was painting a mural of a garden. The receptionist said it not only calmed the patients and their families but made *her* feel a lot more peaceful.

Not that Tessie had limited her hours to twenty-five a week. "I can't," she'd explained to Mike when he reminded her how much time she was spending at the hospital. "Once I start painting, I don't want to stop and clean up. Once the creativity is flowing, I need to follow it." She stroked her hands through the air, her brush dripping ochre paint on the drop cloth. "I never know where the muse will lead."

In a structure built to alleviate pain, the paintings brought a healing influence. Joy lifted some of the sorrow and hope replaced a few moments of fear. Mike believed his mother was inspired, that God worked through her to heal, but he didn't mention it to her. Mom's faith wasn't ready for that yet.

One evening before his shift began, Mike entered the waiting room to see his mother putting the final touches to the garden mural, painting a deep shadow on the edge of a rose petal, a dab of white against the sky. As usual, she wore old jeans with one of his old shirts. And, as usual, Mr. Ramírez sat in a chair watching her every move.

"Isn't she talented?" He turned toward Mike, beaming proudly.

"I've always known she was."

His mother didn't notice either him or Mr. Ramírez, too wrapped up in her creations.

A week later, Ana searched in her purse for the key to her apartment. When she found it, Mike put it in the lock and opened the door.

"Thanks for a great lunch," she said.

He wished he could say something romantic and flowery. But every word seemed to stick in his throat and jam up in his mouth if he tried.

"Yeah. Great," he said instead.

She smiled. "I wish you didn't have to work the early shift, but I'll see you later."

He gave her a quick kiss.

Without bothering to take the elevator, he just ran down the stairs filled with happiness and energy. Life was terrific. Tim had gone to the recruiting office last week, taken a test and was pretty much set to leave for basic training in four months. Before that, he had to meet with the recruiting officer to set things up, but it sounded as if Tim's life and plans were set for a few years.

His mother's creations filled several walls of the hospital. On top of her success, she'd received a raise and an increase in hours to thirty a week. She and Mr. Ramírez were happily courting. When Mike'd asked her if they were getting serious, she'd laughed and waved her hands but given no information. A true Fuller.

The best part, what made him happiest, was Ana. She'd gone with him to church for two more weeks. He knew she'd gone with him the first time to please him, but *she* had reminded him last week to pick her up Sunday. More surprisingly, they'd discussed faith a few times. She was still skeptical but had been willing to listen and ask questions.

All in all, life was good. His family seemed on the right track and he was in love.

Yeah, no use denying it. He was in love and very pleased about it. She was the right woman for him: smart, pretty and caring. Their interest in medicine gave them a strong tie. When he looked back, he realized how shallow the relationship between him and Cynthia had been, based on her beauty and his future. He'd liked to show Cynthia off, amazed that a woman like her could love little Mike Fuller, son of an ex-con. She liked to say, "Mike's in medical school."

Ana accepted him as who he was—well, except that one thing. He didn't communicate well. He'd never been able to, but, as long as life was good, he didn't have to dwell on those old hurts or hide those parts of him he didn't want to share with anyone. He could bury them deep where they wouldn't bother anyone.

He believed Ana cared for him. They were together as often as they could work out. They had fun, as well as interesting conversations. And he really, really liked to kiss her.

By the time he saw Ana at work that evening, he wasn't feeling nearly as great as he had earlier. His head was pounding and his joints felt as if he'd been stomped on by a herd of orderlies. Did he have a temperature? He thought so but didn't want to know. If he did have one, he'd probably feel worse.

Ana didn't let him off as easily. She watched him during staff change, then charged toward him when she saw him in the hall.

"Stand still." She put her hand against his forehead. "Olivia, get Fuller's temperature."

He was running a fever of 101.

Ana put her hands on her hips and glared at him. "Why are you here? Don't you realize your illness jeopardizes both patients and staff?"

"But I can't go home. I need—"

"Listen, Fuller, I'm speaking as Dr. Ramírez so you have to listen to me. Go home now."

Not strong enough to argue and knowing he'd lose anyway, he nodded, went into the staff locker room and got his billfold and keys.

"Okay, what's the matter with you?" Ana entered the room behind him. Now she was both the professional Dr. Ramírez and his girlfriend, a difficult balancing act.

"Headache." He put his hand on his forehead. "Weak and achy."

"Go home. Drink plenty of water and sleep. Take some aspirin to bring down the temperature if your stomach can handle it." She shook her finger in front of him. "Don't come back until you're not contagious and," she said in a softer voice, "until you feel a lot better."

She glanced around the room, stood on her tiptoes and kissed him on the cheek. "Go on. Get in bed and get well."

"I'll be back tomorrow," he said in an effort at humor that didn't work at all. He gave her a pathetic grin and headed for the parking lot.

It was almost midnight when he got home. As he drove down the street, he saw a movement in the bushes next to the window of the bedroom he and Tim shared.

Was someone trying to get in? Not that they had anything worth stealing, but Mom and Tim were in there. He wished he had a cell phone, but his was in the house for everyone to use.

He turned off the headlights and pulled up a few houses past theirs. Making as little noise as possible, he opened the door and slid out. Ignoring his shaky legs, he hunkered down and crept silently around the neighbor's yard and through his backyard.

When he could see between the houses, the shadow

moved and became a person. He sneaked closer to the figure of a man who looked a few inches shorter than he and about thirty pounds lighter. He could probably take him if he had to. Well, maybe if the intruder was also suffering from the flu and had the strength of lettuce, Mike could take him.

Mike slid behind a crepe myrtle to see if the man was breaking in, but he had to lean against the wall to rest for a few seconds first.

No, the prowler had placed the screen against the house—had he already been inside?—and was moving away from it. He had nothing in his hands, but he could have hurt the family. Should Mike check inside the house or chase the man? He'd never catch him, not with his legs still shaking. He couldn't climb in the window due to his painful joints, so he watched.

As the figure reached the front yard, a car drove up, a dark SUV with silver flames on the side. When the man ran toward it, Mike recognized the jacket in the illumination of the streetlight. It was his. Then he recognized Tim's familiar lope and ran after him as fast as he could, which matched the speed of an arthritic snail.

"What in the world do you think you're doing?" Mike said as Tim opened the door of the SUV. "Tim, get back here."

Tim froze. Mike hadn't ever seen anyone freeze like this except in a movie. It was as if the words had fallen over his head and down his body like a blanket of ice.

"Tim, come here."

Tim turned toward his brother but didn't move closer.

"Hey, are you coming?" a male voice asked from the SUV.

"Go on." Tim closed the door and waved toward the driver. "Get out of here."

The tires squealed as the car took off. Step by hesitant step, Tim moved closer to the house. Mike expected him to say, "I can explain," but he didn't.

"Do you want to tell me what's going on?" Mike asked.

He was beginning to feel even worse. With the adrenaline rush when he believed his family was in danger, he'd been able to function. Now the headache throbbed so much he felt as if someone were driving a spike through his eye. He was so weak he had to hold on to the porch column to stay on his feet. Slowly he sank to the ground.

"Hey, what's the matter?" Tim leaned over his brother.

"Don't change the subject." Mike stared up at him from his position on the grass and made an effort to sound intimidating. "Where were you going?"

Tim put his hand on Mike's forehead. "You're hot. You're really sick."

"Where were you going?" He wished he could go to bed instead of carrying on this conversation. Sweat dripped down his forehead and body. When a light, warm breeze hit him, it nearly knocked him over. He shivered.

"You should be in bed."

"Tell me the truth. I'd rather be in bed, but I'm not going to do that until I find out more." Although he feared he might die first.

"A bunch of us were going for a drive."

"A ride after midnight? Don't kid me. Why did you climb out of the window?"

Tim didn't answer immediately. He shifted from foot to foot, an action Mike could see very well from his seat on the ground.

"I didn't want Mom to hear me close the front door. It has a really bad squeak."

Mike's body slowly listed to the left until he allowed himself to lie prone, hardly the most threatening position. "Why?" he murmured.

"You need to go to bed."

"Tim, why?" he forced the words out.

"Rudy wanted to do some stuff."

"Rudy? The kid with the juvie record who lives two blocks over?"

"Yeah, but he's really a nice guy."

"Guns?" He couldn't talk enough to form a complete sentence.

"No, no guns." Tim sat on the ground next to his brother. "Just some fun."

"Knocking over mailboxes? That kind?"

He thought Tim nodded but, of course, with his eyes closed, he couldn't see the action. "When I'm feeling better, you're in a whole lot of trouble." After a few minutes of silence during which Mike almost fell asleep on the ground, he said, "For now, help me up." He reached out his hand for Tim to grab and pull him to his feet. They limped into the living room where Mike collapsed on the sofa, unable to go another step.

As he fell asleep, Mike had an unnerving thought. His brother had felt the call of the wild again, the terrible gene of danger that wandered through his family and had destroyed several of them. What was Mike going to do to stop that?

Obviously nothing tonight.

Three days passed before Mike was able to get to his feet for longer than a few minutes. Ana had visited the day after he'd left the hospital sick. First she greeted his mother, who was hovering over Mike and driving him crazy.

As a doctor, Ana checked on him, diagnosed the disease as a virus, and told him to keep forcing liquids and stay in bed. Then, as Ana, she gave him a bunch of flowers and kissed his forehead. Nice. On the second day, she read the newspaper to him while his mother cooked his favorite food to try to tempt his appetite. It didn't work, but he appreciated the effort more than he had her pillow fluffing.

All those days he was sick, Mike had stayed on the sofa. Although it was too short for him, he didn't notice that first twenty-four hours. Then, even sick as he was, he couldn't rest in the bedroom with a two-foot-high accumulation of Tim's clothing—dirty and clean—empty soft-drink cans and other unidentifiable debris covering the floor. He didn't have the strength to pick them up. Besides, out here he could sleep through a few more baseball games.

As Mike began to feel better on the third day, Tim got sick and spent the next few days on the bottom bunk.

By the time Mike was better, he'd missed five days of work. Although he'd accumulated sick days, he couldn't use them until he'd completed the six-month probation period. That was money he couldn't make up quickly because he was in no condition to do overtime.

Tim had missed three days at the burger place so far, and their mother had missed hours of work taking care of them.

The financial situation looked bleak and was even worse when he found a check for sixty dollars their mother had written for paint supplies. He knew there was a huge charge for the antibiotic for Tim when his virus went into bronchitis. Thank goodness Ana had taken care of Tim. They could never have afforded to pay a doctor.

The evening of his fifth night off, Ana dropped by with chocolate ice cream for Mike to put some weight back on him. When she saw him, she asked, "What are you doing up and dressed?" She glared at him. "You don't plan to go to work, do you?" When he didn't answer, she glared even more fiercely. "You can't go back to work. You're too weak. You won't make it until midnight."

"I'm fine."

"Sure you are." She put a hand on his chest and pushed gently. He dropped down on the sofa. "See." She sat next to him. "Mike, this is a very serious virus. It really saps your strength. We've admitted a lot of people to the hospital."

"See, that's another reason I have to go to work." He stood. "You're not my supervisor and you're not my doctor. You can't tell me what to do."

"Oh?" Her expression hardened. "If I'm not your supervisor or doctor, what am I to you?"

It took a few seconds for both of them to realize what she'd said, really said. She'd asked about their relationship. She hadn't meant to, but it had popped out when he listed what she wasn't.

She guessed he hadn't thought the conversation would turn to this and maybe it was mean to ask him when he was so weak, but she wanted to know.

After a long pause during which he sat on the arm of the sofa and she shoved the ice cream into his hand, he said, "You're my good friend."

That's great. He considered her his good friend? "Do you often kiss your good friends?"

"Shh!" He waved his hands toward the kitchen. "Mom can hear you."

"I don't care." When she took a step toward him, he attempted to move back on the arm of the sofa until he couldn't move farther away.

"No." He cleared his throat. "You're more than that, but I don't know how to describe it. I'm not good at that, and I still feel bad."

His complexion had taken on a greenish tinge on top of the earlier pale gray. He wasn't well. He'd lost so much weight his jeans hung on him. She sighed. Even though he was playing on her sympathy, this wasn't the time to press him. Besides, she feared he'd tell her she was a nice lady next, and her ego couldn't handle that. She took pity on him and changed the subject although he wouldn't like this one, either.

"Mike, you cannot go to work tonight. As you said, I'm not your doctor, but I am *a* doctor. What I say about your condition will have influence in the E.R. A doctor has to clear you for work after this long an absence. None of them will, not after I talk to them."

An expression of relief skimmed across his face. He leaned back and closed his eyes. "Okay. One more day."

"I'll come by and check on you tomorrow. If you're stronger, I'll clear you, but no overtime until I say so."

"Yes, Doctor." He opened his eyes and grinned.

"I'm going to check on Tim while I'm here." She headed toward the bedroom.

"You're a really nice person," Mike mumbled before he fell asleep, still sitting on the sofa with his head resting against the wall.

Not as bad as being a nice lady, but she still wished she hadn't heard those words.

Chapter Fourteen

The next day, Mike felt stronger, but Ana couldn't drop by and check on him. She'd called that morning to tell him she'd now caught the virus, as well, had left the E.R. early and was at her father's home where the family could take care of her.

He consoled her until she stopped speaking and he heard a sharp voice on the other end of the line.

"Ana, you go to bed, now." After a pause, the same voice said, "Hi, Mike, this is Luz. My stubborn sister almost fell asleep while you were talking so I sent her to bed."

"How's she doing? Really."

"Probably about the same as you were on your first day of this stuff." She sighed. "She's the worst patient you can imagine."

"Really?" he asked, not a bit surprised.

"She's so hardheaded. She *knows* she can do anything if she pushes hard enough. She hates being weak, so this is really tough on her, but it's worse on the family."

"I'm sorry for all of you."

There was a pause while Mike heard Luz put a hand over the phone and say, "Get back in bed or I'll drag you there." Then she said to Mike, "Bye," and hung up.

After he showered, shaved and got dressed, he looked in on Tim. The kid had really been sick but that wasn't going to save him from a reaming out as soon as Tim could stay awake for five minutes and as soon as he could force himself to do that.

Mom fixed him breakfast, a nice bowl of oatmeal with brown sugar. For the first time in days, Mike had an appetite.

"May I have another?" He spooned the cereal into his mouth, finished that and held the bowl out. "Please."

"Of course. I've got to get some weight back on you." She placed the second serving in front of him. "I want you to rest until it's time to go to work."

He wanted to protest, but it would be childish. She was right. Maybe that was what becoming an adult was: recognizing that what your mother said made sense. Occasionally.

Breakfast finished and the dishes washed, he went back into the bedroom he and Tim shared and began to pick up clothes, dishes and stuff he preferred not to identify. Once he could walk across the floor without tripping, he pulled the sheets off Tim, who groaned but didn't wake up, and dumped them in the laundry bag with the clothes to take to the Soap and Spin.

"Mom," he shouted from the front door, "You'll need to put clean sheets on Tim's bed. I'm taking these to the Laundromat." He escaped before she could say anything.

By noon, he had a pile of clean laundry but had begun to wish he'd listened to his mother. When he got home, he carried the basket inside. Before he could do more, he dropped on the sofa and fell asleep.

Waking up when his mother called felt like struggling up through deep mud. He lay on the sofa for a few minutes, forcing himself to move, but his body refused to respond.

"It's seven-thirty, Mike." She stood at the arch into the kitchen. "I have your dinner ready and your lunch packed. Are you going to see Ana before you go to the hospital?"

He nodded.

"Good. Antonio wants me to come over. I'll go with you and he'll drive me home." She smiled and her eyes shone with joy.

Everyone was conspiring against her, enjoying her weakened state. Luz had left at noon and put her in the unsympathetic hands of Martita. Her sister-in-law had given her a sponge bath when Ana wanted a shower. This request had been refused *only* because Ana couldn't stand on legs made treacherously unsteady by this stupid illness.

Then Martita, the devious woman, had given her a back rub that lulled Ana to sleep. She napped until almost four o'clock. Now, since Mike had called to say he'd be by on the way to the hospital, she wanted to get up and get dressed, but Martita and her father had refused to allow it.

Martita washed Ana's face again, helped her put on makeup over Ana's loud protests that she could do it herself. That completed, Martita had swaddled her in a warm gown and robe, helped her into a chair in the living room and tossed a blanket over her. As if she couldn't walk to the living room herself. Of course she could, although there had been that one little trip over the edge of the throw rug. She'd never noticed how dangerous that spot was before.

Then Mike had arrived. With a kiss on the cheek, he'd awakened her from yet another nap.

"You're so skinny." Oh, bother. She could feel tears gather in her eyes. What an idiot she was, so sentimental, so emotional. She hated being sick. "I'm glad to see you."

He handed her a tissue.

"I don't need that." She waved it away. "I'm not crying. I never cry."

Why did everyone smile when she said that?

"Querida," her father said. Why would he call her his darling when she was acting like such a cranky person? "You're sick. You can cry over nothing when you're sick."

"While you were asleep," Martita said, "Francie brought you some of Manny's chicken soup. I'll fix you a cup later."

"How nice." She lay back and put her arm over her eyes so no one could see the tears.

"Honey, it's okay." Mike kneeled on the rug in front of the sofa, gently moved her arm aside and blotted her cheeks with the tissue. "You're human."

"What a terrible thing to say."

"You can't reason with her," Martita said. "I've always heard doctors were the worst patients. Don't we know that."

After a few minutes, Mike stood and his mother took his place, brushing Ana's hair back and cooing soothingly.

"Ana, I've got to get going to the hospital. I'll be back tomorrow. What can I bring you?"

"Just you," she said. "Don't overwork yourself. Rest whenever you can."

"Yes, Dr. Ramírez." He laughed and headed outside.

Ana closed her eyes. She had a virus. It would take a few days to shake it, but soon she'd be as healthy as Mike.

But, oh, how she hated to be sick.

The next few days were a nightmare for Mike. It had been a killer virus, as Ana had said. Still not at full strength, he struggled through an eight-hour shift, then went home, called Ana. After that, he'd go to bed and sleep until noon. His mom awakened him for lunch, he read his anatomy book until he dozed off and slept until she woke him up again at eight to eat and go see Ana.

He was so tired when he went into work at ten-thirty he wondered how he'd make it. He had no illusions he could work a double shift. With Tim sick, his younger brother wasn't earning a penny. Fortunately, he was well enough for Mom to work her full thirty hours, but they were so far behind financially.

He hadn't discussed the paint and supplies Tessie had bought. They'd work that out.

What he dreaded most was that he still hadn't talked to Tim about his sneaking out of the house the night Mike got sick. He didn't want to. Confrontation was his least favorite thing in the world. Mike preferred withdrawal, and he knew Tim well enough to know his little brother would make the conversation as difficult as possible.

When Mike got home after his second night back at work, he pulled out the checkbook and looked at his budget. They were okay now, but after he paid the bills there wouldn't be enough money and not much coming in. He'd have to take money from his savings, which would wipe out that account. He dropped his head in his hands. He'd have to work overtime or they wouldn't be able to eat.

He could take the bus home from work, but not to work because there were no connections that late at night. What good would it do to have someone take him and drive home so he could save gas money taking the bus home? None of the other graveyard shift staff lived in this direction, so carpooling was out.

What was left to cut? Nothing. He'd have to work more hours.

The sound of someone moving around awakened him at ten-thirty. "Tim?"

"Yeah. I'm fixing breakfast."

He stood and went into the kitchen. "We need to talk."

"What part—" Tim bit the words off "—of 'I'm eighteen' don't you understand?"

"The part about 'I can do whatever I want and won't get into trouble with the law.' That's the part."

"I wasn't going to get in trouble." He slid the eggs from the skillet onto his plate. "We were going to drive around, that's all."

"No throwing eggs? No paint cans? No vandalism?"

Tim shook his head and shoved two pieces of bread in the toaster.

"Did anyone have a gun?"

"How would I know? You didn't even let me get into the car."

"Tim, you could have ignored me. You could have gotten into that car, but you didn't. That makes me feel that deep down you knew whatever was going to happen wasn't what you wanted, really wanted, to do."

Instead of leaving the kitchen, Tim sat down and began to spread peanut butter on his toast.

"Was there beer involved?" Mike asked.

Tim frowned. "You know I'm not old enough."

"Like that's ever stopped a kid."

Tim shrugged and took a bite of toast.

"Playing chicken?" Mike asked.

"Driving fast, most likely. Maybe shooting paint-balls. I don't know." He chewed and swallowed. "I didn't go."

"How many times have you sneaked out?"

"A couple." He slapped the table with his fist. "You don't know how hard it is to make friends when you're out of school. Everyone I work with is going to college. The Montoyas live on the other side of town, and we have only one car."

"I know that's tough."

"Sure you do." He stood. "You're Super-Mike. You're smart. You're good-looking. You make friends easily. How would you know?" He turned, took a step and tossed the dishes toward the sink. "Everyone says I should be like you, hardworking, responsible, never get in trouble." He scowled. "Well, I'll never be as smart or good as you so I might as well give up trying."

"What are you talking about?"

"You know, Mr. Perfect."

Mike got up and followed Tim into the bedroom they shared. "I'm not Mr. Perfect."

"Sure."

"Tim, I did something really stupid, something criminal when I was eighteen." He leaned against the wall. "I got someone I really love in trouble for that, and I'll never forgive myself."

"What?" Tim swiveled to look at him. "What did you do?"

"I can't tell you."

Tim took off and tossed his T-shirt in the direction of the hamper. "Then I bet it didn't happen. You're making that up to scare me."

"No, I'm not. Believe me. I can't tell you because the person I hurt, the person who ended up taking the blame made me swear never to tell anyone." He put his hands in his pocket. "I broke that promise once for a good reason, and that person got very angry with me. I'm not going to do it again."

Tim ambled over and leaned against the wall facing Mike. "You really messed up? You know what it's like?"

"I was as short as you were in high school, didn't grow until I was a senior. I lived with six or seven foster families in different parts of towns and gave up trying to make friends or playing varsity basketball—and I was a great shooting guard. Yeah, Tim, I know what it's like. Being a teenager is hard."

"Oh." Tim nodded. "Okay, I'll think about what you said." He slipped into his flip-flops and headed toward the bathroom before he turned around and said, "But I'm eighteen and I can leave this house whenever I want to. You can't stop me."

That hadn't gone as well as he'd hoped, but it was going to have to be enough.

When Mike got home, he fell on the sofa and slept so deeply he didn't hear Tim go to work or Mr. Ramírez drop his mother off from the hospital. He did hear her come in and close the door quietly.

"Mom, I need to talk to you." Still half-asleep, he sat up and glanced at his watch. Whoa, almost five o'clock in the afternoon. He'd napped for nine hours.

She twirled to the couch, smiling and happy, and reached down to touch his cheek. "How are you feeling? Your cheek feels cool." Then she sat beside him. "But you look tired."

"I made it." But was he ever thankful he didn't have a double shift today. "Mom, I need to talk to you about the money you spent for paint."

"I should have talked to you when I bought it. I'm sorry."

"Just tell me about it. Wasn't the hospital supposed to buy your supplies?"

"Yes, but you know the hospital purchasing procedure. I knew I was going to run out of paint two weeks ago, just before you got sick. I filled out a purchase order request but it would take a week to process and another a week to ship." She shrugged. "I had no paint or brushes and wouldn't for weeks. I decided it was better to spend the money so I could work and make money than to take time off." She patted his hand. "I'm sorry. You got sick and I forgot."

"It's okay, Mom. We'll cover it somehow."

That meant he'd have to do a double shift tomorrow. He'd be stronger by then. He had to be.

Chapter Fifteen

For Mike, the best thing about the double shift was seeing Ana during his evening break. When he drove over to her house to take her a milk shake, he was glad she felt better but worried because she was determined to work part of her next shift. Of course, there was no reasoning with her.

The worst part about the double shift? Simply that it *was* a double shift. By ten in the evening, he had to take a vertical nap. During a lull at 4:00 a.m., he crashed for thirty minutes in the lounge. An hour before he could go home, a sheen of perspiration covered his face and his legs had taken on an unsteady life of their own. The attending physician took one look at him and told him to go home immediately. Mike didn't argue.

After a quick call to Ana, he hit the lower bunk and slept until three-thirty that afternoon. Groaning when the alarm went off, he wished he hadn't promised to take the second half of an afternoon shift.

Nine hours of sleep. He felt stronger, but he wished

he could sleep nine more hours. That would give him the final shove he needed to be completely well. What he had now was an ephemeral kind of strength sure to desert him by midnight. He'd have to hide from Ana or she'd send him home early.

The thought of seeing Ana at the hospital stopped him right there on the edge of the bed. He dropped his head in his hands to think.

What about Ana? He loved her so much. Who wouldn't? But the relationship was way out of balance. She was smart, successful, beautiful and gave him so much. The only things he'd given her were a few kisses and the flu.

He hated the fact that his thoughts kept ending up in the same place, but with his family problems, their growing debt and his still feeling so tired physically, he struggled to find anything about himself he could offer Ana. Of course, he had his faith, which was such a huge part of his life now. But faith was one thing he and Ana *didn't* share.

"Dear Lord, thank You for all You have done. Please give me wisdom," he whispered. When he searched his muddled thoughts to add more, he reminded himself God knew his needs. "Amen."

In spite of the prayer, his brain circled back. Would it be better to stop seeing each other until he could figure out how to handle the mounting money problems, how to juggle his mother and brother's lives plus the terrible realization he'd have to put med school off for even longer? Right now, as much as he cared about her, he couldn't face Ana's cheerful pushiness, her insistence that he *communicate*. He didn't do it well, not at all well. Couldn't she just accept that?

No, she couldn't, and he didn't want to discuss the mess that was his life with anyone.

At the hospital it was so easy to fall into the routine of kidding and chatting when they passed in the hall or had a free minute. He'd always looked for her during that time, to see if she were free, if they could spend a few minutes together. Life would be easier if he switched to another unit, if he didn't have to be close to her so often.

All in all, Mike wasn't in the best state of mind to go to the hospital. He made it through the half shift from seven to eleven fine, but it got tougher when he saw Ana during the shift change. Although pale and thinner, she looked terrific. She always looked terrific to him. That was the problem.

It would be better for them to be apart now, for him to transfer to another unit until he got his head straight and his life in order.

Ana didn't feel all that great. When she'd checked in the mirror before she left home, she'd looked as bad as she felt: dark circles under the eyes and a greenish complexion the same color Mike's had been. She wore her skinny jeans, the ones she seldom could zip but tonight they closed easily.

Once in the E.R., she revived a little but didn't feel her usual confidence or enthusiasm.

"How're you doing, Fuller?" She passed him in the hall on the way to an exam room.

He nodded. "Fine, Dr. Ramírez. Thank you."

The evening went pretty much like that. He assisted her with patients although he disappeared during a letup in the patient load. Probably helping in another section of the E.R. She was in no shape to look for him.

The hours went by slowly until finally it was close to 7:00 a.m. She'd worked one-third of her usual shift, and exhaustion had dropped over her like a lead cape. Fortunately, she had almost thirty-six hours until her next shift. During that time, she could rest and maybe see Mike this evening or for lunch the next day. The thought made her feel a lot better.

At the end of the shift change, Mike asked, "How'd it go?" when they headed out the door together.

As if he didn't know. As if he hadn't just gone through the first day back after the killer virus.

"Okay for the first shift back at work." She leaned against the wall. "I'd love to talk to you, but I've got to get home."

"Going back to bed?"

"Exactly what I'm going to do. I'm going to sleep all day." She pushed off the wall. "You had the same thing. When do you start feeling better?"

"I'm doing fine tonight. Give yourself a couple more days. Rest, drink plenty of liquids and don't push yourself."

She grinned weakly. "You sound like a doctor."

"And you're going to do exactly as I say."

"Why don't you come over tonight? To make sure I do?" she asked as he walked her to the parking lot.

He stopped walking for a second and glanced quickly down at her. "Um, can't. Sorry, I've got some stuff to do."

"Oh, okay." She could use the rest. She got in the car, started it and headed toward the exit. Through the rearview mirror, she saw Mike watch her drive off. Then he turned back toward the hospital. He must have left something behind.

On her next shift, Ana felt much stronger, but she was *not* happy. Furious would describe her emotion better. Because she didn't see him earlier in the evening, she'd thought Mike was off duty. At 3:00 a.m., Williams said, "I'm going to pedes during my break later."

"Oh, why's that?" she asked.

"To see Fuller."

"What's Fuller doing in pedes?" Ana asked, distracted while adding notes to a patient's history. "Filling in for someone?"

"He got transferred there."

The chart clattered against the tiles when Ana dropped it. "Sorry," she said when everyone turned to look at the source of the noise. She picked up the chart but didn't ask another question. No reason to give the E.R. the juicy gossip that Dr. Ramírez hadn't known Mike transferred and was not happy—actually, she was furious—that he hadn't told her.

"How nice." She smiled. "He loves those kids."

She finished charting, placed the clipboard back in the rack at the nurses' station and headed outside. Once there, she dialed pediatrics and asked for Fuller.

"Yes," he said when he got to the phone.

"Fuller, this is Dr. Ramírez."

Mike didn't answer for a few seconds. "Oh, hi," he said in a cheerful but uncomfortable voice.

She didn't swallow that response for a second. He wasn't a bit glad she'd called.

"I'd like to talk to you." She paused then added, "Soon," because she knew he wouldn't want to talk to her anytime, not in the near future, not in the distant future.

"Meet me in the cafeteria? Seven-thirty?" he suggested.

His complete lack of enthusiasm filled her with dread. What was going on?

Besides, the cafeteria wouldn't work. What she wanted to talk to him about might end up with a lot of yelling on her part because she could imagine the silence and control on his. "I'd prefer someplace less crowded and more private."

When he didn't make another suggestion, she said, "How 'bout the picnic area in the south lawn by the clinic?"

"All right."

"Will you be there?"

"Yes, I'll be there." But he didn't sound at all pleased about it.

Too bad.

Ana chose a bench under a post oak. To distract herself, she studied the contortions the branches of the trees made. She'd begun to look for another diversion when she saw Mike amble across the grass toward her with the eagerness of a child going to the dentist.

The man looked great. He'd put weight on so his

jeans didn't hang from his hips. Strong arms swung from those broad shoulders. The breeze ruffled his hair, but he didn't smile. Not a good sign. Not at all. The sight of his grim features made her catch her breath. She felt as if someone had filled her stomach with balloons that weighed a ton each and burst every few seconds.

When he reached her, he settled at the other end of the bench leaving a good ten inches between them. He didn't show any interest in beginning the conversation. He just sat there, resting his elbows on his knees and looking toward the hospital, all of which made it very clear it was up to her to say something.

She'd never felt so confused and deflated in her life. "When did you decide to transfer to pedes?" she asked.

"Wednesday."

"Why didn't you tell me?"

He didn't look at her, not a glance. "You know I wanted to work there. I thought you'd be happy for me."

Oh, sure. Make this *her* problem. "I didn't realize…" She stopped words that had taken on a sharp edge. Confrontation wasn't the tactic she wanted to use, not with this unapproachable man. "If you thought I'd be happy, why didn't you tell me?"

He shrugged. "Didn't have time."

After a long pause, she realized she'd have to push harder. How frustrating. It was as if they'd moved months backward in their relationship. "I missed your call yesterday morning."

He shrugged again. In fact, he was shrugging so often it looked like a shoulder exercise from the Physical Therapy Department.

"Busy," he said.

This was going great. "Mike, what's going on?"

This time he turned toward her for a second. "Nothing."

She blinked. "What do you mean, nothing?"

He looked down at his hands. "Things are busy for me now."

"Do you want to talk about it?" She bit her lips to keep from screaming at him although he deserved it. If she did, he'd just get up and walk off and she'd learn nothing. As if she was learning so much now.

"Mike, do you care for me at all?"

When he nodded, her temper flared. Bothersome, irritating man! She closed her eyes. *Dear Lord, please give me the wisdom to deal with this impossible man.*

Her eyes popped open. She'd just prayed. On her own because she wanted to. She wished she could share this experience with Mike, but he didn't want to hear anything from her. He made that clear by scooting a few more inches away from her so his body balanced on the end of the bench.

"Mike, what's going on? Do you want a relationship with me?"

He glanced at her. "Yes, but I have to take care of some things first." With that, he stood and headed toward the parking lot.

He had to take care of some things first? What was that about?

She watched him walk away and realized that, for the tiny bit of sharing, communicating and shouting they'd done, they could have had this conversation in the middle of a shift change. No one would have noticed.

She had learned only that Mike was busy and was not going to tell her the tiniest bit more.

Didn't the man realize that there was *never* a time when everything was okay? That there were always rocky places in life? Even in her terrific family, there'd been tough times when someone got sick or they were short on money. Mike was asking her for an on-and-off relationship when *he* felt good, when everything was going well, an arrangement that didn't interest her at all.

She was angry. At the same time, the hurt burned so deeply inside she had to push herself to her feet.

Sunday morning, Ana tried to sleep late but awakened at seven. She read the newspaper while she ate a grapefruit and drank her coffee. That completed, it was only eight o'clock. What would she do with the rest of the morning?

Go to church.

The thought amazed her. She'd only gone three times, but church attendance had become a habit after such a short while. Was she going to allow Mike to keep her from her church? No. Never. She marched into the bedroom and began to get ready.

Arriving a few minutes early, Ana scanned the sanctuary. Mike sat next to Tim. Tessie and her father were in the middle of the pew next to Julie and Francie while Brandon sat on the end with enough space left for another person. She walked down the aisle and slid into the empty space. Brandon scooted over to make more room and smiled at her while Francie reached out to pat her hand and whisper,

"Good to see you." Looking down the row, everyone else waved to her or smiled, except for Mike. She didn't think he saw her because he was so wrapped up in prayer.

He looked miserable, the idiot! It served him right. This must be as hard for him as it was for her, but it didn't need to be.

Maybe she shouldn't be here. Should she leave him in peace? No, she had a right to worship and wasn't about to leave. She relaxed, listened to the prelude and meditated.

After a lovely choir anthem, the associate minister stood, opened the Bible and said, "Reading from the Gospel according to Matthew, chapter eleven, verses twenty-eight to thirty." He cleared his throat before he read, "'Come to me, all you that are weary and are carrying heavy burdens, and I will give you rest. Take my yoke upon you, and learn from me; for I am gentle and humble in heart, and you will find rest for your souls. For my yoke is easy, and my burden is light.'"

Amazing words, healing words. Ana opened the bulletin to the scripture and read it to herself. They made her feel peaceful and renewed. The Lord understood her pain and even took it upon Himself. What a wonderful promise. Then she closed the bulletin to listen to the sermon.

After the last hymn, Francie pulled Ana closer to her. "He's being such an idiot," Francie whispered. "Give him time."

Ana glanced down the aisle. Mike had already left, not even looking at her or talking to anyone in the pew. Right now, he was acting like such a jerk she wasn't sure she even wanted to be with him. "Francie, how are you doing? When are you due?"

"Okay, change the subject, but I'm not finished. Can't you have a little patience with him?"

"Patience isn't one of my virtues. Besides, what's going on isn't my choice."

"He's not an easy person to know, but it's worth it." She grinned. "Now, to answer your question, I'm due in two weeks and am doing great."

"'Come to me, all you that are weary and are carrying heavy burdens, and I will give you rest,'" Mike repeated to himself as he hurried from the sanctuary. Outside, he found a bench in the garden to the side of the church and sat to consider the scripture.

Since he'd found Christ, Mike had tried to be strong in order to follow the Lord, to do His work, but this morning, the words from Matthew struck him in the heart. "'Come to me, all you that are weary and are carrying heavy burdens, and I will give you rest,'" he whispered.

In the turmoil of his life, Mike had forgotten that basic promise of faith. He wasn't alone in his pain. Why was that part of Jesus's teaching so hard for him to remember? Why did he forget that if he turned his life over to his Savior, they shared the pain and burden?

The big problem came with the word *if*. Could he turn this whole mess over to Jesus? Yes, he could, but for him it would be hard to let go of every ugly corner and painful deed. He'd become pretty good at trying to hide them. Because Mike knew himself pretty well, he also knew the task wasn't going to be easy for someone who trusted as little as he did, but he could trust his Savior. That he did know. Besides, if he didn't turn his life over to His healing touch, Mike was going to lose the love of the person he cared for most.

For Ana, the next week passed as if Mike had never worked in the E.R. Not seeing him made her feel as if he'd never existed, never been a part of her life, as if he'd never caressed her cheek or touched her hair, as if he'd never kissed her.

She heard Williams tell Mitchelson that Mike enjoyed working in pedes and was getting plenty of overtime. Other than that, nothing. She didn't see him. No one else mentioned him and she refused to ask questions.

The next Sunday, as Ana got off her shift, she decided to go to church again. She liked the people there, felt a presence like the one Mike had talked about, but she couldn't name. He'd said it was the Holy Spirit. To her, this presence was a feeling of peace and joy, love and healing and something else she couldn't identify, like her soul being touched and changed.

Three hours later, she again slid in next to Brandon. As the associate minister read the scripture halfway through the service, she heard a deep inhalation of breath and saw Francie lean over and gasp. After a few seconds, Francie grabbed her husband's hand and pulled herself to her feet. She whispered to him, "My water broke."

Ana took one of her arms and Brandon the other to support Francie from the sanctuary. Once outside and heading toward the car, Ana said, "How long have you been having contractions?"

"They started this morning."

"This morning?" Brandon said. "Why didn't you tell me?"

"They weren't hard. I thought they were like those false ones I had last month."

Ana opened the car door and helped Francie inside. "How far apart?"

"Oh, five or ten minutes."

"Brandon, you have plenty of time to get her to the hospital, but get going."

Francie reached out the window and took Ana's arm. "I'd really like you to come with us if you don't mind. I'd feel much better with a doctor in the car."

"Sure." As an E.R. physician, she'd delivered babies. Well, one baby. She always called the obstetrical resident, but Francie didn't need to know that now. Ana got in the backseat in time to see the rest of the family running from the church.

"Meet you at the hospital," Brandon shouted and drove off.

After a few hours in the waiting room, Mike was a wreck. Brandon remained in the birthing room and brought frequent reports. Ana had disappeared, but Manny turned up to wait with Julie. They all paced.

Mike went to work in pedes at three but asked Tim to bring him reports. Doing something, keeping busy should make the time go faster, but it didn't. Mike glanced at his watch every few minutes, but it seemed as if the hands never moved. At five, Tim silently dashed through the third floor hall to tell Mike the baby was on the way. After checking out with the head nurse, Mike ran upstairs after his brother.

When they were finally allowed to see Francie and Brandon an hour later, the baby had been whisked off to the nursery.

"What's his name?" Tim held Francie's hand.

"He's Michael Timothy Fairchild," Francie said. "Named for my favorite cousins because you two really are my brothers."

Tim laughed and Mike grinned more widely than he had for days. Mike grabbed his brother's arm and pulled him toward the door. "Come on. We're going to the nursery to see our baby." He waved at the new parents as they left.

Once there, they stood outside the large window and searched the infant's face to see who he looked like. "I think he has your big ears," Tim said.

While Mike tried to think of an insult, he heard someone approach from behind him.

"He's a beautiful baby," Ana said.

"Yeah." Mike guessed he had a huge smile, which became even wider when he saw her. Filled with joy about the baby and from seeing Ana, he took her hand, but she pulled it quickly away. He deserved that.

"Did you know Francie named him for Mike and me?" Tim asked.

"That's terrific." She turned to walk away.

"Ana," Mike said, but she didn't pause. Silently he watched her walk away, furious with himself. What a mess he'd made. Was there any way he could explain to her how messed up he'd felt?

Could he make things right between them again? He had to. He could learn little by little what trust and love meant. Could love heal the break between them?

At seven-fifteen Tuesday morning, Mike waited outside the E.R. for Ana. When she saw him, she said, "Goodbye, Fuller," and headed toward the parking lot.

He deserved that, too. So wrapped up in his misery, so egocentric in his pain, he had treated her as if she weren't important, as if he couldn't trust her. Now, he'd have to paddle really fast to win her back.

He followed her. "Ana, could I talk to you? Please."

She turned toward him. "Why?" she said, only that. Interest didn't show in her eyes nor eagerness in her stance.

"I made a mistake. I need to apologize."

"Oh." She waved her hand toward him. "Don't worry about it." She headed away from him. "I'm fine."

He sprinted behind her and caught up at the edge of the parking lot. "Please. I want to talk to you."

She rolled her eyes. "Mike, you said you're too busy to bother with me."

"I didn't mean it that way."

"Well, that's the way it came out. I don't want to go through this off-and-on stuff. I don't want a relationship with a guy who retreats when the going gets rough because he doesn't care enough to share."

"It's not that I don't care." He took her hand and led her toward the low brick wall that separated the hospital and the lot. "I don't communicate well. I'm sorry. I must have hurt you." He gently tugged on her hand so she'd sit down next to him.

"I'm not going to lie. You did hurt me, but that may

be good. The pain made me realize that the man I want to be with is a lot like my father. Papi drove my mother crazy with his moods." She stood. "I'm not going to live that way no matter how much I care about you. I refuse."

"No matter how much you care?" He got to his feet. "Do you still care?"

"Mike, did you hear the part about how I'm not going to put up with the great stone face, no matter how handsome and charming and smart you are, no matter how much I care? I refuse to do that."

"Please come back. Please talk to me." He motioned toward the wall. "I heard you, I did. Now, at this moment, I *want* to talk. I want to communicate."

With reluctant steps, Ana returned to the wall and sat down.

When he realized it was all up to him, that Ana wasn't going to make this easy, Mike cleared his throat. "Okay, this is why I pulled away from you. Here's what happened. I'm sharing." She didn't look impressed. "I'm worried about Tim. I found him sneaking out of the house the night I went home sick."

"Isn't he eighteen?"

"Yes, but I've told you about my family. We don't make good decisions. I don't believe Tim can handle being out all night with the group of guys he hangs with. He knew this wasn't a good idea or he wouldn't have climbed out the window."

She nodded.

"He was supposed to go see the recruiting officer a couple of times, but he never showed up for the appointments. Now I don't know what he's going to do.

Plus, with our being sick and Mom taking care of us, there's no money coming in but a lot going out." He shook his head before he dropped it in his hands. "I was exhausted from being sick for a long time. I couldn't handle it all. I did what I've always done. I shut everyone out. I shut you out."

Ana sat still for a moment. He watched her face and searched her expression, trying to figure out how she felt, but found nothing. She studied the crepe myrtle, pink and white against the wall of the hospital, while the breeze moved the curling tendrils of her hair.

"Why didn't you talk to me about your problems?"

"I'm a guy."

She sighed. "I believe there may be a few men some-place who communicate. I'm not asking all that much, but you could have mentioned you were having problems and that you'd decided to transfer to pediatrics."

Yeah, he should have.

"Why are you so frightened?" she asked.

There was a moment of silence. Then she looked at him, squarely in the eyes and said, "Do you think if I knew how tough your life is, I'd reject you like Cynthia did?"

He couldn't answer. He felt as if he'd been punched in the stomach, hard, and his breath had been knocked out. Did he really feel that way? "I hadn't thought about it like that." He paused to consider her question, amazed he hadn't recognized what had been so easy for Ana to see. "I guess I did, deep inside."

She stood again. He wished she'd stop doing that. "You have to learn to trust me," she said. "I'm not Cynthia. I'm not at all like Cynthia."

"I know that. I trust you."

"Mike, you don't know anything about trust, and you wouldn't recognize love if it bit you in the leg."

"Do you love me?" He moved around in front of her and took her hand.

"I love a lot about you, but that doesn't change a thing." She pulled her hand away. "I refuse to be in love by myself."

"Ana, please give me another chance."

Gazing up at him, she said, "Mike, I don't trust you."

At least she called him Mike this time, but the part about not trusting him scared him.

"I'm different now."

"You're feeling good because of the baby, but when hard times come again, you'll close me out. I know that. If you love someone, you have to share the good times and the bad, but you won't allow me to be with you and to support you. I can't commit my life to you if you're not able to share your life with me, every bit of your life."

"I don't know how to do that." The confession hurt to make. "I wish I did."

"I know you had a tough childhood and that you're going through hard times." She turned her head away from him. "I can't go through this today-I'm-happy-but-tomorrow-who-knows? stuff with you. It tears me apart." She looked back to study him. "I need to know you're with me for the long term. I need to know if you want that kind of relationship."

"Ana, you have to accept the fact I can't share as much as you want."

She considered his words. "Okay, I can live with that, but I need you to *try* to share, especially the difficult moments. I won't settle for less. Do you love me? Are you willing to make the effort?"

He wanted to tell her how much he needed and loved her but the words wouldn't come. He nodded.

"You can't say it." She took a step toward her car. "When you can promise to share with me, when you can say the words, I'll listen, but I warn you. I'm not going to wait forever."

With the words stuck in his throat, he watched her walk away, unable to stop her. Pain filled him.

Then he remembered the scripture.

"Okay, Lord," he said. "It's You and me together. What I have to do is really difficult, and I need You to share the burden." As the words left his mouth, he felt relieved, as if a load had been lifted from him. He had no idea what to do next, but he wasn't alone.

As she drove out of the parking lot, Ana felt like speeding down the road and shouting at the other drivers to get out of the way. Oh, she didn't, of course, but she *felt* like it. Yes, she was in a real mood because she'd done it again. She'd been Miss I'm-Always-Right, demanding that everything be done *her* way.

She was used to being in control. She was comfortable with that. Being in charge was how she ran her life—but Mike kept her off balance. With him, she wasn't in charge, which completely frustrated her. She had no idea how to handle loss of power and hadn't coped very well today. Yes, she'd blown it. He'd tried but she hadn't.

When she realized she was close to the diner, she slowed and pulled into a parking place by the little park. She should not be driving while she felt this way. Pushing the car door open, she got out, closed it and wandered down the path. Instead of sitting on a bench, she ambled around the rosebushes before kneeling down to yank a weed out here and there.

With each one she jerked out, her stress decreased. Finally, she stood, picked up the bunch of leaves, stems and roots and tossed them in the trash. She smoothed the mulch before surveying the area. It looked better.

Calmer now, she wiped her hands on a tissue and threw it in the barrel on top of the weeds. Then she settled on a bench and stared herself in the face, metaphorically. She did not like what she saw.

In the past few days, she'd attempted to fill the hole Mike's absence had left with work and with prayer. Work was easy. In the hospital, everyone hurried, dashed from place to place and had almost every minute filled with motion. But there were times in the E.R. when she'd look around for Mike, expecting him to be moving a gurney or transporting a patient or assisting her, and he wasn't there.

When she tried to sleep, she imagined the whisper of Mike's finger across her cheek. She wished she could taste the sweetness of his lips against hers. She longed to see his rare smile or run her fingers through his shaggy hair, to rub her hand along the rough shadow of his whiskers. Every thought brought bittersweet tears, but she blinked them back. She never cried. Never—until she met Mike. Tough and determined, she'd always forced herself through every obstacle, climbed all the barriers that had blocked her way, fought every problem.

But not this one. She couldn't force herself to forget Mike Fuller. What a wimp she was to yearn for a man who didn't trust her.

Another worry overshadowed that one. Even if Mike wanted to see her again, she wasn't sure they could make it. And the problem wasn't Mike. It was her. She didn't know how to change, how to give up her need to control.

Her father had told her yesterday that he'd proposed to Mike's mother and felt sure she'd say yes. He'd looked so happy. In fact, he and Tessie always looked delighted just to be together. They didn't fight. They helped each other, understood each other. Tessie did little things for her dad, fixed him special dishes, made cute little drawings. Her father basked in the attention and returned it in the way of small gifts and hugs.

She was so happy for him and for Tessie, too, but their joy made her wonder. Maybe she wasn't meant to be part of a couple. Maybe she was too demanding, too sure of herself and her decisions to allow another person into her life.

As she started toward the car, Ana remembered the scripture from the other Sunday and prayed, "Dear Lord, help me to share Mike's burdens, to be more loving and accepting. Lead me to turn control of my life over to You."

But the thought of actually doing that terrified her, filling her with a strange aimless feeling. In that state, she didn't know what to do next, about Mike, about herself, or their lives.

Chapter Sixteen

"**A**ntonio and I are getting married."

As her words penetrated the information he was reading on diabetes, Mike looked up at his mother and Mr. Ramírez standing in the middle of the living room. He dropped the book and jumped to his feet. "Great." He hugged his mother then reached out to shake Mr. Ramírez's hand. "Congratulations. I'm happy for you."

He moved over to sit in a folding chair and waved for the couple to sit on the sofa. "Tell me about it. When did he propose?"

"Antonio proposed last week, but I asked him to give me a few days to think about it. You know—" she smiled at her fiancé then at Mike "—my first marriage didn't work out too well."

"But Mr. Ramírez isn't at all like my father."

"No, he isn't. Antonio is wonderful." Her eyes shone with happiness. "We haven't set a date yet."

He studied Ana's father. He hated it, but Mike had to

ask, "Sir, do you mind having me for a stepson? After all, I did hurt your daughter."

"Well, it didn't make me happy, but these are your lives, yours and Ana's. You two have to work it out," Mr. Ramírez said. "I learned a long time ago not to meddle in Ana's business."

Mike felt like a father checking out a young man's intentions toward his daughter, but he had to ask the next question, too. "How do you feel about Mom's background, about her record?"

"At first, it was hard to accept." The older man nodded. "But I love your mother. What she did, she did for you boys, and she's never going to break the law again."

Mike watched Mr. Ramírez, who beamed at Mom. Ana had called her father "Mr. Stone-face," just as she had Mike, but Mr. Ramírez didn't look that way. Love had changed one Mr. Stone-face. Could it do the same for Mike, or was he too afraid to try?

"I'd like to get married next month." Mr. Ramírez dragged his eyes from his mother. "We're getting older every day, and I want to share every minute I can with my Tessie."

"Oh, Antonio." She slapped his arm like a girl with her first crush before she said, "I want to make sure everything is fine with the boys first."

"Mom." Mike leaned forward. "Your boys are both adults. You don't have to worry about us anymore."

"But Tim still acts so young."

"If you wait until Tim grows up, you may never get married."

"I thought that army stint was all set up, but the recruiter called this morning," she said. "It seems Tim never kept his appointments."

"Don't worry about Tim. I'll talk to him, try to get that straightened out." He took his mother's hand, the one Mr. Ramírez wasn't holding. "Don't worry about us. Concentrate on the wedding and how happy you're going to be."

Mike paused, then turned to Mr. Ramírez. "Do you mind if I talk to my mother for a few minutes?"

"Not at all. I'll wait outside." Mr. Ramírez kissed his mother's cheek then left the house.

"Are you sure you want to get married?" Mike moved to sit next to his mother on the sofa. "Don't hurry into this because you think it will make my life easier."

"Oh, yes, I'm sure. I love him." She glanced toward the window where she could see Mr. Ramírez standing outside. "He takes care of me."

Mike could see his mother was ecstatic. He really hadn't needed to ask, but there was still something more he needed to know. "But this is so soon. You haven't known him long."

"Sometimes love comes fast."

"Are you sure you want to get married in a month?"

"Darling—" she turned, her gaze capturing Mike's "—when one reaches a certain age, everything in the body begins to go." She whispered the next words. "I want to get married while I can still hold it all together."

His mouth dropped open. He couldn't answer. She tugged her hand from his and spun toward the door in a swirl of her brilliant green skirt.

When she waved and closed the door behind her, he fell onto the sofa and had the best laugh he'd enjoyed in weeks.

For the conversation with Tim, Mike tried to bribe his brother into a good mood with pizza. Before his older brother could say a word, Tim said, "I talked to my recruiting officer today." Then he took a black olive from Mike's side and paused to pop it in his mouth. "I'm going to start basic in three weeks."

"Three weeks?" Mike almost choked on the bite he'd taken. "I thought basic started in two months."

"The recruiter and I decided there was no reason for delay. I'd rather get basic over than keep working at the burger place."

"Makes sense."

Imagine that. Tim made sense.

Both of these events simplified Mike's life greatly. With his mother and brother settled, he could concentrate on his future. What about going back to medical school? And could those plans include Ana, or had he acted like too much of a jerk and lost her?

If he wanted a future with Ana—but there really was no question about that—he wanted to spend the rest of his life with her. He'd have to work hard to win her back. His last effort hadn't been dazzlingly successful, but now he knew what Ana wanted. She'd raised the bar, but this time he'd fight for her. He was determined to get her back.

After a few days, no plan of action had come to mind. He'd considered several alternatives and had wisely decided against kidnapping. A romantic picnic wouldn't work because she wouldn't go with him. Her absence would cut down a great deal on the romance and efficacy. Another thought was a quirky date that would impress her but that wouldn't work, either, for the same reason the picnic wouldn't.

Although he wasn't sure that was true. He'd seen her yesterday in the hall, and she hadn't run. Did that mean anything? Maybe so, which made the last alternative seem possibly successful.

That last alternative was waylaying her. He hadn't ruled this idea out yet but wasn't sure of the details.

Except for a quick glance of her in the hall of the hospital every once in a while, he'd left Ana alone for a few days in the hope she'd mellow. That hadn't happened. At least, he hadn't noticed any sign of obvious thawing like a hug or a huge smile or, well, anything other than a friendly expression. He was looking for a lot more than friendly.

Now he had come up with an idea, a more aggressive strategy.

During his break that evening, he went to the chapel to pray. Although no plan to patch things up with Ana came to mind, he decided this was the place he'd bring her to apologize, to share, to show trust, to say everything and anything Ana needed to know. Here, where God had listened to him and helped him find his way, he'd present his case before God and Ana.

So waylaying Ana and taking her to the chapel became the plan. As sketchy as it was, this was the best, as well as the only inspiration he had. He figured the rest was up to Jesus.

The next morning after shift change, he leaned against the hood of Ana's car and waited for her in the parking lot outside the E.R. The only way she could get away was to run over him. He didn't think her anger had reached that level.

When she showed up, her eyes widened and her lips curled into a smile, but that faded quickly. Oddly, she didn't look angry, but what was that emotion? Disappointment? Guilt? Unhappiness? He couldn't tell because she turned away so fast.

"Hey, Fuller." She jingled her keys. "Need a ride?"

"No, thanks." He walked around the side of the car. "I'd like to talk to you."

She glanced up at him, her keys still jingling as if she were nervous, too. "Mike, I'm very confused right now. I'm trying to make sense of our, um, situation. I don't know how to react, what to say."

"I do." He put his arm on the top of the car and gazed down at her. "I love you."

She blinked a couple of times as he tried to decipher her expression. Did her reaction mean anything? Maybe not. Maybe she had a lash caught in her eye. She didn't move away, but she didn't say anything, either.

"See, I can say the words. I love you."

"Mike," she said in a voice husky with pain and deep emotion. "I've wanted to hear those words, but first I need to talk to you, to figure out what's happening. I haven't worked things out in my mind yet. I don't want either of us to hurt anymore, and I'm afraid that's going to happen."

"Why do you assume I'll hurt you?" He took her hand. "I love you. Do you still love me?"

A long pause followed his question while she considered it. Then she dropped her eyes to the ground. "Yes," she whispered and tried to tug her hand away. "But that doesn't mean everything's going to be terrific. Sometimes love isn't enough. Sometimes people are too different."

"I've changed. At least, I'm trying. I know what you need. You said I need to share every bit of my life with you. I'm ready to do that."

When she didn't answer but stopped pulling on her hand, he said, "Please, come with me so we can talk privately."

Still hesitant and unconvinced, she bit her lip. "Mike, I've been wrong. I have to tell you that first." She walked toward the wall and tugged him behind her. Once they sat, he watched her silently.

"Mike, some of what I said before was true. I can't be in love by myself and you have to trust me enough to share."

"I'm working on that."

"The problem is that you *did* share. You confessed to me that you don't know how to share, and I didn't do anything to help you."

He kept his gaze on her face and tried to comprehend her words. She was apologizing for not helping him? That was an idea he'd never considered. "Ana—"

She held up her hand. "No, this is my confession, and I'm not very good at this sort of thing." With a deep breath, she said, "Did I help you at all? No, I lectured you and walked off. I didn't listen to you or offer to share your burdens. I didn't even *push* you to communicate."

He stretched out his arm and placed it around her. She didn't pull away but leaned closer to him.

"Mike, I walked away from you." Her voice quivered. "On top of that, I acted so superior, as if *I* don't have any faults."

"None that I can see." He smiled.

"Oh, sure." She bit her lip. "How 'bout starting that list with my total lack of compassion and going on from there?"

"Ana, you're being really hard on yourself."

"It's about time. When am I going to learn to accept people, both their faults and strengths? When will I understand that, no matter how determined I am, I can't change other people. Most people are just fine and perfectly happy as they are."

"Maybe they're not. Maybe they're waiting for you to rescue them, to head them in the right direction."

"Right." She rolled her eyes. "Mike, I don't know how to give up control any more than you know how to communicate."

"Okay, we can work on all that. Will you give us a chance to tackle the problems together?"

At her uncertain nod, he got to his feet and pulled her up after him. "Now, it's my turn. Come with me? I need to tell you something, too."

"Why can't you tell me here?" She looked back at the wall.

"Because I'd like to tell you in the chapel. I want to talk to you in His presence."

"That would mean a lot to you," she said, still cautious. "Wouldn't it mean a lot to you, too?"

Ana shoved the keys back in her purse and allowed him to lead her toward the hospital. With his arm still on her shoulder, she remembered his words. He loved her. He'd said that. Mike wouldn't tell her he loved her if he didn't mean it. If she considered herself tough and determined, why didn't she have the courage to try again?

As they turned a corner into an empty hall, she looked at Mike and smiled. He grinned back at her and pulled her closer to him. She knew he wanted to kiss her, but this was neither the appropriate place or the right time. They still had a lot to work through.

When they arrived at the chapel, Mike opened one of the wide doors for her. She stepped inside and heard the loud vroom of the vacuum. Other members of the housecleaning crew dusted the pews and straightened the Communion table. The scent of lemon polish and dust permeated the air.

Mike watched in disappointment before he smiled. "Sometimes plans don't come together," he said. "I thought this would be perfect, but I know another place."

Taking her hand again, he headed toward the bank of elevators. "We should have privacy there."

They got off on the third floor and walked down the hall. Mike stopped before a door. The sign affixed to it said Linen closet 312A.

"Why did you stop?" She studied Mike who was looking back and forth down the corridor. Then he opened the door, shoved her inside and closed it behind them.

"This is the place."

"This is the place?" She turned around. Shelves covered with piles of sheets and towels surrounded them.

"Well, with the chapel busy, I thought of this, the only other private place in the hospital." He followed her scrutiny of the tiny area. "It's private and, after all, God is everywhere, as much with us here as in the chapel."

"Well, yes, but..." She stopped talking when she saw how serious he had become. "Won't we be interrupted?" she asked.

"No, they don't start changing beds for an hour."

The forty-watt bulb in the fixture on the high ceiling didn't emit much light, but it showed Mike's face. She yearned to reach out and smooth away his worried expression but this wasn't the time. Not yet.

"I told you about my family, what's going on with them and about how worried I've been," he began.

She nodded.

"That's why..." Mike started to say.

At exactly that moment, a redheaded man pulled the door open and stood there staring. Ana didn't know the orderly's name, but Mike turned toward him and said, "Hey, Hugo, give us a few minutes, okay?"

"Okay, but we're going to need more towels pretty soon." Hugo grabbed a stack and shut the door.

"Okay, one more time," Mike turned back toward her. "I've shared a lot with you, although most of it was because you pulled it out of me."

"Well, I..." she began in an effort to explain herself.

"I'm glad you did. I don't know how to share. We didn't communicate well in my family or in any of the others where I lived. It was always easier to keep everything inside. That way, no one would laugh at me or use what I said to get me back later or make me feel guilty because I'd made my mother worry. I learned to keep everything in. It's habit by now."

She didn't know what to say. The thought of Mike as a little boy being afraid to communicate hurt.

"But you don't let me get away with that," he said. "That's one reason I love you."

"Because I'm a pushy woman?" She cringed.

He nodded. "I need that. You have to understand I'll never share with you as completely as you want me to. I don't open up easily, but I'll try." He looked at her as if he'd asked a question.

"Okay," she said, although she still wondered what was next. "I can accept that. Go on."

He began looking around, his eyes darting from the bulb to the floor, caressing her face quickly before moving his gaze to the shelves of linen.

"What's wrong? Why are you so nervous?" She placed her hand on his shoulder.

"I'm going to tell you something I've only told one person before. It's hard for me to talk about." He swallowed. "Almost impossible. I didn't tell Cynthia this, but I have to share it with you. I want you to know how much I love you and trust you."

When he didn't say more, Ana rubbed her thumb against his lips. "Go ahead. I'm listening."

He opened and closed his mouth several times

without a word emerging. Finally, he whispered, "When I was eighteen, I knocked over a convenience store."

That was all he said. One sentence, and it rocked her. Mike Fuller had committed a robbery?

"What?" she gasped and dropped her hand. "You did what?"

He turned away, just a little, so he didn't have to see her face. Probably preferred not to see the horror written there.

Recognizing his pain was greater than hers, she took his chin and gently turned his face toward her. "Go ahead."

"Okay." He stared at the towels on a shelf behind her. "When I was eighteen, Francie took me to the store to buy a loaf of bread. For some reason—I don't know what. I didn't know then and I don't know now. Just plain stupidity." He stopped and took another deep breath. "I told you we Fullers don't make good decisions, that we feel the call to the wild side." He paused. "Anyway, I robbed it."

When he didn't speak for almost a minute, she said, "Go on."

"After my cousin let me out of the car, I pulled on a ski mask and walked inside. The cashier saw me, pulled a wad of cash from the register and gave it to me, handed it right over to me." He looked at his hands as if he could still see the money there. "I grabbed it, ran out of the store and got into the car." He stopped and rubbed his hand across his eyes.

"What happened next?" She attempted to keep her voice calm because Mike's trembled and broke.

"That's the worst part, the part I really hate to talk about." He dropped his head and, she thought, whispered a prayer before he started the story again. "When I got to the car, Francie knew what I'd done. I mean, I had money coming out of the pocket of my jacket and held a ski mask. In Texas, there's only one reason anyone has a ski mask, and it isn't to keep your face warm."

"What did she say?"

"Nothing. She drove around the corner, took the money, face mask and jacket and shoved me out of the car. Then she went to the cops, showed them everything, and confessed to the robbery."

Ana gasped. "What?"

"I didn't know until weeks later that she'd taken the fall for me. She was in prison by the time I found out, and I couldn't do a thing about it."

"Did you talk to her?"

He nodded. "When I found out she was locked up, I visited her and told her I was going to confess. She said it wouldn't do any good because they already had her for the job. All she wanted was for me to become a doctor. A prison record would destroy that." He dragged his hand through his hair. "I think it was more her dream than mine at the time. I can never repay her enough for what she did for me. I'm really ashamed about this. The robbery was stupid." He dropped his face into his hands. "It wasn't a big thrill. It cost Francie a good chunk of her life for nothing. For nothing."

Ana didn't know how to react. This man she loved wasn't the person she'd thought. He'd robbed a store and allowed his cousin to go to prison for it. Her effort at acceptance had taken a sharp turn and become harder than she'd imagined.

"Did you ever try to take responsibility?"

He lifted his face. "When Francie and Brandon were dating, I told him. He said there was nothing I could do about it. The case was so unimportant, they'd never retry it. Besides, everyone would believe Francie. She's very convincing." After a deep breath, he continued, "I still feel guilty. Francie and Brandon have forgiven me, but I don't know if I can forgive myself."

She didn't say a word. She couldn't. She was shaken and stunned. None of the thoughts tumbling through her brain fit the situation.

"You wanted me to share, so you'd know I trust you," Mike said. "I don't know what more I can say. Now you know the worst thing I've ever done. I've changed. I believe the years since have made me a better person. Ana, this is who I am, the man my life has made me. Can you accept me?"

"I need to think." She held on to a shelf and lowered herself to the floor. "It's not easy. I wasn't expecting this. It's hard for me to grasp and even harder to understand."

He kneeled beside her. "I know how difficult this must be for you to take in. Because I love you, because I'm working so hard to change, I hope you still love me and can forgive me."

"I can't pretend this doesn't shake me, Mike." She clasped her hands in front of her. "You're a different person than I thought, a man with a criminal background. I have to think about this."

He didn't say a word, didn't contradict her or try to explain.

And yet, he'd attempted to take the blame for the

robbery twice; he'd left medical school to care for his mother and brother, even when it meant losing his fiancée. He'd worked hard as an orderly and was determined to become a doctor. Children loved him, and children always recognized a fraud.

And he'd turned his life over to God.

Could she forgive him for that crime and for allowing Francie to take the fall? But Francie had chosen to go to jail because she loved her cousin.

She glanced into his face and saw such pain, so much suffering and hurt. How could she say she was trying to become a Christian and not forgive a man who looked and sounded so penitent? Who had changed so much? No matter how hard this was for her, the guilt and despair were killing Mike.

"Have you prayed about this?" she asked.

"Over and over. I believe God has forgiven me."

"You said Francie has."

"She was furious I did such a stupid thing, but she forgave me. That's who Francie is. That's why we all love her so much."

Ana remembered her uncle who'd gone to prison. Those years had been hard on his family, but they'd accepted the prodigal back. Wasn't that the whole point of the parable? Of the gospel?

Oh, Lord, lead me. I don't know what to do, but You can guide me. She sat in the silence and listened. In only a few seconds, peace and compassion filled her. Reaching her hand out, she allowed Mike to help her stand.

"Mike, your past is hard for me to accept, even harder for me to understand, but that was six years ago." She searched for the right words. "Since then, you've changed. You've become a fine young man, a person anyone would be proud to know."

"Ana, can *you* accept me?"

"I've seen people change. I know it's possible." She stopped her words. Mike had asked her to trust him. What she was about to say would be irrevocable. She paused to order her thoughts and speak carefully as he continued to study her.

"First, I believe that if Francie and God have forgiven you, you have to forgive yourself."

He nodded and continued to scrutinize her face, so nervous his hand shook a little as he grasped hers. "And you? Can you accept me?"

"I'm trying. Give me a little time, I'm really trying."

He didn't say anything but took her other hand. His eyes scanned her expression as if he were searching for clues. "You know where I've been. You know who I am."

She nodded, still too filled with emotion to say more. What was it her father had said about Tessie? Something about seeing the person she was becoming. Could she do the same with Mike?

He pulled her toward him. "I don't have much to offer, but I can promise you this. I will love you forever."

She allowed almost a minute to pass as she considered and prayed, remembering the robbery had been years ago. Suddenly it was easy. She loved him. Her mind cleared and the words tumbled from her mouth. "You're everything I could ever want in a man, Mike. I love you." When she said that, she felt free, filled with happiness and the conviction this was the right decision.

He put his arms around her and leaned his cheek against her hair. "Thank God," he whispered. "Thank You, God." Then he lifted his face and gazed into her eyes. "I love you, Ana. I'll try to show that in everything I do." He smiled, that wonderful smile that warmed her. "Don't even think of changing. I need you to keep after me, because if you don't, I might go back to the old, silent Mike. Your determination is one of the things I love about you."

"You love me because I'm pushy?" she asked again.

"Well, not always, but most of the time. Sometimes it drives me crazy."

"Then you must really love me to put up with that."

"Yeah, I do. Without your encouragement, I won't know that you love me."

"Oh, you'll know." She put her head against his chest and basked in the knowledge that they were together and sharing, both of them. "You'll always know that."

"It's too soon to ask you to marry me, but I will. I want to be with you for the rest of my life." He held her, his embrace showing her the depth of his love.

Outside, she could hear the chime of the elevators, the sound of people passing and their worried voices, the echo of footsteps getting closer. She figured the latter probably belonged to Hugo who wanted to get his towels.

But here, inside this most ordinary of places, she felt the presence of the spirit. She heard the beat of Mike's heart and felt his loving touch. This was everything she needed.

As she heard the doorknob turn, Ana allowed joy to fill her. In Mike's arms, in a linen closet at Austin University Hospital with the aroma of disinfectants tickling her nose was exactly where she wanted to be.

Epilogue

Mike looked down the pew. On the other end, Francie sat next to Brandon, who held their two-month-old son. As Mike watched, Francie put her hand on her husband's and smiled into his eyes.

Next to Brandon were Tessie and Antonio, the newlyweds. Closer to him were Julie, Quique and Raúl. Of course, Ana sat next to Mike. On her finger she wore a ring with a tiny diamond, the only one he could afford. Ana loved it. When she placed her hand on Mike's arm, he smiled down at her. *Thank You, God, for bringing me this woman who loves me enough to break down my barriers.*

On Mike's left, Tim looked handsome with his short military buzz. One more thing to be thankful for. Tim was growing up and becoming more responsible although Mike doubted if he'd ever be conventional. His own man—that was who Tim was.

Sitting with him on that pew were the greatest gifts anyone could ever receive, his family in Christ. They were all here because a few years earlier, her feet hurting and tired after a long day of work, Francie had entered a church and allowed God to transform her.

Life was truly like a pond, its ripples reaching out to touch others. When she'd entered a church and found faith, God hadn't stopped with Francie. That experience had touched and brought this group together. As crowded as they were into this pew, soon they were going to expand to another as family brought more family and witnessed to their friends.

They were truly blessed.

Dear Reader,

One of my favorite hymns is "Take It to the Lord in Prayer." It reminds me we can share our burden with the Lord. When life was rough, Mike Fuller learned to accept the healing touch of his Savior, as well as the love of Ana Ramírez.

Trying to go it alone is one of my problems. I imagine many of us share that tendency because we've been taught to be strong, to do everything ourselves. As I wrote this book, I was reminded again that we aren't alone, that we find rest with the one who takes our burden upon Him.

You may remember Mike from THE PATH TO LOVE. He's a member of a family with an unfortunate bent toward crime, but a family that has found faith and has changed. In this book, Mike falls in love with Ana, a doctor from a warm and loving Hispanic family.

Ana and Mike's struggles were difficult, but they triumphed through faith. I pray that this victory will inspire and touch each of you.

Jane Myers Perrine

QUESTIONS FOR DISCUSSION

1. Mike's life was a series of wrong decisions, twists and turns. Ana carefully plotted out her life in a straight line leading to where she was determined to go. Which is more like you? As you look back, how did your choices—bad, as well as good—lead you to where you are now? What part did God play on this journey?

2. Mike is lost and doesn't have any idea what to do next. Have you ever felt this way? If so, what did you do?

3. Ana is certain that she can do everything she wants if she works hard enough. Is this realistic? Does Ana change? Can she accept the idea that sometimes there are barriers and that failure is not always a disaster? Can we accept and use failure for good?

4. Ana tells Mike that because Francie has forgiven him and God has forgiven him, he should forgive himself. Do you believe people often hold on to guilt and shame even after they repent? Are there people who find it difficult to forgive themselves? What problems might this cause?

5. Mike discovers something he's always known: Jesus is always with us to share our burdens. When has this been important in your life? Have you seen a willingness to shoulder the load alone in the lives of friends or family members? What often happens when we attempt to carry the burdens ourselves? Why are people so de-

termined to be strong when there are others who can share our problems and troubles?

6. Mr. Ramírez says he loves Tessie for the person she is becoming. Who are you becoming? Are there people you love for the people they are becoming?

7. Have you hidden a dark secret from a person you care about or has someone hidden a secret from you? Did this action hurt your relationship? How? Do you believe there may be secrets we don't need to share with the people we love? Why or why not?

8. What did you think about Ana's reaction to Mike's revelation? How would you have reacted?

9. Ana finally recognizes that her determination to succeed has made her judgmental and controlling. Do you believe she can let go of these traits? Do you know people like this? How can they change? Do they need to change? Why? Can faith help? How?

10. When you're going through tough times, what scripture helps you? Many find the Twenty-third Psalm helpful. Do you? Have you found strength in the verses from Matthew that spoke to both Mike and Ana?

REQUEST YOUR FREE BOOKS!

2 FREE INSPIRATIONAL NOVELS
PLUS 2
FREE
MYSTERY GIFTS

Love Inspired®

YES! Please send me 2 FREE Love Inspired® novels and my 2 FREE mystery gifts. After receiving them, if I don't wish to receive any more books, I can return the shipping statement marked "cancel." If I don't cancel, I will receive 4 brand-new novels every month and be billed just $3.99 per book in the U.S., or $4.74 per book in Canada, plus 25¢ shipping and handling per book and applicable taxes, if any*. That's a savings of 20% off the cover price! I understand that accepting the 2 free books and gifts places me under no obligation to buy anything. I can always return a shipment and cancel at any time. Even if I never buy another book from Steeple Hill, the two free books and gifts are mine to keep forever.

113 IDN EF26 313 IDN EF27

Name _____ (PLEASE PRINT) _____

Address _____ Apt. # _____

City _____ State/Prov. _____ Zip/Postal Code _____

Signature (if under 18, a parent or guardian must sign)

Order online at www.LoveInspiredBooks.com

Or mail to Steeple Hill Reader Service™:

IN U.S.A.: P.O. Box 1867, Buffalo, NY 14240-1867
IN CANADA: P.O. Box 609, Fort Erie, Ontario L2A 5X3

Not valid to current Love Inspired subscribers.

Want to try two free books from another series?
Call 1-800-873-8635 or visit www.morefreebooks.com

* Terms and prices subject to change without notice. NY residents add applicable sales tax. Canadian residents will be charged applicable provincial taxes and GST. This offer is limited to one order per household. All orders subject to approval. Credit or debit balances in a customer's account(s) may be offset by any other outstanding balance owed by or to the customer. Please allow 4 to 6 weeks for delivery.

Your Privacy: Steeple Hill is committed to protecting your privacy. Our Privacy Policy is available online at www.eHarlequin.com or upon request from the Reader Service. From time to time we make our lists of customers available to reputable firms who may have a product or service of interest to you. If you would prefer we not share your name and address, please check here. ☐

LIREG07

TITLES AVAILABLE NEXT MONTH

Don't miss these four stories in October

SLEEPING BEAUTY by Judy Baer
Suze Charles had been sleepwalking her way through life, until she met Dr. David Grant. The sleep specialist offered her hope for a cure—and for lasting love. But could a man who liked order ever fit in to the menagerie that was Suze's life?

LITTLE MISS MATCHMAKER by Dana Corbit
A Tiny Blessings Tale

While dealing with a shocking revelation about his family, firefighter Alex Donovan finds himself temporary guardian to his cousin's children. Teacher Dinah Fraser offers to help him learn to cope and finds herself falling for the unlikely family man.

A SEASON OF FORGIVENESS by Brenda Coulter
Her life was calm and predictable, and Victoria Talcott liked it that way. She didn't need daredevil Sam McGarry swooping in to save her all the time. But he always seemed to be there, rescuing her and setting off sparks in her heart.

OPERATION: MARRIED BY CHRISTMAS by Debra Clopton
Mule Hollow's notorious runaway bride, Haley Bell Thornton, was back. And, not surprisingly, running from another wedding. That gave the matchmaking ladies of the town a secret holiday plan—make wedding bells chime by Christmas for Haley and Will Sutton, the first of her ditched fiancés.

LICNM0907